TRIBAL ETHNOGRAPHY
CUSTOMARY LAW AND CHANGE

ABOUT THE EDITOR

The editor of this volume Dr. K.S. SINGH had conceived of the trilogy in 1976-77 of tribal movements, tribal economy and tribal customary law when he was Director. All the three volumes have now been published. Dr. Singh, now Director General of Anthropological Survey of India, has been the author and editor of a large number of publications relating to the tribal communities of India and the people of India.

TRIBAL ETHNOGRAPHY CUSTOMARY LAW AND CHANGE

Editor
K. S. SINGH
Director General
Anthropological Survey of India
NEW DELHI

CONCEPT PUBLISHING COMPANY, NEW DELHI-110059

ISBN 81-7022-471-3

First Published 1993

Published and Printed by
Ashok Kumar Mittal
Concept Publishing Company
A/15-16, Commercial Block, Mohan Garden
NEW DELHI 110059 (India)

Lasertypeset by
Printing Express,
H-13, Bali Nagar,
NEW DELHI-110015

CONTENTS

VII. Andaman and Nicobar Islands

LIST OF CONTRIBUTORS

DR. K. S. SINGH, Director General, Anthropological Survey of India (An. S. I.) 27, Jawaharlal Nehru Road, Calcutta-700016

DR. S. B. NANDI, Former Deputy Director, Anthropological Survey of India, North Eastern Regional Centre, Lachumiere, Shillong

DR. R. P. ATHPARIA, Anthropological Survey of India, North Eastern Regional Centre, Lachumiere, Shillong

SHRI M. M. DAS, Anthropological Survey of India, North Eastern Regional Centre, Lachumiere, Shillong

SHRI S. K. MUKHERJEE, Anthropological Survey of India, North Eastern Regional Centre, Lachumiere, Shillong

DR. JAYANTA SARKAR, Superintending Anthropologist (C), 27, Jawaharlal Nehru Road, Calcutta – 700016

LATE SHRI PEARSON HUNGYO, Former Assistant Anthropologist (C), Anthropological Survey of India, North Eastern Regional Centre, Lachumiere, Shillong

DR. N. K. DAS, Anthropological Survey of India, 27, Jawaharlal Nehru Road, Calcutta – 700016

SHRI S. K. PAL, Anthropological Survey of India, Andaman & Nicobar Region, Port Blair

SHRI BHABANANDA MUKHERJEE, Former Superintending Anthropologist (C), Anthropological Survey of India, 27, Jawaharlal Nehru Road, Calcutta – 700016

DR. R. K. SAHA, Anthropologist, Anthropological Survey of India, 27, Jawaharlal Nehru Road, Calcutta – 700016

DR. B. JOARDAR, Anthropological Survey of India, North Western Regional Centre, 192/1, Kaulagarh Road, Dehradun. Presently Deputy Director (on Deputation), Ministry of Urban Development, New Delhi

SHRI HASAN ALI, Anthropologist, Anthropological Survey of India, Southern Regional Centre, 2963, Gokulam Road, Mysore 570002

DR. DIKSHIT SINHA, Former Assistant Anthropologist (C), Anthropological Survey of India, 27, Jawaharlal Nehru Road, Calcutta – 700016. Now Reader, Palli Siksha Sadan (Institute of Rural Sociology), Sriniketan, Vishwabharati, West Bengal

DR. R. K. BHATTACHARYA, Deputy Director, Anthropological Survey of India, Eastern Regional Centre, 27, Jawaharlal Nehru Road, Calcutta – 700016

DR. A. K. ADHIKARY, Former Assistant Anthropologist (C), Anthropological Survey of India, 27, Jawaharlal Nehru Road, Calcutta – 700016. Now Lecturer, Palli Charcha Kendra, Santiniketan, Vishwabharati, West Bengal

SHRI P. P. MAHATO, Assistant Anthropologist, Anthropological Survey of India, Eastern Regional Centre, 27, Jawaharlal Nehru Road, Calcutta – 700016

DR. WILLIAM EKKA, Anthropologist (C), Officer-in-Charge, Field Station, Anthropological Survey of India, Ranchi

SHRI D. B. MANDAL, Anthropologist, Anthropological Survey of India, Eastern Regional Centre, 27, Jawaharlal Nehru Road, Calcutta – 700016

DR. I. S. CHAUHAN, Former Deputy Director, Anthropological Survey of India, Central Regional Centre, 11, Seminary Hills, Nagpur

DR. R. K. SINHA Anthropological Survey of India, Central Regional Centre, 11, Seminary Hills, Nagpur

DR. D. K. SAMANTA, Anthropological Survey of India, Western Regional Centre, 16, Madhuban, Udaipur 313001

DR. B. K. DASGUPTA, Former Deputy Director, Anthropological Survey of India, 27, Jawaharlal Nehru Road, Calcutta – 700016

SHRI D. HAJRA Former Superintending Anthropologist (C), Anthropological Survey of India, Central Regional Centre, 11, Seminary Hills, Nagpur

SHRI K. N. THUSU, Former Assistant Anthropologist (C), Anthropological Survey of India, Central Regional Centre, 11, Seminary Hills, Nagpur

DR. B. R. GHOSH, Superintending Anthropologist (C), Anthropological Survey of India, Andaman & Nicobar Region, Port Blair

DR. P. K. MISHRA, Former Deputy Director, Anthropological Survey of India, Southern Regional Centre, 2963 Gokulam Road, Mysore 570002. Now Professor in Anthropology, NEHU, Shillong

DR. B. R. RIZVI, Superintending Anthropologist (C), Anthropological Survey of India, North Western Regional Centre, 192/1, Kaulagarh Road, Dehradun

DR. S. B. CHAKRABORTY, Superintending Anthropologist (C), Anthropological Survey of India, North Eastern Regional Centre, Lachumiere, Shillong

SHRI S. N. MAHATO, Anthropological Survey of India, Southern Regional Centre, 2963, Gokulam Road, Mysore 570002

DR. S. G. MORAB, Former Superintending Anthropologist (C), Anthropological Survey of India, Southern Regional Centre, 2963, Gokulam Road, Mysore 570002

DR. T. S. NAIDU, Former Anthropologist (C), Anthropological Survey of India, Southern Regional Centre, 2963 Gokulam Road, Mysore 570002. Now Reader, Deptt. of Futurology, University of Pondicherry, Pondicherry

DR. J. PARTHASARATHY, Former Research Associate (C), Anthropological Survey of India, Southern Regional Centre, 2963, Gokulam Road, Mysore 570002. Now Lecturer, Tribal Research Institute, Udagamandalam (Ooty), Tamil Nadu

LATE DR. N. V. KAMESWARA RAO, Former Anthropologist (C), Anthropological Survey of India, Southern Regional Centre, 2963, Gokulam Road, Mysore 570002

DR. R. S. MANN, Former Director, Anthropological Survey of India, 27, Jawaharlal Nehru Road, Calcutta – 700016. Now Professor, Deptt. of Anthropology, Delhi University, Delhi

DR. S. H. M. RIZVI, Anthropologist (P), Anthropological Survey of India, North Eastern Regional Centre, Lachumiere, Shillong

SHRI N. K. SINHA, Anthropological Survey of India, North Western Regional Centre, 192/1, Kaulagarh Road, Dehradun

SHRI S. P. LALA, Anthropologist (C), Anthropological Survey of India, 27, Jawaharlal Nehru Road, Calcutta – 700016

SHRI J. C. DAS, Anthropological Survey of India, North Western Regional Centre, 192/1, Kaulagarh Road, Dehradun

SMT. V. SARKAR, Anthropologist, Anthropological Survey of India, Western Regional Centre, 16, Madhuban, Udaipur 313001

SHRI R. SARKAR, Anthropologist, Anthropological Survey of India, Western Regional Centre, 16, Madhuban, Udaipur 313001

SHRI SEM TOPNO, Former Assistant Anthropologist (C), Anthropological Survey of India. Now Education Officer, U.G.C., New Delhi 110002

SHRI N. K. GHATAK, Anthropological Survey of India, Western Regional Centre, 16, Madhuban, Udaipur 313001

SHRI T. N. PANDIT, Former Joint Director, Anthropological Survey of India, 27, Jawaharlal Nehru Road, Calcutta – 700016

SHRI D. K. BOSE, Former Superintending Anthropologist (C), Anthropological Survey of India, Western Regional Centre, 16, Madhuban, Udaipur 313001

SHRI T. LAL, Ex-Cartographer, Anthropological Survey of India

SHRI G. C. MANDAL, Formerly of Anthropological Survey of India, Andaman & Nicobar Region, Port Blair. Now Audience Research Officer, Doordarshan, Nagpur

INTRODUCTION

Tribal Customary Law has been studied as part of the study of tribal society. In the process a distinction has been made between sanction in primitive society and the law of the more advanced society; between the uncodified, unwritten customary rules recognised as binding by a tribal community and the larger corpus of the laws enacted and enforced by formal state system. The critical role of tribal customary law in the maintenance of tribal solidarity – and now tribal identity – has generally been overlooked. In fact the study of tribal customary law in all its aspects has remained a relatively neglected area of tribal studies in the country. With the growing understanding of our pluralism there is now an awareness of the need to know more of the tribal customary laws.

Colonial administrators – turned – ethnographers in their monographs on the tribal people dealt with the administration of justice, land rights, rules of inheritance and succession, chieftainship, bride-price, family, marriage and divorce rules, etc. For instance, C. G. Crawford in *Handbook of Kuki Custom* covered such matters as inheritance, land hire, divorce price, seduction, slave price, loans and oaths. Of all the tribes of the North East, the Garo laws were studied most systematically in the pre-independence period.

A major work was undertaken by W. G. Archer on the compilation of Santal laws in the mid-1940s which remained unpublished for many years. It has now been introduced (1984) by the editor of this volume and published. It is the most comprehensive work on tribal customary law to date. It covers a much larger canvas of tribal civil law and administration of justice among the Santal than any other work of the colonial period.

The makers of Indian Constitution recognised the need for a separate political and administrative structure for the tribes. Special provisions were made to prevent encroachment on tribals' land, uphold tribals' land rights and other customs, etc. There was an appreciation of the need for the codification of tribal customary laws in different parts of India. The Department of Welfare, Government of India, has plans for the codification of tribal customary law which has been entrusted to the Tribal Research Institutes.

In the 1980s pioneering work was done in the field of the codification of tribal law by the Law Research Institute of Guwahati High Court, established on the occasion of the silver jubilee celebrations of the Court in April, 1973. The North Eastern Council approached the Guwahati High Court in 1976 for undertaking the study of the customary laws of the tribes. The institute has embarked upon research into the origin and evolution of various laws prevalent among the tribal people, their historical development, as well as the basic synthetising influences in the North Eastern region.

The Law Research Institute has prepared twelve reports. The reports on the Garo and the Wancho tribes were the first to be finalised, during 1979 and 1980. The report on the Riang of Tripura followed in 1981; the reports on the Ao of the Nagaland, Mizo of Mizoram, Pati Rabha of Assam, and Tangkhul of Manipur were submitted in 1982. These reports covered family, marriage, dowry, adoption, maintenance, minority and guardianship, inheritance and succession, slavery and 'servile' institutions, gift, loan, debit, well, sale, lease, mortgage, land, administrative authority and administration of justice.

The Indian Law Institute, New Delhi, brought out a holistic study on the customary law and justice in the tribal areas of Meghalaya (Kusum and Bakshi, 1982). This study attempts a coverage of the rules, customs and institutions pertaining to the customary laws among the Khasi and Garo. Divided into 19 chapters the work starts with a chronological review of all acts and regulations which have been in operation from the colonial to the post-colonial period. This book also deals with judicial systems among the Khasi/Jaintia and Garo, their village councils, patterns of residence, the female heirs, mother-rights, marriage, divorce, classification of property, adoption and guardianship, inheritance and succession.

It should be noted that in spite of the assimilation of tribal communities into the system of the state laws represented by the Indian Penal Code, the Indian Civil Code and the Code of Criminal Procedure there remains in tribal society a large residual area of autonomy in many matters such as settlement of matters of civil or social nature in the tribal world. The tribal council functions effectively in such cases even today. In recent years with the institution of Lok Adalat, the stress on disposal of cases at the grass-roots level, and the functioning of people's courts in some areas, the processes of the settlement of disputes of minor nature at the local level have gathered momentum. In these circumstances the tribal customary laws need to be codified and integrated with these local level processes.

II

In 1976-77 the Anthropological Survey of India (An.S.I.) had undertaken the survey of tribal movements, tribal economies and tribal customary laws, constituting a trilogy. The works on the first two have already been published (See Singh, K. S.).

This systematic study of the tribal customary law was undertaken to generate uniformly data on all aspects of the customary law among the tribes of India. About 70 tribes were studied under the project and about the same number of papers were presented at a national seminar. However, in this volume we have presented only 40 papers. They discuss ways by which the tribal societies maintain their solidarity and social order, and settle disputes.

The format of this survey has been spelt out under the guidelines (See Annexure I). The mode of the survey was the same as that adopted for the other surveys. The survey was undertaken by the eight regional centres of the An.S.I. The tribes were selected for study from the point of view of their spatial distribution and different levels of economic and technological development. Thus we studied the customary laws of the tribes at hunting and food gathering stage (6), as shifting and terrace cultivators (7), nomads and artisan groups (4), and as peasants (23). Some of the tribes were also identified for study for their special features such as the polyandrous Jaunsari of Uttar Pradesh and the *Rabha* of Assam for the pattern of change from matriliny to patriliny.

The papers highlight the notion and nature of offences tried by the tribal councils, the existing laws and norms of the state, which have a direct bearing on the mode of dispute settlement, the traditional offices and office-holders, the constitution and functions of tribal courts and statutory panchayats, the impact of these institutions, processes and modes of dispute resolution. A few papers deal a little more with ethnography, particularly the type of family, marriage and kinship. However, the focus has been on customary laws and change. It took sometime to organise the material on change because the survey had not been rigorously implemented in accordance with the guidelines. The investigators' professional bias and training in ethnography as different from their appreciation of economy and law partly explained this. There seemed to be a greater stress on tribal ethnography and tribal customary laws as incidental to it than on tribal customary laws *per se*. In view of the nature of the material presented by our scholars we decided to retitle the project as Tribal *Ethnography, Customary Law* and *Change.*

At one stage, we decided to explore the concept of crimes in tribal society (see Annexure II). The tribal languages do not have words for all crimes defined in the Indian Penal Code. There are words for some of the crimes. The Mundas have words for murder (*goe*), theft (*kumburu*), kidnaping (*arkid*), rape (*ota*) etc. There is no word for hastardy, or for many other crimes.

The focus of our study was on the "civil" rather than the "criminal" aspects of customary law. The tribals themselves do not presumably make such distinction. Probably in the pre-colonial phase, the tribal council would decide all such cases which today are identified as civil or criminal under the formal state laws, and disposed of by criminal courts.

The colonial authority took cognisance of the uniqueness of tribal customary laws and the tribal authority that could enforce them. This was particularly so in the areas where the tribals often rebelled or where they were a dominant community. The colonial policy in such matters had four aspects. The first was the recognition of tribal chief or headman. The second was the integration of all civil and revenue functions in the offices created in the scheduled areas, so that the administration of justice to tribals could be made easier. The third was the acceptance of the principle that what the tribals needed was a government by a person rather than a government by system. Fourthly, there was in the revenue laws framed by the colonial authorities recognition of customs particularly the customary rights of lineage to own land and forest, right to pay minimal revenue, enjoy traditional rights in forests etc. In the post-colonial period many of these elements of protection of tribal customary law and rights continued. There was however a gradual movement towards assimilation of the tribal system into the larger, pan-Indian political, administrative and judicial system and formal laws. The single line administration broke down in the post-colonial period. The civil, judicial, revenue functions were separated. The influx of non-tribals into tribal areas exerted tremendous pressure on tribals' resources such as land and forest. Tribal resistance to these developments occurred in the form of a large number of movements of all kinds.

Here we are concerned with only the tribal customary laws. The need for their codification was keenly felt at all levels both in administration and judiciary so that the knowledge of the interesting body of traditional norms and laws is made available to the authorities in deciding matters which affect the tribal people.

The focus of this project in tribal customary law has been spelt out at Annexure I. However, all papers presented here do not conform to the comprehensive format. In fact some of the papers are ethnographically thin, nor do all of them explore the dimensions on the indigenous perception of people's rights and laws, the complex processes of the interaction of the tribal councils and state judicial system etc. The papers generated are uneven in their coverage, and some of them lack in analytical depth. The project should have been rigorously pursued in tune with the guidelines in order to explore all dimensions. This was partly not done because I had left the organisation after the project was launched. When I returned, we tried to put together the material and address the key issues which were raised initially (see Annexure I and II), as far as possible.

III

The main findings of the project on tribal customary law are presented as follows :

- Tribal customary laws are ubiquitous, existing in all tribal groups, cherished, adapted and regarded as intrinsic to tribal identity. This body of law survives even among the numerically small, fragile tribal communities, facing the threat of extinction or dwindling in numbers, such as the Lepcha, Toto, Pando etc. They have shown an extraordinary resilience and pragmatism in coping with the onslaught of outsiders and preserving their institution and traditional law.

- Again, central to this body of customary law is the institution of tribal chief, tribal chief-in-council or tribal council which upholds the sanctity of the law and enforces it. Here there is a whole range of variations. The institution of tribal chief appears to be the strongest in many parts of the North-East where the tribal system survives relatively intact. (See Nandi et al). The tribal chief is the custodian of customary laws and resources; he allots *jhum* plots and regulates use of water; he is the intermediary between his people and the government.
- The statutory Gram Panchayat with its judicial wing, Nyaya panchayat has been introduced all over tribal India except in the North-East. They co-exist with the tribal council. In Manipur, the headman is the ex-officio Chairman of the village authority, a good compromise. The relationship of the two is generally understood by people. The tribals' customary laws are mainly concerned with ordering sex and marriage, and dealing with witchcraft, kinship, inheritance and related matters. It is tribals' own affair. The two institutions co-exist (see Rizvi). The tribal councils often try to adjust to the Statutory Gram Panchayat. Our scholars have reported that the state laws are encroaching on the domain of tribal customary laws particularly in regard to daughter's right in land (*Thusu, Samanta*).
- There are many papers on the mechanism of dispute settlement. N. K. Das discusses the functioning of this system among the Angami-Nagas. Ranjit K. Bhattacharya deals with the.mechanism among the Sauria of the Rajmahal hills, and the dominant British legal system *vis-a-vis* the Sauria customary law in the colonial period. D. Hazra presents the case study in matters of regulation of sex dealt with by tribal council among the Gonds. S. G. Morab discusses the mechanism as it operates among the Malaikudi, a hill tribe of Karnataka. In spite of the dwindling authority of the traditional jural authority, an attempt is made to preserve and uphold traditional norms.
- The Lambadis' tribal council is active (Naidu). Among the Yerukula the system of ordeals or severe punishment is no longer in vogue, but they appreciate the value of solidarity and accept the rulings of their Kula Panchayat (*Parthasarathy*). The Khamti are unique in that they *a la* Manu have a graded system of punish-

ment for the same offence committed by various segments of their society. The late Kameswara Rao discusses the system that prevailed in the Agency tract of Andhra Pradesh, and how the Bagatas from whose ranks the leaders are recruited, have manipulated customary laws to seize power and use it as a handy tool to exploit the weaker sections. Mann reports from North-Western India that an offender is tried afresh by the tribal council even after he or she has been punished under the state laws in order to uphold the authority of traditional system. The institution of the Bhil chief in the Dangs was abolished in 1972, and panchayat raj has come into existence. (Lala) Bose comments on the introduction of a *raja* among the Onges, instead of the band chief-bands in their original form have ceased to exist- and the erosion of the principle of consensus in decision-making.

- The concept of property as we understand it is relatively weak and undeveloped among the small tribes of the hunting and food gathering category. The Irula who have become good agriculturists now demand *patta* rights in land (S. N. Mahato). The island tribal communities have no clear notion of private property. Things of common use are owned in common (*Pandit*) the notion of property appears to be developing among the intrepid Nicobarese (Lal).
- Traditionally, tribals' daughters have no right in landed property in middle India. For example, the Dhurwa do not allow a daughter to inherit the deceased father's property (K. N. Thusu). But the Korkus are reported to have accepted the daughter's right over that of the members of the lineage (Samanta). In the polyandrous society in Jaunsar, the women have no right in the property, either of the husband or of father (Topno and Ghatak).
- J. C. Das who was assigned to prepare an overview paper for the North-Western region presents a fascinating account of the many types of man-women relationship, going beyond the conventional form of marriage, in the Himalayan societies. Their customary law recognises three types of conjugal relations, marriage between a man and an unmarried woman (*byati*), marriage between a man and a married woman and marriage between a widow and a plough man (*haliya*). Their progeny – there are four categories of sons – have a right in property. There is no notion of hastardy in tribal society. Though monogamy is the rule in most of the

tribal communities, a Kol is allowed to keep a concubine (Dasgupta).

– There are many factors of change in tribal customary law. The impact of Hinduism on the Bodo Kachari mediated by *Brahma* movement resulted in the adoption of Hindu norms. Similarly, the influence of Christianity on the Mizo has led to the erosion of many traditional norms. Under the influence of Christianity again, the Nicobarese are establishing elementary families and adopting the Christian way of marriage (Mandal). The Rabha are the process of transition from matriliny to patriliny (S. K. Paul). There were no papers on matrilineal system and the erosion of mother's or daughter's right in land, and the increasing role of the husband and son in management of property and its ownership have not been discussed. In North-Western India, as reported by Mann, the original (or traditional), the borrowed/emulated) and the imposed practices (state laws) coexist in the same tribe.

This study is only the first step, among many others, towards a comprehensive study of tribal customary laws and their codification. There is an urgent need for integrating this body of knowledge with the micro-level processes of disposal of cases which have gathered momentum in recent years, as mentioned above. The need for their codification has been keenly felt at all levels both in administration and judiciary so that the knowledge of the interesting body of traditional norms and laws is made available to the authorities in deciding matters which affect the tribal people.

PART I

NORTH-EASTERN INDIA

1

TRIBAL CUSTOMARY LAW IN NORTH-EAST INDIA

S. B. NANDI, R. P. ATHPARIA, M. M. DAS, S. K. MUKHERJEE

In all societies relationships among individuals are regulated by a body of norms, customs, taboos, traditions, values and moral standards. Tribal societies differ from all other societies *inter alia* in the fact that individuals are relatively fettered by the customs and taboos. But the customary laws of many tribes have been changing fast in the recent decades. In the particular ecological setting of North-East India the traditional economy of many tribal communities, who remained relatively isolated from the mainstream of socio-economic processes of the country, is characterised by shifting cultivation. This area is also the abode of numerous communities having different kinds of socio-political systems. These have laid down stringent regulatory norms and conventions for the prudent use of most important of the resources, viz. land, maintenance of ethnic identity and social order. The papers presented from North-East India mainly concern changes in the customary laws, the varying modes of law enforcement and resolution of conflicts. It will be interesting to examine how the sharing of available resources and sex relations in different tribal communities of North-East India are regulated by customary laws in the interest of harmony and efficient functioning of society.

Among many hill tribes of this region the chief wields power to regulate the use of land and water. The Buddhist Khamtis in the foothills of Lohit and Tirap districts practise wet paddy cultivation. Land is owned by the village chief, *chaofa*, the eldest member of the royal clan. Traditionally, the chief makes allotment of land to different families. Once a land is reclaimed by an individual he remains the owner until he leaves the village. In no circumstance can he dispose of the land. In the event of the family migrating out of the village the ownership of the land goes back to the *chaofa*. If a Khamti of one village wants to migrate to another he has to obtain the consent of the *chaofa* of the village he likes to settle in. Until the enforcement of the Lushai Hills District Acquisition of Chief's Right Act in 1954, the *jhum* land around a village settlement was held hereditarily by thc Lushai chief, *lal*. The chiefs mostly belonged to the Sailo clan. With the assistance of the council of elders or *upas* the chief traditionally distributed the jhum plots to the inhabitants of the village for cultivation. He looked after the water resources carefully and fenced them. An individual violating the customary modes of maintaining the purity of water was liable to pay fine or *salam*. Nowadays the elected president of the statutory village council regulates the use of land and water in the same way as the traditional chief. Similarly, the Hill Karbis of Karbi Anglong District, who as mobile cultivators move from one settlement site to another, have no hereditary right in cultivable land. The hereditary village headman, *sarthe,* distributes land to different families. When a family leaves the village permanently, the *sarthe* takes possession of the land again. A newcomer has to obtain prior permission of *sarthe* for resettling in a village and for cultivation of village land.

Thus, it will be seen that in most cases *jhum* cultivation by the tribes is associated with the chief's right in village land. The ownership pattern, however, is different in areas where settled terrace farming is practised. Among the Angamis (Zoumuo-Keyhonuo) the Naga tribe who practise wet rice cultivation in terraces and also practise *jhum* cultivation, land is owned both individually and communally. The terraced rice fields are owned individually while the *jhum* fields belong to the community. Natural streams and rainwater being the only source of water for irrigation disputes often arise between owners of different plots and even continue for a long period. Conventionally, the owner of the plot whose land is so located as to get the stream water first has the right to use the water for irrigation prior to others, and then the owners of subsequent plots get irrigation water from the some stream.

The Angami have a kinship-based political organisation with well-defined laws and legal procedures for punishment of social offenders through regular courts, called *chape*. The village headman is vested with both administrative and judicial functions and is believed to have the capability to impose supernatural sanctions. His decision is final. Although the British administration introduced regulations banning physical punishment and allowing the village headman to try minor civil and criminal cases, the Angami village authority still adheres to the tribal customary laws in exercising his authority.

The largest tribal group of Assam, the Bodo Kacharis, have a patrilineal social structure. Closer interaction with the Hindus, since the beginning of this century, particularly the spread of the Brahma reformist movement, has affected the customary laws of the tribe. It is not only that the educated Bodo Kacharis, who have accepted the Brahma cult, refrained from making payment for bride or rearing pigs but also significantly modified the marriage ritual in pursuance of the cult.

Marriage by capture and marriage by service now rarely occur. The custom of *ghar-jiva* is also looked down upon. Through the movement the Bodo Kacharis are trying to reform their society and changing many of the customs following the local caste Hindus.

The marriage system among the Bodo Kachari Brahmas is simpler. In a Brahma marriage there is no provision of *hattachuni* feast which is considered important in a traditional Bodo Kachari marriage. But the binding ritual in a Brahma marriage is the yajna. The father of a bride brings his daughter before the yajna-kunda by holding one of her hands in the presence of the priest and other guests. Then the priest ties the nuptial knot, *lagnaganthi,* between the bride and the groom and then both are taken round the burning yajna-kunda seven times. This is similar to the Hindu custom of *saptapadi*. Prayers are offered in Bodo language. This being over, a pair of betel-nut and a leaf is reverentially offered to the yajna-kunda which is immediately followed by sprinkling of *santi-jal* (sacred water) along with the pronouncement of Om Santi three times. In the last stage a paste is prepared from the ashes obtained from the yajna-kunda and a mark is given on the foreheads of both the bride and the groom.

In recent years, the regional committees of the Bodo Sanmelan are taking an active part in reforming their age-old customs. In a meeting held at Kachibari in 1973, the Bodos decided to restrict the marriage ceremony to two days instead of four days in the traditional way. They felt that too much drinking of rice-beer and killing of animals for meat affect their household economy. They will be able to save some rice if they give up the habit of drinking rice-beer. In another meeting at Haludal they decided to reduce the bride-price.

In this session they also decided to use flowers instead of sacrificing animals during Pujas. In this way the Bodo *Sanmelan* is making efforts for reforming their old socio-religious customs and usages.

Under the influence of the Hindu the Rabha customary laws are also undergoing change. The traditions of caste Hindus have not only influenced the customary laws relating to marriage, sharing of resources, etc., but also the laws relating to inheritance and descent. The customary rites, related to worship of ancestors and spirits, are yielding place to the Hindu rituals.

In contrast to the Angami the Karbi have a centralised authority. The Karbi chief, *recho*, exercises traditional authority over all the Karbis in the Karbi territory through the Royal Council constituted of clan chiefs. The Karbi territory is divided into Alongris. The village councils are responsible for maintenance of social order to the Alongri councils and finally to the *recho.* It is the duty of the village chief, *sarthe,* to ensure strict compliance of the tribal endogamy and clan exogamy. It is evident that the Karbis strictly adhere to the customary laws in regard to the regulation of sex. Of all kinds of infringement of social norms incest is considered the most heinous crime by the tribe. Infringement of customary laws is rare particularly among those Karbis who have hardly any access to the statutory legal system.

It appears that the Karbis of Assam had an organised State before the extension of the British rule in the region. This is evident from the existence of the office of the supreme head, the Recho, and the well-defined structure of the traditional council as well as delimitation of specific powers of the different functionaries in the system of social control. There is a definite hierarchy of the traditional functionaries right from the village messenger or *mutiar* to *recho,* the supreme head of the tribe.

The *sarthe* and his co-functionaries exercise social control in the smallest village units. Similarly, the *habe* and his co-functionaries govern the Karbi population in a Longri. But the *habes* are subordinate to the *rechomei* or the royal council constituted of the *lindoks* and the *pimpomar.* Since times immemorial the traditional council has enjoyed unquestioned submission and loyalty to the Karbi chief who is the symbol of unity of the tribe.

The Karbi rely more on pecuniary punishment in bringing an offender to book and ensuring conformity to social norms. In coming to a decision or resolving a dispute, the Karbis follow unwritten traditions. The consensus arrived at in the course of hearing is considered obligatory and the social offender has to abide by the decision of the council or face ex-communication.

The Mizo or the Lusei customary laws are changing fast following the spread of Christianity and education. The study of the Lusei customary laws reveal that the old mode of courtship, mode of payment for bride, the custom of *zawl puan phah* or preparation of lover's bed by mother are giving way to Western marriage customs under the influence of the Western value system. Following enforcement of the Lusei Hills District Acquisition of Chief's Right Act in 1954, the social importance of the chief has waned considerably. A commoner can now marry a member of the chief's clan.

Widow remarriage is allowed in the Lusei society. The bride-price of a widow is less by rupees twenty than that of a maiden. The amount of bride-price is taken by her relatives in the same way as on the occasion of her first marriage. If she has no living kin she can adopt a brother for accepting the bride-price or she can take herself. A widow with grown-up children has to take consent of children for remarriage. If the offspring do not agree she cannot marry from their house, but can do so from the house of anyone of her kinsmen. The children of a widow, who remarries, can live where they like. They may continue to stay with their mother in her new husband's household or may continue to stay in their deceased father's house under the supervision of the father's relatives. Divorce or *inthen* is permitted and may be resorted to by either side. Ground for divorce may arise out of non-fulfilment of the marriage contract, namely, payment of the full amount of bride-price, cruelty, unfaithfulness, adultery, insanity and so on. Barrenness is another valid reason for divorce. When a husband divorces his wife he has to clear the entire amount promised as bride-price and the wife can take back all her belongings including her *thuam*. But if the wife is divorced on account of her committing adultery, which is considered to be the most serious offence, she forfeits rights over all her belongings including her *thuam* and also she has to return the entire amount already paid to her parents as bride-price. At the same time if the man commits adultery and his wife divorces him, he has to repay the entire amount of bride-price and the wife can take back all articles she brought to her husband's house at the time of her marriage. On the other hand when a wife divorces her husband she shall have to return all the amount paid as bride price. If the wife divorces her husband due to his impotency or insanity then the husband has to forgo claims on the bride-price that he has paid. If any husband suffers from impotency or insanity he has to undergo treatment for a specified period.

Thus, the customary laws of many of the tribes of North-East India are in transition now because of Hindu and Christian influences, spread of education and extension of the communication network. The old values have changed but the customary laws connected with sharing of scarce resources and maintenance of ethnic identity or regulation of marriage, more precisely the rules of endogamy and exogamy, are still adhered to in the traditional way.

2

CUSTOMARY LAW OF THE KHAMTI OF ARUNACHAL PRADESH

JAYANTA SARKAR

A custom which is defined as socially sanctioned behaviour of the members of a particular society is transmitted from generation to generation and in the process it undergoes changes in the changed situation. Since customary laws, in a very broad sense, include moral, legal, religious and other aspects of the custom through which the society is controlled, these also undergo change to cope with the new situation.

This paper seeks to examine the changes in the customary laws of the Khamti, a Buddhist tribe of Lohit and Tirap districts of Arunachal Pradesh. The data were collected in the course of field work undertaken during March to May, 1977 among the Khamti of two villages: one nearer to the plains of Assam in the Namsang administrative area and the other away from the Assam plains near the Chowkham administrative area. The area was previously visited by me in 1972-73 in connection with a separate study of the tribe (Sarkar, 1975). Bulk of the material on traditional laws was collected from their chronicles (Thamasat), written in their own script. The data were verified in the record village and at the same time every effort was made to find out the extent of change which might have come due to their contact with the people of the plains.

The Khamti inhabit the foothills of the above mentioned districts. According to their own chronicles they were the settlers of Mungkhamti or Borkhamti of Burma who immigrated to the present place of their habitation as early as the year 1053 of Khamti calendar. This corresponds with 1962 A.D. The Khamti society can broadly be divided into two social divisions: the royal and the commoner. The members of the royal social division usually have a major role in controlling the village affairs. The head of the village, usually the eldest member of the royal clan of the village, takes the responsibility of the traditional chief (*chaofa*) and controls the village with the help of his assistants. Changes in the customary laws of the Khamti have been discussed under the following headings:

(a) The laws as per the Thamasat.
(b) Changes in the traditional council.
(c) The existing situation.

The Laws as per the Thamasat

The Thamasat, meaning the judgement according to religion, as believed, was originally written down by the saints when the Khamti script came into existence. The Thamasat gives advice to the *chaofa* (village chief) regarding the way a judgement is to be adopted in a particular situation. Besides mentioning the details of the composition of the members of the *chaofa's* council it also suggests the qualities which a *chaofa* is expected to possess. It deals in detail the nature of disputes and conflicts and the types of judgement be given by the *chaofa* for such cases, after a proper inquiry and consultation with the members of his council.

Though the Thamasat advises the *chaofa* to be impartial and to judge the cases according to their merit, without considering the social position of the persons involved in the cases, in certain situations it has allowed the members of higher social strata to enjoy more privileges than the commoners. For example, if a person of higher social strata assaults someone belonging the lower strata on the upper part of the body, but not above the neck, one *khan* (Rs.14) should be fined. But if a person of lower strata hits on the head of a person of higher strata the former should be fined three *chois* (Rs.20). If he is not capable of giving the amount, the fine can be reduced to 50 per cent which is more than the fine that should be imposed on a person of "higher" social strata. If the man is not in a position to give even the 50% of the fine he should be asked to serve for the assaulted man of the higher strata. Similarly when a person of higher social strata kicks in any part of the body, other than the head of a person of lower social strata, fifteen *keps* (Rs.15) should be fined but in the reverse case the man of the lower strata can even be taken as slave by the man of the higher strata for his entire lifetime. In cases of adultery, when a man gets involved in illegal sexual relations with the wife of another man of the same social strata with the consent of the women, the guilty should be fined four *khan* (Rs. 56). But when such a case happens with the wife of a man of higher strata than that of the guilty, the latter is fined five *khan* (Rs.70). If the woman is the wife of the *chaofa* the fine increases up to 10 *khan* (Rs.140).

In the past a person of the higher strata used to keep slaves for doing various works. The Thamasat mentioned the privileges which a master could enjoy. For example, when a master gets involved in illegal sexual relations with a slave woman whose husband is also a slave to the man, the master should not get punishment or be fined. But when a master is involved in illegal sexual relations with a slave woman whose husband is not his slave he can be fined and punished. But when a man gets involved with a woman who is not a slave but her husband is, the guilty is only to undergo ritual expiation. No fine should be imposed on him.

The Thamasat lays emphasis on the moral law as it is disclosed from the advice it gives for the nature of punishment the *chaofa* should give in the following case: Two persons were alleged to have stolen fishes from the traps placed by another person. One trap is very simple and is made up of a single bamboo in such a manner that it can be prepared within a very short time. Another trap is complicated and requires skill to prepare. The person who has stolen fish from the simple trap is to be fined more than the one doing so from a complicated trap. It is considered that stealing of fish from such a simple trap proves the person lazy and also a thief by habit. In a similar way the Thamasat's advice for the amount of fine to be imposed for stealing different domesticated birds and animals indicates its emphasis on the moral aspect. Bigger and rare the animal is, lesser the number to be fined. For example, for stealing an elephant or a horse, an equal number of the same animal is to be fined. But, for one buffalo or cattle which almost everyone has, four times of the animal stolen is to be fined. For stealing of one pig, goat, dog, fowl, etc., ten similar animals are to be fined and for even an easily available smaller domesticated bird like a duck, a hundred birds of the same kind are to be fined.

Changes in the Traditional Council

The Thamasat suggests that the *chaofa* should form his council for dealing with the disputes according to the customary laws with the help of the members who should be as follows:

(a) Besides *chaofa,* there should be another leader from the royal clan.
(b) A man who has good faith in religion.
(c) A brave and courageous man.
(d) A good orator and writer.
(e) Apart from them there should be two other officials in the council who will give their impartial comments on the disputes which will be brought before the *chaofa*.

The ideal council of *chaofa,* as described in the Thamasat, has now undergone changes. Usually the eldest member of the royal clan in the village becomes the *chaofa*. In the absence of any such royal clan the village head is selected from the elder persons of the higher clan and in such a case the head is designated as *gaon bura* which the Khamti have adopted from the Britishers.

The composition of the *chaofa's* council has also undergone changes. At present such a council is usually composed of *chaofa*, the head, another person from the royal clan who is considered as leader of the youth, four ministers drawn from four different clans, and one messenger. All types of cases relating to land, non-payment of bride-price, adultery, theft, assault, etc., are dealt with by the council. Such disputes are generally brought to any of the four officials of the traditional village council. The officials discuss the matter among themselves and put the case before the *chaofa*. After consulting his ministers, if the *chaofa* thinks it necessary, he may call the villagers for a meeting through the messenger. The disputes usually do not go directly to the *chaofa*. It is rather a three-tier system. The individuals involved in a conflict or dispute try to solve the problem at the family level first. If he fails to solve, the case is taken up by the clan members, Even then, if they cannot solve the issue it is referred to the *chaofa*. This system was further enlarged in 1954. It was resolved in a meeting of all the Khamti leaders that if a dispute could not be solved within the village, it could be referred to another village, preferably Chowkham, being the largest Khamti village. When the problem could not be solved even at this level the heads of different Khamti villages would sit together and decide the case. In case the dispute still remained unsettled, it can be referred to a government court. This was further re-amended in 1966 through the introduction of the office of the chief. According to this system there is one chief of all the Khamti population of Lohit district. He holds the highest position in the Khamti political organisation. When a dispute remains unsettled even in the body consisting of all the heads of the Khamti village, it is referred to the Chief who is selected from the royal clan. The village without a royal clan, as has already been mentioned, is headed by the *gaon bura*. He is generally selected by the villagers. His council functions with the assistance of the elderly members of the different clans living in the village. But the officials of the *gaon bura's* council are neither selected from specific clans nor have they any specific designation. But like the council of *chaofa* it also plays a significant role in social control through customary laws.

Almost all the Khamti villages have come under the statutory village panchayat system which was introduced by the Arunachal Pradesh administration. In the panchayats the elected members are trying the cases keeping the customary laws into consideration, as far as practicable. Following the customary laws the Village Panchayat may try any case involving any of the undermentioned offences in which the person or the persons accused are resident within their jurisdiction. Theft, including theft in building, mischief by fire or any explosive substance, simple hurt, criminal trespass, assault or using criminal force, the Village Panchayat decides all cases in the presence of at least three independent witnesses of the complainant and accused. The panchayat members, in general, have made it a rule to include some elderly people who are also the leaders of the traditional councils, for giving their comments on the disputes. The attempt of striking a compromise with the customary laws and the Indian laws has proved to be a healthy development. No conflict arises between the traditional *chaofa's* council and the non-traditional Village Panchayat.

The Existing Situation

Like the *chaofa's* council where the elements of change have already entered, the custom itself is undergoing changes in the present contact-situation. For example, traditionally the Khamti are expected to marry within the tribe, but a few marriages between the non-tribals and Khamti girls have been reported. This is a breach of the custom and the persons concerned are liable to face punishment. But, in fact, such marriages are liked and encouraged too by the villagers. The marriage with mother's brother's daughter is preferred and considered as ideal. If someone declines to marry his mother's brother's daughter, the mother's brother can take it as an insult to him and can even ask for compensation. But in practice such marriages are declining in number and this is not considered as a serious offence. Ideally, direct exchange of bride within two lineages is prohibited. But with the change in the times such marriages have taken place, the custom has compromised and restricted direct exchange of brides within the members of three generations; one ascending and one descending generation of the egos, of two lineages. Cases of such prohibited marriages from both the villages under study, though in a very small number, have been reported. It has been observed that in such a marriage the couple or either of the couple has non-traditional education and they belong to the higher strata. No action as per customary laws was taken in such cases. They were recognised as exceptional cases. The children born out of such marriages enjoy the same socio-religious rights as of others. However, some feel that the offspring of such marriages may face difficulties in getting wives from the recognised wife-giver unit. They are to find out a new unit for obtaining a wife (Sarkar, 1977). A fine now a days is usually imposed in cash and not in kind as used to be in the olden days. The cases of murder can not be dealt with by the *chaofa* or even by the Chief of the Khamti as per their customary laws. It is to be referred to the police and ultimately to the government court. In olden days when the Khamti had the custom of keeping slaves there were laws for maintaining the interest of both the master and slaves. Since the custom of keeping slaves no longer exists and some of the services of the slaves are being taken from the labourer, new laws have been introduced. Now a days services from the non-Khamti are generally taken either on a daily-wage basis, or on monthly contract to be paid in kind which the Khamti have learnt from the people of the Assam plains where it is widely practised. The adoption of labourer has also necessitated introduction of some laws for coming into contact with them. They have borrowed the prevailing practices of the people of Assam, along with the system. The system of share-cropping like *meyangtu* (half-half system), *meyang koikhow* (two-thirds system), etc., has been included in the customary laws.

Since such contracts have been borrowed from the plains of Assam along with the rules, these could not penetrate deep into the tradition. Therefore, the case of any breach of contract, specially when the labourer is a non-tribal, is usually referred to the non-traditional village panchayat, instead of referring it to the traditional council.

Besides outlining the privileges sanctioned by the Thamasat to the people of higher social division of the Khamti, the present paper also discusses how in the process of compromise with the new situations the traditional customary laws have undergone change through amendment and also through adoption of certain laws from the neighbouring societies. Even the non-traditional village Panchayat, in general, has been taking the advice of the leaders of the traditional village councils for trying the cases under the customary laws as far as possible.

When any deviation from the custom takes place, a society may react to it in two ways. It may punish the breaker of customary laws or may accept such deviation as an exception. When the members of the higher strata deviate from the customary laws, a stratified society which has long been in contact with the outsiders may like to opt for the second possibility as has been observed among the Khamti. Acceptance of deviation as exception may encourage some members of the society to repeat it. When the frequencies of such deviations increase the society may amend laws and or borrow some rules for accommodating the deviations in the customary laws.

NOTES

Sarkar, J.K., 1975: *The Khamti: ethnography of a foothills Buddhist tribe.* (Unpublished).

——, 1977: A note on avoidance of direct exchange of bride among the Khamti of Arunachal Pradesh. *Man in India.* Vol.57.No.3.

3

CHIEFTAINSHIP AND CUSTOMARY LAWS AMONG TANGKHUL NAGA OF MANIPUR

PEARSON HUNGYO

The chieftainship is an age-old institution among the Tangkhuls. The chief is called *awunga* in Tangkhul dialect which is an equivalent of the English word "king". In every village there is a hereditary chief. In rare cases, there are two or more chiefs in a village. In village Bungpa, there are two chiefs representing the only two clans of the village. In exceptional cases, the leaders of the clan groups during their migration period agreed to settle down in a particular place without submitting their leadership to one another. In such cases, the leaders of the respective groups maintained their identity, and hence we find two or more chiefs in a village. There are many big villages with several clans which have only one chief each. Therefore, the number and size of the clans in a village are not the criteria for having two or more chiefs in a village.

The Tangkhul strictly follow the patrilineal system of descent and therefore the chieftainship passes on from father to the eldest son. If the chief has no male issue, the nearest male kin succeeds him. Under normal circumstances, it can never be transferred to any other person in spite of the influence and wealth a man may possess. In case the chief dies without a male issue and the next man who would succeed him is mentally retarded, or due to extreme poverty and irresponsibilities he could not perform the burial ceremony and other similar functions of the chief, then a person usually from the same clan who is able to perform the burial ceremony in a befitting manner and is capable of shouldering the responsibilities becomes the chief. He must be a man of character who is acceptable by the villagers. In no case does the society allow succession by daughters.

The village *awunga*, besides being the administrative head, is responsible for any affairs of the village including social and religious activities. The religious functions including sacrifice and worship are performed by the village priest but the presence of the chief is essential on all such occasions.

In olden days, defence of a village was a matter of great importance. Due to the practice of head-hunting and animosity among the villages, it was the duty of the *awunga* to keep the village safe from any enemy attack. The village wall and gate must be properly built and constantly guarded by the village braves.

The headman is responsible for the general well-being of his subjects and it is in his interest to keep them happy and contented. In doing so, he must hold meetings of the councillors and village elders from time to time. He looks after a villager whose stock of grain is exhausted due to crop failure for the year. He gives cultivable land to a landless villager. In return, the villagers, as a token of gratitude and respect for his benevolence and status, help him build and repair his house, and cultivate his paddy field. He also gives drink and food to them in plenty on such occasions. Pork and beef are abundantly served. The chief is offered the best drink and food during festivals. He is entitled to a portion of meat of the hunted animal. It is the headman who decides in consultation with the village council the particular block of land to be used for *jhum* cultivation. He has to give the green signal for all the agricultural activities. No one can bypass the decision of the chief who fixes the place and time of cultivation.

Some chiefs become very powerful and wield considerable authority. They command love and respect because of their abilities, benevolent attitude, and bravery shown during the inter-village feuds. However, the headman does not exercise unlimited powers, because the character of the people is highly individualistic. He is guided and advised by the village council on all matters. The real chiefs become only nominal heads and the village council *hanga* controls and takes decisions on all village affairs. However, there is no question of replacing him by another person.

The village chief, as the administrative head, looks after the maintenance of the water supply and village footpaths, opening of new footpaths and construction of bridges across the rivers which are difficult to cross. The dates of village festivals, religious ceremonies, taboo observance and various activities of cultivation are fixed and announced by the chief on the advice and in consultation with the members of the village council. The Tangkhuls have an interesting custom of organising mass hunting and fishing on certain dates in a year fixed by the village council. These are usually consulted with the chief for his consent.

The grazing grounds for cattle are well preserved and the village forest for supply of construction materials for houses is well demarcated. It is the responsibility of the chief that there should not be any beggar in the village. When a household runs short of stock in the granary, due to crop failure for the year, the chief comes to his rescue by asking the fellow villagers to share their extra stock which may be returned after the new harvest.

There is no metric system in the villages for sale of any commodity. The villagers follow certain norms in deciding the price of the commodity. The vegetables are sold in bundles and the meat is sold according to the number of slices cut equally. The chief with the council members ensures that no individual villager sells or buys according to his own whim without following the norm.

The executive power of the chief includes punishing one found guilty of breaking the time-honoured law of the land. Every person is expected to be conversant with the customary usages and traditional laws. No one is excused for pleading ignorance. There are several *gennes* in their religious and agricultural activities. These *gennes* are to be followed strictly and a breach of it is usually punished in accordance with the nature of the cases. They believe that the wrath of the power of evil manifests in crop failure and spread of disease which are due to these law-breakers. The calamity falls on all the villagers and not the individual law-breakers alone. So the wrong doer must be punished.

The village chief, on the advice of the village council, decides all kinds of disputes in the village. In some cases, the disputes may involve the whole village, but in most of the cases it involves only two or three persons. If there is any breach of the executive decision by an individual or a party, it is considered as an offence and action is usually taken against the individual or the party. Fines are imposed either in kind or cash. The councillors may decide to kill an offender's pig, without consulting him, as fine. Sometimes a fine of Rs. 50 or more is imposed.

The headman and the councillors constitute the village court. Whenever a dispute arises in the village in regard to land, theft, divorce, inheritance, adultery, criminal intimidation, incest, assault, breach of executive decision, murder, etc., these are heard and tried in this court. The cases are conducted according to the customary laws and the judgement pronounced by the headman. Disputes between the families of the same clan are, as far as possible, decided by the clan elders. Disputes involving two individuals or families of different clans are also settled by the elders of the two clans. However, if the individual or the parties are not satisfied with the decisions, the matter is referred to the village court. The village court is the highest court of justice for civil and criminal cases among the Tangkhuls.

As mentioned earlier, it is the members of the village council who assist and advise the *awunga* in dealing with all the affairs of the village. In every village, there is a council and chief as its head. It is the principal governing body of the village. Each clan sends its own representatives. Some clans may send two or more if the number of households of the particular clan is large in number. There are several clans in each village. The village council is called *hanga* and the councilor *hangva* in Tangkhul dialect. In exercising his powers in executive, administrative and judicial matters, the headman always takes the opinion of the majority of the councillors.

There are several do's and don'ts according to the customary laws of the land and these are enforced by the village council. The customary laws, though unwritten, are strictly followed and slackness in a case may lead to another.

Some cases of punishing the offenders, according to customary laws, are now obsolete and no longer in practice. Incidence of murder is very rare among the Tangkhuls and if it happens, the aggrieved party would try its best to take revenge upon the murderer or members of his family. Revenge is deeply rooted in the tradition of the tribe and the law of "an eye for an eye, a tooth for a tooth" is followed. The action of the aggrieved is usually endorsed by the village council or the case might never be brought before the council.

The final judgement of disputes, by taking oaths, is no longer in practice commonly as before. The administration also discourages this practice. However, in the olden days, it was a common practice. When the village court could not give any other judgement and the contending individuals or the parties had strong views and would not yield to each other, then oath-taking was the ultimate solution to find out the wrong and the guilty. The nature of oath-taking is usually by diving in the deep pond of the village, river or putting hands inside the boiling water in a vessel. The belief is that the innocent will not be affected by these acts but the guilty will be drawned in the pond and the hands burnt in the boiling water. Such acts were usually endorsed by the village court. Rape is very rare. But if it happens, the offender is beaten, severely by the villagers. Usually they try to break the leg or the hand of the offender. Sometimes the offender may succumb to the beating. This is considered deserving punishment and the village court always endorses it.

Hodson (1974 : 70-115) in *Naga Tribes of Manipur*, writes, "Divorce is a rare occurrence among the Tangkhuls. Barrenness and adultery supposed and proved are the main reasons of divorce. The divorced woman can always bring her case to the village court and the chief with the help of the councillors gives its verdict according to the customary laws and precedents. If a woman divorces her husband on flimsy grounds, she should be fined double of the bride-price paid to her parents and she cannot take anything with her from the house of her husband."

Clan exogamy is strictly followed. Violation of the rule of exogamy is severely punished by excommunicating the offenders from the village.

Land dispute is very common and elders who have long experience of land marks and boundaries are consulted by the village council and the case settled. If the case cannot be settled amicably, then they resort to oath-taking. In land disputes usually the contending individuals bite a little portion of soil under dispute with the risk of dying before the harvest of the year in the presence of the council members. The contending individuals swear that they may not see the new year or may not enjoy the new harvest if they are guilty before biting the soil.

The case of theft is a rare occurrence and the individual found stealing is severely beaten up and the article stolen is restored to the owner.

Tangkhul areas were isolated before the establishment of the British Administration and each village was a sort of an independent republic. There was no outside influence and interference, and they lived exclusively for a long time practising head-hunting among the neighbouring villages. Under such conditions, customary law was strictly followed and enforced by the village council.

"The days of head-hunting and warfare were cut short by the intervention of British through legislation" (Horam, 1977 : 96). The village chief was first contacted by the Britishers when they entered the hill areas for all practical purposes. They tried to win over the confidence of the village chief. He was entrusted with the task of collecting house tax for the British Administration. In recognising his status and symbol, a red blanket called *phrangchi* was given which in those days was considered a rare possession. The red blanket was meant only for the village chief and no other person was allowed to use the blanket.

The traditional way of life and the customary laws governing the villages were not disturbed to a great extent and the old system of village administration was allowed to continue during the British rule. Then came the Independence of India which brought tremendous changes in their political, economic and social life. With the introduction of administrative centres, the customary laws have been losing their importance and people are confused with the enforcement of Indian Penal Code and the Criminal Procedure Code as there are considered time-consuming and too complicated. They suspect manipulation of cases by the officials under the law.

The Manipur Village Authority under the Hill Areas Act, 1956, protects the traditional system of village administration though some changes have recently been made. The village headman is the ex-officio chairman of the Village Authority under the Act. The Sub-Divisional Magistrate has control over the Village Authority under the local jurisdiction. It is the duty of the Village Authority to maintain law and order and for that purpose exercise and perform of the powers and duties are generally imposed on the police under the Police Act, 1961. The customary laws are still in practice in the village administration and the *awunga* maintains the time-honoured law of the land.

4

CUSTOMARY LAW AND SETTLEMENT OF DISPUTE AMONG THE ANGAMI NAGA OF NAGALAND

N. K. DAS

The objective of this paper is to describe the nature of dispute settlement among the Zounuo-Keyhonuo of the southern section of the Angami Naga. The data for this paper is collected from the village of Viswema, which is located on the Nagaland-Manipur State border.

The significant features of the society are : a segmentary social system with a political organisation based on a territorial principle for judicial functions (which in the past was used for military functions of a defensive kind); territorial groups are coordinated with lineage (*sarra*) and clan (*thenu*) groups, the absence of central authority and government organs, presence of informal "court" and village council of elders, the political importance of the lineage/clan system, and the presence of an age-set system which entails certain political and legal functions. We shall describe below at first the age-set system that operates in the village of Viswema in the context of mechanism of social control, as also categorisation of offences, methods of dispute settlement through peaceful compromise and administration of oath, and at last the roles and functions of native arbitrators called *sechomi*.

Age-set System

Among the Zounuo-Keyhonuo persons of the same sex and of about the same age are formally grouped into five distinctive sets, which are usually formed at successive intervals. The age-set is generally defined as a formally organised group of age-fellows. Each age-set in the village of Viswema passes through a series of stages, each of which in the past had distinctive status, ceremonial, military and other activities.

Today the formal constitution of an age-set in the village does not involve any military purpose or any collective ceremonial initiation. In the past when "well-organised wars" were fought by villages, the age-set system served the purpose of providing for military education of the youth. The bonds of age fellowship united the sets of men of a wide area and cut across those of kinship and clan brotherhood.

The whole population of the village is organised predominantly on an age-set basis. However the upper two sets perform the legal and administrative functions. Age is thus a great factor in determining the rank and in conferring rights and privileges. The age confers authority in matters of law and government and the seniormost of the oldest group has the decisive voice in all matters that concern the regulation of public life. It is only the older men who play a leading part in the ritual activities. It may be stated that in the Zounuo-Keyhonuo society the seniority by age and seniority by generation are distinguished. In the life of the individuals there may not be many occasions to follow the rules and norms of age-set system, but at the group and collective levels there are several occasions and situations when the great significance of the age-set system in realised.

Age-set system in the village operates at clan level. Each set in Viswema is commonly called *thechu*. However. the five sets are called and described distinctly as follows :

1. *Pithi-Ketsami*: Included under this set are the seniormost elders, who generally occupy either religious positions or the position of headmen, or *gaon-bura*. The seniormost village-headman (razuo-pithi) is also chosen from the set. In general people above the age of 70 are included in this category.
2. *Mehu-chu* : Included under this set are people between the age-range of 50-70. The elders belonging to this age-set are mostly responsible for carrying out the job of headmanship (pithi) and tribal adjudicators (*sechomi*).
3. *Khrisha-mehu-chu* : The people in this age-set are mainly responsible for all manual work associated with village festivals. Adults of this age-set (between 30-50 years of age) are responsible for performing singing and dancing on important events.
4. *Khrisha-chu*: Included in this age-set are adults of 15-30 years of age. The kinds of activities performed by people of the above

age-set (khrisha-mehu-chu) are also performed by people of this age-set.

5. *Nhachu-chu*: Young boys and girls below the age of 15 are included in this age-set. These boys and girls are not allotted any specific job.

Domain of Social Control

The social order is not an unconscious process; it is an affair of rules, and of keeping or breaking them according to a variety of individual interests, and of responding to conscious obligations and training. These rules form a system. In most tribal societies they are not codified, nor are they always expressed as abstract principles.

The mechanisms of social control, the rules of conduct and the customary laws among the Zounuo-Keyhonuo cover a complex and wide range including the rights and duties of the villagers, marriage laws, rules for the relations between husband and wife, parents and children and between siblings and other kinsfolk, the law of property relating to land tenure, cattle and other animals, and inheritance, and for a variety of legal wrongs against the person.

Categorisation of Offences

The following are some of the offences which could be arranged in several grades on the basis of their seriousness:

1. Murder with intention (*mikedok hwemi*)
2. Murder by accident (*bijo-bimo*)
3. Adultery
4. Theft
5. Physical assault or torture
6. Abusing with dirty words, such as :
    a. *Teikhrunu* (Bastard)
    b. *Kitta* (Refugee)
    c. *Tokyvi* (Monkey)
    d. *Tonyo* (Cat)
    e. *Tehi* (Dog)
7. Land Disputes
8. Dispute over water sources/irrigational channels (*dzulye*)
9. Forgery of money
10. To spit on earth during "dispute arguments".

The offences of different nature demand the intervention of *pithimi* (elders), and *sechomi* (the elder acting as adjudicator), at different social and territorial levels. For the Zounuo-Keyhonuo it is the *thenu* (clan) district or *khel*, that is the most important unit of law enforcement and dispute settlement. Two most important modes of settlement of dispute are "peaceful compromise" and "administration of oath".

Peaceful Compromise (*kezevizhonu*)

As far as the dispute settlement is concerned it is observed that the useful compromise is considered as the basic objective. While such compromise is the only method at intra-lineage level, at the level of inter-lineage dispute settlement too *kezevizhonu* may be applied. The main purpose thereby is not to determine the guilt or innocence but to prevent the internecine strife.

Administration of Oath

If the peaceful compromise could not be reached between two parties, the oath is taken by the parties concerned in order to ascertain and determine the guilt. A person who could take an oath on a much larger number of lives of his kinsmen, as compared to his counterpart, the verdict remains in favour of the former. Depending on the severity of a case, the content of an oath is examined, reviewed and then the *pithimi* and *sechomi* arrive at a decision. Here are some examples of the content of the oath, in local dialect, and their meanings.

An oath starts with this general statement:

A. "*I/Hako tiju meda chusa tepe taye thuvo A/Hako po sa*".

"Let me/let us all not live in this world and let some epidemic destroy me or all of us, if I tell lies. I swear in the name of God."

B. If (any) cattle have destroyed the fields of so-and-so then let the poisonous snake bite me."

The oaths thus involve the life of one single individual or a group of several kinsmen.

An oath involves appeals to supernatural power. An oath is the act of calling upon a deity to bear witness to the truth of what one says. The Zounuo-Keyhonuo people consider an oath to be *opi onu teta zo sheri phoswe (eswe) le ketasa Tso we* (it means, "let there be a big case or a small case, such that of defamation, if a person has taken an oath to prove his innocence, or honesty, the matter is decided).

In settling disputes the question of fact is decided by oath. An oath has the same jural significance either in a village judicial council or in the tribal court located in the Deputy Commissioner's office. An oath in any case if the lives of others are made responsible for its truth as well as the life of the swearer, is usually accepted by either party. Since a false oath is held to entail death or at least misfortune as the result of it, the Zounuo-Keyhonuo do not risk their lives by pledging them to the truth of a statement of a kinsman unless they are fairly well satisfied that the statement is true.

In Nagaland, tribal or village councils regulate the social life. The regulation of 1945 revised in the seventies gives powers to the tribal councils to try criminal as well as civil cases and impose fines. So long as the parties belong to the same area, all civil suits are tried by the council. The punishment inflicted by the council is according to their customary law, though a limit has been put by the Administration to avoid heavy punishments.

Self-help in the Past

Inter-clan blood feud was a common feature in the whole of Naga area before the arrival of the British. Inter-thenu of inter-clan feud was called in Viswema dialect as *thenu-kegie*. General fights between two individuals or a dispute between two families belonging to two clans were not described as *thenu-kegie*. When several members of a clan physically attacked another clan then only it was described as a "feud" chiefly because it explains a state of recurring hostility between groups of people, usually motivated by a desire to avenge an offence against a member of the group. Most often use of iron-weapons, spears, daos (big knife) were avoided and only wooden articles and stones were used in a *thenu-kegie*

Peace accord or settlement of a *thenu-kegie* was always a lengthy procedure, particularly because it was not necessarily a fight between two connected kinship groups. The roles played by the clan-elders from both sides were very significant in this direction. The term *sechomi* is always used in Viswema to describe and address a *pithi* (elder) who is playing the role of an adjudicator, mediator or peace-maker.

Sechomi – The Adjudicator

The *sechomi* emerges in Zounuo-Keyhonuo society as an adjudicator. A *sechomi* is not a political chief but a specialist mediator. The *sechomi* as an adjudicator acts throughout as a go-between. He has no authority to force either of the or both parties to negotiate, and has no power to enforce a solution once it has been arrived at.

Under this kind of social organisation the complex rules of behaviour and code of conduct are viewed in the varied domains of social life. The significance of customary laws becomes observable in both inter-personal and inter-group relations.

An individual's jural status in this society is determined by the facts of birth, adoption and marriage; the jural authority pattern is directly connected with the laws of property which incorporate the rules of inheritance and succession. The rules of descent have their legal significance both at domestic and family levels, and wider group levels. The *pithimi* and *sechomi* guide the day-to-day actions of individuals. It is through these custodians of rules and mechanisms that the social control and social order is maintained in this acephalous, non-State, tribal society of the Zounuo-Keyhonuo Naga.

5

THE RABHA CUSTOMARY LAW IN TRANSITION: FROM MATRILINY TO PATRILINY

S. K. PAL

The Rabhas are one of the major plains tribes of Assam. They follow the matrilineal principles in respect to descent, residence and inheritance. In the pre-independence period the Rabhas were relatively isolated from the mainstream of the Hindu way of life and maintained their cultural homogeneity as an integrated harmonious whole, bound by common sentiments and values. But in the post-independence period the improvement in surface communications, spread of education and integration of tribal areas with the wider economic processes of the region have resulted in closer interactions between the Rabhas on the one hand and different other communities, especially the Hindu caste groups, on the other. As a result of a closer contact with the neighbouring Hindus the Hindu cultural elements have penetrated the traditional structure of the Rabha society. The major thrust of the alien influences on the Rabhas is manifested in the change in the basic principle of their age-old social structure. The Rabha society is, thus, now in transition from matrilineal to patrilineal social structure.

The closer contact with outsiders is due to the developmental and social welfare measures, initiated by the government, which brought to the village the primary school teachers, community development officials and physicians. The improvement in communication facilitated more frequent visits of traders and the Vaishnava preceptors from the plains. More and more of the Rabhas embraced Sarania, the first stage in the conversion process to the Vaishnava cult. The conversion was aimed at elevating their social status and thereby allowing entry into the Hindu fold. The contact with the patrilineal Hindu society has changed the basic structure of the Rabha society with concomitant changes in the customary norms and laws.

The total Rabha population in Assam is 138,630 (Census, 1971). They are distributed chiefly in the districts of Goalpara, Kamrup and Darrang. They are, however, also found in Garo Hills district of Meghalaya State and Cooch Behar and Jalpaiguri districts of West Bengal. But they are mainly concentrated in Goalpara district of Assam.

The Rabhas are primarily settled agriculturists and hence agriculture forms the mainstay of their economy. They are divided into a number of sections, viz. Rongdani, Maitori, Pati, Dahuri, Bitua, Totla, Shunga, Hana, Halua and Kocha. This division is said to be based on the occupational pattern (Rabha, 1974). Barring the Kocha section of the Rabhas, who are found along the north bank of the Brahmaputra river, all other sections are distributed mainly to the south of the said river.

The present study has been limited to the Rongdani section of the Rabhas and is based on data collected from a Rongdani village Salpara under Lakhimpur Police Station in Goalpara district of Assam, about 40 kilometres to the south-west of Goalpara town.

The scope of the present paper is to examine the recent changes of the customary laws of the Rongdani Rabhas consequent upon transition from matriarchy to patriarchy and the factors responsible for such changes.

As early as 1911, Friend-Pereira found that the Rabhas who once had a full-fledged matriarchal base were in a stage of transition to patriarchal form of life. Das and Raha (1967) also noted the process of transition from matriliny to patriliny. The Rabha society still retains some relics of matriarchy.

Traditionally, each section of the Rabhas is composed of a number of exogomous clans, known as *parai.* A profile of the Rabha social organisation is given in the following diagram:

Rabha Tribe

Section (Endo – and exogamous)

Rongdani, Maitori, Pati, Dahuri, Bitlia, Totla, Shunga, Hana, Halua, Kocha,

Clan or barai (Exogamous)

Jhur Hato Majenga Churchung Phenung Hadu Tara Bagur

Huri (Exogamous) Huri Huri

These clans are unilineal matrilineal descent groups. Further, two or more *barai* unite to form *huri* which again is exogamous in character. The members of each *huri* are considered as their friends and according to the emic view of the Rabhas, it is for perpetuation of their traditional friendship that marriage alliance within the same *huri* is prohibited. However, we find laxity in the observance of such prohibition. The question arises how can the friendship ties be strengthened without marriage alliances. One naturally suspects that these had originally been blood relationships among the component groups of the *huri*.

It is observed that the name of some of the Hindu clans like Kashyap and Bharadwaj have been adopted by members of certain clans who have embraced the Vaishnava cult. But so far as regulation of marriage is concerned, they still adhere to the traditional clan exogamy and the offspring of a married couple are known to society after their mother's clan.

The practices of marriage by force and service prevalent in earlier days (Rabha, 1975) are no more practised by the Rongdanis who have come in closer contact with the Hindus.

The negotiated *bhurishinkai* form of marriage (97.10 per cent) predominates in the present situation. In lieu of marriage by service (*Janwaidhankaibia*) the Hindu Gharjamai system (2.90 per cent) has come into vogue. Under this system the groom comes to live in the father-in-law's house with honour and prestige and it is no more obligatory for him to serve the household of the parents of the bride as he used to do before the marriage.

The practice of widow marriage (*Laralaribia*) and remarriage of divorced women are looked down upon and have become scarce now. Traditionally, monogamy is the rule and polygyny, polyandry as well as levirate are strictly prohibited. The incidence of mother's brother's daughter marriage, permitted in their society, has declined in the case of the members of the present generation.

In Bhurishinkai form of marriage, the ceremony is held at the groom's house and the residence of the newly wedded couple is strictly patrilocal. However, certain premarital rites are performed in the house of the bride on Bharkhosakai day when the groom's party comes to the bride's house to finalise the marriage date through a ritual. On that day the forehead of the bride is marked with vermilion by an unmarried female sibling of the bridegroom or his mother's brother's unmarried daughter. The bride's father accepts the *ganodhan* (bride price) from the groom's guardian. In this form of marriage the entire marriage expenditure is borne by the groom's father. But now the expenses are equally shared by both the parties. Sometimes the groom's father bears a major amount of marriage expenditure in the cases where the bride's parents are not economically solvent. Such changes have been adopted in order to ease the economic burden. Nevertheless, there is a recent trend of making gifts in kind as dowry. Nowadays, however, the marriage ceremony is held at the bride's natal house as is the case with the Hindus. This phenomenon is limited to the more Hinduised Rongdanis and is gaining popularity among them. With the introduction of dowry system the bride's parents nowadays face difficulties in negotiating marriage. Simultaneously the outlook of the bride's parents is also changing and they try to find out an educated mate preferably employed in white-collar job for their daughter.

During the marriage the Rongdanis follow some Hindu rites though they do not get the ritual services from the Brahman priest. It is noted that for finalising the auspicious time for marriage the parents of both the parties consult the *panji* (almanac). As among the Hindus they generally avoid the marriage alliance in Vadra (Aug.-Sept), Aswain (Sept.-Oct), Kartik (Oct.-Nov.) Pous (Dec.-Jan) and Chaitra (Mar.-April) which are considered as inauspicious months. But Magh (Jan.-Feb.) and Falgun (Feb.-Mar) have a special attraction for marriage as these two months are considered as most auspicious and suitable for marriage alliances.

Traditionally, the marriage alliances were initiated by the mother's brother who played an important role in the marriage of his sister's son or daughter. His views were respected by the parents of the would-be-couple. But at present, in most instances negotiations are conducted directly by the guardians of the groom and the bride through *ghatak* (match-maker) who is generally related to one of the contracting parties.

The Rongdanis practise patrilocal residence. In most cases (96.23 per cent) the post-marital residence is patrilocal. Even in the existing matrilocal families (3.77 per cent), the authority of the mother's brother has been replaced by that of the father or husband. The traditional extended families (37.74 per cent) have now disintegrated into patrilocal nuclear ones (58.49 per cent). The reasons for split of the extended families are disparity in income, and difference in outlook on life among the individual members of the family. This has weakened the family cohesiveness to a significant extent.

Traditionally, the women belonging to the mother's *barai*, known as *mahari*, had significant roles during all socio-religious ceremonies. For instance, during marriage the mother's brother accepted the *barai tamul* (betel leaves and betel nut) from the groom's party on behalf of the *mahari* to be distributed among the members of the bride's *mahari*. The bride's father was not eligible for such honour. Change of the authority structure in the family organisation has concomitantly changed the role of the kins. The *barai tamul* is now received by the bride's father and they are distributed to all the invitees irrespective of affiliations to the father's or mother's clan of either of the bride and groom.

The Hindu funeral rites have been adopted by the Rongdanis in the recent decades. The eldest son offers *pinda* (made of rice, betel leaves, betel nut, etc.) so that his father's soul may rest in peace. The mourning period is observed by the bereaved family for a fortnight, which is an indication of shift towards the Hindu patrilineal principle. Traditionally, the mother's brother's daughter had the right to offer *ganthi* (pinda) to the deceased soul on the day of the last rites ceremony. She, along with other womenfolk, sang and danced around the *ganthi* after offering. But the role of mother's brother's daughter has now been replaced by the son of the deceased. From the above illustration it is clear that the Rongdanis have also changed over to the patrilineal principle in this respect. It is also observed that the male kins undergo purification ceremony which includes a purificatory bath and head shaving. The service of a Hindu Napit (barber) is requisitioned for this purpose.

The tribal council has also been influenced by the traditions of the caste Hindus. For instance, customarily, *choko* (rice-beer) is offered to the departed ancestors and spirits on the occasion of socio-religious ceremonies. Today, the addiction to liquor is looked down upon by the members of the council, taking it harmful to health and family economy. They have taken the pains in educating the people about the harmful effects of drinking liquor and the habit is on the wane. The tribal council has also undertaken several measures to stop offering of liquor in socio-religious functions. Thus, influenced by the traditional way of life of the upper caste Hindus, the Rongdanis are modifying their old customary norms and rites.

Under the traditional rules of inheritance, the youngest daughter inherited the major share of her mother's property (both movable and immovable) and the remainder was equally shared by other daughters. Succession followed the female line but supervision of landed property was done by the menfolk. At one stage some of the informants suggested that the mode of inheritance became bilineal; the sons inheriting father's property and the daughter getting that of mother's. But soon the rules of inheritance changed over to the patrilineal principle. Today sons inherit both movable and immovable property of their parents. However, a few categories of movable property like handlooms, ornaments and some livestocks are still inherited by the daughters.

Although the overall pattern of inheritance followed the matrilineal principle the males could acquire certain superior position and acted as decision-makers at the village level through their membership in village councils. No female could become a member of these village councils. Each Rabha village was ruled by a *gaonbuda* (headman) and his assistant, a *deoani.* The *gaonbuda* and *deoani* were hereditary positions. A point which flows from this is that although the descent and inheritance principles were in accordance with the matriarchy the general pattern of social control, village administration and judiciary remained dominated by the menfolk, giving certain Hindu-like patriarchal characteristics to their village power structure.

The customary pattern of division of labour between men and women has undergone change, particularly due to the contact with the caste Hindus and with the spread of formal education. In earlier days, the hard manual jobs, like ploughing and house-building, were generally done by the menfolk, while the womenfolk were engaged in all other agricultural operations and domestic chores. Like their counterparts in the caste Hindu families the present-day educated Rongdani women are reluctant to do any agricultural work.

Conclusion

In the preceding pages we have discussed how the Rongdani section of the Rabha tribe shifted from the basic principle of matriarchy. The shift from matrilineal to patrilineal principle as well as the socio-cultural reforms directed towards Hinduisation have resulted in modification of many of the customary rules particularly related to marriage, inheritance and residence patterns. The pattern of authority in family is fast moving towards the patriarchal social structure.

While Hinduisation has affected the life cycle of the people differentially the negotiated Bhurishinkai form of marriage ceremony in particular follows the strict Hindu marriage rites. The father plays the major role during the marriage celebration. He now asserts his authority and takes decisions in family affairs. Divorce is now discouraged and no one can seek divorce for minor reasons.

Transmission of property along the matrilineal line has changed and only the sons now inherit the immovable parental property. But if a person has no male progeny then the parental property is inherited by his daughter. If a man has no offspring all property is then inherited by his brother or brother's son.

To sum up, it is observed that the Rongdani section of the Rabhas had certain cultural elements which were not strictly matrilineal, atleast organisationally, in the history of last one century. This is because the mode of decision-making and village administration was always solely and strictly the responsibility of the male members. Not only were the village councils dominated by the males, but even at the level of a family the mother's brother was accorded special duties to perform. As early as 1911, Friend-Pereira observed that the Rabhas were changing towards the patriarchal social system. As the Rabhas were always in contact with the Hindu caste groups the first could not remain unaffected. The complete changeover to patrilineal mode of property inheritance, on account of Hinduisation, has affected the old social order to a great extent. Even the mode of selection of marriage partners nowadays is in accordance with the patrilineal social system and the same holds true for the pattern of residence after marriage. The current situation reveals a process of transition whereby the traditional social system is fast moving towards patrilineal system.

PART II

EASTERN INDIA

6

TRIBAL CUSTOMARY LAW IN EASTERN INDIA

BHABANANDA MUKHERJEE, R. K. SAHA, B. JOARDAR, HASAN ALI

This report deals with five tribes, the Juang, Bathudi and Jatapu of Orissa and Oraon and Korwa of Bihar. The Oraon and Jatapu belong to the Dravidian family of languages and the Bathudi to the Indo-Aryan family. The Juang and Korwa are Austro-Asiatic language speakers.

The basic organising principles of the social structure of these tribes are patrilineal descent, patrilocal residence and patrilineal mode of inheritance and succession. Therefore, patriliny is the structural landmark on which development and observance of customary laws of the tribes centre.

All of them but the Juang live in multi-ethnic villages. Irrespective of residence in multi-ethnic or uni-ethnic village, all live in nexus with the non-tribals. Each of the tribal village is under a secular and religious head. Over the segmentary political structure at village level, there was/is the superarching federal organisation at the regional (*pargana or pir*) level.

Every village is self-sufficient in the matter of social control. The village and the regional political institutions look after the observance of customary laws besides the built in structural unit, like lineage among a few tribes.

In course of time many changes crept in. The historical relation of these tribal institutions with the then raja or zamindar of the region was snapped. The statutory panchayat has been introduced. Education has spread and conversion to Christianity has taken place among some tribes Shifting cultivation almost disappeared and diversification of occupations made them mobile. Contact with the non-tribals intensified and gradually the tribal value profile received a new orientation. Nevertheless, the tribal political structure continued to remain viable at least at the village level.

Social Control Mechanism

It seems that each system is unique though there is something in common. Tribal method of social control has a fairly uniform form in Bihar and Orissa.

The Juang of Keonjhar in Orissa live on hill slopes clad with forest and those of Dhenkanal in the plains. The former are shifting cultivators in the hills and live in uni-ethnic villages. The latter are the peasants in the plains and live in muli-ethnic villages. They are also in contact with the Hindus and worship the deities of the Hindu pantheon.

The social organisation of the Juang in general may be called clan lineage-based segmentary system. Once they were exposed to centralised political authority. They had their *pir* organisation at the regional level. Its headman was called *sardar*. The Juang in two villages have a tribal council. It deals with all internal problems. Among the Juang of Dhenkanal there is, in addition, a *jati* panchayat. Its head is called *bada behera*. The Juang adopted it from the low castes of the area. It has under its jurisdiction a number of villages and deals mostly with cases of divorce and adultery.

Tribal Council and *jati* panchayat function at village level and are viable organisations having sufficient control over the Juang. Tribal Council has five officials and the pradhan is their secular head. There is also the priest *dihuri*, the religious head.

Extra-structural organisation is the statutory panchayat both for the tribals and non-tribals. The Juang are the majority in the statutory Panchayat but they do not bring in any of their tribal problem.

The Bathudi are also a tribe in Orissa. They were studied in two villages in Mayurbhanj district. These villages have different ecological and social environment. Village Padmapur, which was their traditional habitat, is now more exposed to outside contact. The tribals here are poor day labourers. The Bathudi of Aganpat on the other hand are less exposed to contact. They are mostly peasants and prosperous. Their social organisation is based on joint family and lineages. They live in multi-ethnic villages.

The Bathudi have a village council and caste council (*jati sabha*).

The village council consists of elderly members of different caste and tribes, and each caste and tribe has a *jati sabha.* Besides these two, they had *pir* and *pargana* organisation at Padmapur. *Pir* and *pargana* organisation still continues in Asanpat village. *Pir* controls three or four villages and its head is called Beschatia. *Pargana* controls several *pirs* and its head is called *deo pradhan.* Formerly the Bathudi Zamindara used to control the *pargana* organisation. Being dominant they also control the statutory panchayat.

Among the Bathudi the village council and the *jati sabha* are viable organisations. *Jati sabha,* which consists of elderly persons, is headed by a *pradhan*. It deals with all social offences and breaches of social customs. At the structural level the other viable unit is the lineage (bakhuri). This is a built-in power centre whose heads have also the authority over its members. Besides these there are also heads of small hamlets. But the *jati sabha* enforces the strict observance of customary laws. They impose fines on outcaste offenders and re-admit ex-communicated persons through expiatory ceremony.

The third tribe of Orissa is the Jatapu, a Telugu-speaking group and an off-shoot of the Khand. They, like other two tribes, namely, the Juang and the Bathudi, have both *gram* panchayat, at village level and *mandali* panchayat at regional level. Saonia, the head of the *gram* panchayat and the elders of the village look after petty cases and litigations. The *mandali* panchayat, headed by *mandali naidu,* settles cases which are complicated and have a bearing on the prestige of the whole community. The village priest is invariably consulted, when there is any breach of socio-cultural norms, particularly violation of lineage exogamy. Besides, public opinion is mobilised when it is apprehended that an offender is likely to subvert the decision and verdict of the *gram* panchayat.

Among the Juang and the Bathudi, law does not differentiate between the two sexes. But among the Jatapu the women have unusual freedom and special status. A woman can desert her husband, if she is not satisfied with him. Normally therefore premarital and exmarital cases are not dealt with by the *gram* panchayat.

In Bihar, the Oraon were studied in the Badar Sub-division in Ranchi district. One village is in relative isolation. Both of the villages depend upon plough cultivation. Their social organisation is based on clan and family. The villages are multi-ethnic. The group includes both Christian and non-Christian Oraon.

They have the *gaon* panchayat at village level and the *parha* panchayat at regional level. The two are their traditional institutions which are still viable. *Gaon* panchayat deals with all disputes of the village and breaches of social customs. It also executes the decision of the *parha* panchayat. *Mahato* is the head. Divorce is effected by the *gaon* panchayat and a case of pre-marital pregnancy is taken over by it. Parha organisation is a sort of an appellate court and settles all disputes which the *gaon* panchayat fails to do. Being a traditional institution, these two are responsible for enforcement of customary laws.

Originally, the functionaries of these two institutions derived their authority from the association with the rular of Chhota Nagpur and thus like the Juang they had association with centralised political system. *Parha* panchayat appears to have a royal court structure which has remained unchanged. But following the abolition of zamindari, the functionaries did not have the same power.

The Oraon customary laws appear to have changed a little as far as these two villages are concerned. Relaxation of commensal rule is noticed. Even the commensal restriction between the Christian and non-Christian Oraon seems to be a thing of the past. Now they interdine and inter-marry. Still violation of the ruler endogamy, clan exogamy, incest and premarital pregnancy are looked down upon. The Christian Oraon observe some of these rules.

The Korwa of Bihar have been studied in the context of ecology and social situation of Ranchi and Palamau. In Ranchi, the village Malom is situated in the hills and is clad with forest. Sera Seam in Palamau is in the plains and in contact situation. Economically the Korwa of Ranchi are agriculturists and sharecroppers and traders in forest produce whereas in Palamau they are agriculturists and day labourers. As regards social organisation it is clan-based in Ranchi whereas in Palamau they have forgotten their clan names. Such a small group widely scattered and living in small villages or settlements have two traditional social control institutions. These are *gaon jati sabha* at village level, headed by *panch* or *mahato*. The *pargana sabha* or panchayat operates at regional level. Cases concerning marriage, divorce, adultery, etc., are dealt with by *gaon jati sabha* but cases which are not settled by it are dealt with by *pargana sabha*.

Customary laws regulate the Korwa social relationship both within and without. Rules regarding endogamy, bride-price, clan endogamy, observance of prohibited degrees of kinship in marriage and the rule of inheritance are rigidly followed. But there are flexibilities in other rules, namely, the rule of residence. They are patrilocal but many of them often live in the house of wife. There is also no rigidity about the order of marriage of siblings. The younger siblings may marry before the elders without violating the norm. A number of spouses were found separated without any formal meeting of *gaon jati sabha*.

While observing the customary laws, the Korwa also see to the necessity and convenience and have a rational outlook. The same body of customary laws operate in two villages having different ecology, economy and exposure to outside. But the major differences are due to urbanisation and Hinduisation. The Korwa of Palamau take the services of barber and washerman. New values and ethics seem to have prevailed there.

Social Forms

Social forms in terms of family lineage, clan, marriage, etc., can not be properly documented in view of lack of uniform data among the five tribes.

Family organisation among the Juang is nuclear. They have exogamous clan organisation. Each Juang village comprises the members of one clan. Therefore marriage is interdicted within a village. Age at marriage is 15 or 16. Most marriages are now settled by boys and girls themselves. Bride-price is just symbolic. Marriage by negotiation and capture and love marriage are general modes for acquiring mates. monogamy is the rule but polygyny is not rare. They marry classificatory mother's brother's daughter. The kin categories are consanguineous (*kutom*) and affinal (*bandhubok*). Marriage within a clan and prohibited degree of kinship and premarital conceptions are serious social offences for which one may be ex-communicated. But an ex-communicated individual is re-admitted into Juang society through performance of expiatory ceremony. Land ownership is both individual and collective. Individual ownership of land is a later development.

As regards observance of customary laws for family, marriage, etc., the old and new have different attitudes. Hence a conflict is developing.

Among the Bathudi, family organisation is nuclear in Padampur village whereas in Asantpat it is joint. Extended lineage structure (*bakhuri*) is well intact in Asantpat where the heads of lineage have considerable authority over its members. Thus lineage (*bakhuri*) acts also as a repository of the customary laws of the tribe.

They have exogamous clan organisation. Bride-price is not symbolic like that of the Juang. The amount depends upon the wealth and status of the bride's family. In all cases of divorce it is refunded.

Marriage by negotiation, intrusion and *sangha* and love marriage are modes of acquiring mates. Marriage by *sangha* is a remarriage of divorced, widower and widow. Social position and legal right of the children, born of second marriage, are the same as those of the children born of the first marriage. As to the order of marriage of female siblings, the eldest daughter is married first and there is no departure in this regard. Monogamy is the general rule but under some circumstances one is permitted to have more than one wife. The widows are not denied any social right. They can perform all social ceremonies like any married woman.

Divorce is effected by *jati* panchayat and involvement of any spouse in crime and conviction by court is also taken as a ground for divorce. Property is inherited by sons. But all have usufructuary right over natural resource.

Among the Jatapu of Koraput, Orissa, the dominant family type is nuclear. Household with married sons is rare. As regards marriage rule, importance is given to lineage exogamy. Any marriage within the lineage is a serious social offence. Most of the marriages are arranged by grown-up boys and girls. Very often they resort to *donga palli* marriage which is performed in secret. These marriages are common due to demand of bride-price (*oli*). Bride-price is claimed back, if a woman re-marries but not if she lives with her parents after separation. There is another mode of acquiring a mate, which is known as *raja-ote*. This is marriage by force. Generally they are monogamous. Because of the Telugu influence marriage between maternal uncle and sister's daughter is in vogue, unlike the other tribes covered here. Marriage among the Jatapu is very simple. Living together of a man and a women on mutual consent is a sufficient social fact to be recognised by society as husband and wife. Because of the above notion of marriage and the freedom and independent status of women, illegal union and birth of illegitimate child are not seriously considered as violation of normative behaviour. The sons inherit property to the exclusion of daughters. Like the Juang, the Jatapu own *padu* field (shifting cultivation land) property. •

Family organisation among the Oraon is nuclear. Clan exogamy is strictly observed. Most of the marriages are settled by negotiation. The other modes of acquiring mates are elopement, intrusion and love marriage. Divorce is effected at the meeting of the *gaon* panchayat. Sons inherit property. Landed property of all unmarried men is divided among his brothers or their sons after their death. In Oraons' conception, land belongs to lineage and hence, according to their customary laws, land cannot pass over to daughters who cease to be lineage members after their marriage. But in contradiction to this traditional rule, one Oraon transferred his land through registration to his daughter. Though this is legal, he could not escape criticism of his lineage members and clan members for breaking the tradition. They value social approbation more than legal sanction.

Nuclear family is dominant among the Korwa of Bihar. The Korwa of Ranchi, however, observe clan exogamy but those of Palamau do not. In Ranchi, violation of clan exogamy occurs. At both the places the rule that no body can bring a spouse from outside the *kuri* (tribal section) still prevails. Infringement of the rule of endogamy is treated among the Korwa as the most serious offence. Marriage is prohibited not only with the consanguineous but also with some affinal in. Monogamy is common but polygyny is also found. Most marriages are settled by negotiation but love marriage is also common. The younger sibling may marry before the elders without violating the norm. Both husband and wife have the right to divorce, which is effected by *panch* or *sabha.* Knowledge of black magic by a woman is not a ground for divorce. Adultery is discouraged in Korwa society. If a woman runs away with a non-tribal, she is excommunicated. But if she leaves him, she is re-admitted after an expiation feast is given to the *panch.* Re-marriage of widows and divorced women is common but their children, by the former husband, do not get the step-father's property.

Rules regarding tribal endogamy, clan exogamy and inheritance are strictly observed.

Conclusion

There are institutions of social control at the village and regional level among the tribes of Bihar and Orissa, which have not become dysfunctional. All customary laws still have the social and supernatural sanction. Scale of social organisation and built-in authority structure, like lineage, maintain the structural form of social control mechanism among the Oraon and the Bathudi in full vigour. Customary rules are not disparate ecology. Social change appears to have caused erosion of customary iaws in contact situation among the Bathudi in one village and the Korwa of Palamau. Rational thinking, due to modernisation, has led to disregard of the rule of commensality among the Oraon (both among the Christians and non-Christians) and the order of marriage among siblings and separation of spouses among the Korwa. There is a conflict between State law and customary law among the Oraon regarding transfer of land to daughter. There is inner contradiction among the Juang as to the attitude towards customary laws between the old and the new. Statutory panchayat among the tribals which is an exogenous mechanism has an impact over the endogenous tribal social control mechanism. Although general concepts are shared by the tribes some variations are observed in conceptualisation of marriage among the Jatapu, distribution of shifting cultivation land or *padu* field among the Juang and the Jatapu and about illegal union and illegitimate child among the Jatapu.

As regards social forms conformity is maintained among these tribes. Family pattern, monogamy, form of marriage, prohibition of incest, laws of inheritance are, by and large, similar. As regards order of marriage among siblings, and sharing of property among male siblings, there are variations. Structural principles regulating marriage, tribal endogamy, clan and lineage exogamy, rules of inheritance and succession and categorisation of consanguine and affinal kin are the same.

7

CUSTOMARY LAW AND CRIME AMONG A HUNTING AND GATHERING TRIBE — THE CASE OF THE HILL KHARIA OF BIHAR AND WEST BENGAL

DIKSHIT SINHA

Customary law of primitive societies of India has received scant attention from anthropologists. But there can be hardly any dispute regarding its importance because if we are to integrate the tribes more meaningfully with the formal institutions of the State without endangering their cultural identity, understanding of the customary law of primitive societies becomes a *sine qua non*. One of the major difficulties inherent in studying customary law is the lack of clarity regarding what we understand by the term customary law, especially in societies which lack formal institutions. Radcliffe-Brown (1952) differentiated between "sanction" of primitive societies from "law" of more advanced societies. Recently Pershit (1977) characterised the "precapitalistic" societies as having "mono norms", that is, societal norms which make it obligatory on each member to adhere to and abide by the norms of his society. Pospisil (1972) points out that 'law' in contrast to what is merely customary (internalised norms of the society everybody obeys) is a relative phenomenon. Even what is custom at societal level may be law at a group level (clan, lineage, etc.). According to him from the dynamics of intergroup and interperson behaviour certain repetitive generalised pattern of decision regarding what ought to be the behaviour of a community can be abstracted. These are again backed by four attributes, namely, authority, intention of universal application, *obligatio* and sanction. But not all societies have well-defined authority backed by social sanction, especially simple societies like the Hill Kharias with whom we are concerned here. In such societies the absence of authority is made up by the presence of people's "conviction of its indispensability and desirability". Violation of customary law in such cases generates tension and anxiety in the individual apart from the general opprobrium he receives from his contemporaries.

The Problem

The Hill Kharia, traditionally a hunting and gathering tribe, live in the hilly regions of Western Bengal, Orissa and Bihar and do not have any written authoritarian law. This tribal group, who now combine hunting and gathering with agricultural labour is unique in the sense that in the region, especially in West Bengal and adjoining districts of Bihar State, they are regarded as criminals. The dwindled forest wealth and impoverished agricultural system of the region from which the peasant scrape their bare necessities have pushed the Hill Kharias into a situation from which they find no ready route of escape. The pervasive feature of factionalism in the villages and the Hill Kharias' own impoverishment draw them in various criminal activities (Sinha, 1976). This particular feature is no less important because it give us a clue regarding not only the nature of the Hill Kharia society but also their relationship with the other dominant societies who control the law-enforcing institutions. Although this itself does not allow us to understand the customary law of the Hill Kharia society it will enable us to understand the nature of inter-ethnic relationship. In this paper apart from delineating the salient features of customary law of the Hill Kharia society we will focus and try to explain why the Hill Kharia participate so widely in criminal activities.

Area of Field Work and Method

The field work was carried out mainly in two villages, one in Purulia district of West Bengal and another in Singhbhum district of Bihar. The total length of field work carried out for this purpose was three months. It may be pointed out that before this I carried out five months' field work among the tribe.

An Outline of the Social Feature of the Tribe

The Hill Kharias or Erenga Kharia who now call themselves as

Sabar, the mythical figure of Ramayana, are widely spread over six districts of West Bengal, Bihar and Orissa. The Hill Kharia of Bengal and Bihar differ from the Hill Kharias of Orissa in dialect, clan organisation and certain ritual observances. In West Bengal they live in Purulia, Bankura and Midnapur districts. Except in few isolated pockets they now live in close proximity of peasant villages. In none of the census enumerations they have been separately counted. A rough estimation made in 1975 indicated that in Purulia their number would be around five to six thousand.

In Kulabahal there are altogether 24 Hill Kharia families. Besides the Hill Kharia there are nine other ethnic groups including a Muslim caste called Mal. But the Kurmi Mahatas are numerically dominant as a single ethnic group (49.38 per cent). They are the people who control nearly 80 per cent of village land and also dominate the political institution like Panchayat. The Hill Kharias occupy the lowest social rung in the region because of their unorthodox food habits.

Economic Deprivation

The landless Hill Kharias of the village eke out a precarious existence by combining their traditional occupation of gathering and hunting with agricultural labour, selling forest produce like sal leaves, firewood, medicinal roots, etc., objects fashioned from bamboo such as fish trap, broom-stick. The depletion of forest has made their getting fruits, roots and tubers difficult. Hence people are trying to participate in the agricultural system as much as possible. Young boys from the age of 7-8 years are hired by peasants as full-time cowherds or agricultural-cum-domestic labourers (*bagal*) at a negotiable annual rate of wage. But this has anything but solved their economic problem. Starvation for days on end during lean periods has become part of their life. In contrast they are confronted by the spectacle of other communities of the village, secure in their knowledge of possession of land and economically relatively much better off. Consequently, the tribe suffers from a sense of felt economic deprivation.

Ray (1937) found the presence of only two clans among the Hill Kharias of Mayurbhanj. In Purulia informants listed 18 clans. But the clans at the present time do not play significant corporate and ritual roles. Rather it was found that the lineage groups (*bangsa*) play an important role in organising their life. In their atomistic social life occasion for the need of leadership seldom arises. In group life they are guided by the principal of avoidance of conflict.

The Supernatural World

Like their social system the supernatural world is segmented. The chief spirit is known by the name of Dharma. Each significant aspect of nature is conceptualised as controlled by a particular spirit. Their two religious ceremonies are held on the first day of *Magh* (middle of January) and in the month of Baisakh when new flowers and fruits are offered to the deities. Each of the village has a *laya* who performs this puja on behalf of the people.

Before we deal with their customary law it may be pointed out that the Hill Kharia society is characterised by marginality vis-a-vis the peasants, felt economic deprivation and a notion of hopelessness. The last trait arise out of their peculiar socio-economic position as well as their regular persecution by the police as criminals.

Marriage Rules

Marrying and establishing one's own family is a prerequisite of attaining the full adult status in Hill Kharia society. Three kinds of marriages are prevalent among the Hill Kharia : (1) *Seja biha* or marriage by negotiation, (2) *sikar biha* or forced marriage, (3) *sangha* marriage or second marriage. Of these, *sikar biha* nowadays occurs very infrequently. The negotiation for marriage must be initiated by the groom's side. In the past there were elaborate procedures of marriage negotiation called *panr base*. Negotiations, especially the fixation of bride-price, are carried out using symbolic terms. Residence is usually patri-neolocal. Recently some cases of uxorilocal residence were recorded. The choice of residence is governed by the availability of food. The decision is, of course, entirely the husband's prerogative.

Nowadays bride-price varies between Rs. 20 and 40. Although clan exogamy is said to be the rule this remains a notion only. In Purulia it was found that while negotiating for marriage alliance care is taken to eliminate the possibility of the prospective groom or bride being the direct descendant of one's own *bangsha* (patriline) or that of the F.S., M.S., M.B., and F.M.B.'s *bangshas*. Therefore, in practice the Hill Kharia marriages occur between a set of lineages. Kharia informants stated that if one's parents, F.S., M.S. or M.B.s are dead and marriage can take place between these lineages. It was pointed out that supernatural sanctions are invoked after every marriage (*khatabara*) and it was seldom objected to by supernatural deities (marriage between collaterals).

S. C. Roy (1937) recorded that marriage with classificatory M.B.D. is practised by Hill Kharias. No such preference was expressed by the Hill Kharias of Purulia. Junior levirate and sororate marriage although optional is present among the tribe. In Singhbhum one junior levirate marriage and in Bhutam (P.S. Puncha, Distt. Purulia) one sororate marriage were recorded. If the husband dies after the birth of a few children wife prefers to remain as widow and bring them up.

Divorce Common

Among the Hill Kharia divorce occurs frequently and the process is very simple requiring no intervention and mediation of any institution. The grounds for which divorce is sought are : ill-treatment, denial of food, barrenness, incompatibility, etc. There was no case of adultery for which divorce occurred. It is significant that no divorce was recorded after the couple was blessed with a child. When husband and wife see that they can no longer adjust together they generally take the recourse of moving off from their common place of residence. Usually the husband takes his wife or, the wife herself goes back to her father's village. After this kind of visit it is customary among the Hill Kharia that the husband will take back the wife to his village. If he fails to do this then it is thought that the husband has decided not to live with her. After waiting for a reasonably long period the wife then takes off the iron bangle that was ritually slipped on to her wrist by her husband and waits for the second marriage (*sangha*). Sometimes a protracted quarrel results in the husband taking off the bangle from his wife himself.

Interaction with Kin

In kinship relationship it was found that due to impovisation it was difficult for the people to abide by the conventional norms. For example, it is customary to invite parents' M.B. besides one's own in-laws and F.S., M.S. during marriage and sradha ceremonies. But nowadays economic constraints prevent extending invitation to such kins. Only few close lineally related families are invited. Visitation and mutual help during crisis period is very rare.

Although we have stated that hunting is a part of Hill Kharias' occupation they hunt only small games, like snake, lizards, hare, fox, etc., which require hardly any participation of a group. But when such groups are formed sharing is a must. If the group is formed exclusively from among lineage members then the hunted game is shared equally. But if there are non-lineage members the person who strikes the first blow or arrow will receive the right hind leg and two ears of the head and a portion of the other share.

The Concept of Property and Inheritance

Among a hunting and gathering people usually the concept of property is weakly developed. But they had a strong sense of territory. In Purulia this sense of territory is also lost because after the promulgation of the Forest Act they roam about without any stable habitat. Moreover, they do not have any control over the territory they settle down for temporary or permanent residence. In former days, it was reported that the Hill Kharias had to pay a token tax on roots and fruits once a year to the king in lieu of their right to extract a living from the territory they used to live in. In some places of Mayurbhanj where jhumming is still practised the family which clears the portion of the forest retain the use of it for jhum cultivation. Nowadays some Hill Kharias have acquired certain amount of cleared forest land converted into agricultural land. These properties are inherited according to the convention of the local villager which singles out the eldest son as the person largest beneficiary, that is, he is entitled to the largest share. The remaining amount is shared equally by the other sons.

Each son as he establishes his own family gradually acquires the necessary hunting implements, like digging stick, traps, nets, etc. Therefore, the question of inheriting the father's hunting implements becomes obsolete. However, at the time of the father's demise the son with whom he was staying inherits the movable property.

The office of the *laya*, the priest, is a hereditary one. The eldest son inherits the office of the *laya* after the death of his father.

Avoidance Best Method of Social Control

It was pointed out that the Hill Kharias do not have any institution of social control. The domestic mode of production and poverty-stricken situation has imposed an atomised form of social relation. But this lack of any formal social control has been partly replaced by *lasan* or black magic. Through lasan one can seek redressal of one's grievance against any person. But not all people are experts in performing lasan. Nevertheless, the danger of this prevents any person acting in such a way as to attract such reprisal. Another belief which prevents people from unduly injuring any person of his community is the notion of guardian spirit. Hill Kharias believe that every person has a guardian spirit which sees to it that its protege does not fall into danger. Nevertheless conflicts arise frequently in the Hill Kharia society too. How does one resolve conflict without any mediation of any authoritarian institution ? It was pointed out that Hill Kharias try to avoid all overt conflict. Although due to the lack of any effective authoritarian institution it is not possible to strictly impose even the norms of avoidance it was found that in a conflict situation this is the way by which conflict is resolved. In Kulabahal village practically all the families suffered from social boycott. Although the sentence of boycott was passed in a group there was no method by which social boycott could be withdrawn. For example, Sambhu Sabar is said to have misbehaved with the laya when his son who married Sambhu's daughter drove her off from his house. The laya, Bhim Sabar, sat nonchalantly all through when Sambhu came to his hut with a bamboo staff and rained abuses on him and his son. When at last Sambhu went out his brothers and neighbours came out and discussed Sambhu's "misdemeanour" and decided that he should be taught a lesson by boycotting him. The Kulabahal Sabars are divided into two major lineages, Sambhu and Bhim representing each of them. As Sambhu's own kinsmen had quite a few grievances against him they too concurred with the social boycott. When Sambhu heard this he did not become repentant but showered another dose of abusive language on his neighbours. It was noticed that Sambhu's own brother continued to visit him. A few of his own lineage members also visited him stealthily when they, driven by hunger, sought food from him. (Relatively speaking, he was well placed as far as supply of food was concerned.) Gradually the rigour of social boycott fell off and only Bhim continued to adhere to it.

In another conflict too Sambhu was involved. Sambhu, it was alleged, occupied a portion of garden land of Arjun. This problem proved to be intractable as neither of them possessed the requisite cadestral map and were not enterprising enough to seek recourse to other methods of arbitration, that is, land revenue department or the help of village people. Arjun said bringing on *amin* (land surveyor) requires money. Even the persons of the village who know to whom the portion of the disputed land belongs demand money. To his kin, busy in securing a hand-to-mouth existence, this is a far-fetched problem. Therefore, the dispute has survived through a decade. In the past people frequently resorted to the method of migrating from the village where he finds little hope of getting peace. Nowadays the density of population pressure has increased to such a proportion that migration has become difficult. Therefore, intra-group tension is mounting among the Hill Kharias.

Crime and its Cause

For a hunting and gathering tribe the Hill Kharias' brush with the police is quite frequent and intensive. This coupled with their impoverished economic situation and marginal social position has generated a kind of hopelessness in the tribe. They have given up any hope of securing a better deal for themselves — either economical or social justice. In Kulabahal as many as 76 per cent of the total adult males were arrested by the police for various crimes. The police believe that the Hill Kharias of the district are habitual criminals who are associated with various forms of crimes like burglary, dacoity, rioting, arson, etc. Mortally apprehensive of police catching them unaware the Hill Kharia adults sleep outside their hut during night. They keep a wary distance between all kinds of strangers.

Why the Hill Kharias participate in criminal activities? Do they have some inner compulsion ? Our study suggests that poverty and the consequences that flow from it affect his behaviour which draws them into the crime and factional rivalry that goes in the peasant village. In discussing this in an earlier paper it was pointed out :

> Through his long knowledge of peasant's way of life he knows that he lacks many things that the peasants have. Also the past ways of life of themselves make him intensely aware that in present day the easy way of life of his forefather is no longer possible. The

lure that the peasants' promise hold to him is precisely which his forefathers were fortunate to have : at least some days relief from the anxiety of food supply and happy abandonment. Peasants not only promise this but also assure them safe conduct from the village after the dacoity has been committed. In theft and burglary also they are drawn in by the village people (Sinha, 1976, p.11).

But the guardians of law do not have so much time to look beyond the surface. They are happy that they have such helpless people at their thumb's end. They just nab any Hill Kharia from a village situated within the region where a crime has occurred, sometimes even beyond the region and charge them with having committed the crime. The poor Hill Kharia pay dearly for this. The stigma of being criminal also sometimes leaves no other alternative but to act in a way that other people want them to act. For this to happen their marginal position and relationship with the people is in a way responsible. In Kulabahal the Hill Kharias are reported to be involved in three dacoities.The Kharias themselves admitted their involvement in two dacoities. They themselves did not participate in it directly but helped their kinsmen residing in a distant village to commit dacoity. The villagers themselves, it was reported, came to them and detailed them regarding the date and the manner by which dacoities were to be committed. Similarly some people also instigated them to steal paddy from the fields of their kin to settle some long-standing score. Thus dacoities were committed in G. Kar and A. Mahato's house. Analysis of these cases showed that the factionalism amongst the villagers culminated in the dacoities. These economic blows were considered to be the most serious blows which effectively curb the fighting capabilities of the adversaries. It may be pointed out that neither the Hill Kharias' social organisation nor their customary law has anything to do with it. There is no evidence that customary law or interactional pattern among the people legitimises the participation of the Hill Kharias in criminal activities.

Lastly it may be pointed out that most of the criminal activities of the Hill Kharias are perpetrated among the peasants. Within their own society incidence of crime like adultery, theft, etc., seldom occur. A few cases of death through *lasan* were reported. But this is a legitimate weapon sanctioned by the society.

Conclusion

In sum, it may be seen that among the Hill Kharias the customary laws were mainly concerned with ordering marriage, kinship and such other primordial relationship. The hunting and gathering Hill Kharias, in the past, mainly used to live in small groups made up of one's close relations. The economic activities were in the forest to which all people had equal access. The method of sharing was very simple — equality among the close kin and equal sharing in case the group was madeup of non-kin. With change in economy there occurred a qualitative change in their world-view. Proximity to peasants also led to inevitable acculturation. The believe in spirit and *lasan* kept the people away from injuring others. In case of conflict people tended to take recourse to the method of avoidance frequently culminating in moving to another area away from the scene of conflict.

The Hill Kharias are supposed to be criminals. Their criminal acts are mainly committed against the peasants under the tutelage and guidance of the different factions of the peasant villages. The Hill Kharias are drawn into these criminal activities by the peasants due to their poverty and marginal social position. However, incidence of crime among their own communities is rare.

8

TRIBAL CUSTOMARY LAW: A STUDY ON THE SAURIA OF THE RAJMAHAL HILLS, BIHAR

R. K. BHATTACHARYA

The paper is a descriptive account of some aspects of Sauria customary laws. In March, 1977, I was assigned three months' field work among the Sauria. I did a month's field work in the interior of Litipara; a fortnight's work among the Christian Sauria living on the plains of Boarijore and finally one more fortnight's study in a village in the hills of Sahebgunge where the tribe had come comparatively more in contact with other communities. I spent still one more fortnight visiting a couple of interior villages in the hills near Borio and a few well-known market centres of the district — Borio, Banjhi and Barharwa.

The Saurias call themselves Māler meaning men. They are indigenes of the Rajmahal Hills, Bihar. Usually the Māler have their villages and hamlets in the high forested hills, especially on isolated peaks which are normally flat, while valleys and plain land below are spotted with villages of an agrarian tribe, the Santal. The Māler also live on the plain. More than fifty thousand people — approximately half of them males while the rest females constitute the population of the Māler. For decades their population has remained rather constant. The Māler speak Malto, a language having no script of its own. The language is classed under the Dravidian family. The Māler are swidden hill cultivators. They use for cultivation hill slopes which are often strewn with huge granite blocks and loose weighty boulders and rocks. They clear these slopes by cutting the shrubs, leaving them for some time to dry and finally by burning them. They grow crops on the cleared land for two successive years and then keep it fallow for some years till wild plants grow on the land to certain heights. There is no irrigation beyond what they get by way of rainfall. Women as well as children along with adult male members of the community take part in all agricultural activities. On plain land they practise wet cultivation. Though the Māler live in the jungle, they are no keen hunters. But they are gatherers. They collect timber, firewood, grass for thatching houses, bamboos and various seasonal edible or otherwise useful fruits, flowers, creepers and leaves which grow in abundance in their jungle either in weekly markets or to itinerant traders visiting them at their hamlets mostly on horse-back.

The Māler have no clan. They have, however, awareness of lineage among them. Topographic isolation of the villages has given rise to certain territorial divisions of the tribe largely in terms of habitat, dress, food, certain customs and variation in the dialect. Some Māler villages have youth dormitories (*kodāddā*). The Māler allow polygyny and marriage of divorced or widowed persons. At the beginning of the British rule in the Rajmahal hills in the last quarter of the 18th century, hills were divided into *pargana* or *tāppā* each under a chief called *sardar*, who, sometimes, had one or more assistants called naib. Each village claimed separate hill or a separate range of hills and was presided over by a village, chief or headman called *manjhi*. The British carried on their transactions mainly administrative with the hill people through the *sardar* and *manjhi*. They granted allowances of Rs. 10 a month to all *sardars* and Rs. 5 a month to all naibs. This system with some changes still survives there in certain areas. After Independence the system of Panchayati Raj under the Bihar Panchayat Raj Act, 1948, along with the scope of participation in the general elections has been introduced. This has brought in an added structural aspect in the tribal polity of the area.

Every Sauria village has its own headman, *manjhiye* or *tikri manjhi* and one or two village messengers. The other village officials include personalities like the village priest and his assistant, if any, and *demano*, the man who gets possessed by spirits during ritual performances.

The main religious ceremonies of the tribe centre round the offering of harvested crops, viz. maize (*gangi*), beans (*kasre*) and fruits. In certain areas sauria villages organise *Kali puja*. Christian missionaries have converted a very small section of the tribe.

Area of Study

Two contiguous hamlets of Chhota Surajbera and Bada Surajbera constitute Surajbera, known as Kanchna Surajbera. Surajbera is situated on a hill-top in the interior of Litipara block of Pakur sub-division. The whole *Damin-i-koh* Government Estate (for a note on *Damin-i-koh* see Government of India 1964 : 524-530) of the district is divided under Dak Bungalows and Kanchna Surajbera is under Kunjabona Dak Bungalow. Kanchna Surajbera has earlier been referred in anthropological literature (see Sarkar: 1938 : 14 and 30 and Vidyarthi: 1963 : 8).

Bada Surajbera had 13 households having 26 males and 20 females; of whom 14 were adult males and 16 were adult females.

Chhota Surajbera had 30 males and 28 females; of whom 16 were adult males and 20 adult females. Total number of households in the hamlet is 14.

The old British offices of *manjhi*, *sardar* and *naib* are still in vogue in the area along with the post-Independence system of Panchayati Raj.

There was a free primary school having two teachers in Chhota Surajbera run by the State Government's Paharia Welfare Office. Students were given monetary aids plus their course material from the State Government. The block had separate nutrition programmes for villagers and schoolchildren. The school was established in the year 1951 under the aegis of the then Paharia Seva Mondal.

The Christian Saurias were studied in the village Kusumghati on the plains of Boarijore block of Godda sub-division. Earlier the village was under the jurisdiction of Rajavita Dak Bungalow. The village has four sections or *tola*, namely, Duligodda (officially known as Ramaitola), Pachhevita Tikritola (*tikri* means high or barren) and Bedogoda. In Duligodda besides the Saurias, the Santal and the Goala lived. All other sections were solely inhabited by the Sauria.

More than a hundred years ago the Saurias of the area came in touch with the European Christian missionaries. The close contact with the missionaries improved the literacy of the Saurias of the area. During my study missionaries were not active.

Chhota Pachruki (see Sarkar 1938 : 21) in the hills of Sahebgunge is a small hamlet of the Saurias. The steep hill sites here are by the Ganges and the fertile plains of South Bihar. These Saurias had frequent contact with the market centres at Sahebgunge mainly as sellers of fruits such as mango, jackfruit, guava, custard. They were often referred to as Bar or rather Barer (meaning by the side of the Ganges) Paharia by their brethren in other parts of Rajmahal, e.g. Litipara.

Appointment of Sardar

As per the Santhal Parganas Rural Police Regulation No. 4 of June 20, 1910 (see Government of India 1964 : 116-125). I quote here a few relevant facts as regards appointment of sardar to show how statutory State rule was made to control appointments of important positions in the tribal society of the Sauria.

. . . . The Deputy Commissioner may, from time to time, by order in writing.

(a) declare any local area or group of houses to be village for the purposes of this Regulation;
(b) form any such village into circles; and
(c) appoint a sardar for each circle (Ibid : 118)

Nijri was a well-known *sardar* of Kachna Surajbera. He was known to many Saurias beyond his jurisdiction. After his death his second son, Baidyanath, became *sardar* in Surajbera. After his appointment as *sardar*, a coveted position, his elder brother Narendranath (a State Government employee) spent quite a bit of money in throwing a feast to the *manjhiye* (*manjhi* or *pradhan* in official parlance) who voted, especially in favour of his brother. In Annex. I copies of the inquiry report and order sheet in connection with Baidynath's appointment are given.

Besides being the *sardar*, Baidyanath was manjhiye or tikri manjhi of the hamlet Chhota Surajbera. *Manjhi* was often referred to as *tikri manjhi*, perhaps to distinguish him from the stipendary *manjhi* commonly known as *talpia manjhi*. Baidyanath held the position of village priest, *nado*, for both the hamlets of Chhota and Bada Surajbera.

The offices of *sardar* and *naib* were not found in Chhota Panchruki and Kusumghati. In Chhota Panchruki I was informed that during the British rule the offices were in vogue in the area. In Kunjabona bungalow there was no *naib*. However, the adjoining bungalows, namely, Singlom and Dharampur, still had a *naib* each. [For details on *sardar* see Vidyarthi: 1963 : 65-66 and Bradely Birt (1905 : 59-60) as has been referred to in the former.]

Rights and duties of the *sardar* and *naib* were governed by statutory rules of the State (see Government of India 1964 : 425).

Appointment of Manjhi

According to the Record-of-Rights of Sauria Paharia tract in Godda and Rajmahal (see Government of India 1964 : 420-427), I quote here rules in connection with appointment and dismissal of *manjhi*:

> "On the death of the *manjhi* his nearest male heir, if duly qualified, will ordinarily be appointed by the sub-divisional officer to succeed him. The *manjhi* is liable to dismissal by the Deputy Commissioner for default in payment of the village rent, for misconduct or other sufficient cause. When a *manjhi* dies leaving no heirs, or is dismissed, one of the resident Paharia raiyats elected by the villagers will be appointed *manjhi* with the sanction of the sub-divisional officer," (Ibid : 425).

Due to these statutory rules the *manjhiye* of a Sauria village might be selected by the villagers themselves but his appointment would require sanction of the sub-divisional officer. His rights and duties were elaborately pinpointed in the rules (ibid : 422-423).

Here I may relate an old case of the British period, where the villagers of Chhota and Bada Surajbera in their confrontation with the statutory rules, eluded the government authority with a view to coming to a decision of their own. Rama Paharia was *tikki manjhi* of Bada Surajbera. In course of time he became poor and wanted to sell his position of *tikri manjhi* to his wealthy cousin Begda. The villagers agreed to Rama's proposal; but in order to circumvent the government procedure, the villagers lodged a complaint against Rama and prayed his dismissal and appointment of his elder brother (in actuality a cousin) Begda in his place. True copies of villagers' application for dismissal of Rama and *kanungo*'s report plus the court order are given in Annex. II.

Pirka (Senior, i.e. Bada, the riche *sinare*, literally means rich) one person in the two hamlets was acting for a few years as *tikri manjhi* of Bada Surajbera having inherited this hereditary position about three/four years ago. In 1977 he was made permanent in the post. He inherited another hereditary post, viz., stipendary *manjhi*, i.e. *talpia manjhi* of Bada Surajbera in 1976. With the consent of the villagers he handed over this latter post to his cousin Jogya.

Besides a *talpia manjhi*, Chhota Surjabera had a *chowkidar* too.

Social Offences

I gathered information regarding two adultery cases dealt in Kachna Surajbera. A council (in Sauria dialect *bichar saba*) dealt with cases. There is no separate council for the two hamlets. The council dealt with issues requiring decision at village level. The village officials, *sardar*, two *tikki manjhi* (of both hamlets) *talpia manjhi* (from the two hamlets — one from each hamlet), and *chowkidar* of Chhota Surajbera were all *ex-officio* members of the council. In both the cases the council punished the male offender by fine.

In one of the cases Kalu, the eldest son of Jama of Bada Surajbera, had relations with Kabri, wife of Bamna of Chhota Surajbera. He was married and had a few months old son. Bamna was the eldest son of Deva, an ex-military man residing as a *ghar jam* or *arkbejdoki* in Sauria dialect (i.e., "a son-in-law who comes to live with the parents-in-law, and works as[1] a son of the family" (see Datta-Majumdar: 1955 : 42) in Bada Surajbera. Bamna was *gharjam* in Chhota Surajbera. Kalu had relations with his wife while he was in jail.

Kabri's father Bada Gugara (i.e., Gugara, senior) spent Rs. 12 to 15 serving liquor to the members of the council. The council fined Kalu Rs. 120 and gave the sum to Bada Gugara.

The second concerned Deva, son of Surjya of Chhota Surajbera. He was charged with raping his neighbour Badu's wife. He was fined Rs. 100, of which Rs. 40 were given to Badu's wife while the rest was spent for buying a cow which was slaughtered and shared among the members of the council.

In Chhota Pachruki where the offices of *sardar* and *naib* were not found, the council was headed by a sarpanch, an office created by the Government after the introduction of Panchayat Raj. Pradhan or mukhia was the head in the panchayati system. His major role was earmarked for developmental work and the *sarpanch*, a junior official, was given charge of the council. The *pradhan* (i.e. pradhan) was, however, an ex-officio member of the council. Village messenger(s) were also ex-officio members.

Though both husband and wife have the right to divorce among the Sauria, the Christian Saurias of Kusumghati village in the Borijore block of Godda sub-division were reported to be debarred from such right by the church (*girija* in Malto dialect). The disapproval of the church was manifested in the fact that divorces were not allowed to any second church wedding. The Christian Saurias had no social sanction for polygyny.

In the different areas of my field work it was reported that theft (galway), dacoity, homicide (malpite) and suicide were, in general, dealt with by the State law. However the State law took cognizance of other social offences too, when those were brought to the notice of the judiciary of the State. e.g., Subash Malto, a matriculate now pursuing studies at a mission in Ranchi for becoming a pastor, was sued against in the formal court by his former fiance whom he abandoned and married an Oraon woman of Ranchi. The fiance claimed in the court to have financially helped Subash while he was a student. She was a nurse in the Holy Family Hospital at Kurji in Patna. Because her engagement with Subash broke, she was dismissed from the Hospital which showed rather too stringent rules as regards relations between unmarried boys and girls. From the court it was decided that she should get a share of the produce from Subash's land till she married.

Conclusion

I would discuss the two major issues of the paper in the backdrop of the few cases referred to in the preceding pages.

The issues are :

(1) Confrontation of a tribe, more specifically of the Sauria with the statutory legal system of a colonial period namely, the British; and
(2) Customary vis-a-vis statutory laws.

The confrontation between the dominant British legal systems and the local law of politically subordinate Saurias *ideally* presents a legal situation supporting Fallers' exposition. But from the preceding cases referred to hereunder the subheads, "Appointment of Sardar" and "Appointment of Manjhi" it becomes apparent that the dominant legal system, in reality, overcontrols the situation giving little scope other than theoretically for the politically subordinate community to take course of free choice in using its local law. The offices of *sardar* and *manjhi* were in vogue among the Sauria before the advent of the British rule. The dominant British legal system recognised and supported these offices to the extent that it could bring these within its fold. Its recognition and support were not in favour of free functioning of the local law. Instead it took charge of the control of certain offices of authority having importance in the functioning of the local law of the politically subordinate community of the Sauria.

The Saurias were studied both in interior areas and in relatively contact situation having a large market centre close by. The State law comes handy for police and forest guards to exploit them at both the above situations. But in areas where the Saurias had formal education, such atrocities were rare.

9

RULES, DEVIANCE AND MEANS OF SOCIAL CONTROL AMONG THE LEPCHA

R. K. SAHA

The Lepcha's traditional village organisation consists of three officials, namely, *latsen* (Mandal), *yumi* and *ngapoon*. *Lasten* of Mandal is the head of these officials, *yumi* (the communication agent), his assistant, and *ngapoon* is the bearer and messenger too.

Lasten or *mandal* is a hereditary post. During the period of king, after the death of a *mandal*, his son was formally selected by the villagers and then he was recognised by the king as *mandal*. The villagers still now select the son of a deceased *mandal* to be recognised as *mandal* by the District Collector. If a *mandal* dies without any issue the villagers select a man from the same (patrilineal clan) *putso*. In no case it goes to any other *putso*. For example, the post of *mandal* of Tingbong belongs to Aram Ajet *putso*. Once in the past the king had no correct information about the selected *mandal* of Sakyong. So he recognised a man from a different *putso* as the *mandal* of the area. The villagers objected and ultimately the king had to cancel his recognition and recognised the selected man of the same *putso* to which *mandal* belonged. If the son of a *mandal* is incapable the villagers select a man belonging to the same *putso*. *Yumi* is elected by the villagers. In some villages it is elected for lifetime like the *mandal* and in others it is elected for three years. But it is never hereditary. *Ngapoon* is selected for three years, by rotation, from all the households.

In early days *mandal* used to judge all the disputes within the village. He used to look after the discipline in society as also collect revenue. He was the spokesman of the villagers too. *Yumi* was mediator between the villagers and the *mandal*. So *mandal* used to contact villagers through *yumi*. *Ngapoon* was messenger as well as a bearer. Nowadays the official function of *mandal* is to collect revenue from the villagers. The villagers, though they seek the help of the Village panchayat in settling disputes, cannot forget their *mandal*. So ultimately *mandal* is to settle everything that arises out of deviation from social expectation. *Yumi* is almost defunct. The main duty of *ngapoon* is to look after the comfort of the government officials during their visits.

The panchayat system was introduced about 12 years ago. At the beginning the villagers selected the members and informed the same to the king. The king made one President, one Vice-president, Secretary and panchayat members out of these selected members. Now the villagers elect the panchayat President, Vice-president, Secretary and members. For example in Tingbong panchayat unit the villagers elect one President, one Vice-President, one Secretary and two ordinary members. The panchayat members are the communication agents of the government. They inform the villagers of all the government orders, notices, etc., The government help is given through them. They also try to settle all sorts of disputes.

Autocratic Right Recognised

The panchayat members, the traditional village officials or the village elders cannot work independently in matters related to their society and culture. They work in unison. And any decision is arrived at jointly by the *mandal*, panchayat members and the village elders. Thus in the body of controlling authority there are both the democratic and autocratic features. They cannot forget the autocratic right of the *mandal* and this autocratic right is again democratically recognised. Theoretically it is the fact that the democratically elected panchayat members should deal with every matter. But the Lepcha cannot accede to it fully. So the autocratic right of the *mandal* and the village elders is recognised in dealing with any matter.

The Lepcha normally do not tell a lie. So they do not take the help of supernatural world and ordeals in the process for settling any deviations from social expectation or any breach of rules. They do not try to judge who is right and who is wrong. Rather they try to identify how far the behaviour is deviated from social expectation in the presence of all the participants. Anyone present is allowed to speak. Trials are frequently used, participants are identified, evidences are submitted and witnesses are presented. The decision is arrived at unanimously. No one should have the feeling of dissatisfaction. The motive is to re-state the deviation.

The Lepcha use social pressure as a means of social control. They do not prefer public ridicule but criticise the improper behavior of any villager through gossip by nicknaming and satire. For example a man of Kusung became so habituated that he tried to establish sexual relations with any woman or girl whoever he met. The society permits sexual connection with other women but the society criticises that man to prevent his being habituated in that behaviour. So they criticise the man through gossip and satire.

When social pressure fails they resort to the fine system. The social rule permits three types of fines. They are: (1) if a man elopes with another man's wife, the man has to give a fine–either replacement of another wife or the total expenditure the former husband incurred to marry that woman. This fine is recoverable if there is no loss of peace. *Mandal* of Tingbong recovered such fine. His third daughter was married to a man. After some time another man eloped with her. So the earlier husband of his daughter demanded the replacement of a woman, *mandal* took fine from the lover of his daughter, the second husband, and then he replaced another woman for the first husband of his daughter; (2) If an unmarried girl becomes pregnant by a man and the man is unable to marry her the man has to give the following fines: (i) one ox, (ii) one *maund* of Chi (fermented liquor), (iii) 10 *takfre* (a kind of basket measurement) of rice, and (iv) Rs. 15. If the unmarried girl gives birth to a son the fine recoveries would he given to the son and if a daughter the fines will go to the mother of the daughter. The biological father of the son of an unmarried mother of Pentong neither could agree to marry her nor paid the fines. The villagers became silent because they did not like any loss of peace. Moreover the man was very clever and the villagers were not clever enough to tackle with such a man; (3) If the younger sister is married before the elder sister, the elder sister receives the following fines from the younger sister's husband: (i) one *maund* of Chi, (ii) one *mon fung*, i.e. foreleg of pig, (iii) *khadaw*, i.e. scarf, and (iv) Rs. 15. The informants told that the cash amount varies. In Tingbong it is Rs. 100. The third daughter of the *mandal* of Tingbong was married before the marriage of the second daughter. But the second daughter could not get the fine because she was then reading in school and was away from home.

The controlling authority of the Lepcha society, consisting of the *mandal*, panchayat members and the village elders try to resolve any issue arising out of deviance under the laws of the society. In this regard it would be worthwhile to cite a few cases :

Case No. 1: A man of Tingbong became old but he did not hand over authority to his elder son. Instead, he used to live separately in a separate house with the wife of his younger brother. The man's elder son was married and had children. He used to live in the natal house along with his brother and mother. After two years he sought the help of the village authority, the members of which held a meeting and advised the old man to divide his property equally between his two sons keeping aside a portion for his own maintenance. Ultimately the old man obeyed the rules.

Case No. 2: A man of Linko is at present 54 years old. His only son died in an accident. His wife became too old to beget child. So he went to village officials and village elders. The village elders decided as per rule that the relatives of his wife should supply another woman as his wife and they were informed of it. So they showed the man's wife's brother's daughter, a girl of 18 years, as the man's second wife. The man married her. Now this man, aged 54, forced his second wife aged 18 to sleep with him. But the girl did not like to sleep with the old man. The Bek-bu and the village elders say that this is the rule. They do not allow the girl to mix with the young boys. They think that by dint of this pressure the girl will surely sleep with the man and they believe, if a child is born to her she will not run after any young boy.

Sometimes the authority accept a case of deviance if it does not threaten the society with a view to maintaining peace. Let me here cite a few cases:

Case No. 1: One Lama left his wife and co-habited with his younger brother's wife and ultimately she became his wife. The village elders requested the Lama not to do that and advised him to leave his younger brother's wife. But the Lama did not obey their advice. Ultimately the village authority tolerated this breach of rule when the woman threatened them that she would commit suicide. So the village elders did not want to make any further loss of peace.

Case No. 2: One individual of Tingbong has no issue In such a situation it is socially permitted that he can take a second wife if a first one permits. The man's wife does not allow him to marry second time. To satisfy his wife he cannot even take the help of the authority in this matter.

Case No. 3: An individual of Tingbong deprived his brother, one way or the other, and got *patta* for maximum amount of his father's land in his own name. The authority did not like to take up the matter in order not to create any further disturbance.

Case No. 4: A girl of Pentong became pregnant by a man. She gave birth to a son. This man already had two wives. These wives warned that they would kill this woman if she is taken into home as third wife. So the man neither married her nor took charge of her son. He even did not pay the money to be spent in connection with the ceremony for the social recognition of the bastard son. The village elders did not take any step against the man because that would lead to loss of peace.

The Lepcha are a peace-loving people. So they tolerate the breach of the laws simply to maintain peace. This tolerance is not limited among themselves but is also extended to the Nepali. For example, we may mention two cases — one happened in the village Lik and the other in Tingbong. In both cases the Nepali coolies, while living in the house of their masters, ran away with the daughters of their masters. It has also been reported that some of the coolies have, though rarely, sexual relations with the wives of their masters. The Lepcha criticise this behaviour. They, however, do not take any action because they think this may lead to the loss of peace. Sometimes they express their grievances against them but do not ultimately go beyond that.

We may cite another case in which the Lepcha tolerated wrong behaviour. The socio-ritual aspects of the Lepcha and the environmental condition make drinking essential in their life. But they never become angry and do nothing wrong under drunken conditions. It happened one night in my presence that the nephew of my host became very much angry and chased my host with a sword. The cause of his anger, as per his argument, was that half of the natal house of my host is on the plot of his nephew. Other people tolerated this wrong behavior on the ground that they did not like to create any further disturbance. They said that the boy is a very bad one and unlike the Lepcha his nature is that of a Nepali. They suspect admixture of Nepali blood in him.

The instances of rules never lead to a change in the law. These are limited to individual cases. These do not threaten the society. So the Lepcha can tolerate these.

Theoretically any decision should be unanimous. So they arrive at a decision after prolonged discussions when each and every individual agrees to it. In practice, though decision is unanimous it is influenced by the idea of any dominant man. If a dominant and clever man takes a decision other people think that this is his decision. In this regard two cases are cited here.

Case No. 1: During my stay at Tingbong, the Governor visited the area. All the village elders, panchayat members, traditional village officials and local M.L.A.s held a meeting to decide as to how to greet the Governor. They could not arrive at any decision even after long discussion. Then one M.L.A. suggested something as final and others also thought that was their opinion. In this way the M.L.A.'s suggestion was accepted unanimously as final decision.

Case No. 2: People criticise a man of Nung because this man is not as simple as other Lepchas are. His two daughters were reading in Tingbong high school, when I was there at Tingbong. These two girls did not pay attention to their studies. One Nepali teacher insisted that all the students should be sincere. So the teacher rebuked these two girl students and possibly slapped them. Father of these girls became angry and thought that he should get punishment. So he called an M.L.A., the headmaster and some other members of the panchayat. They held a meeting. Even after long discussion they could not arrive at any decision because the man and one or two others wanted that the teacher should get punishment while others could not agree to it. At last the M.L.A. told them they should give a warning to the teacher and they should also try for his transfer to some other place. Others accepted the proposal as their opinion

To sum up, it may be stated that like every other society the Lepcha have social expectations. These are based on the value system of their society and culture to which they belong. The Lepcha have some rules framed by their society which facilitate action and prohibit others so that the social expectations are fruitfully achieved.

People are accustomed to these happenings through the process of socialisation. Still people deviate from these expectations. For the purpose of settlement of such matters the Lepcha society has formed a body of village officials. The mode of settlement is such that it does not result in any gain for one and loss for the other.

10

CUSTOMARY LAW AMONG THE TOTO OF WEST BENGAL

B. JOARDAR

Totopara, the home of the present-day Totos, is situated in the district of Jalpaiguri under the subdivision of Alipurduar, West Bengal. The village Totopara is encircled by Titi reserve forest, river Torsha, Bhutan and the stream Hauri. One can reach Totopara after a hard trek through deep forest full of pythons, snakes, elephants, hoars, bears and tigers, dry riverlet beds and over hills and loose sand. In the rainy season reaching Totopara is next to impossible. Of course, sometimes in great need they do venture to go to Lankapara *haat*, a market-place.

Nearly a decade ago their number was 322 only. In 1941 it was 321 and in 1951 it came down 248. She authorities were misled and came to the conclusion that the Totos are a vanishing tribe. But this is far from what the actual picture is.

Major Economic Activities

About 60 years back orange trade was the main source of Totos, livelihood. They also used to practise slash and burn cultivation until two generations ago. After the death of the orange groves, and to cope with the changing situation, the Totos invited the Nepali families to settle at Totopara and to leach them agricultural techniques.

Their major crops today are maize, *kaoni,* Nepali *marua* and Toto *marua*. The agricultural implements are very simple. Elephants, boars and deer cause serious damage to their crops.

The Totos can carry on for about seven months with their agricultural produce. For the rest of the year they have to make do with the roots and tubers collected from the nearby forest. They also sell bamboo, pigs, cocks and arecanuts.

Toto families earn a good amount of cash, during October and November, as toto porters carry oranges from the orange groves of adjacent Tading Bhutan to Totopara, the gateway of Bhutan orange trade to India. A few of the Totos purchase small quantities of oranges from Tading Bhutan and sell it at Ramjhora, Lankapara or Dalsingpara market.

The Panchayat

The Totos perform the *puja toli* of Mahakali during July-August and August-September (Toto's Kati and Agai months). During this *puja* a panchayat court sits where cases are tried and its judgements are respected by the Totos.

The Totos have their traditional panchayat. Ten to 12 village elders form the panchayat. After hearing the deposition of both offenders and defenders, the bench gives the verdict and the person found guilty has to obey the decision. Generally the offender has to give a pitcher full of liquor *(ewe)* to the persons present over there. Most of the cases, in such bench, relate either is cattle trespass or quarrels between two persons or families or groups. The structure of the panchayat consists of the following:

(i) *Kaijee* or *subba* (the religious head)
(ii) *Mondal* (the Headman who is in-charge of land and revenue)
(iii) Panchayat (the Panchayat head)
(iv) *Karbari* (Messenger), selected by the *kaijee, mondal* and panchayat.
(v) *Chowkidar*

Kaijee or *subba* is the religious head. This post is hereditary. It is the *kaijee* or *subba* who settles any dispute or question regarding social customs or manners.

After the Bhutan war of 1864-1865 the western Duars and so also Totopara under Bhutan were annexed to India November 12, and the final treaty was signed on November 11, 1865 (Sunder: 1895 : 20). Before this transfer of Totopara to the jurisdiction of India, the office of *kaijee* and *mandal* were held by the same person.

Amepha, the panchayat head, says that with the growing complication of work after the British annexure, the office of *mondal* was separated for the smooth function of the panchayat.

(ii) *Mondal* is the headman, who is to settle in consultation with the village elders any dispute among the Totos about land. The present *mondal* is Dinesh Toto, son of the late Dhanapati Mondal. This office is also hereditary.

(iii) Panchayat post is hereditary and panchayat's duty is to assess *chowkidari* tax and also to realise it. In consultation with the village elders he settles the dispute like quarrel between two Totos or any matter pertaining to a breach of the law and order in the village (Totos only).

The duty of *karbari* is to carry out the *kaijee's* (*subba*) order and summons to the villagers. This post is not hereditary. Nowadays there is also a statutory gram panchayat of Totopara. There are eight members of which four are Nepalis.

The structure of the statutory Gram Sabha is as follows :

i Adhyakhya--Dinesh Toto
ii Upadhyakhya--Amepha Toto
iii Members--Lamsing Toto
iv Marang Toto--Marang is the Chowkidar and ex-officio member of the Panchayat.
v Manbahadur Rai (Nepali)
vi Dilbahadur Tamang (Nepali)
vii Jetha Moktan (Nepali)
viii Ambahadur Rai (Nepali)

Divorce not Difficult

The common practice for divorce is that the person who intends to pray for divorce goes to the *subba*, or *kaijee*, the religious head, and prays to him for divorce or *paiesua*. The *subba*- Sirong Toto instructs his orderly or *kaijee-nang-puiling* to call the village men, generally the elderly persons.

Subba fixes the time and venue of the hearing and informs his *kaijee-nang-puiling* who later goes to every *gaon,* like Panchayat Gaon, Mitrong Gaon, Dumchee Gaon, etc., and gives the notice to assemble to *subba's* house for the *paiesua* case. Generally the *kaijee-nang-puiling* selects a central place of the *gaon* and place the verbal; notice loudly. Moreover, on his way he tells about the notice to the suitable persons he comes across. As per notice the village elders and the respected persons assemble of the place in time. In some cases, both husband and wife come for *paiesua*. But when only one of them comes, the *subba* also informs the other person, may be husband or wife, to appear before the court. But he or she may not attain the court and this behaviour is not offensive.

The person who seeks the divorce comes with a piece of banana leaf, a few areca-nuts, betel leaves, and generally 50 paise. On behalf of the court the *subba* keeps these articles on a *chang-dai-ing* (wooden seat, platform-like).

The person who seeks *paiesua* will have to offer a pitcherful of *ewe* — country-made liquor. If both the parties are present, the *subba* instructs the person who seeks *paiesua* to give the betel leaves and areca-nuts to the other person concerned.

The court listens to the deposition of the person seeking *paiesua* or both the parties (where both the parties appear before the court). Hearing the deposition, the *subba,* after discussing with the other members of the court, instructs them to exchange the betel leaves, areca-nuts and banana leaf.

The members of the traditional panchayat (obviously except *subba* or *kaijee*) may not also be present in this court.

After hearing the deposition *subba* or *kaijee* declares that from that day (with effect from that time) they cannot be regarded as husband and wife, and they are free like unmarried persons and have every liberty to marry.

In case of divorce the husband concerned gets some compensation. Of course in such a case the husband concerned would appeal for divorce.

We can cite the case of Dinesh Toto, the present *adhyakhya* of the Totopara statutory *gram* panchayat. Aguni Totani, the third wife of Dinesh, wanted to live with Agashe Toto and so she went with Agashe Toto to live with him. Now, for this, Dinesh went to the *subba* or *kaijee* for divorce.

Subba called both Agashe and Aguni to his court. He also informed the villagers with the help of his orderly or *kaijee-nang-puiling*. Here in this court of *subba* decision was taken that Agashe should pay a fine of Rs. 150 only, and this amount should be given to Dinesh as compensation. Divorce is settled in the court of Subba or Kaijee. This is the rule. But if *subba* or *kaijee* himself is involved the *mondal* settles the case.

We can cite one such case here.

Both Sirong Toto, the *subba* or *kaijee,* and Dirpa Toto's wife (first) were eager to live together. So Dirpa's wife went with Sirong Toto. Dirpa could not appeal for a divorce as divorce should be settled in the court of *subba* or *kaijee.*

The villagers (Totos) went to Dhanapati Toto, who was the *mondal* at that time, and asked him to settle the issue. Dhanapati Mondal was also willing to arrange for a trial. So he asked the orderly and *chowkidar* to arrest Sirong Toto. They did accordingly and took him to the court of Dhanapati Mondal. Here Dhanapati with the assistance of other village elders (Totos only) decided the case. In this case Dirpa — now employee (part-time) of the Totopara Tribal Welfare Centre, Government of West Bengal, received a sum of Rs. 25 only as compensation. Sirong Toto had to pay this amount to Dirpa, and there was no other way out, though Sirong himself was empowered to judge the case of divorce.

Adoption Common

Adoption or *puia-aiama* is very common among the Totos. The adopted sons may by taken back by the old family. But such cases are very few. After adopting if the person concerned gets a son, and if by that time the adopted son remains a minor, the original parents of the adopted son generally wait to take their son back. The original parents of the adopted son appeal to the *subba* or *kaijee.* If the adopted son is grown up, he himself can appeal for his release to the *subba* or *kaijee* and only after getting he necessary permission he can go back to his original parents.

It is worth noted here that if both the parties agree, only then can the adopted son be released and go back to his original father.

The person or persons who make such an appeal have to give two pitchersful of *ewe.*

We may mention a case here.

Agashe Toto had no son. So, he adopted Onje's son. But later Agashe's wife divorced him and married Bhusan Toto. Agashe later married Dinesh Toto's third wife Aguni Totani, now here Aguni gave birth to a son.

A few days after this, Aguni gave back the adopted son. For this Onge had to give a pitcherful of *ewe.* In this function *subba* was not present. It is worthy to mention here that, in case of adoption or release *subba* may not be present. The village elders take the decision and settle the matter. Here in this case *subba* was not present.

He who is willing to adopt any boy has to go first to the *subba* or *kaijee*. But there is exception to this custom which I have already pointed out above. He should inform him about this in detail including the name of the boy and the *gaon* from which they are. The person who is willing to adopt should go to *subba* or *kaijee* with two pitchersful of *ewe*. In this ceremony the presence of the boy is very much necessary.

Generally in this *puia-aiama* function some villagers are called. But there is no hard and fast rule that the villagers must participate in this court or even be invited.

Now in the presence of the court the person concerned informs the house that he is willing to adopt the boy concerned, who is the boy and so on. The *subba* or *kaijee* and others over there discuss it for a few minutes and agree to give the necessary permission. The *subba* on behalf of the court informs them that from that day and time the boy is the adopted son of the person concerned.

Premarital and Extramarital Relation

Premarital and extramarital relation with non-Totos is a grave offence. In such a case the *subba* or *kaijee* deals with the case.

After hearing the deposition of both the persons, *subba* or *kaijee* consults the house, and on deciding the guilty, orders his *karbari* to drive him out of Totopara.

Pre-marital or extramarital relation with non-Totos is more among the Toto female than male. Out of 13 cases of excommunication only two relate to Toto male.

Naibong Totani, the daughter of Sirong Toto — the *subba* or *kaijee* — is unmarried. She had sexual relation with Janardan Prasad Kesari, a Bihari boy, son of Sarganath Kesari. She had also established sexual contact with Harka Bahadur Bombjan, a Nepali.

Before the sexual relation with Harka Bahadur Bombjan she lived with Dipendra Nath Mondal, a Mechia (means a person from the Mech tribe). She lived with him for a few months.

For the sexual relation of Naibong with non-Toto, the Totos nursed some grievance.

The panchayat — Amepha along with other Totos went to *subba* and asked him to settle the case and to call the hearing of the court as soon as possible.

After a lot of discussions in the court, Sirong Toto — the *subba* agreed to perform *sangailampami* (penance ceremony) within 15 days and he did so.

The court thought that there should not be any excommunication and that's why the court decided that *sangailampami* would be sufficient punishment.

Offence against property is settled in the court of *mondal*, and social offence like murder, homicide, infanticide, abortion and rape is absent. But if any such offence happens, the panchayat would settle the case.

Concluding Observations

Though there is a statutory panchayat, the traditional panchayat's role is vital in Toto society.

In case of divorce, adoption or any offence, etc., the Totos settle the case in their traditional panchayat. On the other hand the statutory panchayat settles the case where both the Totos and non-Totos are involved.

In their internal affairs they never take help from the non-Totos or statutory panchayat. Of course, in most of the cases they invite the Toto Welfare Officer, Government of West Bengal, stationed at Totopara for taking part in their court. In fact, in any trial, the Welfare Officer's opinion is of a considerable value.

It has been seen that in case of some minor disputes the Totos generally go to the Welfare Officer who settles the issue. His verdict is final and the case rarely goes to the traditional panchayat.

To cope up with the changing situation the Totos have changed some of their customs related to death.

Only three or four years back, the mourning period was one year. During the mourning period one could not cut hair and nails, and had to sleep in someone else's house. He or she had to keep a piece of bamboo of the size of the dead for one year.

Previously they never had to go outside Totopara, beyond Phuntsolling (in Bhutan), Hasimara, Dalsingpara and Lankapara *hat*. But now they are to go to Jalpaiguri, Madarihat and such other places in the interest of their own. So obviously it is not possible to go to the plains like Jalpaiguri, Madarihat with beard and nails and a big bamboo in hand, said the Totos.

Once Amepha, the panchayat of the old traditional Panchayat, had to go to Madarihat for community work and he had to go with long hair, beard, nails and a big bamboo.

This is the first time the Totos faced such a crisis. After this the Toto leaders decided that the mourning period should be 12 days instead of 12 months. This decision was approved by the Totos.

Previously rules of excommunication were very rigid. For sexual relation with non-Totos, excommunication was must. But nowadays the Totos are not at all eager to excommunicate. The Toto leaders pointed out that previously excommunication was, in fact, a heavy punishment, as it was very difficult for a Toto to live outside Totopara and at the same time it was not possible for such a person to disobey, and live within Totopara or even he could not dare to live in any place adjacent to Totopara.

But with the changing situation such a person may live outside Totopara very happily with his employer in any Tea Estate or somewhere else, or he may even live just outside Totopara village boundary and he wouldn't bother at all. Even he may remain at Totopara and the panchayat cannot exert its power over him.

The Toto elders and traditional panchayat leaders added that only 20 years back their number became so small that they were really afraid to excommunicate anyone. Moreover till now sexual relation with non-Totos has not posed any problem.

Nowadays the Totos try to ignore such incidents. When any one complains only then can the panchayat (traditional) take up the case. These days one rarely brings this to the notice of the panchayat. Even if it is noticed, the panchayat (traditional) rebukes the person concerned and asks him or her to perform *sangai-lam-pami*. Nowadays the panchayat simply warns the person concerned. The minor disputes are settled by the village elders and they rarely go to the traditional panchayat.

11

LEVEL AND MECHANISM OF SOCIAL CONTROL AMONG THE KORWAS OF BIHAR

HASAN ALI

The Korwas are concentrated in Surguja, Bilaspur and Jashpur districts in Madhya Pradesh, in Ranchi and Palamau districts in Bihar, in pargana Dudhi in Mirzapur district in Uttar Pradesh. It is said that they migrated from Palamau and Surguja districts. They are also found in a small number in Orissa and West Bengal. In West Bengal their concentration is in Purulia district. According to the 1971 Census the Korwa population in Bihar is 18,717.

Some earlier accounts of the tribe have been furnished by scholars like Dalton (1879), Risley (1891), and W. Crook (1896). More recently (1944) a detailed ethnographic account of the tribe is available in D. N. Majumdar's work.

The two major endogamous divisions among the Korwas are (i) Diharia or Dih Korwa, who live in village (*dih*) and are cultivators and (ii) Paharis or Ban Korwa who are also known as Benwaria, on account of the fact that they practised *bewar* or shifting cultivation in the past.

The present description is an outcome of the field work conducted among the Korwas in Ranchi and Palamau districts in Bihar for three months during 1977. The focus has been on their customary laws.

The two villages, namely, Malom in Gumla Sub-division in Ranchi district and Serassam in Gorhwa Sub-division in Palamau district have been studied.

In Malom, a fairly scattered village, the Korwas live much isolated, deep into the forest and hills. They are surrounded mainly by the other tribes, viz. the Oraons, the Asurs and the M. W. Das. In

Serassam, a comparatively less isolated and exposed village, the Korwas live amidst the Hindu castes and other tribes such as the Khairwar and the Oraons. According to Orierton (1965) the Korwas speak a dialect of the Memdari branch of the Austric family of languages. But, in fact, the people of younger generations have almost forgotten their traditional dialect and rather excelled in the local dialect (Sadri in Ranchi and an admixture of Bhojpuri and Magahi in Palamau.

Traditional Social Control

The traditional institution for social control among the Korwas is known as panchayat or *sabha.* The head of the panchayat or *sabha* is known as *punch* in Ranchi and *mahato* in Palamau. *Panch* or *mahato* plays the most decisive role in all matters though elderly and reputed individuals among them also influence the decision-making. Another important functionary of the panchayat or *sabha* is the *piyada*, also known as *barik*. He serves as a messenger. His main function is to go around the village(s), informing fellow tribesmen about the date and venue of the panchayat meeting and the parties involved. The posts of *panch* or *mahato* as well as that of *piyada* are hereditary, being succeeded by the eldest son of the respective family or lineage.

Apart from the *mahato* or *panch* and other functionaries, the person occupying a most significant place in the Korwa society is the *baiga* or *pahan*, the traditional Munda priest of the Korwas. He is considered by the Korwas as their religious and spiritual leader and all tiapropitory rituals during festivals and other occasions are conducted by him. The person next to *pahan* is the *pujar* who acts as an assistant to the *pahan.* The post of *pahan* like that of *mahato* is hereditary while any male member of the *pahan* lineage could assume the role of *pujar*.

The Korwa panchayat functions at two levels, (i) village level known as *gaon gati* panchayat or *sabha* and (ii) inter-village or religion level, known as Pargana panchayat or *sabha*. The pargana panchayat at Malom included five villages while at Serassam it included 17 villages. The jurisdiction of Korwa pargana panchayat, both at Ranchi and Palamau districts, are found to be the same as those of the statutory panchayats of the respective areas.

The entire Korwa population is considered formally as member of the panchayat at both village level and pargana level, though all are not allowed to participate in the deliberations. At pargana level the *mahatos* or *panchs* decide a case on the basis of a general consensus among themselves.

The main function of the Korwa panchayat is to safeguard their customary laws and social norms through regulating the interpersonal relationships among the individual members of the tribe as well as relationships of the tribe vis-a-vis other tribes and communities in the regional milieu. The panchayat has the power to impose fine in cash or kind, inflict physical punishment or ostracise a person or family accused of violating any social norm.

Strict Marriage Code

Marriage and/or sexual relationship outside the tribe or more specifically outside the *kuri* are considered serious infringements of the tribal code and as such the individuals or the family involved, very often, is ostracised. The news of excommunication is communicated to the *mahato*(s) of the villages within the pargana by the *piyada* or *barik.* The ostracised individual or family is required to be re-admitted by the panchayat on the pargana level only and *gaon gati* panchayat is authorised do so on its own.

An individual having sex relation outside the *kuri* is considered polluted and is hence required to be readmitted to the community through the purificatory ritual called Bhat-Bhittar.

Normally 70 to 80 kilograms of rice, 10 to 15 kilograms of pulses etc., are demanded by the panchayat from the accused by way of a fine. The members of the panchayat along with the villagers present entertain themselves with a feast. Meanwhile the purificatory ritual of Bhat-Bhittar is conducted on the individual or the all members of a family as the case may be in the presence of the *mahatos* of the pargana panchayat. The salient feature of this ritual is to slay a white cock and collect a few drops of oozing blood in a pot already containing water. This is then offered to the accused or the offender to drink.

An individual having undergone such ritual is supposed to have become purified and thus re-admitted into the *gati.* Till this ritual is performed against the offender nobody accepts water or tea from his/her hand.

In one case it was found that a married Korwa woman developed intimacy with a Chamar boy. By the time villagers came to know about it, they eloped. After a couple of months they had a chance encounter in Mirzapur with a few Korwas of the same village who had gone there to work as labourers. The news was communicated back to the village and her husband along with one member of the panchayat went to Mirzapur and brought her back. The Chamar boy somehow escaped. A meeting of the pargana panchayat was held and she was severely reprimanded by the *mahatos*. She was even beaten by her husband at the instance of the panchayat. As she lived for some time with a person other than their own tribe, she had to be ritually re-admitted to the community. In one case one Korwa was found ostracised for over two years on the ground of being responsible for the break of the norm of tribal endogamy mainly due to his negligence of a guardian's duties.

In another instance, B, an elderly Korwa had two daughters. One of them two married a man of Teli caste, while the other eloped successfully with a boy, again a Teli by caste. B had received a severe warning by the panchayat when the first incidence occurred. With a view to getting his second daughter married B brought one Korwa boy. But his daughter announced her dislike for the boy and eventually refused to marry him. Knowing this the members of the panchayat asked B to immediately arrange his daughter's marriage with the boy. But B did not do that till his daughter eloped with another Teli boy. B was summoned to the *gaon jati sabha* or panchayat vehemently reprimanded and threatened him with ostracism unless 80 kilograms of rice, 15 kilograms of pulse, one he-goat, etc., are given to the panchayat by way of fine. B refused to do so and got ostracised.

Sometimes the panchayat negotiates a marriage also in order to avoid any untoward incident. A Korwa girl on her husband's death came back to her parents' home and started living there. Meanwhile, the first wife of one Korwa had died and the second one whom he married later on had eloped with a Korwa boy of an adjacent village for over six months and remained untraced. The *sabha* under these circumstances negotiated marriage between the widow and the person who had lost both his wives, one way or the other.

Statutory Panchayat an Important Institution

As such, all the affairs of the tribe including marriage, divorce, remarriage, widow-marriage, etc., are dealt with in their panchayat or *sabha*. Cases of general nature like land dispute, quarrel, theft, etc., are usually taken to the statutory panchayat by all the ethnic groups.

The statutory panchayat or *gram* panchayat is another important institution for social control among the rural folks in general.

Malom *gram* panchayat along with Malom includes five villages, while Rabha *gram* panchayat has 17 villages under its jurisdiction including Serassam. The *gram* panchayat has two major wings, viz. the executive committee headed by one *mukhiya* with one *upmukhiya* and six members and the judicial wing headed by one Sarpanch with one Upsarpanch and six members. Election for the post of *mukhiya* and *sarpanch* is held every three years.

The main function of the executive wing is to help execute the governmental rural development schemes and to look after the general welfare of the people, while the law and order situation is maintained by the judicial wing of the *gram* panchayat. It is empowered to settle both civil and criminal cases of minor nature. Of lade, the *gram* panchayat is alleged to have become quite popular among the relatively isolated Korwas. They do not feel reluctant while bringing their cases to the Gram panchayat.

Though the statutory panchayat is becoming more and more popular with passing years eroding the role of the *gati* panchayats of various ethnic groups, yet the traditional *gati* panchayat of the Korwas, for all matters, still plays the most important role. The *mahato baiga* or *pahan*, etc., still remain the undisputed leaders and continue to play a vital role in the Korwa society.

The Korwas seem to be no more confined to their *gati* panchayats alone but are closely linked with the statutory political bodies like the *gram* panchayat. The articulation and contact with the outer world has widened and moulded the native worldview, making them more dependent on the public-political institutions, while the primordial nature of their traditional panchayat has been retained in greater proportion.

12

CUSTOMARY LAW AMONG THE JUANG OF ORISSA

A. K. ADHIKARY

The Juang are a primitive tribal community of Orissa. In the 1961 census total population of the Juang was recorded as 21,890. They were distributed primarily in the districts of Dhenkanal (11,551) and Keonjhar (9,768). They were also found sporadically in the districts of Cuttack (416), Koraput (154) and Mayurbhanj (2). The original habitat of the Juangs was in the district of Keonjhar from where they migrated to Dhenkanal and other districts.

It was said that the Juangs were previously under the rule of the king of Mayurbhanj state. The then capital of the State was at Khichching near Keonjhar. But later on the king shifted his capital from Khichching to Baripada which was situated far away from Keonjhar. From Baripada it was somewhat difficult for the king to look after his tribal subjects, like Juangs, who lived in Juangpirh that covered the hilly tract bordering Dhenkanal and Sundargarh. In spite of their exposure to the centralised political system the Juangs are found to operate their traditional system of social contract at the village as well as the ethnic level.

The primary economy of the Juang in Keonjhar is shifting cultivation on hill slopes. In Dhenkanal the Juang practise both shifting cultivation and wet cultivation. In most of the areas of Dhenkanal the Juang have switched over to *taile* (shifting) cultivation in high lands and wet cultivation in low lands. The Juang of Pellahara (formally a princely State), a Sub-division of Dhenkanal, have almost given up shifting cultivation under the restriction of forest rules. Now they have adopted wet cultivation. but owing to low yield most of them are found to take recourse to basketry as their main source of economy.

Field investigation was conducted for a period of one and a half months in the districts of Dhenkanal and Keonjhar. The Juangs of Keonjhar live on hill slopes and are in less contact situation while those of Dhenkanal district mostly live in plain areas and are in regular contact with different local Oriya caste groups. The Juang, in Dhenkanal district, live in multicaste villages. In Keonjhar the Juang live mostly in uni-ethnic villages though there are always a few households of Gonds and Patra castes living in separate hamlets.

For intensive field investigation two villages, namely, Guptaganga (Keonjhar) and Aluajharan (Dhenkanal) were selected. Guptaganga is 10 Kms. away from Keonjhar-Pallahara bus route and is located on hill slopes near the source of the river Bitarani. Aluajharan is about 8 kms. away from Kamakhyanagar sub-divisional town and is located about 2 kms. away from the Dhenkanal-Kamakhyanagar bus route.

Village Organisation

The Juang society is traditionally characterised by clan-lineage based segmentary system. In the following pages the present norms and customs, with reference to certain institutions, will be described.

Two important levels of territorial organisation are found among the Juangs—one at the level of village and the other at the level of *pir*. While the village (*gram*) is a cluster of households living together, a *pir* comprises a number of villages.

Every Juang village is traditionally inhabited by a single clan (*bak*) and has the following main officials : (1) *pradhan,* (2) *dihuri* or *nagam*, (3) *nayaka,* (4) *kaji* and (5) *dangua*.

Pradhan is the secular head of the village and is usually selected hereditarily. Sometimes he may be recruited otherwise. If the *pradhan's* sons are not grown up and experienced enough, the oldest knowledgeable man of the village is selected for this position. In fact, the most competent and rich men of the village become *pradhan.*

Dihuri or *nagam* is priest or the religious head of the village. In every matter of the village he is consulted. In any ritual affair he is assisted by all other village officials.

Nayaka and *kali* assist the *dihuri* in all the ritual activities of the village. In village rituals the *pradhan* sacrifices the animal while *dangua* helps him either by stretching out the legs of the animal or pulling apart the collar rope.

In some Dhenkanal and Pallahare villages all the above officials are not found. *nagam* is, however, found in every village. Apart from the council of these officials there are certain other informal mechanisms for the maintenance of social order.

Any meeting of the village is held at the dormitory (*majang*) of the village. The dormitory is the biggest house in the village. One side of the dormitory is kept open. It is usually built in the heart of the village. Though it primarily functions as the sleeping house of the young unmarried boys of the village, all the informal and formal gatherings are held in the dormitory. The jurisdiction of the village officials does not go beyond their own community people, and is mostly confined within the village. Punishment is given usually in terms of ostracism or fines in cash or kind. No physical punishment is meted out.

The young unmarried boys, who sleep in the dormitory, operate as an informal group among themselves. They maintain the dormitory house. They bring firewood for the fireplace, which is always kept alive, and preserve a basketful of paddy for the village guests. If there is any guest in the village, he is entertained by the unmarried boys of the village with the paddy stored up in the dormitory. Occasionally unmarried boys and girls from one village may visit another village, in such cases the guest boys and girls sleep in the dormitory house and are entertained by their agemates of the village.

Boys, of about seven to eight years of age, are initiated to the dormitory. At the time of initiation the parents of the boys provide them with one *maan* (about 1/2 Kg) of rice, one chicken, one bottle of liquor, one shirt and one small piece of cloth; and ceremonially send them to sleep in the dormitory along with other boys.

Pir Organisation

Apart from the village council of the officials mentioned above, the Juangs have an inter-village organisation which may be described as *pir* organisation. The Juang territory is known as Juangpirs. It is divided into six smaller divisions (*pirs*) namely, (1) Jharkhand Pirs comprising 17 villages, (2) Rebana Pirs comprising 16 villages, (3) Kathuapira having 12 villages, (4) Satkhand Pirs having 7 villages, (5) Charigarphira having 6 village and (6) Hunda Dandapat Pirs having 11 villages.

Each *pir* had one headman, called *sardar,* who was appointed by the then king. The function of the *sardar* was to collect revenue from the villages under his jurisdiction and to give it to the king.

Every year, at the time of the Dussehra festival, the *sardars* had to collect goats from their villages and present them to the king. In the month of Pausa the *sardars* had to collect crops like *rasi*, Paddy from the villages under their respective jurisdictions and give 25 *pai* of *rasi* and 11 *khondi* of Paddy (440 kgs appx.). *Rasi* were offered to the temple and the paddy directly to the king as revenue. At the time of the car festival, in the month of Ashad, the *sardars* had also to take coir to the king's palace for pulling the car. The king, in turn, presented red or black turbans (*Shiropa*), *dhoti* and shirts to his *sardars*.

The *sardars* were appointed by the king. At the time of appointment the king took the votes of the *pradhans* of the village. The man, who was supported by the majority of the *pradhans*, was given the appointment as *sardar* of the *pirs*.

The *sardar* had to look after the villages under his jurisdiction. He had not only to collect the revenue for the king but also to settle the disputes or litigations within his jurisdiction. In case of any inter-village dispute all the *pradhans* of his villages were called at convenient place and a meeting was held under the leadership of the *sardar*; no official could exercise arbitration. Decisions were taken unanimously.

It may be mentioned here that the *pir* organisation is no longer in vogue. Some of the Juangs in Keonjhar still remember the system. The *sardars* are still found to be respected. The villagers, under his jurisdiction, often ask for his mediation in mitigating any litigation among them.

The constituent villages of a *pirs* are related by kinship ties. There is, thus, a continuity between their traditional mode of social control by kin-based non-centralised social system and the territorial organisation introduced by the king of the State.

Panchayat System

In Goansika panchayat 17 *mauzas* were grouped into 12 wards, each having one member. Of these eight were from Juang community one from Patra, a Scheduled Caste community, and three from Bhuiyan, another major tribal community of the area. The secretary was a Gonda by caste while the *sarpanch* was a Juang.

Although in the *gram* panchayat the majority of the members are from the Juang community, they hardly bring any internal problem of their community to the panchayat for trial. Rather, cases involving other non-tribals are brought to the panchayat. Sometime if any land or property of any Juang is forcibly occupied and enjoyed by any non-tribal, the case is invariably brought to the panchayat, or even to the police station.

Internal problems are handled within the village and among community members.

Jati Panchayat

In Dhenkanal the Juangs, like other low castes, of the area have caste councils of their own. Such a caste panchayat comprises a number of villages and has three important officials, namely, *bade behera, sai behera* and *pai behera.*

Bade behera is the head of the *jati* panchayat. He is also known a *sabhapati*. He can call for any meeting at any time. No *jati* meeting can be held without his notification. *Sai behera* is the head at the village level. Every village has one *sai behera.* There may be more than one *pai behera* in a village. The function of a *pai behera* is to announce the date of a meeting among the community members of the village and to help *sai behera* in various other matters.

The cases of divorce and adultery within the community are usually dealt with by this panchayat. There is no definite place where the meeting is held. It can be held in any village within the jurisdiction of the *jati* panchayat.

The officers are not hereditary. Experienced and knowledgeable persons are appointed to the offices through election.

Nuclear Family

In the districts of Dhenkanal and Keonjhar the families are nuclear in type. A few joint families are also found. Authority rests usually in the hands of the father or husband, according to the composition of the family.

It may be mentioned here that in Keonjhar the sons, on marriage, may run independent households, but usually they along with their father hold and cultivate land jointly. In such cases authority rests, to a great extent, with their father.

Age of Marriage

Boys among the Juangs are married usually after the age of 15 or 16 years. Girls are married after they attain puberty. The Juangs' belief is that girls attain puberty usually at the age of 11 years or above. Though maximum marriages are settled on the mutual liking of boys and girls, it is hardly found that younger brothers or sisters are married before their elders.

Bride-price

The Juangs of Keonjhar have the custom of bride-price. At the time of marriage the groom's party has to give one rupee to the bride's mother's brother and another to her father. This system of bride-price seems to be symbolic in nature.

Marriage is performed on auspicious days that are ascertained by the village priests, and involves much preparatory functions. Whether a particular marriage will be a good one or not is also ascertained by the priest through his usual method of divination. Three grains of paddy are kept in such a way that one remains above the two. Then these grains of paddy are covered with a basket, and kept there for one night. After lifting it, if the grains are found undisturbed, it is presumed that the prospective marriage will be a good one.

There is one major difference between the marriage practices of the Juangs of Dhenkanal and those of Keonjhar. While in Dhenkanal the Juang grooms go to the bride's village for marriage in Keonjhar the bride has to come to the groom's village.

Different forms of Marriage

There are different forms of marriages among the Juangs. These include (1) *kamandiria kania*, (2) *digar kania*, (3) *mana mania.*

Kamandiria Kania: This marriage is by arrangement or negotiation. Someone acts as middleman. After marriage is settled and the date is fixed a party comprising women, unmarried boys and girls of the bride's village take the bride to the groom's village. The boys accompany them with their *chengu* (musical drums) and dance and sing in the groom's village. The groom's father has to entertain this party. However, in the case of poor parents ceremonial part is less elaborate.

Digar Kania: It is a form of marriage by capture. From the dancing ground or from the bathing *ghat*, or from the jungle a bride may be captured by the friends of a groom. After capture the groom's father sends information to the bride's parents asking for their consent in marriage. After marriage is over the new couple may pay a ceremonial visit to the bride's natal house and pay money, clothes, paddy and other things as taken of bride-price.

Mana Mania: It is a form of love marriage and is widely prevalent among the Juangs in Keonjhar. Mutual love between a boy and a girl is expressed at the time of *chengu* dance. A girl expresses her liking by touching the feet of a boy. Afterwards they start visiting each other's village and exchange gifts. The boy, later on, informs his parents of his liking who, in turn, request the girl's parents for consent.

If parents do not agree the boy and the girl may flee to another village and settle there as married couple. After several years, when the things appear to have settled down, the boy may come back to his natal village. This is locally known as *serum kania* or marriage by elopement.

Sometimes intense love may lead to sexual indulgence and the girl may become pregnant. In such cases the parents of both the girl and the boy are fined (a few rupees) by the Village Council. In addition to this the parents of the boy have to offer a feast to the villagers of the girl. The boy is forced to marry the girl. This type of marriage is locally known as *udung kania*.

Monogamy is the rule but polygyny is not rare. A man may keep more than one wife at a time. In Keonjhar I found one man having four wives at a time all living together but in separate huts. The reason of polygamy, as told by my informants, is usually barrenness of wife. but this is not the only reason. There are certain social and economic reasons too.

The Juangs are divided into a number of exogamous clans (*bok*). Some clans feel themselves related to one another and are referred to as *kutum bok*. The people of these clans trace their descent from a common stock, and do not marry among them. The clans with whom marriage is permissible are known as *bendhu bok*. There is another category of clans which is known as *surya bok*. They are like *kutum bok* or brother clans. While the clans of Surya *bok* can trace their genealogical connection with one another, those of *kutom bok* feel themselves related mostly on the assumption that they have descended from a common ancestor. Marriage among these clans is prohibited.

Since almost every village is inhabited by a single clan or members of a *Kutum bok*, marriage within the village is not usually permitted due to the principle of exogamy.

Consanguineous kin like grandmother, mother's, daughter's, granddaughter's brother's, daughter's sister's daughter's, etc., are prohibited in marriage. Similarly affinal kins like wife's mother, wife's elder sister, wife's sister's daughter, etc., are also prohibited.

There is a slight tendency towards mother's brother's daughter marriage. The Juangs, however, try to avoid actual mother's brother's daughter, and prefer to marry classificatory brother's daughters.

The Juangs have no custom of marrying elder brother's widow. Younger brother's widow is, however, avoided. Junior sororate, i.e. marriage of wife's younger sister, is permissible among the Juangs if the first wife is dead. Divorce is permissible among the Juangs. Locally it is known as *charpatra*. It occurs usually in the case of wife's barrenness. It may also happen if the wife does not like her husband and if she develops any love affair with another man.

In case of any separation the issue is to be raised in the village assembly where it is decided. If it is found that the husband is guilty, he has to give his wife Rs. 20 to 30 and one sari. If the wife has any child in arms, the husband has also to bear the expenditure for the child until it is grown up. The husband, however, has the right to take away the child after it has weaned.

Premarital sex indulgence is permitted, but it should not get socially exposed. Premarital love leading to pregnancy of the girl is socially looked down upon. In such cases the person involved is forced to marry. Marriage within the prohibited range of kins is a serious social offence. They are sometimes ostracised from the community. Such a couple has to live in some distant village. The ostracised man can return to his natal village if he can fulfil some conditions. He has to plant a tamarind tree in the village. When the tree starts bearing fruits, the man may come back. He invites all the villagers and treats thm to feast rice and curry of tamarind.

Property Ownership

In Keonjhar land is owned both collectively and individually. The Juangs in this area practise shifting cultivation on hill slopes. One has to clear jungles. The amount of land one is able to clear is owned by him. Household comprising a nuclear family of husband, wife and unmarried children is the usual production and consumption unit of the Juangs. Sometimes several such households related agantically own and cultivate land collectively. The produce is, however, distributed and consumed in terms of individual households.

In every village there are a number of jackfruit and mango trees. Some of these are owned by a group of related families, some by the entire village community and some by individual family. The trees are owned by the man who plants them. After his death the ownership goes to the head of his descendants. The trees of the man who dies without any descendent become village property, and are shared equally by all the villagers. If any man leaves a village for ever, he usually donates his trees to the village people.

Moveable properties are transmitted in the male line. Married girls may sometimes get their share of fruits from the trees in their natal villages. Sometimes mothers may give their ornaments and clothes to the daughters. There is, however, no prescription for this.

Conclusion

At present the Juangs, like most other tribes of India, are much exposed to the exogenous socio-economic influences of the region. All the Juangs of Orissa are, however, not equally affected. The Juangs in Dhenkanal and Pallahers areas live in plains areas along with different local Oriya caste groups. They have wet cultivation in low lands besides swidden cultivation on hill slopes. Through the government's developmental and welfare programmes they have got land and aid in cash and kind. As a result, individual ownership of land and other types of property have emerged. They also often resort to the Block Officer and police station for settlement of any disputes regarding land, especially with the people of other community.

Since the Juangs in Dhenkanal and Pallahara areas constantly live and interact with the neighbouring caste people, they are found to emulate certain features of social control mechanism from the regional caste-based Hindu society. For instance, *jati* panchayat among the Juangs of those areas is one. Like the low-caste people, any dispute among the members of the Juangs is settled by the *jati* panchayat where several villages are involved.

Besides, the custom of the groom's going to the bride's house for marriage as well as the prohibition of the custom of *chengu* beating is a new phenomenon adopted from the macro social system. In spite of these changes in their customary behaviour, the community is regulated primarily by their traditional customs and institutions.

The Juangs of Keonjhar, on the other hand, are less exposed to the larger socio-political contexts. Though in every village there are some households of Gouda and Patra caste, the Juangs are dominant in every sphere. In case of any dispute in a village even the Gouda or the Patra people seek justice from the traditional village council of the Juangs. The Gouda and Patra are always in service relations with the Juangs. The *pir* level of territorial organisation, though appears to be a mechanism of social control introduced by the kings of the princely States of Mayurbhanj and Keonjhar, is, in fact, on extension of the mechanism of social control characterised by clan-lineage-based segmentary system. The Juangs of the villages headed by a *sardar* were all related through a common kinship tie. The members belonged to one or two clans which traced their descent from a common stock and were referred to as a *kutum bok* or brother clans. Though the centralised authority of the King in his State is, no longer present, the people still seek the help of the *sardar* in case of any dispute among the villages under his jurisdiction. The institution of *sardar* is still there. Now the office is hereditary.

Law is usually supposed to exist only where there are courts and codes supported by a fully politically organised state. In this sense the Juangs have no formal law. However, they have the experience of being under the rule of the centralised authority of politically organised state. After the abolition of the princely States they are exposed to the regional socio-political processes of social control. At present we find that the Juang society is regulated primarily by their traditional norms and customs and the sphere of social control is limited within the domain of kinship.

There is, however, a perceptible difference between the young and the old generations as regards their outlook towards their customary law. Among the Juangs of Orissa the young and educated Juangs appear to be more enthusiastic about the socio-political aspects of the larger society while the old are proud of their traditional mechanism.

13

CUSTOMARY LAW OF THE BATHUDI OF ORISSA

PASHUPATI PRASAD MAHATO

A good number of tribal groups, namely, Santal, Gond, Bhuiya, Sounti, Ho, Kharia and Bathudi live in the districts of Mayurbhanj and Keonjhar of Orissa. They constitute 24 per cent (12,88,610) of the total tribal population (50,71,937) of the State of Orissa. Total number of the Bathudi was 130,792 in 1971 and their concentration is in Mayurbhanj and Keonjhar. The Bothudis are Oriya-speaking people, yet they frequently use some words in their speech that belong to the Dravidian family of languages.

The district of Mayurbhanj has four sub-divisions: Sadar, Bamanghati, Kaptiapada and Panchpir. Each of these sub-divisions has two levels of revenue units known as Pargana and Pirh. The former unit is under the control of Tahsildar who supervises the work of revenue matters relating to five or six lesser level units (*pirh*). Each unit of the latter is again managed by respective *desh-pradhans* or *desh-chatia*, who is directly concerned with the collection of revenue from five or six villages with the help of the headman known as *pradhan*. Being headquarters of a Pargana in Panchpir sub-division, Jashipur is a small town on the Bombay road situated at a distance of 70 miles from the District headquarters of Baripada. In the record of *tal-patra* (Palm-Leaf) of Jashipur Matha the following historical account of the local Bathudis is available.

A Short History of Bathudis

At some point of time, the entire Panchpir, a sub-division of Mayurbhanj District, was under the control of the Kharia tribe. But they had to recede from this place by surrendering their control to the Bathudis who came from Nandipur village in Simlipal.

In course of time, the Bathudi chief was able to secure the title of Mahapatra for rendering military support to the Maharaja Mayurbhanj in the battle of Tenta-posi against the invasion of a Gond chief. Later on the Bathudi chief became tyrannical and the tenants had no alternative but to revolt against him. Having dismissed the then zamindariship of the Bathudis on account of their oppressive rule, the Maharaja of Mayurbhanj decided to introduce a new system of revenue collection, by auctioning the entire area to a person, Karan by caste, who arrived in Jashipur from Cuttack to work as Tahsildar. According to the local information the Jashipur area was the homeland of the Bathudi tribe. Although a few among them are still in the habit of drinking indigenous wine and taking termites and red-ants, together with other animal diet, many of them refrain from this and prefer clean food. It is for this reason that the Bathudis of Panchpir sub-division where they are numerically strong have acquired a status of *jal chalniyas,* i.e. from whom water can be accepted. Generally the Bathudis engage Brahmins to officiate as priests for their various ritual performances. They are highly caste-conscious and refuse work in the houses of the Kurmi-Mahatos who are good peasants and are regarded by the Bathudis and other Oriya people as unclean and untouchables.

Padmapur Village — First Phase of Field Work

The first phase of the field work among the Bathudis was carried out in a village named Padmapur, under Bhanda Pirh within the jurisdiction of Jashipur Pargana in the sub-division of Panchpir, in the district of Mayurbhanj. Padmapur is at a distance of one and a half miles from Jashipur town. It is a multi-ethnic village with four hamlets, each of which is referred to after the name of the communities who are numerically strong than others. These are Bathudi Sai, Khandwar Sai, Kol Sai and Mahuljola Sai. Various ethnic groups present in the village are Karan, Khandwar, Sounti, Kol, Muslum, Bathudi and Mahakur. Out of 130 families in Padmapur village, the number of Bathudi families is only 40. The surrounding villages have a similar ethnic composition. The ethnic groups are Kurmi-Mahanta, Telis, Maharana, Mauri, Muslim, etc.

Asanpat Village — Second Phase of Field Work

The second phase of field work was carried out at Asanpat village under the jurisdiction of Baria police station in Champus Sub-Division of district Keonjhar, Orissa. Asanpat is a big multi-ethnic village, under Asanpat Gram Panchayat, where Bathudis are numerically dominant. The number of hamlets is nine which are found to be scattered. According to 1971 census, the total population in the whole of *gram* panchayat is 4,013. All the members and the head (*sarpanch*) of the *gram* panchayat are Bathudis. The other ethnic groups are Kol, Barik, Mahanta, Gour, Maharanas and Dom. The tribal people are not only numerically strong, they are also economically dominant. They are educated too. Forest and hills cover an area of 250 acres, whereas an area of 1,600 acres is meant for cultivation. For the purpose of studies, I selected three hamlets (Upar Sai, Majh Sai and Tal Sai) in Asanpat village.

The following is the description of the normative rules that govern and regulate the traditional socio-cultural life of the Bathudis.

Mechanism of Social Control

While collecting information on this aspect, it is observed that the normative rules operating in the Bathudi society are executed through three distinct spheres. The first two are related to the systems of revenue and development activities. As mentioned before, the former operated through the units like *pir* and *pargana* whereas the latter has formed a three-tier structure. Constituted under the Panchayat Act of the State Government, the village panchayat (*pallisabha*) occupies the lowest level being concerned with the development activities of the village only. The elected members of this unit send their own representatives to the next higher unit known as *gram* panchayat headed by a *sarpanch.* The highest body conducts its business at Block level and it is referred to as panchayat *parishad* in which all the *sarpanchs* of the constituent units are the members who elect one among them to act as Chairman.

Last but not least is their traditional caste council known as *jati-sabha.* No doubt the Bathudi zamindars, particularly of Bathudigarh of Jashipur, had at one time exerted their influence in bringing about some stability in the social relationship among their brethren in different villages but there had occurred considerable erosion in this respect, due to relegation from their erstwhile position and also for being landless now.

As a convention, all the elderly persons of different caste groups including the Bathudi tribe in Padampur village constitute the traditional village council (*gram* panchayat) presided over by the Pradhan, the chief headman, whose post is hereditary.

In Asanpat village, the Bathudis being numerically strong and dominant in all spheres, not only control the traditional caste council but also the modern institutions like *palli-sabha* and *gram* panchayat. For this reason, the *pradhan* has a considerable hold in the *jati-sabha* and takes due note of the instructions given by higher officials belonging to *pirh* and *pargana*, namely, *desh-chatia* and *desh pradhan.*

I observed that though these units (the traditional village council and case council) take a leading part in the over-all control mechanism yet there are constituent units which operate at the level of social organisation with restricted powers. Apart from the control exercised by the family head in the domestic sphere, the heads of the lineage have authority over the members residing in the lineage settlement (Bakhuri), for they decide the dates and plans, the arrangement for feasts during marriage and funeral ceremonies. The same is the case with the heads of hamlet (*sai*) who are invested with appropriate authority to decide the dates for the worship of village deities for the protection of the crops. But the village council (*gram* panchayat) has great responsibility for announcing the actual dates of village festivals like Rajh, Ura, Doljatra and Chaitra-Parab.

Customary Laws

When an unmarried girl becomes pregnant by a boy of her tribe, the traditional village council imposes a fine on both the parties. Effort is also made to influence the boy to marry the girl. But if a non-Bathudi boy is implicated, the girl's family is immediately excommunicates. But if an identified person refuses to accept the fatherhood, then it is the woman who has to prove it to the caste council. Bathudi members neither accept water nor fire from such socially degraded persons. For attaining normal condition, admission into the society is granted by the village council on providing a feast along with a penalty of Rs. 100 to Rs. 200. When a Bathudi man commits such an offence with the woman belonging to a non-tribal group, the caste council steps into this affair to outcaste the guilty person. When a person suffers from an obnoxious skin disease as a result of infection by flies (Machhiapat), he too is made either outcaste or has to undergo the appropriate purification ceremony (*suddhi* or *pravaschita*) to avoid such expulsion . The priest who is a local Brahmin conducts this ritual. The afflicted person thereafter invites his relatives (consanguineal and affinal) as also his friends to attend the feast. Not only the *suddhi* ceremony is performed in such cases but it has to be observed in the case of killing a cow or calf, even in the case of killing one's wife. In the absence of the priest an assistant to the priest can officiate. It has been stated that the priest in Jashipur and *desh pradhan* in Asanpat area take part in the feasts given by outcast persons for getting readmission to the society.

As a result of dissensions in a joint family, the villagers preferred to take the help of the village council or caste council (*jati sabha*) for bringing about an amicable partition (*apas bhag*).The nature of cases dealt mostly by a caste council, and the breaches of social norms are very strictly dealt with by it. Authorities generally impose fines ranging from Rs. 5 to Rs. 200. If one fails to pay the fine, he or she is outcasted. However, it depends upon the nature of the offence. Any wrong against a person and offences like defamation, abuse and assault are considered in the village council. The offender has to take oath by touching a cow's tail or tiger's tail (*bagh langur*). The Bathudis are very much afraid of tiger. To tell the truth, an oath is a serious matter because of the belief that telling a lie will get them leprosy. Bathudi village council does not tolerate pre-marital or extra-marital sex relation, theft, etc. It does not deal with murder, homicide, rape, etc., which are reported to the police and court. The Bathudis are not involved in criminal suits. However, there are some civil suits in which they are involved.

The constitution of the caste council is not a written one. It is to control the social offences committed by the members of the village or tribe in its traditional way. Recruitment to the offices is made through the hereditary process. In the absence of any suitable heir, the function of the office is performed by the newly elected person. The service land also passes to the successor to the post. When there is an outbreak of cholera or small-pox, necessary fund is raised through subscription and the village council performs a ritual at the village shrine (Thakurani Sai). With the help of *rawriya* (sorcerer) and *deori,* the festival of Mahima to Thakurani, the Chandani of Jashipur Math, Sirakuri Chaitra Jatra all are organised by the village council.

The village priest (*deori*) who is a Kharia in Padmapur and a Bethudi in Asanpat village are mainly responsible for the worship of the village deities. After the completion of rituals at the village shrine, the head of the *bada* (male goat), which is sacrificed, is taken by the *deori* and the body of the goat by the villagers. The village council supervises the cooking of the meat. The members eat it near the Thakurani Sai. No woman is allowed to take the meat of the goat.

Marriage Age

The age at marriage for the girls ranges from 17 to 18 years and that for boys from 20 to 21 years. Whenever any pre-marital relation takes place, the family elders try to minimise the issue. Marriage must be performed within the tribe. But marriage within the same clan or same lineage or with close kin is strictly prohibited.

The usual practice is to marry off the elder daughter first. Any departure in this case would create subsequent difficulty in arranging her marriage. People of the region may take it very seriously and suspect that something is wrong in the family. Such family is marked as Deshighar.

The bride-price (*kañya pan*) depends upon the wealth and status of the bride's family. The bride price is settled at the time of negotiation. In general, it ranges from Rs. 200 to Rs. 300 in cash. Besides, five maunds of rice and a he-goat are also given for a feast. As an obligation to the wife's mother, who brought her up with breast milk, she is given a cloth too as compensation.

For the other elderly women related to the bride, 20 to 25 saris (cloth) are demanded. There is also demand for ornaments mainly of silver and gold. The recipients of the bride-price are mainly the elderly members of the family for generally father, mother, brother, uncle, etc. Actually it is not shared by them. The elderly members of the family purchase ornaments for the bride with the bride-price. Saris are distributed to the mother's wife of mother's brother, wife of father's brother, etc.

The refund of bride-price takes place in case of divorce (*chara-chari*) only. According to the decision of the caste council it must be refunded within six or seven months. But in the case of death of the husband the question of refunding bride-price does not arise.

There are four kinds of marriage within the Bathudi community.

These are: (i) marriage by negotiation (*sambandha*), (ii) marriage by *sangha* (in case of death of husband or a wife and after divorce, a male or female can marry again), (iii) love marriage or *ghar dhuka*, (iv) marriage by intrusion, in which the girl comes on her own accord to reside with a man as his wife (*sambandha*).

Jhulam Baha

The Bathudis are generally monogamous. But after the death of the spouse (husband or wife) one can remarry. If the wife is barren, then the husband may take a second wife with the consent of the first. The wives live in common house. Second marriage must be within their tribal group. The Bathudi can practise territorial endogamy in case of marriage. If any case of incest is ever reported to the villagers they take serious note of it. Only junior levirate and sororate are prevalent among the Bathudis. They are patrilocal. After the marriage a woman is absorbed in the clan group of her husband. A son-in-law who lives in the father-in-law's house is called *ghar jamai*. Generally, it happens when the daughter is the only child. If a widow or divorced woman prefers to remarry, she may either go with her breast-sucking child, to live with her new husband or she may leave the children in her father's house and go along.

Generally the children, born of previous marriage, reside in the paternal house of the mother. Social position and legal rights of the children born through second marriage are the same as those of the children born of the first marriage. There is no distinction between the two. The widows are not denied any social right. No social stigma is attached to them. They may perform the social ceremonies like other married women. As divorce (*chara-chari*) is permissible by the Bathudis, the matter is first referred to the caste council. If the husband is idle (*arshua*) and he is not in a position to maintain his wife (*ki-akare pushibe*), then the divorce is effected by the caste council. If the husband is suffering from leprosy, then it also grants the prayer for divorce. On the charges of adultery, desertion, neglect of duties, contagious disease and barrenness against the woman, the husband gets the grant of divorce. On the other hand the woman gets the permission when charges are there of impotency, cruelty and adultery against the husband. Divorce is also granted to husband, when wife is believed to practise witchcraft (*dakini vidya*). Both husband and wife may demand divorce in case of insanity or incurable disease.

Similarly involvement of any spouse in crime, punishment and conviction by court of law is also taken as a ground for divorce. When the *jati-sabha* grants divorce it is implemented immediately. The question of repayment of bride-price is considered at the instance of the caste council. It must be paid within six to seven months. However, the wife may demand a compensation as maintenance (*khoraki*) for six to seven months; it is for a year if she is in the family way.

Head of Family

There are joint and extended families among the Bathudi living in Asanpat village, whereas nuclear family is dominant in Padampur village. In the family, father is the head. In his absence, if the children are all minors, mother assumes the authority.

After marriage, the son inevitably gets separated from his parents to take up his new residence with wife. This separation is a must in Padampur village and only son is no exception to it.

Adoption

Regarding the adoption of a boy (*pusuna putra* or *posha putra*), the Bathudi have no hard and first rule. The son of wife's sister and a brother's son may be adopted. He gets social recognition when the members are given a good feast by the adopter. On such social recognition, he can only inherit the property of the adopter.

Property

The different types of property include land, paddy, rice, homestead land, houses, money, cattle, ornaments, plough, bullock-cart, agricultural implements, etc.

The title of the land is recorded by the settlement authorities during the time of settlement operation. This is known as Proja Swatts. Nobody can oust the tenure holder. But if there is no successor, then the settlement officer may give the Patta of the land to another person.

The arable land (*khet*) is demarcated with a plot number. One's landed property may be scattered in different places of the Mouja. During the time of raja, when a subject failed to pay the annual rent, his property used to be auctioned.

The produce of land, namely, paddy, *kodo, gundlu,marua, jonar, sarisa* and vegetables of different kinds are also regarded as property. The non-agricultural produce like cotton of *smiul* tree, fruits of *mahua, sal* flower, *kendu* leaves, honey, etc., are regarded as property; livestock are also regarded as property by the Bathudi. The other movable property are ornaments.

Landed property and other properties are inherited by the sons or by sons' sons, sometimes also by the daughters. The son of the daughter may inherit the property if the man has got no son.

Villagers enjoy a few customary rights over the natural resources. These are grazing ground (*to-char*) for the cattle, *go-dandi*, the place where the cattle are kept, *pakhari* and *baguvet*, the pond and the garden. These are village properties. The water of streams or the river and other natural resources is used by all the villagers. The burning place of dead bodies (*sasan*) is a common property.

Bathudis have no right of hunting in the forest. But they can collect fruits, herbs, honey, etc., from the village forest. They have the usufructuary right only.

Changes in the Customary Laws

The Bathudis of village Padmapur, who live in their traditional habitat, are found to be more exposed to outside contact than those of the village Asanpat. The local businessmen and peasants usually refer to the Bathudis as lazy. Living in forest habitats for a long time, the Bathudis have gradually moved towards the Jashipur township where they are exploited by the local upcountry businessmen who control the sources of trade. There are Telis and Mahatos who control land. On the other hand the Bathudi men and women work mostly as labourers in road construction in the forest department and in the mines. Owing to their mobility and poverty, the cohesive character of the group behaviour and maintenance of social control have become loose. Their village council is weak. The political, social and economic control is no more in their hands.

In Asanpat, the Bathudis are very much conscious about their social position. No change has occurred in the caste council in which all the elected members are Bathudis. Their village council as well as the caste council have a firm grip on all. We find cohesive social behaviour in any decision of the council. Every member is afraid of the village council and caste council. Social organisation of the Bathudis is based on extended or joint families and lineages in Asanpat village. They are good peasants also. They are extremely caste conscious. The political, social and economic control in the village is in their hands. In Padmapur village, which is in contact situation, the Bathudis are gradually losing their identity whereas in Asanpat, their identity is alive.

Conclusion

The Bathudis observe in general all the customary laws which are part of their cultural heritage. The rules are rigidly observed in Asanpat where the social organisation as well as the village council are strong. Whereas in Padmapur, where the Bathudis are poor and day labourers, the caste council is weak and the customary laws are not rigidly binding. Tribal identity, peasant economy and compact and strong social organisation, as found in the former village, consolidate the traditional norms and values.

14

CUSTOMARY LAW AMONG THE ORAON OF BIHAR

WILLIAM EKKA

Numerically the Oraons are the largest tribe in Ranchi district, Bihar. In 1981, they numbered 10,48,066. The area of their distribution too is as vast as their number. They are spread practically throughout the length and breadth of the district. Their population density, however, is not uniform everywhere in the district. In Khunti sub-division they have rather a thin population. In its Simdega sub-division too they are relatively low in number. However, in Kurdeg Anchal of this sub-division the Oraons have a preponderant population because of its contiguity with the Oraon belt of Raigarh district, Madhya Pradesh. The two other sub-divisions, namely, Sadar and Gumla, have the main concentration of the Oraons.

The Oraons are spread over a very vast area and, therefore, are likely to have at least some variation in their culture. However, the customary laws, delineated in this paper, are restricted in their generalisation to the neighbouring areas of two villages, Bhita and Kachmachi, where the field work was undertaken.

Both the villages are very close to each other, the distance being hardly one kilometre between them. Of the two, Bhita is a bigger village having 366 households. Out of these, 295 households belong to the Oraons. Seven of them are of the Christian Oraons. The remaining households belong to Baniya, Gorait, Kumhar, Lohra, Modi (betel-seller), Mohammadan, Nagbansi, Sonar and Teli. Kachmachi has 88 households. Of these 80 belong to the Oraons. They include 25 Christian Oraon households. The other castes living in the village are Ahir, Gorait, Lohar and Nagbansi.

These villages are in Lohardanga Anchal of Sadar sub-division of the district. They are about 16 and 20 kilometres away from Rañchi and Lohardanga respectively. In spite of this, they may be regarded as interior villages mainly because of their relative isolated location.

Social Control Mechanism

The social control mechanism of the Oraons of this area operates both at village and regional levels. At the village level it is called *gaon* panchayat and at the regional level, the *parha* panchayat.

In general the *gaon* panchayat settles the disputes of the tribesmen of the village, takes decisions on rituals and ceremonies to be performed for the village duties and the evil spirits when epidemics such as cholera, small-pox, etc., break out in the village, settles the disputes arising out of dissolution of marital unions, executes the decisions of *parha* panchayat and deals with the breaches of social customs and exercises its authority by punishing the offenders with fine or excommunication.

The traditional functionaries of *gaon* panchayat are *mahato, pahan* and *bhandari.* In the past they were village servants of the Raja of Chhotanagpur who had given them some rent-free land for their services. By virtue of their association with the raja they had great influence over the people of the village. It was the source of their authority. These persons particularly the *mahato* and the *pahan* formed together the decision-making, body for the village affairs. They commanded the respect of the villagers who looked upon them as their leaders. *Mahato* and *pahan* usually belonged to the Oraon tribe and, therefore, the tribal leadership in the village was automatically assumed by them. This authority structure in the village is still continuing to function even after the abolition of zamindari.

Mahato is the head of the *gaon* panchayat. The post is hereditary and follows the rule of primogeniture. In the absence of a son, the *mahato* is succeeded by a male member of his clan who is closely related to him. Now the service land, called *mahatwai khet*, is no longer tax-free. But still it is inherited along with the post.

Pahan is the village priest. The tenure of his office is for three years. After every three years a new *pahan* is selected on the day of *sarhul* festival.

Bhandari is the village messenger. In addition to this he was entrusted with the task of looking after the grain store, locally called *bhandar*, of the raja in the past. Therefore now the *bhandari* is found in only those villages in which the raja had a grain store. Rent-free service-land attached to this post is called *bhandari* or *bhandargiri khet*. It is no longer rent-free now. It is inherited along with the post which is hereditary like the post of *mahato*.

Parha has a sort of federal structure comprising neighbouring villages whose number may vary from nine to twelve or even more. The *parha* to which Bhita and Kachmachi belong has nine villages including these two. The remaining seven villages are Amboa, Bamandia, Baragain, Cherma, Kanjo, Khijri and Nagdi. These villages are located within about 5 sq kms.

Parha panchayat acts as an appellate court, settles the disputes which the *gaon* panchayat fails to do, takes the offenders to task who do not accept the decisions of the panchayat, deals with serious breaches of social customs end punishes the offenders suitably by either excommunicating them or imposing a fine on them according to the nature and gravity of offences. It promotes social solidarity among the tribesmen of the component village summoning them to its meetings and involving them in deciding any case, tribal or non-tribal. Besides, each year a group of people of the component villages of a *parha* is led by the *parha* chief to a traditional tribal fair held in Murma, a village near Mandar, where they take part in the dances. Some of the dances are competitive in nature and rivalry among the dancers of different *parha* becomes quite evident. Furthermore once in a year *parha jatra* (dance) is organised in every *parha*. Where there is a scope for hunting or where there is jungle, people of a *parha* organise a *parha sikar* (Parha hunting expedition) once in a year. The women also of a *parha* go on a hunting expedition once in 12 years. It is known as *jani sikar*. Such things reflect the social unity of the *parha* and the people of its component villages.

The functionaries of the *parha* panchayat are *raja, dewan mantri. painbhara* and *kotwar*. These posts, except the last one, are traditionally held by the *mahato* of Cherma, Bhita, Nagdi and Kachmachi respectively. The post of *kotwar* is collectively held by the young boys of Kanjo village.

Raja being the head of the *parha* presides over its panchayat meetings. *Dewan* is his assistant and *mantri* is their adviser. *Painbhara* is entrusted with the task of making arrangements for the supply of food and water to those attending the meeting. All these posts are hereditary. *Kotwar* act as messengers and volunteers for *parha* panchayat. If necessity arises the *parha* raja awards corporal punishment to the offenders through the *kotwars*.

Authority in Family

The Oraons are patriarchal, patrilocal and patrilineal. In the old age the authority of a man automatically passes down to his eldest son. A widow can exercise authority in the family if her sons are too young to undertake the responsibility of running the household. In case of horizontally extended family the authority rests with the eldest brother.

Bride-price

Bride-price is known as dali which is more symbolic than real. In cash an amount of Rs. 7.50 p. is paid to the bride's father. In addition to it about 10 pieces of cloth are given. They include *maisares barki* (a cloth used for covering the body while sleeping) and *maisaree* (saree) for the bride's mother, *sara dhoti* (dhoti) for her younger brother, *aji ledra* (saree) for her father's mother, *nani ledra* (saree) for her mother's mother and 4-5 sarees for such relatives as her paternal aunts, maternal aunts, elder brothers. wives, etc. Bride-price is not refundable for any reason.

Modes of Acquiring Mate

The most acceptable and prevalent mode of acquiring mate is the negotiation initiated by the boy's parents or elders. The other modes of acquiring mate are elopement, intrusion and mutual consent. All these three modes are sometimes combined and the marriage resulting from any of them is called *dhuku.* In order to obtain social sanction for the marriage resulting from any of these modes a feast has to be given to the tribesmen of the village. Another mode of acquiring mate is by service. Locally it is known as *ghar-damad.* The term actually denotes relationship rather than the mode by which a mate is acquired. For such a marriage the entire marriage expenditure is borne by the bride's father. The bridegroom is exempted from paying even the bride-price.

Polygamy and Polyandry

Among the non-Christian Oraons polygyny is not prohibited though they do not have any instance of it in the two villages. Theoretically one can have any number of wives depending upon his economic ability to maintain them. Christian Oraons are forbidden to practise it by their religion. Polyandry is not allowed in Oraon society.

Rule of Endogamy

The Oraons are an endogamous tribe. Transgression of the rule of endogamy is seriously dealt with by the *gaon* panchayat. The offenders are excommunicated as well as fined. For readmission into the tribe they have to sever all their connections with their non-Oraon spouse, undergo a purificatory ceremony and throw a feast to the tribesmen of the *parha*. Christian Oraons also abide by this rule though their religion allows them to marry anyone of any caste or tribe if he or she is a Christian.

Clan Exogamy

The Oraons have several totemistic clans, and the members of a clan believe to have descended from a common ancestor. Hence, they practise clan exogamy. The breach of this rule amounts to commission of incest which, as they say, is a matter of great abhorrence. Sexual relation with any consanguineal kin is forbidden. One cannot have it even with some affinal relatives also as wife's mother, wife's elder sister, wife's sister's or brother's daughter, wife's brother's wife, etc.

Preferential Marriage

The Oraons do not, as a rule, have any preferential marriage. Though they are a Dravidian tribe they do not show any preference for cross-cousin marriage, nor is there any instance of cross-cousin marriage in the two villages. Cross-cousins are related to one another as brother and sister and use in terms of siblings.

Among the Oraons senior levirate is allowed, and there is instance of it in Bhita. Junior sororate also is permissible among them. There exists a joking relationship between a man and his two such kins. Such marriages, however, are not obligatory on the part of anyone. Practice of either junior or senior levirate and senior sororate is forbidden. One has avoidance relationship with these two kins.

Rule of Residence

The Oraons follow patrilocal rule of residence. But under certain circumstances the rule is overlooked. For instance in case of marriage by service one often has to live in his wife's parents' house.

Remarriage of Widow and Divorcee

Oraon society permits the remarriage of widow and divorced women with as well as without children. For remarriage also paternal clan exogamy is observed.

The children born of the previous marriage generally reside in their house. If a woman having a suckling child becomes a widow and is remarried soon, she may take the child to rear it up. But later on it may be sent back to its own father's house or it may stay with its mother if its step father consents. In case of remarriage of a divorced woman having a suckling child she may be asked to take it along with her to rear it up. If she is willing, she is given some money or grain on demand for feeding the child. The social position and legal rights of the children born of remarriage are the same as those of children born of the first marriage. A widow has the right to continue to live in her husband's house. If she likes, she is free also to get remarried to anyone deferring to the rules of the society. None of her deceased husband's kins has marital right over her as spouse.

Divorce Permissible

Though it is not looked upon as something good or desirable, divorce is permissible in the Oraon society. Every year about 10-15 divorce cases occur among the non-Christian Oraons of the *parha*. Locally it is termed as *chhuta chuuti*. A man may divorce his wife on the grounds of adultery, desertion, neglect of duties, barrenness and incompatibility of temperament. Similarly a woman may divorce her husband on the grounds of cruelty, impotency, neglect of maintenance and adultery. Witch-craft, sorcery and crime are also grounds for divorce. The Oraons hold contagious disease also a justifiable cause for divorce. Such a case, however, has not come up for consideration. But divorce is not granted to any of the spouses for insanity, prolonged illness or non-curable but uncontagious disease. Divorce is effected in the meeting of the *gaon* panchayat. The grievances of the aggrieved party seeking divorce are heard and, if needed, witnesses are called to testify to the charges. The defending party also is given a chance to be heard. Generally the panchayat tries for reconciliation and persuades both the parties to live together peacefully. But if the aggrieved spouse insists upon getting divorce on justified grounds it is granted to him or her.

Divorce generally results from desertion by the woman. She goes on her own to her parents' house and refuses to come to her husband. She may be persuaded to come back. But she would leave him again and go back to her parents' house at the first opportunity. So her husband goes to her father along with the *mahato*, *pahan* and some elders of his village. A meeting is held in her father's village which is attended by the *mahato*, *pahan* and elders of that village. In the meeting the woman is asked to go back to live with her husband. If she decides otherwise her father is asked to pay marriage compensation. This is locally known as *bihodi* and amounts to Rs. 200-300. The woman's father generally refuses to pay it. Instead he leaves it up to the people attending the meeting to persuade her to go back with her husband. If their efforts fail she is left to live in her parents' house. The realisation of marriage compensation is kept pending until her remarriage. Then it is realised from the person who marries her.

Adoption

A man having no child of his own may adopt any Oraon child. If it is a girl she is married off and she goes to her husband's house. If it is a boy, he succeeds his foster-father and inherits his property. But if the adopted son happens to be of a different clan then the members of the clan would vehemently object to his choice of adoption of a child against the sons of his brother or of such close relatives of his clan as traditionally they are the first to have any claim on his property.

Children of Unmarried Mother

Any unmarried girl found to be in the family way is required to present herself before the *gaon* panchayat and to name the person who is responsible for getting her into trouble. If her statement is found to be correct that person is asked to accept her as his wife. If the decision of the panchayat is agreeable to him, a simple ceremony is held to bind them together into marital union. It is followed by a penal feast to the tribesmen to make amends for their misdeed. Unless he marries the girl he is under no compulsion to have any duty or obligation towards the child. The child, however, does not suffer from any social stigma as the Oraons hold that such a child did not choose to be illegitimate of his own accord.

Concept of Property

An average Oraon's concept of property is as simple as few are his possessions. To him land, cattle and house constitute property. The more a person has these things the richer he is regarded to be. As agriculture is the main source of their livelihood they attach great importance to the land. These three things are necessarily divided among the brothers when their paternal property is partitioned.

Land Tenure

The land tenure system prevailing in that area is ryati under which a landowner is required to pay land tax to the government annually for all his land. It is applicable to the Oraons also.

Residential Land

Every village has a residential area on which one can build a house. His descendants acquire hereditary ownership right over it.

Arable Land

Distribution and demarcation of arable land is beyond the pale of customary law of the Oraons. Land is directly under the control of the government. It maintains a record of the land possessed by individual farmers. It has got maps also showing the boundaries of each piece of land. The land which a man holds is registered in his name. It gives him the right of permanent ownership over it, and, thereby, his sons acquire a hereditary right to inherit it.

Inheritance

The landed property of a man is inherited by his sons. As far as their custom is concerned, a woman is seldom given a share from her father's land. In case of her having no brother her father's land passes into the hands of her paternal uncles. In the case of marriage by service a man may continue to live in the house of his parents-in-law, and his wife may be given a portion of her father's land. But he enjoys usufractuary right over it. If the members of her father's lineage agree, she may continue to enjoy usufractuary right over it even if she goes away elsewhere to live with her husband. Her sons may inherit this land and enjoy the same right over it. With the permission or concurrence of the members of her father's lineage she may get the land registered in her name, and, thereby, her sons acquire hereditary right of ownership over it.

Contravening their custom a man may give whole or part of his land to his daughter provided he is the sole registered owner of his land, i.e. it is not held by him jointly with any member of his lineage. For this he has to transfer the registration of the land into her name. This is, however, not a common practice. Only one such instance was reported from Bhita village. A person taking such an unconventional measure for the transfer of his property has to face the opposition and criticism of the members of his lineage or close clan relatives. It created ill-feeling and enmity among them. Their grievance lies not only in their being deprived of the extra share from their ancestral property but also in its passing into the possession of the members of other clans.

The landed property of an unmarried man is divided among his brothers or his brothers' sons after his death. Generally an unmarried woman has hardly any landed property. But if she comes to acquire any, her brother's sons divide it among themselves.

Among the Oraons the eldest son is treated as the successor of his father. But they seldom adhere to the rule of primogeniture. The land of a person is divided equally among his sons as far as possible. They, however, have a practice called *jethans*, by which the eldest son gets a little more of his father's land than his younger brothers. But this practice is followed only when a man possesses or leaves behind a large area of land.

It may not be out of place to maintain here that the partition of a man's property among his sons is not treated just as a household affair. The *mahato*, *pahan* and elders of the village are requested to come and divide it among them so that if ever any dispute crops up among them over its division, they would be available for its settlement.

Categorisation of Social Offences

A wrong done against a person such as defamation and abuse are settled by the parties concerned. Such cases are seldom brought before the *gaon* panchayat. Assault of serious nature on a person is dealt with by the police.

Seduction of a woman is a wrong done against family which is taken as a very serious offence. The culprit is fined a certain amount by the *gaon* panchayat and he is socially boycotted until he gives a penal feast to the tribesmen. If the seduced woman is unmarried, he is asked to keep her as his wife. On his refusal to do so he is asked to pay for her maintenance until she is married to someone. In case of adultery also the offender is fined by the *gaon* panchayat. The adulterous woman is generally divorced after realising *bihodi* from the man if he keeps her as his wife. But if she is left to live separately *bihodi* is realised later on from the person who marries her.

Extra-marital or pre-marital sex relation with any kin is forbidden in the Oraon society. There exists joking relationship between certain kins of opposite sex but if they are found guilty of sex offences, no exception is made to them by the *gaon* panchayat in giving punishment to them.

Oraons do not have the concept of trespassing upon the land of others, at least in the rural areas. However, encroachment upon the land is taken very seriously which often leads to litigation. Damage of crops, theft of cattle, etc., are considered as criminal cases which are, however, handed over to the police.

Homicide and infanticide cases are also handled by the police. If a rape case is settled by the *gaon* panchayat it would be treated as a case of seduction. Cases of abortion also are dealt with by the *gaon* panchayat if they come to its notice. The woman is asked, if unmarried, to tell the name of the person who is responsible for her pregnancy. The man is fined a certain amount and, in addition to it, he is asked to accept the woman as his wife. In this case also a penal feast has to be given to the tribesmen.

Among the Oraons a person who is excommunicated for violating the rule of tribal endogamy, interdining with the people of other castes and tribes has to undergo a purificatory ceremony for his re-admission into the tribe. Re-admission is termed as *jait udhar*. He is made to drink water from a receptacle in which a few drops of blood of a white cock or goat, a copper coin and a few leaves of *tulsi* (ocimum sanctum lin) are put. After this ceremonial purification a penal feast is given to the tribesmen. A person coming back from jail or after performing a long journey also has to get ceremonially purified in the same way before he could interdine with his tribesmen. His purification is witnessed by the *mahato*, *pahan* and a few elders of the village who are entertained with food and drinks later on. Children born of an Oraon man but of non-Oraon woman of *paniha* caste or tribe (from whom the Oraons accept drinking water) also are admitted into the Oraon society by subjecting them to this ceremonial purification after their heads are shaved. It is also followed by a grand feast to the tribesmen of the *parha*.

Conclusion

Oraons have certain customs which may ordinarily be called their laws for regulating their interpersonal behaviour within the tribe as well as their relationship with the people of other castes and tribes. For the enforcement of these customary laws they have traditional tribal councils, *gaon* panchayat and *parha* panchayat. The functionaries of these councils were the village servants of the erstwhile king of Chhota Nagpur. From their association with him they derived their authority to assume leadership. *Parha* panchayat appears to have had a royal court structure which has remained unchanged over the years and is being carried on by force of tradition as a legacy of the past though the Chhotanagpur king has ceased to have any control over his subjects after the abolition of zamindari in India.

Though the tribal councils did not undergo any apparent structural changes as a result of abolition of zamindari, the authority of their functionaries did not remain the same. In the past it used to be said that *Mahato aur Pahan gaon chalate hain* (*Mahato* and *Pahan* govern the village). They were a sort of autocrats. But in the present changed situation they have turned to be democrats in that they seek and endorse the opinions of their tribesmen while taking decision on any issue. In spite of it the councils are not less effective today than they were in the past as even now they equally strive to prevent the breaches of social customs and to maintain as well their ethnic identity.

The Oraon customary laws appear to have changed little as far as these two villages are concerned. Little changes that have crept in may be attributed to the inescapable processes of modernisation.

Thus, it may be found that the commensal rule of the Oraons with other castes and tribes has relaxed. While they visit a town they cannot adhere to their commensal rule. It also holds good for those who are employed in the towns. Commensal restriction between the Christian and Non-Christian Oraons has become a thing of the past. With its disappearance it paved the way for removing their social differences and rebuilding social solidarity in spite of their religious differences. Now not only they interdine but intermarry also. In such marriages, however, Christians have the upper hand. In spite of relaxation in a commensal rule both Christian and non-Christian Oraons observe it in their traditional setting especially with regard to the people who belong to the lower castes and tribes.

By embracing Christianity, the Christian Oraons have changed their religious beliefs and practices. But in many other respects they appear to have changed very little. It would sound contradictory that the converted Oraons of these villages have not yet fully shaken off their traditional religious beliefs altogether. They tend to believe in the existence of village deities and their power, and directly or indirectly they participate in their worship because of their small number, the social milieu in which they grow and live and certain situations in which they find themselves. Save religious matters, the non-Christians conform to other basic customary laws more or less as much as an average non-Christian Oraon.

The Oraons do not have hard and fast rules as to the type of family they should have, marriage age, marriage of younger children before that of the elder ones, number of wives one nay have. Most often they are subject to the necessity and convenience of individual members of the tribe.

Nevertheless, they have some customs which regulate their social life. The violation of certain established customs arouses the wrath of the society and it sets them right by punishing the offenders. In spite of the changes that are creeping in their society as a result of the processes of modernisation the Oraons follow them and other customs for maintaining their ethnic identity as they set them apart from the people of other ethnic groups.

15

MECHANISM OF SOCIAL CONTROL AND SOME ASPECTS OF CUSTOMARY LAWS OF JAMATIA

D.B. MANDAL

Tripura, an erstwhile princely State, has a total population of 15,56,342 (Census, 1971) of which 29 per cent are tribals. The territory is inhabited by 19 Scheduled Tribes. The nine major tribes are Tripuri (2,50,382), Riang (64,722), Jamatia (34,192) Chakma (28,662), Halam (19,076), Noatia (10,297) Mag (13,273), Lushai (3,672) and Kuki (7,775).

According to Hunter (1876), the Tippera are divided into four classes : (1) Tripuri (locally known as Deh/Durma), (2) Jamatia, (3) Noatia and (4) Riang, With the exception of the Jamatia each of these classes is sub-divided into several sub-classes. Maharaja Birchandra Manikaya conferred the Kashagapa gotra on all the Jamatias so that the latter do not face any difficulties in getting the services of Brahmins for their rituals and rites of passage in the absence of any such gotra.

The Tripuri, Riang, Noatia and Jamatia speak a common dialect, i.e. Tripuri, with minor local variation which is intelligible to all. Besides Tripuri language, Jamatia could speak Bengali fluently. The Jamatia belong to the Mongoloid stock and claim descent from the lunar race.

The Jamatia is an important well-organised tribal group in Tripura, who are still confined in a small geographical area. They are numerically third in position among the tribal groups of Tripura, with a population of 34,192 (7.59 per cent) as per the 1971 census. Their main concentration is in Udaipur, Amarpur and Khowas subdivisions of the South Tripura district in the central region of the State. There are about 600 villages inhabited by 6,000 households of the Jamatia.

Two Jamatia villages, namely, Hadra, a traditional big village of Udaipur sub-division, and Hadrai Khamarhari, situated nearer to an urban centre of Khowai sub-division, were selected. Data for the present study were collected from these two villages during March-April, 1977. The former is a very old village and the latter was established only 40 years ago. The people of the Hadrai-Khamarhari have migrated from Amarpur sub-division in search of plain wet-land as well as forest for collection and hunting. Village Hadra is located about 15 kms away from Udaipur town by the side of Gomati river and is not even connected by a mettalled road. Inhabitants of Hadra village immigrated from an extinct village named Tepamia, which was situated near Udaipur town. As the town extended, the Jamatia shifted towards the interior areas and settled at the present Hadra, Totahari and Shilghati villages. The total number of households of village Hadra is 64 and population is 480 of which the males mumber 254 and females 226. The average size of the family is 7.5.

Democratic in Nature

The political system of the Jamatia is democratic in nature. The system is simple and effective. Every village has a council of elder persons. Besides the village council, the supreme council exercises the highest legal and judicial powers. All levers of social control of the Jamatia rest on it. The political organisation of the Jamatia is divided into three units, i.e. *luku* (village level), *mayal* (regional level) and *hada* (community level).

The Village Council (*luku*) mainly consists of one headman (Chowdhury) and two or more assistants (*khandal*). Usually Chowdhury is selected from the senior persons of the main lineage of the village. He is regarded as the secular authority for maintaining the administration. Only the married persons with children participate in the selection of members of the council. But if he is found to be inefficient, the five-year tenure of office is reduced.

The Village Council deals only with minor socio-economic disputes. Function of the Chowdhury is to supervise all sorts of social events like marriage, death or any other ritual and also look after the law and order and welfare work of the village. He keeps direct relation with the head of the society, i.e. *hoda akra*, and participates or sends two representatives (*along*) to the annual supreme council meeting, held on the occasion of *gang* festival (goddess of water). It helps to maintain the solidarity of the society. The agenda of the meeting is circulated all Jamatia villages. The *chowdhury* is the most respected person of the village. Besides the headman and his assistants, some aged and influential persons (i.e. ex-*chowdhuri*, educated people, etc) of the village also take part in the council meeting.

The Jamatias have a full-fledged regional council (*mayal*). A regional council consists of 30 to 50 villages of a geographical area. There are 13 regional councils of the Jamatia of Tripura. In a *mayal* panchayat, there are two headmen (*sardars*) who are elected by *chowdhurys* of all the villages under that particular *mayal*. Elections for the *sardars* are usually held after three to Five years on the occasion of regional *gang* festivals. Besides judicial functions, each *mayal* also performs *gang*, durga, Ker, Rakkhakali festivals. The function of the regional council is to maintain law and order and socio-economic development of the region. *Sardars* are empowered to decide all kinds of inter-village disputes of the region with the help of *chowdhurys* after proper hearing of all sorts of cases including divorces, adultery, and so on.

Hoda is the supreme council of the Jamatia society. There are two *akras* (supreme men of the society) functioning since 1974 in two divisions of the territory. They are selected by the representatives (*abong*) of all the villages on the occasion of *gang* festivals. Selection usually takes place after three to five years. Besides the above two *akras, hoda* consists of eight executive members (*upadesta*) selected from all over the Jamatia tract. They are secretary (*sainai*), messenger (*mizakda*), bearer (*gamta*), cashier (*hanbdari*), etc.

The function of the *hoda* is to arrange for some annual festivals like Garia, Gang, Delai Matai, etc. The Garia festival is held in the house of Kherpang lineage only and the God is worshipped by the priest who belongs to Kherpang lineage. Besides the religious function, the Hoda has judicial function too. All kinds of cases like divorce, adultery, kidnapping, love affairs or any other anti-social activities and complicated cases which could not be solved by the *chowdhurys, sardars*, are dealt by the *akras*.

Procedure of the Traditional Council

On a complaint lodged by an individual of the community, the complainant has to offer one bottle of beverage or Re. 1 to the *chowdhury* as fee. Then the headman fixes a date, time and place for the meeting. Usually meeting is held in the *chowdhury*'s house. Both the parties assemble with witnesses. The headman (may he *chowdhury, sardar* or *akras*) and some elder persons constitute the jury. Meeting is called by the *khandal* in the evening. The headman takes his seat and directs the complainant to place his case before the assembly. After hearing the complaints the headman asks the accused to defend himself. Then the witnesses are asked to give their statements. Then the members of the jury discuss the pros and cons of the case among themselves. In this discussion the opinion of the *chowdhury* and elder persons are sought first. The headman's decision is final and is usually accepted by all including the plaintiff and the defendant.

The council punished an offender in different ways, say imposition of a fine in cash or kind, ostracising a person from the village or society and so on. Punishment to the female offender is sympathetically considered. Fine in cash is a recent development. In the past, lashing with a cane stick was in practice. The money collected through fines is utilised in organising the common festivals. The mechanism of social control is so strict that the violation of law is seldom done in the Jamatia society. When the *chowdhury* fails to settle the case or his judgement is not accepted by either of the parties, the case is referred to the *mayal* which in turn sends it to a non-related village council for settlement.

Besides the traditional councils of the Jamatia each village has statutory bodies, i.e. *gaon sabha* and *naya* panchayat of the Government of Tripura. The function of the three statutory bodies is mainly to deal with all types of welfare work in the rural areas and it also settles minor disputes of the village.

Some Aspects of Customary Laws

Family: Father is the head of the family who controls the family affairs and allots duties and responsibilities to each member of the family. Besides domestic work women are also engaged in various activities such as agricultural work, collection of firewood, weaving of cloth, etc. Monogamy (*nakhum*) is the rule. Out of 64 marriages in the Hodra village, 29 (45 per cent) are monogamous. Polygamy is rare. Polygamy is permitted only in certain cases. Frequency of extended family (50 per cent) was more in Hodra village. Usually when any dispute or quarrel occurs within the family, and if it is not so serious it is solved by the senior members of the family. Usually ill-feeling within the women is ignored by the males. In the Jamatia society, besides the plaintiff, the members of the family have to share 50 per cent of the punishment. Of course this happens when the accused is young and not separated from parents.

It is customary rule among the Jamatia that after marriage the groom has to live with his father-in-law for about three years to assist him in agricultural work. Though nowadays this rule is not strictly followed due to the impact of neighbouring Bengali people, education and changing economic conditions.

Marriage: Among the Jamatia no man or woman can marry within the same lineage (*gosti*). Spouses should be selected after the third ascending generation. Marriages take place within the endogamous groups, i.e. Jamatia. Marriage by service is most common among the Jamatia. Marriage by intrusion and by mutual consent is also noticed occasionally. In such cases, a normal compensation has to be paid to the village council. Adult marriage is the rule. Occasionally father also brings an older bride for his minor son in the expectation that she will assist in the domestic as well as agricultural work. In a reverse situation the groom has to stay in the father-in-law's house till she attains maturity. It is also observed that due to affection of parents for the elder or younger daughter, the son-in-law stays in the house of the bride. Marriage of the young son and daughter before the elder usually does not happen, but it is permissible. Cross-cousin marriage rarely occurs. Parallel-cousin marriage is strictly prohibited. Levirate is allowed, though frequency is less. It is customary law that a widower or divorced man can marry only a divorced woman or a widow. There is no restriction on marriage between the divorced person and widower/widow. If anyone violates the basic traditional rules of the society, he is penalised by the village council immediately. If they fail to decide, he may go in appeal to the supreme council.

Remarriage was widely practised in the past. Nowadays a person can remarry once in his/her lifetime. In case a person desires to remarry more, he has to paya fine to the village council. Previously a person could remarry any number of times, but as they thought that such a marriage had some bad affect in the society, the headman restricted remarriage to a single time. However, if a person remarries second time outside his own society, he is ostracised in keeping with the norms of the society. However, he may be readmitted after paying a fine.

Marriage within the same village is possible and bride from a relative's village is preferred.The girls are not permitted to marry a person of Riang, Morsum, Kaipong, etc., who are considered as lower than Jamatia. Among the Jamatia there is no prescriptive form of marriage, but usually bride or groom from the affinal side is preferred. Patrilocal residence is the common rule. Nowadays in place of bride-price, dowry system has been introduced among the educated and well-off families, though the council members are against it.

After remarriage, if a woman brings her children, born out of their previous marriage, to her second husband's house, they do not get the property of the second husband. The children of the previous marriage will be denied some social rights. A male child is rarely adopted among the Jamatia society. Adoption takes place after preformance of *lampra* worship by the village priest (*ochai*) and if the adopted son belongs to another community, the child is purified by sprinkling holy water (*ochaitai*). It is observed that a new custom favourable to the society, has always been accepted by all without any objection. The councils are very alert in accepting and rejecting the old as well as new practices. Through annual meetings with the Akras, if needed, an old custom may be changed or modified.

Property

To a Jamatia, the belongings of a person, having monetary value and which could be exchanged, mortgaged or sold, are considered as property. Property includes land, house, utensils, furniture, trees, ponds, ornaments, grains, etc. The property is equally inherited by the sons. The son living with the father at the time of the latter's death inherits the residential houses and some of the movable properties. When a man dies without having any issue the property remains under the possession of the widow till her remarriage. If she marries another man the property will go to her deceased husband's close relatives. The father usually divides his property among the sons during his old age. Land is the most valuable property among the Jamatia. If a person likes he may allot one-eighth portion of land to his daughter. The unmarried daughter and widowed mother get one share of land for their maintenance.

Step-sons cannot claim any property from the step-father.

Residential land also can be obtained either by purchase or by inheritance. Usually well-to-do men divide their residential land equally among the sons and sons-in-law if the latter live with their brothers-in-law for a long period. If any dispute regarding the division of property could not be solved within the kins it is referred to the council. The council solves the problem according to the customary rules. Thus the council is working as the key-body for maintaining harmony of the family and the society as well.

The Jamatia have no personal right over natural fallow land and forest. but they can collect forest produce, firewood, etc., from the neighbouring forest. Each village possesses a well-defined area which in general is demarcated by natural objects and within this area the villagers enjoy paramount rights for hunting and fishing. Hunting is one of the most important sources of livelihood as well as recreation. The kins take part in hunting. Except the first shooter all other participants get equal share of the flesh of the game. The former gets the head of the game as an extra share. Previously all male members of the village used to participate in annual hunting and get a share of the game. The council members strongly oppose any breach of its autonomous laws. The council keeps record of the cases. If the occurrences of a particular type of breaches are more, immediately council members meet together and devise ways to control such deviations. The office of the secular headman of the village, region and society as a whole is not hereditary. These posts are filled on the basis of selection by the headmen of the families. The succession of the office is restricted only to the male line. The office of the village priest and medicine man is also not hereditary. Specialists hold these posts on the basis of their efficiency, power and popularity. They give preference to efficiency rather than hereditary right. Only the priest of god Garia, called *chantai*, belongs to Kheropang lineage and his office is hereditary.

Summing-Up

There is little difference in the customary laws of the Jamatia living in exposed and unexposed villages. Owing to constant contact with the neighbouring Bengalis some Hindu traits have been adopted by the tribals. Even then they have to abide by their own customary laws. Contact with the wider society could not bring about any change in the judicial system of the Jamatia. Changes are observed more in material objects and language. There is no marked change in the socio-ritual aspects of the society. Though there is a slight change in their way of life, the old customs are still intact. Violation of the customary laws is rare even in the exposed area, among the semi-urban settlers, who are in close contact with the wider society. Nonetheless the Jamatia in general have been found to make little use of the courts and panchayat. This may be due to the strong hold of the traditional customs. In Tripura, the Jamatia have been following customary laws strictly because of their well-organised political councils and compactness of the habited area. It does not mean that there is no change, but such changes are accepted by the society only when these are approved by the political councils, which are the watch-dog of the society. These, together with their belief in automatic punishment by a supernatural power and the awareness of the children about their customary laws through their attendance in the council meetings, discourage them to deviate from the customary laws of their society.

PART III

CENTRAL INDIA

16

TRIBAL CUSTOMARY LAW IN CENTRAL INDIA

I.S. CHAUHAN

There is a strong common consciousness among the Gond, Kolam, Kol, Pando, Korku and Dhurwa tribes in the Central Region to retain the traditional rules and regulations. But this, of course, is not always possible. The changes have occurred and they frequently reoccur.

There are, however, two distinct but overlapping areas of life. One is clearly within the realm of the custom while the other within the jurisdiction of the State laws. With the passage of time the first has shrunk and the second has widened. There are situational variations too. In some cases the proximity to the dominant Gonds has influenced the processes of change while in others the frequent intermixture with the caste people has helped the erosion of the influence of the customary laws.

What clearly falls within the realm of the traditional customary laws is sex which is the most used or abused area of the tribal life. An intricate web of rules and regulations is knit around the simple act of love-making. There are sets of rules and regulations regarding sex before marriage and sex after marriage, sex with one's life partner and one's friend and divorcee and what not. There is a range of behaviour within the limits of permissibility. There are alternatives and choices.

Sex results in childbirth and then there come in the problems of inheritance, land, property and economy in general upon which the influence of the State is certainly more imposing than that of the customary law. In the economic sphere the State laws penetrate through forest, revenue and developmental bureaucracies which also act as agencies and instruments of change.

Another feature found commonly in all the tribes relates to the mode and means of dealing with the breaches of the customary laws.

In almost all the tribes such cases are dealt with by the traditional council each of which has a headman and a few functionaries. These bodies are organised strictly on the principle that age and experience will get priority over youth and achievement. There is absolute conformity with the rule of the traditional council. Each decision is considered binding.

According to the tribal code of conduct in Central India, the effect of an offence is not ever lasting. An offender's honour is easily redeemed after undergoing a punishment which generally takes the form of excommunication or derecognition of a certain set of rights. Punishment invariably involves hosting a feast or paying a fine in cash which is utilised for wining, dining and merry-making. This act is almost always given supernatural overtones by involving ritual propitiation of offended tribal deities. It appears that the crime and punishment have both been turned into a "source of entertainment". This, of course, is not to suggest that a breach of the traditional law is not taken seriously by the tribal society.

The imposition of the State law, the pace of which has certainly increased during the past three decades, is invariably considered illegitimate, undesirable and a phenomenon against which the tribal is utterly helpless.

Tribal Faces a Dilemma

The tribal, exposed to the forces of modernisation and change, faces today a dilemma. He constantly ponders over the question whether his own customary laws are more appropriate vis-a-vis the new State laws. He finds it difficult to shake his faith in the old, the tried and the established. The problem becomes all the more acute if the dispute involves a non-tribal party. The details of customary laws and practices as mentioned in the "Tribal Customary Law of the Kol" by B.K. Dasgupta (Ch. 19) indicate the range of norms and customs which are still distinct from those of neighbouring communities. Although members of this community come under the purview of the village panchayat in matters of intra-village anomalies, yet whenever two Kols are involved they prefer settlement of the dispute through their *malik* (headman), thus refurbishing their faith in traditional mechanism of social control. This retention of social values is further accentuated by observance of rituals associated with sacred pantheon which comprises tribal gods. Their priest (*panda*) belongs to the same community which does not accept any services from the Brahman. This non-acceptance of services of a Brahmin also helped them to maintain their tribal boundary. The system of keeping a mistress (*rakkelu*) has acted as a safety valve against occurrence of polygyny. It is interesting to note that in spite of their long association with the caste groups, they have not adopted the practice of child marriage nor attempted to adopt measures to up grade their social position in the ethnic pyramid of the region.

From the details of the customary practices of the little known tribe of Pando it is apparent that due to their sparse settlement and distribution over a large territorial area, it is striving hard to regulate their social relations, marriage alliances and socio-religious practices. The impact of forces of recent change did not make any dent in the age-old customary practices. However, the influence of Hinduism followed by their neighbours did have an impact specifically on the aspect of purity and pollution. This may be due to the presence of the feudal structure prevailing in Surguja and its adjacent areas. This feudal structure has had a long history of rule in these areas. The rehabilitated section of the Pando, however, presents a different scenario.

17

SOME ASPECTS OF CUSTOMARY RULES OF THE PANDOS

R. K. SINHA

The Pando, a little known tribe of Madhya Pradesh, are mostly found in the dispersed villages situated in the forest and hill tracks of Surajpur and Pal tehsils of Surguja district. Some of them also live in the plain multi-ethnic villages and in the rehabilitated colonies. According to Hiralal, Pandos are akin to Kawar, the descendants of the Kauravas of the Mahabharata, whose cousins were the Pandavas, a theory which is not supported by the notice regarding their customs, while, Shootbort noticed a marked similarity between them and the Kawar. But, the present Pandos identity themselves to be a separate ethnic group and claim to be the descendants of the Pandavas of the Mahabharata. They do not acknowledge any association either with the Kawar, or even with the Bharia-Bhumia or Bhuinhar-Bhumia. Since 1921, Pandos have been amalgamated with Bharia-Bhumia or Bhuinhar-Bhumia. Their mixed population is 92,639 in the census report of 1961, out of which 31,036, 26,606 and 12,041 are residing in the districts like Jabalpur, Surguja and Raigarh respectively. However, the *District Census Hand Book of Surguja, 1961*, very specifically states that nearly 95.5 per cent of the Pando population is residing only in Surguja. Pandos are patrilineal, patrilocal and patriarchal. The head of the family holds the supreme authority. Nucleus type of family is more popular in comparison to extended family. Composite type of family is very rare.

They are divided into two endogamous groups, viz. Surguja and Uttaraha. The former consider themselves to be superior to the latter. Previously marriage between these two groups was not practised but now they have started inter-group marriages. However, in practice Surguja accepts an Uttarahas girl as bride but is very much reluctant to give his girl to the latter.

The traditional group of Pandos live in the forested and hilly surroundings, where food-gathering, basketry and to some extent hunting constitute their main source of livelihood, and wage earning job is considered to be a degrading one. They also practise agriculture but only for namesake. It hardly provides much relief to them. On the other hand, Pandos living in the multi-ethnic villages and in the rehabilitated colonies depend more on the wage-earning job for their subsistence, although agriculture and forest produce also help them in earning their livelihood.

Pandos Prefer Isolation

The Pandos, in general, prefer to live in isolation, surrounded by their own kith and kin, away from the civilised world, where they have their own rules and regulations. In other words, it is a world where outward forces are least active and they are least aware and concerned with the external affairs. In such a situation they are ordinarily keen and interested with the affairs of their own surroundings and ethnic groups. Here, they prefer to live a peaceful life in isolation in accordance with their own traditions, customs and norms.

The present paper is an attempt to understand the customary laws of the Pando tribe, which is of immense value to them as the interpersonal relations of the members of an entire society are regulated and controlled by customary rules. The customary rules of the Pando society can be fully conceived by its traditions, customs and norms, which are operating in the day-to-day life of the members of the society.

An Orderly System

The Pando maintain the traditionally approved interpersonal relationships and have an orderly system of social relations under the council of elders (*darbar* or *panchayat*). Most of the Pando villages have a *darbar* which functions in accordance with the traditions, customs, ethics and moral values of the society. The *mukhia* or *patel* is the head of the *darbar* and every adult male of the village is recognised as member (*panch* or *punch-bhai*) of the *darbar*. This village *darbar* works as watchdog and keeps a strict vigilance on the interpersonal relations of its members. Whenever necessary or when anybody violates any of the customary rules, the Pando *darbar* interferes and corrects him by punishing such a person. Here, the *mukhia* or *patel* presides over the meeting, the offenders or involved persons are called, their grievances are heard patiently in the *darbar*. In the last phase, the matter is discussed by the members of the *darbar* where they come to a decision by consulting each other. On certain occasions, when the decision of a village *darbar* is not accepable to the offender, the matter is referred to the Regional Council (*jati darbar* or *bara-darbar*). But in the rehabilitated colonies and such other villages many new posts of office-bearer have been included in the village council.

The *jati-darbar* consists of at least five village heads, members of the nearby village *darbar* and one messenger. The combination of village heads varies depending upon the spot of incidence and propinquity of the villages. Again, the jurisdiction of this council covers a radius of about 10 miles which includes about 10 villages. The head and place of this council are always changing. Ordinarily, it meets at the offender's village and the head of that village *darbar* presides over the meeting. The offender or the concerned party is called and heard. They are given full opportunity to speak against the charges. But, if the charges are proved, the offender is bound to act in accordance with the verdict of the council. Here, too, every decision is taken in consultation with all the present village heads. This regional council meets on inter-village issues or something relating to he whole ethnic group, usually for excommunicating a social offender or for readmitting such a person into the community fold.

Among the Pandos certain deeds or activities are looked down upon by their customs and traditions. If anybody is involved in such deeds, he is taken to task, sometimes fined, punished, asked to fine a communal feast or excommunicated from the society, subject to the sanctioned customary rules of the society. Here, mention may be made of those customary rules regarding hut-making, eating and drinking, marriage, for losing one's ethnic identity, for killing a cow, ox or calf and for many other such violations.

Ek-Duaria and Du-Duaria

The Surguja Pandos usually make two doors if it is one-roomed hut, one in the front and the other in its backside. Adjacent to this room, there is a small apartment called *bhitar-ghar*. It is the abode of ancestors and clan deities. The entrance to the *bhitar-ghar* is just near the front door of the main room. The women of the Surguja Pandos do not use the front door and *bhitar-ghar* during their menstruation and childbirth. However, the Uttaraha Pandos have only one door in the frontside of the main room, which is used by both sexes for all purposes. They locate their *bhitar-ghar* in one corner of the same room but do not observe all the restrictions and observances like the Surguja. It is because of this distinction and restricted observances that Surguja Pandos are considered superior to the Uttaraha Pandos and the former are also called Du-Duaria while the latter Ek-Duaria.

Again, Pandos are very orthodox in the observance of eating and drinking rules. They are very strict and do not accept cooked food, water and tobacco not only from the inferior tribal or caste people but even from their own excommunicated family members. In an unavoidable circumstance, Pandos may accept only raw food from the latter and cook for themselves there. If, this customary rule is violated, they are taken to task by the council of the elders.

Pandos' Sense of Superiority

In regional social hierarchy Pandos consider themselves to be superior to Chamar, Chirka (a musician caste) or Kuar, Oraon (Dhangar), Ghasia, Pahika and Agaria, but inferior to the Gond, Rajwar, Binjhwar, Ahir (Mahato), Bargah (Rout, Kumbhar, Nai and Cherva). So, usually a person is excommunicated from the society, if he or she is found eating or drinking with or in the hut or food cooked or served by the inferior caste or tribe man. Such a person is readmitted into the society only if he or she obliges the villagers with a communal feast. But, in the rehabilitated colonies and such other villages, such excommunicated persons are firstly purified by the village *baiga* (Priest). Here, village *baiga* and some of the villagers sprinkle coldwater or cowdung water on the head of the excommunicated person. Later on, villagers accept communal feast from him or her. Hence, it appears that the purificatory rite is a new development among them. They learnt and copied it from the neighbouring groups. Similarly, a man is excommunicated from the society, if one is beaten by an inferior caste or tribe man. Such person is readmitted into the society by throwing a communal feast to the villagers.

The award of imprisonment by the state is also not tolerated by the society and one who returns from the prison has to face the

Pando *darbar*. It is said that a man is sent to prison only if he does a wrong. Again, during the period of one's imprisonment one eats the food and water served by unknown caste or tribe men. Hence, as soon as one returns from prison, he or she is excommunicated on the said ground and is readmitted by charging a communal feast. Previously, he-goat was a must in such a feast, but now this feast custom has been liberalised. With the great insistence of the villagers, the involved man obliges the villagers with a sum of Rs. 20 towards this feast (*jail-bhat*).

Pandos' *karma* dance is governed by the joking and avoidance rules of kinship. They play *karma* dance with joking relatives and unrelated Pandos but avoid such relatives who are to be avoided. This *karma* rule is strictly observed and a violator is subject to fine or a feast.

Again, the cases of *kantuti nathe-bhathe* and *gau-mari* are dealt very severely in a uniform way, although the treatment of offenders depends the nature of cases.

Injuries: a Divine Punishment

The term *kantuti* stands for the cut injury of ear which may occur during fighting or while underfalling economic pursuits. Such injuries are taken to be a curse and believed to be caused by some divine power against one's wrongs secretly done. Therefore, the sufferer is required to serve a communal feast to the whole village, otherwise his or her whole family members are excommunicated by the Pando *darbar*.

The literal meaning of *nathe-bhathe* means losing one's own or caste identity, on account of violation of some customary laws. Ordinarily, a person is taken to *nathe-bhathe* as soon as one acquires or goes to live with a non-Pando life partner. Here, a man is ordinarily readmitted into the society but if a woman once loses her tribal identity, she can never be readmitted in her lifetime. At first, a man has to divorce his non-Pando partner and has to pass through prescribed rituals. For this purpose, a date is finalised and villagers assemble at some distance of the concerned man's hut on that day. The man is asked to sit there after taking bath and the village *baiga* sprinkles coldwater or cowdung water with a mango leaf on his head. It is followed by other village *punches*. Later on, he offers bread, fried grains, water and tobacco to all the assembled persons. Now, all of them proceed to the hut of that man where *baiga* leads them by sprinkling the coldwater throughout the way. When, they reach the hut, firstly all the earthenwares are thrown away by the family members. Again, the *baiga* sprinkles cold water in and around the hut, then, he-goat is sacrificed on the door by the *baiga* and the man enters the house by stepping on the blood of the goat. It concludes with a communal feast and all the family members are readmitted into the society. But in the rehabilitated colonies and nearby village, Pandos of these villages employ the services of barber and washerman on such occasions. The barber shaves at least one member from each family of the village, while the washerman collects at least one cloth for cleaning from each family of the village. This practice appears to be a recent borrowing from the neighbouring groups.

Phul-Pari: a Curse

Similarly, the term *phul-pari* stands for the worms or insects which develop in the wounds of human beings. It is also believed by the Pandos to be a curse which is sent down by God against some secret or unknown deeds or sins of a man. Hence, as soon as a case of *phul-pari* is noticed, it is reported to the village *punches*. Soon all the family members are excommunicated, until they get purified and throw a communal feast after the cure. The feast of *phul-pari* is of two kinds depending upon the nature of suffering. They say that if the larvae develops in the wound, it is subject to a vegetarian feast, but if worms develop in the wound, a non-vegetarian feast is charged from the sufferer. After cure, all the members of the family have to get purified through the prescribed ritual process and then a feast is served.

In the same way, the term *gau-mari* denotes the act of killing a cow, ox, or calf. For *gau-mari* also, the killer is required to go through a number of prescribed rituals. Firstly, one is required to proceed for a purificatory bath (*Ganga-Banaras*) in the tank located at the shrine of *Gai-Mari-Devi* (near Kathghora in Bilaspur) or at the shrine of Vimsendarh (near Ambikapur, on Ambikapur-Raigarh Road). Again, one is required to reach the sacred tank by begging and drinking water at least from five villages. After the purificatory bath, one returns to one's own village with one pot of water from the sacred tank. In the village, one again takes bath and sits outside the hut in an open space, surrounded by the village *punches*. Here, the village *baiga* purifies the cow-killer and his family members by the prescribed ritual process. In the last phase, a non-vegetarian feast is served to the villagers and the entire family is readmitted.

Rules Regulating Pando Life

Besides the above mentioned details, Pandos' marriage rules, remarriage rules, rules regulating children of unmarried mothers, rape cases and abortion are very much important in regulating their way of life. A short description of these rules will help in understanding the customary laws of Pandos to a greater extent.

They practise adult marriage in which a sum of Rs. 20 is given as a bride-price. It is never refunded in any case but they have a custom of claiming *bunda* (compensation for one's wife) which varies from Rs. 200 to Rs. 300 and is claimed from the man who flees away with one's wife or lives with another's wife. These days marriage (byah) is one of the standard forms of acquiring a life partner, while *barokhi*, *bandhwa, udalia* (marriage by elopement) and *duku* (marriage by intrusion) are other ways of acquiring a life partner. Polygyny is also recognised but is an exception.

Again, Pandos practise clan exogamy and avoid incest. Marriage within the village is no bar but such alliances are avoided. Prescriptive and preferential marriage ties are not the rule of the society, while senior levirate and junior sororate marriage are permitted.

Remarriage of deserted, divorced and widows is allowed and children are no bar. Ordinarily, children born of the previous husband live with their father's family or one of the close relatives. But, if there is none to take care of such a child then only he or she is carried by the mother. After marriage, her new husband gets full marital right over such woman. At the same time, she also receives her full right in the home affairs of her husband. But, she cannot enter the *bhitar-ghar* of her husband as long as necessary rituals are not performed for her.

Children of Unmarried Mothers

If ever, it comes to the notice of the Pandos that an unmarried Pando girl is pregnant, the matter is taken very seriously. Everyday the matter is discussed in their Darbar until the name of the responsible man is disclosed in public.

If he happens to be a Pando, he would be pressurised to accept the girl as his wife, provided she also agrees. Otherwise, the man would be required to pay a fine of Rs. 5 to Rs. 20. Now, there would be no hesitation and difficulties for anyone to accept the girl as life partner. She may marry anyone even by *haldi-ghasai*, and the child would be recognised as *logiti* to offspring of the couple.

But, if the responsible man happens to be a non-Pando, the matter takes a very serious turn. Here the responsible man is pressurised to accept the girl as his wife. If he obliges the Pando community by accepting the girl, it is all right. Now, the father of the girl will have to oblige the villagers with a feast for not paying due attention towards the affair. In case the man does not accept her as his wife, she will be excommunicated and no Pando will accept her as his wife. If her parents or anybody who gives her shelter, he will also be excommunicated from the society. But, in practice her parents give her shelter in the outer shed of the hut, where she does not enter the main part of the hut and does not cook and fetch water for the family. Food and water are served to her there only. In other words she does not do any such work which may result in the pollution of the family. When she delivers the child, he or she is not accepted as a member of Pando society. Such child may be brought up by Pandos but ultimately he or she is accepted by one's father's ethnic group, latest by the time of his or her marriage. Because his or her father's name is already disclosed in public during the Pando *darbar*.

The Rape and Abortion

The cases of rape although very rare are handled by Pando *darbar*. The rape by a Pando male is not taken very seriously. Here, the responsible man is fined a sum of Rs. 5 to 20. Besides this amount he is required to give a *saree* to the girl for covering her chastity because he is believed to have robbed her of chastity.

But, the rape by a non-Pando is taken to be a very serious matter. If caught in action, the offender is beaten very severely by the villagers. The matter is finally reported to his caste panchayat or village panchayat. Here, ordinarily, the involved man is forced to accept the girl as his wife. If he really accepts the girl, the case is closed, otherwise he is left simply to the mercy of his caste panchayat.

In the last state the girl is excommunicated along with her family members. Such girls are never readmitted into the societal fold and no Pando accepts them as life partner for fear of excommunication. She may be accepted by a Pando of the same category (*nathe-bhathe*). But her other family members are readmitted after a communal feast.

Abortion is taken to be a very sinful act which is just equal to killing one dozen she-calves. Therefore, it is not reported from their society and at the same time there is no mention of any customary rules against such deeds.

Conclusion

Through the simple mechanism described in the foregoing pages the Pando society controls social relations. Here, whoever violates or goes against the established customary rules is treated as a social offender and the whole Pando society turns against the offender. So, it is the collective responsibility and the power of the *darbar* which compels an offender to act according to its verdict.

The impact of the modern forces of change on the customary laws of traditional Pandos has been very little due to Pandos' negligible interactions with the outer world. At the same time it is also very true that Pandos' customary laws seem to be very much influenced by the Hindus' notion of pollution and purity. It may be due to the impact of Hindu rule of feudatory States of Madhya Pradesh who reigned in this region for quite a long period.

But, if the customary laws of rehabilitated Pandos are taken into consideration, the impact of recent changes is seen to a little extent. It is evident that these days Pandos of these villages require the services of barber and washerman during purificatory rites. Again, some new positions have been incorporated in the Darbar for those villages which have the statutory panchayat, although system of functioning is more or less the same. Similarly, the custom of giving communal feasts also seems to have been less strictly observed which is evident from the *jail-bhat* and lesser number of non-vegetarian feasts.

18

ADAPTATION : A CASE STUDY — THE KORKU OF MAHARASHTRA

D. K. SAMANTA

Following Indian independence the need to know the character of tribal customary law has been felt on an urgent basis. The tribals in general are socially as well as economically backward. To bring them close to the general Indian population various development programmes were undertaken to improve the life condition of the tribals.

Similarly the tribals have also been brought under the jurisdiction of statutory laws. It is very much necessary to understand the pattern of reaction of the tribal groups towards such legislation. How the people face the situation is most important. A tribe may respond positively or negatively and there may be a conflicting situation. The knowledge about a tribal's response is imperative for the fruitful implementation of legislation. Our attempt would be to study the pattern of reaction of the Korku towards those legislations which are at odds with their customs. Stress will be laid on highlighting particular customs through case histories.

The Korku are a Mundari-speaking people who live in the western part of Satpura Hills. Their concentration is in the districts of Betul, Chindwara and Khandwa of Madhya Pradesh and Amravati district of Maharashtra. Being surrounded by other castes and Dravidian or Indo-Aryan-speaking tribal groups, they form a pocket of Mundari speakers widely separated from the mother stock. They have social and economic interaction with the neighbouring tribal groups as well as with the Hindus for a long time.

Till recently the Korku living in hill areas used to practise *binder*, a type of cultivation which may be said to be a form that comes in between shifting cultivation and settled agriculture. However, with the strict imposition of ban on shifting cultivation, they have now adopted wet cultivation. Except in the case of forest areas, agriculture forms the main basis of their economy. In the forest areas the rate of yield is quite low. To substantiate their meagre agricultural output they work as labourers in the forest department. They are expert in forestry work. Hunting of wild game is totally banned and a violator is liable to be prosecuted. Fishing they do in the rivulets only occasionally. The revenue department has allotted some plots of land to each family and accordingly they have been provided with the record of rights. Through this, their ownership rights have been established. This has enabled them to qualify for getting loans from governmental sources. Efforts are being made to bring the Korku villages located deep in the woods under the jurisdiction of the revenue department. This will induce change in the administrative set-up at the grassroots level. At present some officers of the forest department have been given revenue powers.

Precedence Given Importance

Among the Korku there are customs regarding marriage, property inheritance, succession, etc. They are guided by these customs while taking a decision. Precedence is always given due importance while dealing with a particular dispute.

A single-tier system is followed by the village council to look after the maintenance of customary laws. The council acts as the arbitrator. Disputes of civil nature as well as those involving minor quarrels are settled by this council. For criminal cases like murder, etc., they go to the court of law. Here the State legislation intervenes.

The head of each household is a member of the village council. He is normally the oldest male member of the house. Each household has to be represented in the council meetings by a member. The *patil* or the village headman presides over the council meetings. The post is hereditary and honorary. He gets a honorarium only in the case of girl's marriage in the village. There is a *chowdhury* of the village, messenger and a *bhagat* (priest). Both of these functionaries get a yearly remuneration from each household for their services. There remains a *bhumka* or the medicineman in the village. For any council meeting the *patil* asks the *chowdhury* to inform the villagers about the date and time of the meeting. The *patil*'s house is mostly used as the venue for the *panch* meetings. The views of the *bhagat*, old man and *bhumka* carry weight. The final verdict is announced by the *patil*. It is obligatory for the parties in a conflict to accept the verdict.

Besides this *panch* (village council), there is another functionary, i.e. *jato patil*. His jurisdiction is over 12 neighbouring villages. He is the head of the regional council. All the *patils* of these 12 villages are the members of this council. The *jato patil* presides over the regional council meetings. Such a council has the power of excommunication as well as to pardon those who have been earlier excommunicated. If a Korku man marries a girl from Nehal, who are lower in status, he is liable to be excommunicated. He may gain his old status through some purificatory rites. It is the *jato patil* who takes the decision on this count. After a grand feast offered by the offender the council announces the acceptance of the person. This regional council has ceased to function in various areas and *jato patils* are not always found. In the absence of such a council the *panch* takes the decision. For inter-village disputes the councils of both the villages sit together to settle it.

As stated earlier, following the country's independence and intensive development of communication channels at various levels, the tribal villages and the inhabitants have been exposed to outer influence. Legislation is one of the important things which have affected the tribals.

Specific Inheritance Rules

The Korku have specific rules regarding the inheritance of ancestral property. Their society is patriarchal. The sons are the legal heirs of their father's property. After the father's death, his property is equally shared by his sons. The daughter has no right over the father's property. After a girl's marriage she becomes the member of her husband's clan. This membership she loses when she becomes widow but is revived through her second marriage with her husband's younger brother. A daughter has no claim in her father's property. In the absence of a son the property goes to the deceased's brother or brother's son. The property cannot go to a person other than that of the same lineage. The widow also can not inherit the property from her husband. However, she has to be provided economic security by the person who enjoys the property. In most cases the husband's brother's son looks after his father's brother's widow. As a whole in

Korku society the woman's claim over property has been denied. The state law, however, gives equal right to the woman. The daughter should get the share of her father's property equal to her brother. The widow can be the legal heir of her husband's property. The revenue department, following the state law, has accepted the daughter's claim on her father's property.

The situation evolving out of it is interesting. One illustration in this regard may be more communicative and self-explanatory. Rama Kasde had only one daughter whom he married off nine years back. Initially she was living with her husband and children. After three years of her marriage she with her family started living with her parents. In the year 1973 the *patta* (record of deeds) was given by the forest department, who also have the revenue powers, to Rama where he was declared as the owner of some plots of land. Following Rama's expiry the question of right over his property came up. Who would inherit the property? Rama's brother's sons or his daughter? The forest department declared the daughter as the legal heir. There was a hue and cry among the elders on this issue. It was against their customs. But the other section advised that they cannot do anything against the government's decision. There were a lot of informal group discussions in the village on the subject. There was a feeling of discontentment. They were also aware of their inability to impose the traditional custom. Realising the situation they decided to call a meeting of the village council. The *patil* called the meeting and the issue was discussed in detail. On one point they were of one opinion that the state law could not be ignored. They reached an agreement on the point of making an amendment of their customary law. It was resolved that if the daughter was the only issue she would be the legal heir. But they could not claim equal share in their father's property with their brothers. This way they avoided in clash.

Similar cases have also been placed on record from another village. One Bhailu was the only son of his parents. His mother was the lone daughter of her father. Her father died at an early age. So her mother got the right over the property which she inherited. In this case too there was a lot of discussion in the village council. Finally, the rule of the state law was accepted and accordingly the customary law was modified. Several respondents remarked that the widow of the deceased had a right over his property. And if there were sons they could share the property with the widow. On the point of sharing the property between mother and sons the respondents differ. They do not have a uniform opinion. The daughter is to justify her right of ownership above that of the lineage member (brother, brother's son).

Similar disagreement has also been observed regarding the succession rules relating to public office. The office of the village *patil* (headman) is hereditary. It follows the male primogeniture rule. The eldest son of the *patil* succeeds his father to the office. Only in such extreme cases as mental disorder or physical unfitness the second son may replace the eldest son. It is not necessary that the eldest son has to be exceptionally brilliant. Even if he be an infant the council may work. His presence then is more of a ritual. The elders take the decision which is announced through him.

Administrative Set-Up

During the British rule throughout the state each village had a headman who used to be called *patil*. He was the revenue collector who used to preside over the village council. He used to get remuneration as honorarium for his service.

After the introduction of the three-tier system of Panchayat Raj in rural India the situation became different. For several interconnected reasons *patils* were not popular. A new generation of leaders has recently come up as elected representatives in the Gram Panchayat. The Gram Panchayat, being an elected body, wields more powers than the traditional single headman. But the post of *patil* has been retained even to this day. His jurisdiction, however, has become very much limited.

During yearly revenue collection he assists the *patoari* in his work. He is now called Police *patil* and in case of any criminal incident in the village he is asked to give his report. He is an agent of the Police at the village. In the Korku land, the situation is not the reflection of what we have stated here. Because, the Korku lives in both revenue and forest villages. The Panchayat Raj has not come into effect in the forest villages. In forest villages, the Korku village headmen do not get any remuneration. But in the revenue areas they receive the honorarium, In near future the *patils* of the forest villages will also get the remuneration. A decision in this regard has already been taken. Now from the Government side certain criteria are laid down for selecting a person as *patil*. Of these criteria education and contact with outside are most important. The officials say that it helps in good communication. An illiterate *patil* having the hang over of the tradition is rigid and not easy to tackle. he is apathetic towards new ideas. So it is better to go for a person who is literate and has open mind. The eldest son of the traditional *patil* satisfies these new requirements. In the village Hatru, the present *patil* is the third son of the previous *patil*. The council organised the meeting after it was made clear by the resident forest personnel about the requirement of the post. The council in its meeting discussed the issue. Here too, they knew that they could not go by the tradition. An amendment was done. The council arrived at an agreement, that any son of *patil* will succeed him. He may or may not be the eldest son. As the first son of the *patil* was illiterate and the second son was poorly literate, the third son, who left his studies when he was in the ninth standard was selected as *patil*. The council accepted him the Kalme, the present *patil* has visited the small towns of the district.

In Kusumkot the present *patil* succeeded his maternal grandfather. Along with the property he has inherited the office of his mother's father. He has studied up to the sixth standard. The eldest son of the present *patil* lived separately with his family. He is illiterate too. His second son has passed the lower matric examination. The present *patil* is also a member of the Group Gram Panchayat.

Traditionally, the *patil* holds the office till death. After the expiry of the *patil* the question of successor arises. The present *patil* wishes to retire due to bad health and other responsibilities. He feels that his second son who satisfies the requirements (educated, well behaved, physically fit) should inherit the office. There are other aspirants who go even to the extent of ignoring the hereditary right to the office. The present *patil* has interest in his son. If not the eldest son, at least another son who is educated should get the office. As a *patil* has to give the report of criminal incident in writing, he should be educated. The village council is in support of the present *patil*'s view. The conditions are also favourable for the *patil*'s son. Another aspirant for the post is a matriculate. His brother is a teacher in a middle school in the district town. He is a member of a political party. The teacher tried to use influence for his brother but could not succeed. As remarked by one of my respondents the important fact is that the hereditary right over the office of the *patil* has been challenged.

Discussion

Adaptation is a process and a state (Hankins, 1954). It is used to indicate the end result of modifications on the state of being adapted. In the latter sense it is equivalent to "adjustment" or such harmonious relationship between external stimuli and the essential conditions of life as to ensure peaceful co-existence, in order to avoid conflict. Here we find that some of the customary laws of the Korku differ from the State law. But the State law has been imposed on them. Under this situation the Korku society has made an organised attempt to adapt to the changed condition so as to maintain the harmony in interrelation. Here we find conflict, rivalry and emulation as part of the whole process. The woman's right over the property has a negative response from the society. But the council as we have seen finally agreed to accept the daughter's right over that of the lineage members. A widow can legally be a heir to her deceased husband. We have also seen that the existing rules regarding succession to public office are in conflict with the present requirements. Here, too, the society has agreed to compromise. Any son of the *patil* who has the required qualifications can be an alternative for the eldest son for the office of the *patil*. The council has resolved the differences and has made necessary amendment in the customary laws.

19

TRIBAL CUSTOMARY LAW OF THE KOL

B. K. DAS GUPTA

The Kol are spread over the central uplands "extending from Kolhan in the district of Singbhum to the Chitor Hills in the West". Guha (1946) states that "contact with them was from the earliest as shown by the name Kolarian still used by many in a generic sense, for the languages and people of the Munda groups". At present, the people who categorically go by the name Kol are primarily scattered in 23 districts of Madhya Pradesh and nine districts of Uttar Pradesh. In Madhya Pradesh, they are the predominant people in the Katni and Sihora tehsils of the district of Jabalpur which has the maximum concentration of the Kol. In this district again, in the Sadar tehsil, i.e. Jabalpur tehsil, the concentration of the Kol is almost negligible so much so that *District Hand Book, 1964* records the number of the Kol, in this tehsil, as nil. According to the same Hand Book the other three tehsils accommodating a fairly large number of Kols are as follow.

Katni tehsil :	14570	(Male) 14632	(female) =	29202	(total)
Sihora tehsil :	12496	do 12661	do =	25157	do
Patan tehsil :	1161	do 1174	do =	2335	do

In Madhya Pradesh, where the Kol are only next to the Gond in number, they also inhabit the districts of Rewa, Mandla and Chhindwara. As is evident from the population figures of the three tehsils of Jabalpur, women outnumber men and the 1971 Census Report also depicts the male-female ratio as 100 : 1006. Jagannathan (1964) reports "only 4.2% of them are literate and only 3 in 10,000 have received education up to matric and higher stages".

The Kol are included in the Proto-Australoid ethnic stratum that formed the ethnic matrix of central and south India by submerging the Negrito. The Kol, therefore, are a category of Munda-speaking tribes, along with Baiga, Korku, Munda, Kharia, Ho and Santal in central India. It is noteworthy that the territory inhabited by the Ho of Bihar is also known as Kolhan. This on the one hand describes the ubiquitousness of Kol nomenclature in the central part of India and on the other exhibits the affinity that exists between the Kol and the groups that go by the generic name "Mundari or Munda-speaking tribes".

The Kol today have changed a lot and many of the norms and practices that brought their distinctiveness have been lost due to contact with the non-tribal neighbours. As early as 1946, Griffiths found them as "greatly acculturated with Hindu ideas and beliefs" and asserted "that the Kol do not retain their original practices in the same form and extent as those living in the interior areas of Rewa". It is understood that the Mandla Kol, too, retain many of the traditional traits of especially these of the totemistic septs. Even then Griffiths who concentrated on the Jabalpur Kols has exposed a number of interesting features centring on their supernatural belief practices and the importance given by the Kol to sept or clan structure in the organisation of their society.

The accounts of Crooke (1896), Risley (1916), Russel and Hiralal (1916) too accommodate information on their culture. Of late, Hasan (1972) has also delineated the changing facets of Kol culture in UP. The present study undertaken in 1977 based on a well defined parameter estimated to throw some light on the customs practised by the Kol of today. The work was mainly carried out in the Sihora tehsil of the district of Jabalpur where the Kol always inhabit the heterogeneous village, of course, forming a separate settlement cluster of their own.

Today, the Kol are engaged in varied occupations from day labouring, quarry work, wood collection, petty service to agriculture. Griffiths (1946) identified three strata among the Kol from the economic standpoint. These three strata are: (1) factory workers who are better off, (2) forest people and agricultural workers who have enough to eat but no money for anything else and (3) those having primitive occupations of wood and grass cutting.

The Kol are believed to be hard workers but not very good agriculturists. Therefore, today, in many areas of Jabalpur district where the Kol are surrounded by at least 13 other communities, Kol are mainly presented as landless labourers. The bulk of the landholding is in the hands of other communities. Kol are agricultural labourers, factory or mine workers or the like. There has not been any instance where a Kol family has augmented the landholding through calculative measures.

The Kol of the Katni-Sihora tehsil believe that they were earlier in the Mewar side and used to occupy the hills of that area. They have inherited a tradition of martial character and firmly believe that with the help of the Kol and the Bhil only, Rana Pratap, the great king of Mewar, could fight against the Moghuls. In view of this they feel that they were adapted to hill setting. Therefore, as later on they came down to valleys, they could not take to wet-rice cultivation and continued with the earlier tradition of shifting hill cultivation. Therefore, today in the district of Jabalpur the Kol are seen in a number of occupations and many have been avoiding agriculture and have taken to daily labour, collecting forest produce, wage earning in lime quarries and the like.

During the time when the zamindari system was in vogue, the landlord used to donate land to *malgujars* who used to enjoy the ownership right over the village or villagers in lieu of their allegiance to the landlords. (Das Gupta : 1978). There was no Kol *malguzar* in Katni or in Sihora tehsil. Most of the Kols were initially *sarkari pattadar* enjoying free ownership right over a patch of land for three years and after that period became *bhumi swami* (lord of the patch of land). As a result, they cannot sell the land without the expressed permission of the District Collector. The forest wherefrom they collect wood apple and fuelwood belong to the government and they are to pay nothing to the government. They graze cattle in the fallow *khas* land for which no tax is given whatever. Most of the Kol families have been living at a bare subsistence level and many are in debt. In 1977, the government of Madhya Pradesh did away with many of the outstanding debts or bonded labour with the help of Debt Relief Inspectors visiting different SDOs' courts on specific days to settle pending cases. In this way in 1976 only, 10 cases in the Katni tehsil area and four in the Jabalpur area were settled in favour of the Kol. Of them four relate to parties bound as bonded labour to richer people while the others are regarding repayment of loan made against the pawn of utensils, ornaments etc.

Settling Intra-village and Intra-group Disputes

The Kol of any settlement depend on a council comprising three *mukhobar* (elderly personalities) including a *malik*, who are selected by the villagers. The *mukhobars* within a village are contacted whenever there is any case of involvement with other's wife or a marriage within one's *baenk* or the like. In case a man leaves his wife immediately after marriage, he is treated rigorously and is accepted only after a feast is thrown to the *biradari* (group brethren). Most of the trials end in the award of fine in the form of a feast for the fellow brethren. Only in the case of adultery a fine to the tune of even Rs. 300 (three hundred only) is awarded. The feast often is prescribed for two days – *kacchi khana* comprising rice, dal, vegetable curry to be given on the first day and then on the next day *pakki khana* is thrown when *puri* (bread fried with clarified butter) and vegetable curry are served.

In the selection of *malik* no definite system of primogeniture or ultimogeneture is followed. In one village one DK became *malik* only after the death of his elder brother and for holding this office the *malik* does not get any special privilege. But these villages with a fair concentration of the Kol have a malik while others do without that. In matters concerning illegitimate child, keeping of *rakhelu* (concubine), dealing with witch and such matters of social significance, the *malik* has an important role to play.

The amount of fine is utilised for constructive works concerning the community. Thus in the village of Ghatsimuria (Sihora tehsil) durries, gaslight, utensils, etc., required for Kol council meetings and for a community gathering have all been purchased out of the amount of fine. One very important decision, of late, decided by the *malik* of Ghatsimuria was about a Kol girl of a village who allegedly had illicit relation with a Doman boy and hence refused to go to the village of her husband KK (of another village) Three men of the husband's village implicated the girl with the Doman boy and brought the matter for the consideration of the elders. Since it involved a number of villages, a big congregation of about 200 Kol elders sat in the village of Ghatsimuria under the chairmanship of JK, the *malik* of the village. In the absence of any definite evidence, the girl's guilt could not be proved and the three men who thus tried to defame the girl were fined Rs. 60 only the amount was spent on feasting.

Again, one MK's step-mother of village J was driven away from her house by her husband. She left and MK's father brought another woman (a widow) from village T and lived with her and could beget a son (MK). MK's step-mother had a son MHK who was also staying in the family. Naturally after the marriage of MK and MHK when they tried to live separately a dispute arose over the sharing of land. Kol *malik* of the village arranged a *kacchi khana* where the elders also participated and the matter was settled. The council decided that no discrimination should be shown in this regard and MK and MHK should be treated on an equal footing.

In case of any dispute involving a Kol and a non-Kol residing in the same village, the matter is put to the village panchayat. In the two villages under study there has been hardly on cases involving the Kol and all these have been settled. But whenever the cases are inter-village in nature or if any dispute cannot be resolved by the village panchayat, it is referred to the *nyayapanch* which covers about five, six or so number of villages (Das Gupta, 1978). The *pradhan* who is the chief of *nyayapanch* is assisted by an *upo pradhan* and a few panches of which one may be a Kol. In one *nyayapanch* till 1976, about 34 cases came up in the previous eight years and of them only four involved the Kol. The nature of these cases was: (1) quarrels with neighbours on various grounds, (2) dispute over land boundary and (3) dispute over payment of loan. *Nyayapanch* as a judicial body superior to the village panchayat is important in the Katni area. But in the Sihora tehsil area *nyayapanch* is not that important in the Kol life. In the latter area, whenever any inter-village dispute arises the maliks of several villages and a few important Kol personalities from Jabalpur town assemble to decide upon the case. Nyayapanch can fine Rs. 50 in criminal cases and Rs. 100 in civil cases. As a matter of fact, the case in the Sihora area which needed months and months of deliberations with the active participation of four Kol *maliks* and two influential Kol personalities was about a Kol man involved in relationship with a non-Kol girl. This remained unsettled at the level of the Kol council and hence as a last resort it went to the SDO's court wherefrom it is learnt it was ultimately withdrawn. Cases of theft, homicide, etc., are not within the *nyayapanch's* purview.

Adoption

Adoption, *godnama*, does not require any formal permission or feast nor the malik has to be informed beforehand. Only the *kotwar* has to be communicated verbally who in turn intimates the *sarpanch* of the village who often is not a Kol. Those who can afford often throw a feast to solemnise such an occasion. A child, male or female, taken on *godnama* will get a share (in case there are other sons) or the whole (in case the individual has no other sons) of the property. Thus one PK of village Ghatsimuria adopted his daughter's daughter NH at age of seven and since then she is staying with PK as her own daughter. PK tells that his landed property will be owned by NH only when his wife dies because PK has no son of his own. Similarly, in another case one RK adopted the son of his younger brother DK because RK himself had no son. RK desires that all his landed property should go to his adopted son.

Residence in Wife's Village

The patrilineal Kol follow the rules of patrilocal residence. But there are instances when a man, on marriage, decides to stay on in the wife's village primarily goaded by reasons of convenience to look after the property of his wife. Even if a man is staying with his wife he will get the share of the parental land and cattle. Such matrilocal residence does not need any prior permission from the *malik*. In one village (Ghatsi Muria) with 28 Kol families, there are two instances of matrilocal residences:

> One SK is staying with his wife at her father's place in the same village. Her father has enough landed property. One BK is putting up at the house of his wife's father at Maharajpur. Since BK earns his daily wages through carrying goods in a push cart, he says staying at Maharajpur is advantageous for him.

Rules of Inheritance

Movable and immovable property is shared by the sons. The share is equal among them and no additional share is earmarked for the eldest or the youngest. A daughter, after marriage, does not get any share of the father's property nor can claim any share. If a person dies leaving behind married daughters only, then they will inherit the property, whereas if a person leaves behind his wife only, the widow will own her husband's fortunes. In case there is none, the siblings (male only) of the deceased will inherit the property. Below a number of actual cases have been cited and depicted to assess the nature in which the property is inherited.

1. One SK had one and a half acres of land. On his demise, the land is being jointly cultivated by his five sons and the crop yield is being equally shared by them though they are staying in separate households. SK's widowed wife who is staying with the youngest son also gets a share. But the silver ornaments of RT (wife of SK) were sold out and the money equally shared.
2. PK inherited 39 decimal of land and two bullocks from his father. His father purchased the same pieces of land from a Brahman of Jwelha. The house where he is now living belonged to his mother's father after whose death it was jointly inherited by PK and his two brothers and his mother and now on the death of the mother the house has come to PK.

Of these 39 decimal of land ideally one-third should come to PK, one-third to his brother RK and the remaining one-third to their mother. PK is staying in his wife's village and has not claimed any share of his property. Moreover on performing the last rites of his mother the one-third share of the mother has also come to PK who is thus the owner of the whole lot of 39 decimal. CB and RN, the two married sisters of, PK have no claim over the property. If any person dies without leaving behind any son/daughter, then the property will be inherited by his widowed wife after whose death it will go to the male siblings of the deceased.

When there is any controversy regarding the boundary of the landed property, measurement of land is done by the village *patowari* in the presence of the Kol *malik*.

If a widow is kept as a concubine (*rakhelu*) by a man, her children from the earlier husband are to get a share of the land, cattle and house of her keeper and they are not to be deprived of this legitimate share. In case of any discrimination, the elders are contacted and they sit together to decide such cases.

If a girl after marriage is deserted by her husband and has to stay with her parents or with her brother (if parents are deceased) she is not entitled to any share of the landed property for her maintenance. She has to adjust with her brother/brothers in this matter.

A man XK owns five acres of land and left behind two sons from his wife and one son from his *rakhelu* (concubine). The two sons got two acres each and the son of the *rakhelu* got one acre. Had the *rakhelu* got one daughter only, the five acres of land of XK would have been equally shared by XK's sons.

Had XK left behind no son and only his widowed wife and a childless *rakhelu*, out of the five acres of land, three acres would have gone to his wife and two acres to the *rakhelu*.

If a man dies living behind no child, wife, siblings, and *rakhelu*, the Kol elders sit together with the *malik* and his house is converted into a club house or shrine or for any other purpose for the cause of the whole community. Under such circumstances, the Kol living in multi-ethnic villages have to take the Sarpanch and the village Patwari into confidence.

Marriage Rules

Monogamy is the rule. A man cannot have a second wife during the lifetime of the first wife. Polygyny does not become necessary because of the existing system of *rakhelu* (concubine) who invariable belongs to the same community (and may be of different or the same *baenk*). A *rakhelu* behaves like a wife in asmuch as she also wears vermilion, *kangan* (heavy bangle) and *mahau* (red liquid painted on the either edge of feet). *Rakhelu* is kept in a separate hut if the wife is alive. Among the Kol, the girls marry between 14-18 years and the boys between 20-24 years of age. They must have adopted child marriage imitating the upper castes of the neighbourhood. Marriage with cross cousins, parallel cousins, sister's daughter, wife's elder sister is strictly disfavoured and the persons indulging in such marriages are to pay a fine of Rs. 25 or so and throw a *kacchi* feast. Wife's younger sister can be kept as concubine after the death of the wife and the elder brother's wife can be kept as *rakhelu* after the death of elder brother. Any form of involvement with wife's elder sister and younger brother's wife is forbidden and the involved person may be asked to leave the village. It is thus clear that the rules of avoidance have not been framed in terms of the kin but taking the relative seniority and junior position into consideration. Thus among the wife's sisters, the elder one is to be avoided and the younger sister can be accepted and among the husband's brothers, the elder one is respected and avoided whereas the joking relationship with the younger one is tolerated and liked.

Bride-price *chari* consists of Rs. 20 or so in cash, a calf or a goat and ornaments (*kang*– bangle, *lachatoi* ornament). In recent days *chari* is giving place to *dahej* i.e. dowry that comprises cash of Rs. 50

or so and some utensils. *Dahej* is a mark of prestige too and hence to get good educated boys especially those who are in service, guardians of girls even offer better *dahej*, in kind, comprising cycle or the like. For the poor Kols, *chari* is still continuing to be in practice. Bride-price or dowry, whatever is parted by the boy's side or the girl's side, is not to be returned in the case of divorce or *chhorchhuthi*. The Kol are clear about the avoidance of the following kins in marriage. Thus, marriage with wife's mother, wife's elder sister, brother's daughter, mother's brother's daughter, father's sister's daughter, father's brother's daughter, step-mother, daughter's daughter are prohibited. Elder brother's wife, younger brother's wife can be kept as rakhelu, i.e. cocubine.

If any of the above prohibitions are ignored, the guilty would be fined and a feast of rice, pulses and bread has to be thrown to the *biradari* and co-villagers in which the *malik* and *mukhobari* have to be invited.

Village endogamy is generally avoided but then there are occasions when marriage within the village has actually taken place. Thus in one village, out of 37 marriages, only two marriages have been solemnised within the village while in 35 other cases brides have been taken in from about 29 other settlements.

The families are mostly simple in nature with very few cases of joint families where two simple families have united under a common roof and kitchen. Thus in one village the following family types are discernible. Self, wife, married son with wife and without children (6), with without unmarried son, daughter, widow, widower with unmarried, son daughter (5), single individual (1), self, wife, unmarried children (16), self, wife, any agnate with/without unmarried children (4), tow brother staying together (1). This shows that while about 50 per cent of the family composition is simple in nature, families comprising any affinal kin are non-existent. Moreover, the size of each family is also not big and in our sample village maximum five members are seen in a family.

Institution of Rakhelu

Among the Kol bigamy is not allowed. But if a Kol desires to accommodate a second woman in his house or desires to have access to a second woman, he can keep *baithalu* or *rakhelu* (concubine). For this it is desired that he throws a *kacchi khana* (meal in the preparation of which clarified butter is not used) to his *biradari*.

In the matter of inheritance of property a *rakhelu* along with her children gets a proportional share of the property that has been detailed elsewhere.

Rakhelus, in most of the cases, are widowed women. Kol custom debars a widow from remarrying but she can stay with any person as concubine in his house or in a separate house. In the Kol society where the number of women is more than that of men, there are always excess women who cannot find out partners. Therefore, the institution of *rakhelu* has been acting as a safety-valve against any societal chaos.

A *rakhelu* girl may use vermilion, *kangan* and *mahau* because she is regarded as a woman with *marad* (man). Only some selected agnates and affines of the *rakhelu* are to be invited to a feast. Whether the *rakhelu* will stay with her children or not would depend on her keeper. On many occasions, a *rakhelu* lives under the same shed along with the wife often with such cohesiveness that it may become impossible to distinguish the two. There have been cases too when Brahman and Bania men have taken a Kol widow as *rakhelu*.

Divorce (*chhorchutti*)

In the case of divorce, the children are to stay with the father. The babies, if the elders decide, may go with the mother. The wife when divorced is not given any compensation and is not likely to get any share of property nor any allowance for maintenance.

Reasons for seeking divorce are (1) incompatibility, (2) adultery and (3) barrenness.

Among the Kol, it is not the wife but the husband who mostly takes the initiative in asking for a divorce. When granted, the children stay with the father and the divorced wife cannot take them. The divorced wife can take with her the sukling baby and that too after the husband's consent. If through agreement a boy or a girl lives with his/her divorced mother he/she is not deprived of the share of the property of his/her father. In no case is the *dahej* (dowry) or the *chari* (bride-price) returned.

Baenk (Agnatic Segment)

The Kol comprise seven *baenk*. Theoretically a *baenk* is endogamous and there is some amount of territorial limitation in the distribution of these brotherhood groups.

But then in some of the cases an amount of laxity is there in the matter of endogamy. Thus Ratuel can marry with Khotaha and Khotaha can also marry with Dessao. In most of the cases, the Kol inhabiting a village or occupying a hamlet of a village belong to one and single *baenk*. Thus in Ghatsimuria village (Sihor Block, Jabalpur district) all the 33 families belong to Rautia *baenk*. Again in the village of Mansukra in the same block, of the 28 families, only eight belong to Thakuria and the remaining 20 to Rautia. The villagers assert that Thakuria being a higher *baenk* must follow *baenk* endogamy. People, however, admit that the prescription of *baenk* endogamy is not always adhered to.

Again, Thakuria is believed to be the superiormost followed by Rautia. Most of the villages are inhabited by one *baenk* or the other. Thus Rautia and Rautel are more to be found in Katni tehsil and the Gharbaria is found to the east of the Rautia tract. The Thakuria is more spread in Sihora tehsil of Jabalpur district while the Dahait is seen in Mandla district mainly. Marriage between one *baenk* and the other is forbidden but not totally absent. Thus though the Thakuria are hierarchically superior, the Rautia feel that they can marry with them because they are "almost equal of each other". Each such marriage has to be brought to the notice of their chief. Anyway, the spatial relationship of each *baenk* reminds us of clan-land relationship among many Austric-speaking groups such as Munda and others. However, though villages are dominated by a single *baenk* which is as a rule endogamous, yet village endogamy is neither preferred nor practised.

Leading Persons in Kol Society

The influence of the *malik* in Kol life was earlier all-pervasive and in a village there would not be any important matter of which he would be ignorant. In keeping a concubine, adopting a child, husband and wife separating from each other, the *malik* must be informed. But the *malik* now says "we are not honoured", while some people say "our *maliks* do not take care of us now-a-days. *Maliks*, however, insist that at present many of the happenings in a village go without their knowledge. Villagers feel that the government should formalise the institution of *malik* and of tribal council. A *malik* is generally male but his wife can perform the duties on his death till a new malik is selected. If a *malik* dies leaving behind a son fit to inherit the office, the villagers select him to that post. Thus though *malikship* is not intended to be hereditary, it often lies in a family for quite a long period. The Kol elders who help the *malik* in deciding a case are called *mukhobari*.

A *panda* happens to be an important official to preside over the rituals that typically belong to the Kol. These rituals centre round the worship of Desai Devi in the month of April and of Gorokhi Devi for the health and prosperity of the inmates of a house The *panda* also serves as *onjha* and is requisitioned by the villagers. . . (even by those who are not Kol) in cases of chronic sickness. In the Katni tehsil area, the malikship and the *pandaship* have been held by two different persons but in Sihora tehsil (both of Jabalpur district) these are held by the same person. We know that among the Mundari group of tribes the offices of headman and village priest are always held by one and the same person. Among the Kol, if perchance the *malikship* is temporarily held by a woman, a man must be made the *panda* because the women are not allowed to officiate in rituals. In Sihora tehsil, the Kol worship Khermai in a shrine of three mounds under a margosa tree and opine that Khermai is the combination of three distinct deities — Khermai, Didai and Mahamai — all the deities being benevolent and responsible for the welfare of the people and the land.

Thus we know whenever any two Kols are involved, they would go to *malik* for settling the dispute. On the other front, a *panda* looks after the sacred pantheon and cater to the priestly requirements because the Kol do not accept the services of Brahmans. It is, therefore, seen that the offices of *malik, mukhobari* and *panda* have been instrumental in maintaining the tribal boundary of the Kol even in the background of the caste-ridden environment.

The Kol do not possess any tradition of kingship nor is there any single individual leader of all the Kol of Madhya Pradesh or of the whole of central India. One CK of Jabalpur town is now regarded as the *mukhiya* of all the Kols of Jabalpur district and as such in settling any inter-village dispute his presence is sought and his verdict becomes final. But then this is a recent phenomenon and CK's authority is accepted because he is town-based, educated elite and thus be commands considerable reverence from his group brethren.

Concluding Remarks

Griffiths (1946) contended that "there is a definite hardening of the social divisions within the Kol tribe . . . and the Kols are apparently forming a miniature caste system". In practice the sub-divisions have not become that strictly endogamous though theoretically they are and the villagers are truly dependent on the non-Kol service castes around. Griffiths listed about 22 *kurhi* (*baenk*) and Crooke gave a list of nine septs; but now, excepting six, others have been lost into oblivion though they are conscious about their seven traditional *baenk*. However, today no one can overlook the important roles of sacred and secular offices, viz. *punda* and *malik* in maintaining their group cohesiveness in the face of tremendous social-cultural changes taking place around them.

The above, in brief, outlines the major elements of the customs that bind the Kol together primarily in the Jabalpur area where they form a sizeable population and where Griffiths too undertook his pioneering ethnographic work in 1946.The Kol who have moved away from their forest environment have not seriously taken to agriculture and are not truly regarded as cultivators. They are engaged in assorted jobs such as quarry work, daily-wage earning, forest products gathering, agricultural labour and petty agriculturists. Side by side, education has stealthily crept in and higher educational institutions of the area have a few Kol enthusiasts. On the other hand, they are eager to have a judicious leader whose words can be effective in the whole Kol tract. This is partly to put a check on the traditional village level headmen who gradually have been losing importance to those Kols who are educated, urbanite and progressive. Thus subtle changes have been engulfing the Kol in various aspects especially in their economic and social dimensions.

20

AUTHORITY, STRUCTURE AND MODE OF SOCIAL CONTROL AMONG THE GONDS

D. HAJRA

The Gonds are one of the most important tribes of Central India. They are spread all over Madhya Pradesh and are found in good numbers in the adjacent parts of Maharashtra, Andhra and Orissa. The Gonds of different regions are designated in various ways, forming an endogamous group in each case. But some important features are usually found common among most of such groups. The presence of a self-designatory term *koitor*, system of phratry for regulation of marriage, common tongue Gondi, etc., are some of the common characteristic features found among most of the Gond groups. A field investigation was undertaken in the Jabalpur-Mandla region during May-July, 1977, in connection with the study of customary laws among the Gonds of this area.

The Jabalpur region may be said to form the extreme northern limit of the distribution of the Gonds. Here they are found to have undergone many changes due to their location in the peripheral region being surrounded and influenced by alien cultures. They have given up their own Gondi dialect, adopting local form of Hindi; they usually go by the name *kisan*. Likewise, in some parts of Jabalpur district they have adopted certain characters pertaining to the higher castes of the Hindus. It is found among the Gonds of Dargarh, a village under study, that they have contrary to some universal practices as found common among other Gond groups elsewhere, stopped rearing chickens in their houses; drinking of liquor within the village is very much resented and discouraged; marriages with some near kins like father's sister's daughters or mother's brother's daughters have now become an obsolete practice.

The Gonds of the Mandla region, on the other hand, have

retained many of their common tribal characteristics. They still retain their own Gondi dialect, though it is found corrupted much by the local Hindi. They still use the common generic Gondi term *Koitor* to designate their own group of people. They also practise cross-cousin marriages as found common among other Gonds.

It is noticed among the Gonds in the area under study that even under sweeping changes in recent years, they still adhere to their traditional system in having their tribal council as a means of control in dealing with various social offences in their society. It deals with all breaches, particularly in matters of sex, and with inter-village disputes on social matters. The introduction of statutory panchayat system among them is of recent origin, but at present its activities are found to be, on the whole, directed towards welfare matters. The traditional authority structure (*gaon* panchayat or *panch*) though enjoying control over matters of social breaches is gradually losing control over the matters relating to economic disputes, particularly those arising out of land issues. Criminal matters like petty thefts may also be dealt with by the traditional panchayat if the members of their own community are involved; but those of a grave nature are reported to the police. Adultery and elopement though generating under general state laws, are still well within the purview of the tribal panchayat. In dealing with such cases nowadays, they have adopted certain procedures as per the requirement under the general criminal law that apply to the Gond society as well.

In case of any inter-village dispute, *gaon* panchayats of the concerned villages sit together to decide. If there is no solution, the panchayats of a few other neighbouring villages are called for a joint meeting, and the majority decision arrived at in the meeting is obligatory on the concerned villages to accept.

Gaon Panchayat or Tribal Council

The formal composition of a traditional tribal council in the area includes a few office-bearers, and they along with the elderly male members of the village constitute the council body as indicated below.

Patel : He is the village headman; formerly the designation was *mukaddam*, but it has now become obsolete. Formerly the post of a *mukaddam* was of hereditary nature, and the eldest son used to succeed his father. But now the *patel* of a village is appointed by the government on being selected and recommended by the majority of villagers. As such, this post cannot be said to be of hereditary nature, but in practice selection is made from the same family, if not from the same lineage.

Though the post of a *mukaddam* has become obsolete the legacy is still present as is observed in Dargarh; here, the eldest son of a dead *mukaddam* is still recognised as such. He is given due respect and he enjoys certain privileges and some command in the council.

Diwan : He comes next to the *patel*; he presides over a meeting in the absence of the *patel*.

Siphahi: He acts as an errand-man; his main function is to carry any message of the village *panch* to the villagers, to summon the litigating parties before the *panch*, to announce the date and time of a council meeting, etc. This post is hereditary.

The *kotwar* of a village (belonging to an inferior caste) sometimes acts as a *sipahi*. Besides the abovementioned office-bearers, the elderly male members of the village also take part in a council meeting and they are free to express their views and givew comments in dealing with a case.

In the following pages rules regarding regulation of sex life under various social situations and the function and responsibility of the tribal council in dealing with such cases have been discussed; some illustrations from case studies have also been cited for better understanding in the context of their customary laws.

Regulation of Sex Life

According to traditional law marriage (*marmi*) is settled by negotiation between the parents of a boy and a girl. It is solemnised in an elaborate form, following all the traditional marriage rituals. A man may have a number of wives marrying them in the *marmi* form, provided the girl in question remains unmarried. But, for a woman, she can have only her first marriage performed in the traditional form. As she loses her maidenhood at her first marriage, her procuring any husband at a subsequent occasion can be effected through elopement (*rareli*); a widow can also remarry, and it is called *gaban*. So, the term *marmi* is not applied in all such cases. As a normal rule, an unmarried man is not expected to take a widow or a divorcee as his wife, but it is not strictly followed.

If a man elopes with a married woman and takes her as his wife, he is to compensate the former husband by paying the requisite fine (*dawan*) as fixed by the councils of the two concerned villages; the meeting is held at the new husband's place. Both the men have to entertain the council members of their respective villages with feasts. If an unmarried boy and a girl belonging to marriageable groups elope, the question of paying any compensation by the boy does not arise. When the boy comes back to his village with the wife, their marriage is formalised hurriedly in some short form of *marmi*, known as *kalwan-marmi*, in which only a few important rituals are observed. The boy has to arrange a feast for the whole village.

In case of an elopement, if both the partners, i.e. the boy and the girl, happen to belong to non-marriageable groups on account of their sharing a common clan or phratry, the families of both the partners are excommunicated. If they want to be taken back in the society, the *gaon* panchayats of the two concerned villages meet together with those of a few other neighbouring villages for taking a just decision. In such cases, both the boy and the girl have to undergo certain expiatory rites. They are taken to the riverside in company of all the council members and village members (only males), where their heads are shaved by the tribal barber (*shermia*) ; they take purificatory bath in the river and necessary rituals are observed by sacrificing goats and chickens. Then a feast follows. All these are done at the expense of the boy. He has also to feed all the villagers after they return to the village. The locks of shaved hair are attached to a pole which is erected on the side of a road as a warning to others.

According to their social norm, it is the prerogative of a husband to seek divorce (*chhor-chhuti*) from his wife. Some of the evil qualities like quarrelsome nature, lethergy in domestic work, bad character, etc., if found in a wife, may prompt the husband to demand the dissolution of marriage. A wife, on the other hand, has no right to ask for a divorce for any reason whatsoever like drunkenness, ill-temper, lasciviousness, etc., on the part of her husband, and she has to reconcile and remain passive. But she is free to leave her husband at her sweet will, if she finds her marital life miserable. In such a case, she may elope with a man of her choice.

In a divorce case, both husband and wife are to appear before the village council. The council first attempts to mediate and settle the case in an amicable way. If the husband is adamant, the marriage is dissolved. If there are children, it is the right of the father to stake a claim over them. But the infants may stay with their mother till they grow up. A woman, after getting a divorce, usually returns to her parents, and in most cases, she takes another husband. A divorced woman is entitled to claim maintenance cost from the husband as long as she does not take another husband. Now there is a trend to go for record when a marriage is dissolved and accordingly a written document is prepared to that effect in some cases, bearing the signatures or thumb impressions of the husband and wife. For formal recording, the village *kotwar* is to inform the concerned police station.

When a divorced woman remarries, the new husband need not pay any compensation to the former one. As already stated in the case of a married woman, the question of paying compensation arises when she takes another husband through elopement or otherwise leaves the former one. In such a case the dissolution of the earlier marriage in a formal way takes place in the presence of the *gaon panchayat* of the two concerned villages which meet for deciding the compensation issue as claimed by the former husband of the woman in question. The bond of the earlier marriage is broken in a symbolic way whereby the former husband tears a piece of a kind of grass (*sirkarisi*). The former and the new husband then exchange good wishes with each other, and as a gesture of goodwill they exchange a coin (rupee) between them. Thus, an amicable settlement is reached between them and from then onwards they are not supposed to bear any animosity or hatred towards each other.

If an unmarried girl bears a child, the village *panch* attempts to ascertain the man involved in the affair. If the fatherhood of the child remains unknown, the girl is declared as out-caste; but if the father is found to be from within the community, the man is forced to accept the girl as his wife. He has to marry the girl in the traditional form of marriage immediately observing only the important marriage rituals. Both the families involved in such cases have to entertain the village *panch* with feasts. But if the man happens to belong to some other group, the girl in question loses her community affiliation and remains as an outcaste.

When a man brings a woman from some other community and they live as husband and wife, he is excommunicated. He, however, may be taken back in the society provided he forsakes the girl and undergoes the prescribed expiatory rites like shaving of head, etc., and gives communal feasts.

An illegitimate son of a man enjoys all the facilities enjoyed by his other sons, without any stigma attached to him. He is affiliated to the clan of his begetter and, like other sons, has full claim over the property of the man according to the prevailing tribal rules. But all these depend on the condition that the mother should be from the same group, i.e. Gond. Otherwise, the boy loses all such claims. In case a man is an outcaste, he does not lose any right over his father's property which is due to him.

When a married woman is detected having an illicit relation with another man, the matter may be referred to the village council by the aggrieved husband. In such cases, if the man belongs to some other group, the woman is outcast and loses her tribal affiliation. But if such an affair happens within the community, the man involved in the case is punished, and he is to provide a feast to the village council, while the woman goes unpunished on the ground that otherwise her poor husband would suffer by having to hear the cost of feast without any fault of his. If the husband of the guilty woman so likes, he can desert his wife, who is free to take another husband if she wants.

Case Studies

Some case studies of breaches of different nature recorded during the field investigation are stated in short as below:

Case No. 1: In 1976 Komlu and Bhaiyalal, father's brother's sons of Gnansingh Pusam, sarpanch of Dargarh village, Jabalpur district, filed a case against Gnansingh in the Jabalpur court regarding the possession of some ancestral agricultural land possessed by him on which they claim as rightful owners. This case was first brought to the notice of the *gaon* panchayat but it failed to take any firm decision. The claimants thought that Gnansingh being the *sarpanch* had much influence over the villagers, and as such, they might not get due justice from the village council. So they preferred to go to a court of law.

Case No. 2: Sometime in 1975 there was a case before the village council concerning the restoration of conjugal life of Vijaysing Soriyam, the eldest son of the Mukaddam of Dargarh. Vijay's first wife who was from Ramhepur (a constituent village under the same statutory panchayat) left for her parents' house leaving her husband's place. She continued to stay over there for long without caring to return to her husband in spite of several requests from him. After hearing the case, the council also insisted on sending the wife back, and pressed the parents to send back the girl, but without any result. There was no counter-move of any kind from the girl's side through its village council clarifying the position as to why the girl intended to stay away from her husband. Ultimately, the boy married again on May 19, 1977, assuming his first marriage being void due to absence of any response from the wife for a considerable length of time.

Case No. 3: As reported in Silpura in Mandla district, an unmarried girl from Thonra and a boy from Gangpur, both lying not very far from Silpura, eloped sometime in 1974. Both of them were Gond. After three months, the girl was brought back by her parents, and she was not allowed to go to the boy again.

The boy after consultation with his relatives and friends decided to bring liquor to his in-laws in order to patch up the differences caused by elopement. But when the boy with another man visited the place, they were murdered. There was a police case which continued for a year or so. The final outcome of the case is not known to the people.

The cause of the murder could not be ascertained. The point was not clear as to why the girl's side had to take recourse to such a heinous crime without any apparent provocation from the boy. Under normative rules such types of elopement cases are very normal among the Gonds, and these marriages are subsequently regularised on payment of fine and through communal feast as decided by the village council. However, violation of marriage rules is not ignored and clan-exogamy or incestuous marriages is a matter of great concern to the people. But the society never, at present, encourages such an act of violence.

Case No.4: Harlal, a married son of Jharu Pando of Bujbujia, seduced a married girl from Panka caste of Silpura, an adjacent village. He started living with her in Bijbujia itself. This happened in the year 1971. Now, the Pankas are considered to be an inferior caste by the Gond. So, Harlal was excommunicated by the villagers. Social intercourse of any type was totally stopped. Even Harlal's parents and other close relatives used to keep distance from him. His Gond wife went back to her parents in Amatola, a neighbouring village, leaving the husband, and subsequently took another husband. Harlal had a son by his Gond wife who was then living with his grandfather in Bujbujia.

On the other hand, the Panka people also severed all connections with the girl; it was said that even if she left her Gond husband, she would not be taken back in the Panka society. She had a young son by her first husband who accompanied the mother and was living in Harlal's house.

It was said that if Harlal so liked, he might be taken back within the Gond fold, but in that case he would have to forsake the Panka girl and undergo the prescribed rituals followed by the communal feasts at his expense.

Case No. 5: The marriage among the Gond is regulated by the rules of clan and phratry exogamy, that is, a man must select his mate outside his clan or phratry. The breach of any rule in this respect is not tolerated. The people scrupulously avoid any intra-clan or intra-phratry union. But if anything goes contrary to this rule, the persons involved in such cases are penalised and are required to undergo the necessary expiatory rites as prescribed for the purpose, in case they wish to remain within the tribal fold. The exogamy rules relating to a clan are much more stringent as compared to those concerning a phratry. So, a breach under phratry exogamy rule is dealt with less severely and may be reconciled on easier terms.

Fatnu, a young man of Bujbujia, eloped with Dholia Marvi, a married and issueless girl of Silpura. Fatnu was the grand son of Jharu Pandro (a reference is also made in Case No. 4). He was formerly married, but his wife left him ad went back to her parents at Khursipar quite some time past. Though Fatnu and Dholia belonged to two different clans, viz. Pandro and Marvi, but both these clans are affiliated to the same 7 god phratry. As such they were, according to rules, debarred from marrying each other. So, for the breach of the existing marriage rules, Fatnu and Dholia had to observe all the prescribed rituals. In addition, Fatnu had also to arrange a communal feast for all the panchayat leaders and the villagers. For eloping with Dholia, he had also to pay a fine of Rs. 150 as compensation to her former husband, Sukrat Parteti of Bhainsadaha.

Case No.6: Kamli, a daughter of Barelal Paraste of Silpura, was married to Phulsingh Marvi of Jarga about 16 years ago. Three children, one daughter and two sons, were born to them, the youngest being an infant of about one and a half years. Their married life was happy in the beginning, but trouble started for the last few years. Frequent brawls became a regular feature, and thismarred their family life. Ultimately the wife was driven out of the house by Phulsingh, keeping all the children with him and taking away all her ornaments. Kamli returned to Silpura in May, 1977. Naturally her parents and other members of the house were very much displeased with Phulsingh. Their annoyance further increased when Phulsingh took two women as wives one after another through elopement within a short span of one and a half months, paying due compensation to the aggrieved husbands in respective cases.

The major grievances of Kamli and her kins against Phulsingh were that as she had been forsaken by the husband, she should never have been deprived of the articles given her by her parents during marriage, over which Kamli had legitimate claim. The articles included two brass plates (*tatia*), one metal waterpot (*lota*) and a half-grown bullock (issue of the cow presented to her during marriage which had since been dead). As the ornaments given her by her parents-in-law had been claimed and retained by Phulsingh, so she had the full right over the articles given by her parents. In addition, she had also the right to claim some portion of the cultivable land from Phulsingh for the purpose of her maintenance.

Of her near kins in the family, Gnanlal, her father's brother's son, was considered to be very sensible. He was very firm to fight out the case, and he wanted Kamli to exert her right over her due share. He was so firm that he wanted to move the court if the village councils failed to bring about the desired results.

On June 16, 1977 Gnanlal with a party of two, brother of the *mukaddam* (*patel*) of Silpura and another elderly man of the village, went to Jarga to meet the village elders of that village and to put forth their claim. (The author had the opportunity to accompany the party).

They came to the house of Jamlal Akke, the *mukaddam* of Jarga, where some other village elders including the *diwan* met for discussion. Phulsingh was, at that time, out of the village; instead of him came from his house his old mother and one of the two newly procured wives. In the meeting when the question was raised about Kamli's claim, it was made clear by the village elders of Jarga that the matter under reference was a household affair of Phulsingh. Moreover, it was a fact that nothing came to the notice of the village council in a formal way; Phulsingh never sought the divorce (*chhor-*

chhuti) from Kamli before the village panchayat and there was nothing on record to that effect so that their marriage be declared as void. Hence any claim for maintenance or over the property in question as put forth on the part of Kamli could in no way be accepted. Gnanlal returned with the party; he was thinking of revisiting Jarga to meet Phulsingh and to press their demand before taking any further step in this regard.

21

DHURWA CUSTOMARY LAW AND STATE LAW

K. N. THUSU

By customary law is meant the body of traditional and normative rules which maintain the social order in a particular (tribal) group and regulate the continuity of its culture. Owing, however, to the social changes taking place in a society, the infractions of these rules may also take place from time to time.

Admittedly, all the major criminal offences, whether committed by the Dhurwa or others, are dealt with at present by the police and the courts of law. Quite apart from such offences, we find that while the social and religious life of the Dhurwa is mainly regulated by their tribal councils, without, in the least, being interfered with by the prevailing state laws in force, it is in their economic life that the workings of the state laws (e.g. in the form of Land Revenue Code) is having a direct effect, often of a disturbing nature, on their long-cherished customary laws. For a proper understanding of this situation, it is desirable to give a brief outline of their socio-cultural life.

Mention may, in the first instance, be made of the fact that it was on different occasions (that is, previously, from 1958-60, with breaks, and, then, in March-April, 1977) that the basic data on the socio-cultural life of the Dhurwa, with particular reference to their customary laws, were collected by me, primarily, from their traditional habitat in the area of their maximum concentration, viz. the village of Marenga and its surrounding villages. For comparative purposes, due inquiries were also made from other areas of the Dhurwa habitat in Bastar district.

The Dhurwa, who were previously known as Parja, occupy the central-eastern portion of Bastar district of Madhya Pradesh. The number of persons returned as Dhurwa, as recorded in the 1961 Census, is 36,599. They speak the Parji language, which is linguistically, an independent member of the Dravidian family, but those living in the northern portions of their habitat have adopted Bhatri/Halbi as their mother tongue. They generally assign a "higher" rank to such (Hindu) castes as Brahmin, Dhakar (or Chatri), Halba, Kallar, Kumhar, Rawat and Sundi as well as the Bhatra (tribe); but while Raja Muria (tribe) is regarded as their "equal", Maria and Maria-Lohara (tribes), along with Mahara and Ghasia (caste groups) are given a "lower" position.

Agriculture Main Occupation

Agriculture forms the main occupation of the Dhurwa — those owning land as tenure holders treat their close agnates as co-sharers. They are patrilineal in descent and patrilocal in residence. Their basic social groupings consist of various levels of segmentation — the relationship at all these levels being characterised by agnatic brotherhood. Thus, in Marenga village (which lies 35 miles south of the district town of Jagdalpur and contains 125 Dhurwa households out of 164 households of the village), a number of founding (minimal) lineages are grouped together under a single segment, which is combined with other (localised) segments, forming thereby the main lineage group of the village, which in its turn remains connected with a particular stretch of territory covering four neighbouring (Dhurwa) villages, hence, following Bailey (1960, p 47), it may be termed the "territorial" clan.

No Centralised Authority

The Dhurwa lack a centralised authority to regulate their life. Instead, they possess what may be referred to as traditional tribal council (locally termed panchayat), which exercises social control over the Dhurwa living in certain specified villages. Such a council meant for the Dhurwa of Marenga and its (three) adjacent villages is headed by the *cetia* or *naik* (of Tongpal). Thus, those who essentially recognise the authority of the *cetia/naik* of Tongpal belong to the territorial clan covering the four (Dhurwa) neighbouring villages. In other areas of the Dhurwa habitat, too, there exist such areal councils, but their headmen are known as *bat-nail*. In any case, the office of the *cetia/ naik/bat-naik* is hereditary passing generally from father to the eldest son. His mainly function is to sprinkle the holy water on the ex-communicated person who is required to be re-admitted to their fold.

It may, however, be noted that the deliberations regarding breaches of the serious social rules are always held in the tribal council, being attended by the elderly Dhurwa males of the concerned villages, of course, in the presence of the *cetia/naik*, who never acts alone. For that matter, their tribal council has neither a standing body nor does its membership remain fixed. The *cetia* also does not directly select the elders for the meetings.

The main function of a tribal council (at present) is to take cognizance of the breaches of the following social offences:

(a) Ploughing by Dhurwa womenfolk;
(b) Acceptance of cooked food from persons belonging to the "lower" ethnic groups;
(c) Entering into wedlock with a non-Dhurwa woman.
(d) Incestuous marriages between such agnates as belong to any segment which is included within the territorial clan of the area under study.
(e) When a Dhurwa man or woman is released from prison where he/she was sentenced for having committed murder, etc.

The violations of the above rules require expiatory ceremonies to be performed by the *cetia/naik*, and entail great expenditure for providing communal feast (with pigs, chicken and drinks) to the assembled members of the tribal council and the *cetia*. In addition, the Dhurwa inhabitants of Marenga and its adjacent (three) villages, also, take cognizance of the breaches of below-mentioned rules, requiring, however, merely the imposition of nominal fines:

(f) Eating new crops or fruits without performing, first of all, the rituals in the common shrine which is associated with the territorial clan;
(g) constructing a house or a part thereof, or performing a marriage ceremony, during the period when the ceremonial sowing of the consecrated rice-seeds is being celebrated, jointly, by the Dhurwa belonging to the aforesaid territorial clan;
(h) Holding the fair-festival of Mandai/Bazar in any of the four constituent villages comprised under the territorial clan, ear-

lier than the celebration that takes place annually in Hamirgarh, for the Pargana(of Hamirgarh) as a whole.

Apart from the tribal (areal) council of the above description, yet another panchayat is at work at the level of the village, which is participated by the elderly males drawn from the Dhurwa and other ethnic groups living in the village under study. Its composition varies from time to time, while its functions relate largely to matters affecting law and order in the village, specifically to settle the terms of compensation demanded by an aggrieved husband whose wife has eloped with a man living in that particular village; to persuade the concerned parties to come to an amicable settlement whenever any quarrel arises between them; to decide about the amount and rate of subscription for celebrating a joint festival or ceremony or to meet the Govt. demands for taxes, labour, etc.

Customary Law Supreme

The Dhurwa in the area of our study, as also elsewhere, have been left practically undisturbed by the state laws insofar as their social and religious life is concerned; even the minor, petty cases of quarrels, etc, are allowed to be settled by them, collectively, at the village level. The result is that it is mainly through their tribal (areal) councils that social control is enforced among them — according to their customary laws, without being affected in the least by the prevailing state laws in any form. Those found guilty by their councils, too, accept the punishment, and undergo the necessary expiatory ceremonies, for otherwise social boycott would follow.

In contrast to the above situation, we find that state laws are enforced on such economic matters as pertain to ownership of landholdings in the concerned villages. Thus, according to the Land Revenue Code, the ownership of the respective land holdings, with all its concomitant effects, is recognised and declared in the relevant revenue records, year after year, and, as such, it is vested among the various Dhurwa and non-Dhurwa tenure-holders. On the basis of the entries made in the respective revenue records of 1954-55 and 1967-68, and corroborated by the relevant local inquiries made in this respect, I have discussed elsewhere (1977), how the changes in the ownership of agricultural lands in the village of Marenga have occurred, due to inheritance and otherwise, during the last few generations.

It has been shown there that the system of land control (among the Dhurwa) was traditionally exercised by their main descent group and/or their constituent lineage group, but, at present, the growing demand for land among them is met by their keen efforts to secure the individually owned separate proprietorship of village land, exclusively, in their favour. And, further, the landed property passed on to the eldest son of the deceased, is acquired by him (and accordingly entered and declared in the revenue records), in an undivided, compact form, without any partition taking place, but with the surviving close agnates treated and recognised by him as his co-sharers (*shamil kashtkar*).

According to the well-established customary law among the Dhurwa of Bastar, a daughter is strictly excluded from inheriting the landed property of her deceased father. But, the recent official entry in the revenue records (pertaining to the period 1976-77) shows that a married daughter of the deceased Dhurwa has been declared as the tenure holder of the land measuring 12.59 acres in the village under reference. It is a fact that the Noutak-affiliated Cheetu (since deceased, whose wife had pre-deceased him) had only one child, Mitki by name, who has been duly married to a Dhurwa belonging to the adjacent village and is residing there with her husband since her marriage.

It may be added that during the life-time of Cheetu, his step-brother, Kola by name, was recognised and declared as his co-sharer, and, so, on the demise of Cheetu and Kola, it should have been one of the surviving sons of Kola, if not his eldest son who was reported to be living then in a distant village, who should have been recorded as the tenure holder of the land in question. When the Dhurwa villagers of Marenga learnt about this official entry in the *patwari*'s records, they expressed their resentment for, according to them, no married daughter could be recognised as the owner of agricultural land, even if she be the only child of her father.

No Land for Married Daughters

On making further inquiries in this connection, it was gathered from a well-informed Dhurwa of another village (who is a retired Revenue Inspector) that in his particular lineage group, there were three cases where the married daughters were granted agricultural land for cultivation purposes; but in no case was the land put permanently in their possession, only the same was to be cultivated by them and its produce was meant for their consumption for their life-time only. The reasons as to why married daughters are not given any land is (as explained by him) that, otherwise, disputes were sure to arise between the married daughters (and their issue) and their brothers (and their issue).

This version was corroborated by the Dhurwa informants living in the hamlets of Jabalpur town, who maintained that (after the marriage of the girl), she is welcome to visit her natal family, and in case of death of her husband or in case her marriage is dissolved, she may return, if she so desires, to her parent's/brother's house, which remains open to her. But in case she gets landed property on the death of her father, then the door of her brother's house would remain closed to her.

In view of the strong feelings of resentment expressed by the Dhurwa villagers of Marenga (any by others, too), it is interesting to know as to why no appropriate action has so far been taken by them, insofar as the mutation of land in favour of a married daughter is concerned. It is obvious that the concerned entry was made in the relevant revenue records when the long due regular settlement operations in the area under reference took place some years ago, and the concerned revenue officials were led to believe, for reasons of their own, that justice demanded that the only daughter of the deceased Dhurwa should be declared and recorded as the tenure holder of the agricultural land in question.

The present position with regard to the case cited above is that, in conformity with the local practices in vogue, it is actually under cultivation by the surviving sons of Kola and others, who contribute towards the payment of land revenue and other cesses (through the *patel* of the village), although the same is officially declared in the name of Mitki as per the workings of the state laws exercised through the revenue officials. Now that the Dhurwa inhabitants of the village under study have come to know the real (legal) state of affairs, two courses appear to be open to them : (a) to accept the official declaration as final and binding, (b) to make some efforts to get it annulled by making representation. As things stand at present, neither their traditional tribal council, nor their village-council is interested to take any concrete steps to set right the official entry in the revenue records, even though it goes very much against their customary laws, perhaps because it is realised by them, in the ultimate analysis, that it is the working of the state laws that prevail, whenever there is a clash or conflict with their customary laws in such matters of economic concern as ownership of land holdings.

Reference may be made in this context the fact that while the ownership of agricultural land is declared in the revenue records as being vested in his individual capacity, by customary usages, he is granted the right and privilege of distributing different plots of his agricultural land to his close agnates (who, too, are often recognised as the co-sharers in the official records). It may be remarked that howsoever dissatisfied these co-sharers may be with the specific portions allotted to them in the (otherwise common) land holdings, they do not openly demand their partition for their shares, neither do they approach the village/tribal councils to come to their rescue in this regard. Of course, it is asserted by the respective tenure holders that the distribution of land holdings is based on the criteria of the relative size of the concerned families of the co-sharers and other such considerations as the needs of the situation are taken into account by them, while distributing (unequally though) the portions of the land holdings among their co-sharers; but, it is clear that they reserve, for their own use, the largest share in the best available land.

It may be added that some co-sharers have been recently allotted specific plots of land from the unoccupied government land, with the consequence that they have been shown as the independent owners of the individual land holdings, but, simultaneously, they are recognised and (officially) recorded as the co-sharers of the (otherwise commonly held) land holdings. It has also been noted that during the last 2-3 years, some Dhurwa tenure holders of Marenga village, who owned large areas of land in their individual names, have made formal applications to the Revenue authorities, with a specific request to partition their land holdings among their co-sharers in accordance with their mutually agreed arrangements. The result is that the necessary changes have accordingly been made in the concerned revenue records. On making inquiries from them, it was learnt that they had come to know that in view of the Ceiling Land Act, the excess of their land holdings would be taken over from them by the Government, and so it was considered prudent by them to come to terms with such state laws whatever be their customary laws in this respect.

In the light of the above discussion, it may be concluded that it is only in respect of economic matters, specifically relating to the ownership of the land holdings, that State laws are encroaching upon their customary laws. It is, nonetheless, realised by the Dhurwa of Bastar that in such matters, State laws would ultimately prevail howsoever strong their initial feelings of resentment may be.

22

ISOLATION AND CULTURAL IDENTITY — A CASE STUDY OF THE KOLAMS

B. R. GHOSH

The Kolam are one of the least known tribes of India living in Maharashtra and Andhra Pradesh. They are concentrated in Yeotmal district of Maharashtra wherein resided 41,013 souls in 1961, the total Kolam population of Maharashtra is 43,788. In Andhra Pradesh the Kolam are confined to the district of Adilabad only.

Rev. Hislop first excluded the Kolams from the Gonds but later included them. The Kolams and the Gonds do not intermarry, but being neighbours they attend each other's marriages and even accept food from each other's hands. The Kolams and the Gonds dress similarly.

Today the Kolams stay in the villages and do cultivation; till recently they were not settled cultivators. They had their symbiotic relationship with the Gonds who being politically powerful and influential enjoyed the status of a "ruling race". The Gonds were the patrons of the Kolams and Pradhans. The Kolams were employed as priests of some of the important gods of the Gonds and were called "pujari" by the Gonds. Living with the Gonds for long in the some area, Kolams have adopted many Gond customs.

The Kolams, however, speak their own dialect, Kolami, which occupies a position similar to Gondi between Kanarese, Tamil and Telugu. Though conversant with the local dialect of the area in which they live, their own dialect is very much in use even today in their home.

The Kolams construct their houses at some distance from the other multi-ethnic villages. It seems from the pattern of their settlement that they still desire isolation and maintain a separate habitational identity. They are never seen living with the other groups of people. It may generally occur that the Kolam villages may be, at places, very near to the settlement of other communities, but at least they have some distance and their village boundary is at least vaguely marked within which they install their deities and celebrate the worships and festivals of the community.

These independent hamlets of Kolams are called *pod*. It is also recognised by others as Kolam *pod*. In Kolami, the term for village is *oor*. For their own reference they add the word *oor* for the full village settlement, but an extension of the village having a spatial identity is called a *pod*.

The Cultural Focus

It is this practice of maintaining a separate habitat by the Kolam's which appears to a large extent responsible for the continuation of their cultural identity on the one hand and backwardness on the other. In fact this separate habitation is part of the cultural focus for the Kolams allowing them to maintain their cultural independence to some extent.

Thus their foremost ritual of festival concerns with the *pod* or rather the boundary of the *pod* by the name Gaon-Bandhani. By means of this festival they emphasise the separateness of the *pod* and demarcate its boundary every year.

Gaon-Bandhani is a festival celebrated every year by the Kolams in their *pods*. This is a gathering of the people to wish one another happy life for the whole year. There is not a fixed date for the celebration of this festival, but it falls after Baishakh puja. They collect contributions for both of the festivals simultaneously and purchase two goats from that collection of money and they are sacrificed to the deity.

The purpose of celebrating this festival is to avoid the entry of the wild animals to their *pods*, protection from supernatural spirits and diseases. It is believed that by celebrating this festival, they will be free from evil spirits, diseases and other destructions.

This festival is officiated by the *bhagat*. If there is no *bhagat* in the *pod*, they call one from another *pod*.

Gaon-Bandhani is celebrated for two days. In the evening of the first day, they worship the main deity of the *pod* by applying vermilion and sacrificing a goat. This sacrifice is performed by the Naik. This deity is a female deity. A booth of leaves of black berry is erected. This booth looks like a cottage. This deity is generally installed in the middle portion of the pod in the courtyard of the *chawadi*. A fire burns for whole night in front of the deity.

After worshipping the deity and before sunset, the *pod* is tied with mantras (secret incantations) by the *bhagat*. After performing this ceremony, the deity is propitiated. Then they go to the north-east direction where *pettachiyam* deity has its shrine. They keep there a reversed plough. The deity and plough are worshipped traditionally by applying vermilion, turmeric, etc. Here is installed a post of three stones and inside that a cock or chicken is placed. The *bhagat* goes there with a spear and marking a line proceeds towards the west. The Kolams follow him from inside of the *pod.*

The Kolams beat the drums and some persons play on flutes. Then the *bhagat* is possessed by the deity and in a trance visits the corner stones of the *pod*. The people assemble there to dance and sing. Now they become free from all types of supernatural spirits, because the *pod* becomes a preserved area secured by the secret incantations.

The Kolams never go outside during this Gaon-Bandhani celebration. If anyone is left outside, he enters through the east gate. But, it is not observed that any Kolam remains outside of the *pod* during this festival. The entry of the outsiders is strictly prohibited in their area during this festival and if any body enters he is penalised according to their custom. They permit outsiders if permission is sought from the *naik* to observe the festival.

Today, the trespassers are tied to the trunk of trees, and are released only when they pay the amount of the fine. It also happens that the people, who did not accept their fault, were released after worship on the next day.

Sometimes, it happens that the people living in the neighbouring villages do not remember the day of celebration of Gaon-Bandhani and they enter the *pod* after the start of the festival. They are fined from Rs. 5 to 10 and are left free after the payment. It does not mean that the Kolams are cruel. They have good relations with Patils and Kunbis, but they do not tolerate any infiltration during their Gaon-Bandhani celebration.

Once a truck driver took his truck from the side of the *pod.* He was stopped and when one of the labourers paid them Rs. 10 they became happy and danced there.

But the Kolams are not accustomed to this big money, they only ask for Rs. 2 or Rs. 3. If it is impossible, then a lesser amount or a coconut and vermilion is charged. Once a cartman touched their territory. He was caught by the Kolams. The cartman was not having a single paisa to pay them, then he was asked to offer his cap. He did the same and got free.

After the completion of the celebration, the Kolams take their food and again gather at *chawdi.* They dance and sing for the whole night. The women, children and persons of all ages participate in it. Some men disguise as women and dance. Drums, flutes and other instruments are played. They shout, vigorously wave hands and legs to-and-fro and whistle. This celebration is most enjoyful, when it is celebrated after the rains start. They are very fond of dancing in showers. If there are no rains, they throw water and dance in mud.

They hope that nobody will sleep at night. If anyone sleeps, he is awakened by sprinkling water and mud on him. They sing songs. The English translation of one such song is as follows :

> "Mahur Devi why did you come, did not come we worship you after 12 months. The women and children of the *pod* assemble for what? To see only the Gaon-Bandhani festival."

In the early morning, the *bhagat* is again possessed by the god. He holds a whip and knocks at every door of the pod by saying "Bhutai do. Vaghai do" by whipping his hand. A few persons surround the *bhagat* to control him. He is provided with chicken, etc. The *bhagat* is assisted by a pseudo-*bhagat* who asks for leaves from the people. The collection is offered to the main deity. The goat and chickens are dressed and cut into pieces. The mutton is fried and the dance is continued. The persons are given mutton pieces and water, which is known as *tirthiprasad*. It is performed by *ghattaya*.

In the morning, the celebration is completed. The booth is unrooted. The place of the deity is besmeared with mud. A maiden of 7-8 years worships the *bhagat* and 2-4 children are also seated there. Th water is poured on the deity. Then they proceed towards east. It is led by the *naik*. The *bhagat* lies on the gate where the bunting of mango-leaves are hung. He is worshipped before crossing the boundary and hunting is cut by a knife. Then the people cross the *bhagat* and go out. After their passing, the *bhagat* stands and follows them, and only after this, the people become free to go outside of the *pod*.

The group of people led by the *naik* goes to a certain place with

Devi at a distance of 1-2 kms. and she is put down, the people throw the wooden swords, jingles, etc., there and worship the Mahasaba deity. To free the *bhagat* from the possession of the deity, an egg is thrown into his mouth and if yet not released, he is thrown on the ground and is freed from possession.

Having thus ritually asserted the spatial entity of the *pod* the Kolams have to arrange its governing, and they have evolved a functional system of control which continues even today partly because of their separate habitat. Today, however, due to the introduction of the statutory panchayat usually one Kolam member is present in the statutory body as well. But Kolam disputes traditionally never reach the statutory panchayat and are usually settled at the level of *pod* itself excepting the welfare activities: it is only nominally that the Kolam *pod* is under the statutory panchayat.

Independent Political Organisation

The Kolams' political organisation is independent and separate from other communities. It has some qualities of its own which are clearly visible when we study the panchayat system of the Kolams.

In every *pod* there is a body which is called panchayat or *panchmandal*. It has got a significant place in a Kolam's life. The Kolams were till recently almost unaware of other judicial bodies. Even today they do not generally go to the police *patel* called *kotwal*. The disputes are solved by the *panchs* in their own panchayat. They do not go to the local courts.

Following are the officials of the panchayat:

Naik : He is the president of the Kolams. He is called *nikun* in the Kolami dialect. He is the headman of the Kolam-pod. He officiates as head in festivals/meetings. Previously, he was entitled to officiate in land disputes among the family members. Still he is powerful and called but not so frequently as the usufructuary right has stopped. The people obey his decisions.

He is accorded respect by the people. The children as well as the women do not stand in front of him. During meetings the women are not supposed to face him. The *naik* leads in many festivals. He takes initiative in the agricultural works.

Mahajan : *Mahajan* is the Vice-President of the Kolam Panchayat. He is called *mahajanyak*. He is shown deference in society and the children do not come in front of him. After the *naik* he seconds the decision. On their new year day, they celebrate a festival called *Phanmori* which is in honour of the *mahajan* and is connected with agriculture.

Karbari : *Karbari* is the secretary of the panchayat. He holds an important place in the panchayat. He raises contributions for the community festivals and keeps the record of the expenditure and collection of the money. Through his work, he is always in good contact with the public.

Ghatya : He is also a key man of the panchayat. He makes the necessary arrangements and calls the Kolams for the meeting. He also goes to the other *pods* to call the people concerned with the case. He is responsible for the absence of the persons in the meetings. The pitchers (*ghat*) which are kept in marriage places are looked after by the *ghatya* and so the name *ghatya*.

The abovementioned officials are the backbone of the judicial body. *Ghatya* is praised for his services. *Naik*, *mahajan* and *karbari* are venerable members of this council. These members take decisions collectively. There is no autocracy. Firstly, decisions are taken by these members, then are put before the public and when approved by the public become final.

The officials of the panchayat also look after the social problems. They make necessary arrangements for different festivals and are assisted by other people, if necessary.

1. *Terama or Bhumak*: *Terama* or *bhumak* is the bailiff. He extends his cooperation for effective implementation of the duties in *pod* matters. He is entitled to collect alms from every house of the *pod*. He is entertained with respect and offered loaf. He prepares the community dinners, arranges tea for the members in the meeting, cleans the *chawdi* utensils, etc. Sometimes women are also assigned this work and then they are known as *dhumkin*.

2. *Deokari or pujari*: He initiates the worship in the community.

3. *Phulkari or daphkari*: The persons who play on flutes are known as *baskari* in Kolami and *phulkari*. The person who plays the *daph* (a musical instrument) is *daphkari*. They play these instruments on festive occasions.

4. *Songadya or betalak* : He is the bhat or bard of the Kolam tribe. He composes poems, and keeps the record of the tribe. He entertains the public, dances and guides them. He also fixes the date of marriage which is the work of the *pujari*.

Panchayat Meeting

The meetings of the Kolam are held in the courtyard of the *chawdi*. The *panch* sit on the platform and other Kolams sit beside them. The Kolams are free to give their opinion on different matters, but they never violate the decision of the *panchmandal*. The details for performing festivals such as the *Gaon-Bandhani, Acari*, etc., are decided in these meetings.

Justice

The Kolam do not quarrel. They do not like even to visit the nearby villages due to fear. They are afraid of outside. They rarely fight with their community brethren.

The persons who commit any offence are fined or excommunicated from the group. At Dhoti in Yeotmal district, a Kolam boy and girl left the *pod* and spent some days together. When they came to the *pod* they were fined Rs. 50 each and were fastened tightly with rope to a pole and were lashed. In these matters, the Kolam panchayat is very action.

The women who give birth to children in their maidenhood are punished. The Kolam women are also kept as concubines by Moslems due to their poverty. But the Kolam panchayat is not silent on these matters and takes rigorous steps.

Prohibited Words

Even mention of shoe-or chappal-beating has its severe consequences. Persons uttering these words are kept at a distance. It is known as *vithal*.

The person, who falls under *vithal* stops in the outskirts of the *pod* and makes it known to the villagers in a loud voice. The men and women go there and worship the boundary by turmeric, water, etc., in a traditional way. Then the man enters the *pod*. He arranges for *posta* (see below) and then is admitted into the group. If any Kolam is abused by his master (farm master), he comes under *vital* and he leaves the job. The same ritual is observed in this case also as has been described in chappal-beating.

Posta : The accused man brings jaggery. The god is washed with jaggery and water which is distributed in the public. It is known as *posta*. The persons who are excommunicated from the groups can not smoke with others, are not allowed to take water from the well and are sometimes abused and beaten.

A person who is excommunicated can be readmitted to the group by the following process. He is asked to go to the river, wash his head with water. His beard and moustache are shaved and is "burnt" in the fire and then someone cries that "he is pure and not polluted". He drinks the water after washing the feet of the elders. The women are also purified in the same way.

Dog-cat Killing Prohibited

To kill a dog or cat is strictly prohibited among the Kolams. If a person kills a dog or cat he is excommunicated and is admitted when he observes the above ritual.

The Kolams are afraid of going to courts. They teach their children that it is not good to go to court. It is better to follow the judgement of the panchayat. The Kolams have faith in their community elders. They are honest and peace-loving people. They do not lock their houses.

The Kolams have an understanding for different types of guilt. Theft is regarded as an ordinary guilt while adultery or any guilt concerning women is a major one. In cases of theft, they are fined Rs. 5 to Rs. 20. Mostly the cases of theft are concerned with stealing of cotton from the fields. The persons who do not pay the amount of the fine are excommunicated.

Marriage by elopement is a serious offence. Keeping concubine is not allowed. In these severe offences, cases are decided by the Panchayat of 3-4 *pods*, if they are involved.

Formation of Panchayat

The Kolam panchayat is not a permanent body.

On the day of *Mandows*' i.e. the Kolam new year day, all the Kolams gather at the *chawdi* and review the activities of the panchayat. Anybody has the right to criticise the working of a particular office-bearer, who has to justify his action. They do not follow the present legal philosophy of "innocent till proven guilty". If there is sufficient backing of the person criticising or if the criticised officials fails to extricate himself he has to step down and a new person is selected/elected.

Such a meeting generally continues till consensus is reached. No actual election has so far taken place. When someone gets elected to a new office, he is installed by the seniormost person of the *pod.*

PART IV

SOUTHERN INDIA

23

TRIBAL CUSTOMARY LAWS IN SOUTHERN INDIA

P. K. MISRA, B R. RIZVI, S. B. CHAKRABORTY

This paper is based on the data collected on the customary laws among seven tribal groups in the southern region. The selection of the tribal groups for the study was arbitrary and based on the convenience of the individual researchers. This paper focuses on dispute settlement among these tribal groups. It examines the disputes which most frequently and persistently crop up and their relationship with society.

Andhra Pradesh is the largest State in the southern region and it also has the largest concentration of tribal groups. Obviously the number of tribal groups selected from Andhra Pradesh for this study was more. The tribal groups selected from each State for the study were as follows : Andhra Pradesh — Koya, Bagata, Yerukula, Sugali; Karnataka — Malai Kudi; Kerala — Kadar; and Tamil Nadu — Irula

First some background of the economy and history of these tribal groups may be given.

The Kadar, the Irula and the Malai Kudi are forest-based. Of these the Kadar are a relatively much smaller group. Their total population is around 1,926 and they are confined to a small area in Palghat and Trichur districts of Kerala State. The Kadar were reported as food gatherers and hunters by Thurston (1909). Coming almost after 35 year Ehrnfels did not find them different. The field work done in 1977 shows that though the bulk of the Kadar population is engaged in the collection of forest produce, good part of that collection is done for the market. A few of them are also engaged as wage-earners. The area the Kadar have lived in is progressively getting exposed through a network of roads. Developmental activities have been undertaken and there is general extension of economic interests of different groups in the area. The size of the forest has dwindled and at the same time there is much less to collect and hunt in the forest.

The Malai Kudi is relatively a bigger group. Their population is about 7,000, and they are found in the forest areas of the districts of South Kanara of Karnataka. The Malai Kudi practised shifting cultivation and also raised cardamom but gradually the area they were dependent on passed into the hands of outsiders who changed the economy of the region from subsistence collection of cardamom and other forest produces to massive exploitation of timber and capital-intensive farming. In this process most of the Malai Kudi became labourers, earning daily wages. A few of them are employed by the Government.

The Irula is a much bigger group having a population of about 89,000. They are spread over several districts of Tamilnadu but their concentration is in the forest areas of Coimbatore district of Tamilnadu.

Their larger population and spread in several districts of Tamilnadu themselves suggest that this group is different from the other smaller groups like Kadar or Malai Kudi. There are stories which suggest that Irula were a widespread group and they were rulers. Unfortunately a systematic study of their history, though very much required, has not been undertaken. They mostly live in the forest areas, which are now fully exposed. Most of them have forest lands to cultivate but they also work as labourers in the forests as well as in the fields of other farmers.

Historically the Bagata are a known group who have been interacting with the peasantry. Their population is 71,657, and they are concentrated in Vishakhapatnam, one of the most populous tribal districts of Andhra Pradesh. In the plains the Bagata live in villages which are inhabited by other tribal groups too, with whom they have complementary roles. The Bagata consider themselves a superior group and claim the highest rank in the local hierarchy. They are landowners and agriculturists. They are a dominant group in the region.

In the erstwhile feudal estate of Jeypore, the Bagata were one of the functionaries. The system was called *muttadari* where groups of villages called *mutta* were entrusted to influential individuals called muttadars, for management, maintenance of law and order and collection of revenue. *Muttadars* used to have a number of functionaries.

One of the functionaries was *pettandars* whose job was to collect revenue. This post was hereditary and was invariably held by the Bagata.

The Koya are a large group and extensively distributed in the belt adjoining Andhra Pradesh, Madhya Pradesh and Orissa. In Bastar district they are also known as Dorla. Their population is around 28,85,226 in Andhra Pradesh. They live in multi-ethnic villages. They were settled agriculturists but nowadays most of them work as labourers. They also make baskets. The Koya women too go out for work. The Koya land is now exposed, so to say. There is considerable infiltration of outside population in the area.

The Sugali are known by several names. They are widely spread out in different parts of Andhra Pradesh and Karnataka. It is well known that they were a nomadic group and at one time they were transporting goods particularly grains and salt and supplying them to different parts of the country. Gradually they lost their occupation and settled down at various places. To some extent they have adopted the language and culture of the regions they have settled in. They mostly depend upon agriculture and labour. Their labour force is often seen repairing roads, etc. Though they live in multicaste villages their settlements are separate and they have retained their cultural exclusiveness.

The Yerukula are known by several names like Koracha, Korava, etc. They were a nomadic population and like many other nomadic groups they are also gradually settling down. They are experts in making baskets and ropes, but they engage themselves in several other occupations. Those who have been able to acquire land do agriculture, others combine their crafts with trade, fortune-telling and labour. The "popular" belief is that the Yerukula are "congenital thieves". Generally, even now police keep a watch on them.

The sample of these tribes presents a fairly good range of variation. The Kadar is the smallest group, they have shown a remarkable resilience and in spite of tremendous changes in their neighbourhood and market forces reaching out to them, they try to stick to the food-gathering economy. The Malai Kudi were ejected out of their forest and were converted into wage-labourers, which means they have to depend on outsiders for their survival. The Irula, comparatively a large group, with a historical belief that they were once the rulers, are now fully oriented to peasant economy but live near about forests. In this respect the Bagata and Koya are different. They are like any other peasants, the main difference, however, being that the Bagata occupy the position of a dominant group in their region and the Koya are the dominated and exploited group in their own region. The Sugali and Yerukula present entirely a different picture. They were nomads, while the former were traders of some repute the latter did all kinds of residual occupations in order to subsist. Sugali lost their occupation, once the network of roads and mechanised transport came into being. They settled down in the peasant villages taking to agriculture or working for wages. They, however, remained an exclusive group. The Yerukula still continue to do residual jobs along with their craft but for some it is essential that they become bonded labour to earn their livelihood. One of the essential points to be noted in the case of the Sugali and Yerukula is that they interact with the Hindu peasantry in many ways and yet retain their exclusiveness a central feature of the Indian caste system. Economically they are dependent, in spite of the fact that the Yerukula are skilful.

This background would suggest that the Kadar, Irula and Malai Kudi operate in a dual legal system, one recognised by their own group and the other which is sanctioned by the State. But in the case of the Bagata, Koya, Sugali and Yerukula, they have to participate in a three-tier legal system, namely, their own, the norms laid down by the dominant group and the norms of the State. In our sample the Bagata themselves happen to be a dominant group but that position itself makes them party to a traditional multi-group social system.

Law and Society

We need not go into the controversy as to what law is. The studies conducted so far suggest amply illustrate that anthropological studies of law do not form a single systematic body of data and concepts. However, the prime concern in the general field of anthropology of law is the study of processes, and in particular the processes of dispute settlement. If this be our major focus, then the most productive unit of study particularly in the societies where the law is not codified will be empirical disputes. In fact even in the literate societies where full documentation of formal laws and rulings are available, the most productive unit of study will be to follow the disputes, if the idea is to find out how the cases are actually decided. No case is decided in social or cultural vacuum; hence the study of disputes will reveal how the levers in society are actually operated.

In this paper it will not be possible to go into the actual cases of dispute among the different tribes and make a comparative analysis. Instead we will indicate what are the issues which frequently cause friction and then I make an attempt to give their interpretation. Before we go into this it will be worth knowing the institutions that exist to settle disputes among the different tribes under discussion here.

Dispute Settling Institutions

The Kadar do not have any formal organisation to process the disputes and settle them. They seem to have a headman but his role in society is somewhat hazy and in any case he does not have any authority to settle disputes. It appears the king of Cochin used to confer the title of *mooppan* (headman) to some Kadar men. This was apparently done to have some kind of a link person in the jungle areas. Interestingly enough, after this kingdom of Cochin was abolished, the forest department restarted this practise and they gave recognition to some Kadar as *mooppan* in order to have a link with the tribe as such. The Kadar settle their disputes in a simple and direct manner. As already indicated they do not have any mediators, the disputes are resolved by direct negotiation, arguments and fights, failing which one of the parties withdraws from the actual scene of conflict. Thus, the physical distance between the disputants is used to resolve the issue. This is perhaps one of the major reasons for the fluidity of the membership of their settlements. The Kadar in this respect are so much similar to the food gathering groups reported from different parts of the country. The Jenu Kuruba in Karnataka also resolve their disputes by the process of withdrawal from the actual scene of conflict. But it is being increasingly noticed that they are left with little room to withdraw. This situation is bound to create more tension in their society unless they find some other procedure to settle their disputes (Misra, 1969). Haimendorf has discussed "settlement of disputes by avoidance" in some detail comparing Chenchu, Onge, Great Andamanese, and Sermang of Malaya (Furer-Haimendorf, 1967).

The Irula have a formal institution to settle disputes. Besides the headman it has other functionaries. It appears that while their council has a right to adjudicate, its power to enforce its decision is greatly limited or has dwindled. Now when they are unable to settle their disputes they want forest guards to intervene and decide them. It is another matter that the forest guards have some vested interest in mediating into the affairs of the Irula or even encouraging them to seek their mediation.

The Malai Kudi seemed to have had a council of elders called panchayati and the institution of headman which was started by the Hebbars, the then rulers of the region. They were interested in the collection of wild cardamom. The collection work was done by the Malai Kudi. In order to have a better control over the entire community, the rulers used to bestow the title of headman on some of the Malai Kudi and also presented gold bangles to them. Later, the Hebbars lost control over the area and it got distributed among several owners who exploited the area for extracting timber and later for plantation. It is reported that in the process, the headman and the council of elders lost much of their authority. It seems probable that even when this institution was functioning in its pristine glory much of its authority was derived from the power of the then rulers. To-day the council of the elders has no authority to impose its decision, it cannot even reprimand or persuade people to accept its adjudication. It often invites the local strongmen to intervene and adjudicate on their behalf.

The Koya have an elaborate organisation called *kulam* panchayat to process disputes. They have councils at hamlet, village and regional levels. Each level has its head and other functionaries. The position of the head is hereditary. The authority of the *kulam* panchayat is greatly eroded because of factional fights, violations of various norms by the powerful in the community, challenge from outside which the members of the community face particularly when their women get more attracted by hard-working men of better economic status than men of their own community who are relatively easy going and are fond of liquor and existence of the outside legal system.

The Bagata, the dominant group in their region, have a hierarchy of councils to process their disputes both among themselves, and also with other groups. Their system of adjudication is called *guruvu* and the leader is known as *pedda guruvu.* Along with these institutions, the statutory panchayat also exists in Bagata villages. In the interior villages the Bagata rule supreme and, therefore, they are easily able to dominate the statutory panchayat also but in more exposed villages of each council is more or less demarcated. The local level council is entrusted with the role to protect the purity and high status of the members of the tribe. The councils at higher levels are more concerned with the issues of compensation, divorce and property. The councils are empowered to impose fines, punish or excommunicate the guilty. The guilty are not only required to abide by the decisions of these councils but are also expected to undergo expiation and purificatory ceremonies and thereafter offer a feast to the members of the community. The existence of the powerful forces outside is making a dent on the *guruvu* system. Factionalism has undermined its authority. Some of the educated tend to advocate that the *guruvu* system serves no other purpose but the vested interest of the leader.

Every Sugali *tanda* has its chief called *naik*, and has a council called *gor* panchayat. The post of the *naik* is hereditary. The *gor* panchayat has a number of functionaries. The Sugali clearly distinguish between criminal disputes and property disputes. The criminal disputes are adjudicated by the *gor* panchayat of the *tanda* but if the dispute is between the members of two *tandas,* then adjudication is done by the *gor*-panchayat of another *tanda*. The *gor* panchayat has the authority to impose fine, punish or excommunicate the guilty. The guilty have to bear all the expenses of food and drinks consumed by the members of the council and elders during adjudication. The Sugali are great liquor consumers. Meeting only these expenses could be quite burdensome.

Each Yerukula settlement has a council of its own called *kula* panchayat which adjudicates all disputes arising in it. The members of the *kula* panchayat are the elders of the Yerukula settlement. Each *kula* panchayat has a headman called *berumonushya*. The *kula* panchayat processes all disputes between the members of the Yerukula settlement but any dispute involving Yerukula and non-Yerukula has to be resolved by the village panchayat or through the legal institutions of the State. When the *kula* panchayat is not able to get the truth through negotiation and oral examination, it subjects the accused to various sorts of ordeals to get the truth out which may include such activities as dipping fingers in boiling oil, lifting of a red hot crowbar etc. They believe that an innocent person will not be harmed whereas the guilty would get hurt and thus exposed. When the *kula* panchayat yet has the authority to impose fine, punishment and excommunicate the guilty. The guilty has to expiate himself and undergo purificatory ceremonies and also give feast to the members of the community. Factionalism within the community undermines the authority of the *kula* panchayat and also of the headman. Nowadays the *kula* panchayat cannot openly conduct ordeals, as that is against the law of the State. Some of the powerful members of the community have resisted the idea of conducting ordeals and threatened that they would take the help of police.

Discussion

The disputes and the mechanism through which the same are resolved occur neither in cultural vacuum nor are static. The issues which are likely to cause disagreement leading to disputes differ from one society to another depending upon how far the interests of the community are diversified. Diversification of interest is itself connected with the historical development of the community and general development of the economy of the region. The issues arising out of this cannot be discussed here. The diversification of interest will enlarge the range of relationship and determine its quality. Thus the more the diversification the more are the chances of conflicts and disagreements.

One of the common causes of conflict in all the groups is the sex relations. Whether a group is in food-gathering stage or is involved in a sophisticated production system it has to regulate the relationship between the sexes. Regulation is necessary because each time a socially unacceptable sex relation is established between a man and a woman, somebody's rights have been infringed, interfered with or denied, in relation to some body else in a cultural context. As a result of this some shuffling of social relations, adjustment of mutual loyalties, obligations, rights, and establishment of new reciprocal ties are bound to take place. These relations have a cultural and economic value. These values and the expected violations determine the norms in a particular society. The machinery to regulate the norms also develops in the context of society. One may hypothesise that the higher the values of relationships the more elaborate will be the norms and the more frequent will be their violations. Machinery to regulate the norms will grow out of the elaboration, which may emerge as a force by itself. It may be expected that the consequence of this process will be the rise of mediators who are likely to develop vested interests in the prolongation of disputes and institutionalising the process. So the sex relations are not only primary but are of great importance.

The Kadar do recognise the rights on ranges and right of extraction of forest produce from such ranges. These may cause some disagreement but most of these are resolved by direct negotiation between the concerned parties, or withdrawal from the scene of conflict. But the most recurring cause of friction is due to sex relations. Most of the sex relations are established by mutual attractions which suggest that there is equality of sexes. Apart from biological differences there is not much of role differences between sexes, in this society, in other words no special value is attached to one sex. Ripple action which follows sex relations concerns only those with whom the couple has direct relations. It has the potentiality to disturb the harmony of the group. Elopement of a couple to a supposedly unknown place is sine qua non. Elopement is in reference to the group and therefore by definition temporary. The elopement announces the new relationship between the couple and gives time to other members of the group to rearrange their ties and come to terms with the disturbance. The Kadar have small range interests in all aspects of life. Their range of relationship is accordingly limited.They have use-value of the commodities though cash economy has started penetrating among them. The mating prescriptions are a few. The disagreement if any is to be resolved directly failing which they physically avoid the conflicting situation. There is no scope of reaching solutions via mediators. There is no economic evaluation of the social relations.

The Malai Kudia have a different history. They have been more severely exploited. The cash economy has fully penetrated among them, diversifying their interest and thereby the range of their relationship is relatively larger. As expected the Malai Kudia do not recognise mating based on mutual attractions and direct negotiation between the concerned parties. The mating partners are to be selected by the mediators which may be parents and relatives. There are clear mating proscriptions and prescriptions. There is a clear notion that a girl goes from her father's side to her husband, which means equality of sexes is not recognised. The girl-losing side has to be compensated by an amount of money and in kind previously agreed upon by the negotiating parties. This process is set in motion by celebrating the attainment of puberty by girls which is an announcement that the girl has attained social adulthood.

Elaborate norms presuppose disputes. As expected the disputes relate to the negotiation of marriage, pre-marital and extra-marital sex relations, sex relations with outsiders, and disagreement between husband and wife. All these emanate from the central issue that the girls have a value which is different from that of boys, and this value can be paid in cash and kind. From this a number of formulations can be generated such as a more desirable girl will be more sought after than others, which may mean some stratification on the basis of those who have more desirable women and those who have not. A distinction is also bound to occur between those who can easily pay and those who cannot, and have to offer their labour to pay the amount which means a distinction is bound to develop between those who offer labour and those who can hire that labour. All this has the potentialities of causing friction in society. As they rule out the direct negotiation to resolve the disputes in the first place, they cannot have it at a more complicated stage.They have a body to adjudicate but adjudicating authority is unable to enforce its decision, the major cause of which is that the Malai Kudia are dispossessed people. Their land and resources have been acquired by outsiders and all of them have become equally dependent, the middlemen and others, upon the wages they earn. The middlemen being in the same economic level as others, being equally dependent and having not generated any populist movement on any commonly felt issue they have no power to enforce the decisions of the group. Though perfunctorily the disputes are taken to the council, nothing much happens there and it is not expected either. The local non-Malai Kudia landlords and plantation owners do interfere in the disputes of the tribes but obviously their interests are different which we need not discuss here. The Koya are almost in the same position as the Malai Kudia though far removed from each other. The disputes relating to sex are almost the same with the difference that the frequency of cases are more. It may be noted that the range of relationship of the Koya is relatively larger than of the Malai Kudia and they have far more elaborate norms and a hierarchy of council functionaries. The adjudication by the councils is openly violated by the people. The society is under crisis and this a crisis is being fully exploited by the outsiders. The Koya have a very high percentage of broken families. Like Malai Kudi, the Koya too are a dispossessed people and their main source of livelihood is labour. Their economy is totally interfered with and exploited and all of them stand at the same economic level. This position gets itself repeated among the Irula in Tamilnadu.

The Bagata present a variation to this model. They live in multi-tribal settlements. Their interests are much diversified than any of the groups discussed so far. Their range of interaction is far wider, penetrating into the political arena. They represent a typical case illustrating Martin Oraon's concept of a tribe in search of a great tradition undergoing the pangs of emulation-solidarity conflict.

The sexual relations are controlled by the Bagata by having elaborate mating proscriptions and prescriptions. They announce the attainment of social adulthood of girls by celebrating puberty ceremonies. The women have a price and it is much higher than among other groups. Bagata are not a dependent group. They are producers and dominate the local region. The women are the potential source of contamination and may affect their claim or aspiration for high and pure status and hence are to be protected. In the process the women lose their freedom completely and become objects for attainment of power by the vested interests.

There is a significant change in the nature of the cases which come up for adjudication among them. There is hardly a dispute which infringes their own sex conduct. How could it be? The tribe does not intend to "fall" from the high pedestal it is wanting to reach. So if there is any dispute involving infringement of sex norms of the community by its members, which must be there, it is to be suppressed, and prohibited from coming into the open and hence has to be resolved directly among the disputants. There is some resemblance between the food-gatherers and Bagata peasants in this respect though for entirely different reasons.

The Bagata have even a norm that if an adultery is reported to the council, the guilty should be severely punished leading to excommunication but the one who reported should also be punished. It is a deterrent for people to bring such cases for adjudication. The Bagata are seized of the problem of maintaining the purity status of their people. Since purity is closely associated with status, that, is higher status people are more pure than the lower status people, the Bagata do not allow sex relations with the people belonging to the lower groups. Such cases are a cognizable offence and are frequently brought for adjudication. The guilty are not only punished but have to undergo expiation and purificatory ceremonies. The symbols adopted for purification are significant. The same cannot be discussed here but may suffice to mention that gold and silver tongue cleaners are made red hot and the tongues of the guilty are touched by them.

There are many factors responsible for the adjudicating body to enforce its decision but the most important is that the community has been made conscious of its high status and that it should rise still higher. This has not only brought in the Hindu puritanical ideas into the community but also the Hindu gods and goddesses and the rituals.

The Yerukula and Sugali live in a caste society where their status in the total hierarchy is fixed. Both the groups are economically dependent, but culturally exclusive. Their exclusiveness is slightly more pronounced because of their nomadic traditions. They have a diversified interest and therefore their range of interaction is also wide. They do get involved in various kinds of disputes of which property and theft issues are fairly well pronounced.

The Yerukula and Sugali have elaborate mating proscription and prescriptions. The women have a price and in their case we get the logical extension that a man can keep as many wives as he can afford to. The Yerukula and Sugali are conscious of their status, they do not prohibit an open discussion of the dispute arising out of sex relations. In fact such discussions and the decisions on them give strength to the adjudicators. Each case brought before the council for adjudication is accompanied by much feasting and drinking by the adjudicators on behalf of the would-be guilty. The adjudicators develop a vested interest. It pays them and their personal power enormously increases. As each settlement has its own council the system is decentralised enough for the leaders to collide, but this has started happening now.

The Yerukula consider that sexual offences can be adequately compensated. A woman if raped gets compensation in the form of cash, the normalcy is restored once again. It is interesting to note that in such cases while the fine to the *kula* panchayat is paid immediately the compensation to the aggrieved party if cannot be paid immediately can be paid in instalments.

The Yerukula too are caught up in maintaining their status whatever it is. They prohibit sexual relations with the people of lower castes. If discovered, the punishment is fine and excommunication. Readmittance is allowed after expiation, and purificatory ceremony. Among them too, the tongue is touched by hot gold to purify.

Our hypotheses seem to be validated and also the argument that sex relations which appear peripheral encompass the whole society.

Though the modern administration and law have penetrated almost all areas of life, the small men out in the forests and in the fields exercise their own choice as regards sex relations. What they have is apparently residual powers but the same are significant. This even appears to be applicable to men in the industrial society. The high incidence of broken families among the Koya or Malai Kudia is also found in the modern society. There must be some common denominator for the common phenomenon. We have shown that some resemblances exist in the establishment of sexual relations between food-gatherers and peasant tribes aspiring for a high status. This discussion can be further carried with some profit. It may be mentioned in passing that some resemblances are noticed among the food-gatherers and the members of the highly industrialised societies of the West in respect of choosing mating partners directly, and in having minimal norms regarding sex relations and all disputes relating to sex relations are to be individually tackled. Is it the unity of the opposed?

It may be observed that the rigid prescriptive form of cross-cousin marriage and the usual mode of acquiring a wife by capture could not stand before the onslaught of changing world view of society in general and of women in particular. Thus, the inbuilt rules of marriage have helped to increase celibacy and spinsterhood.

The large-scale participation of Koya women in labour activities is not primarily an economic activity making a contribution towards subsistence. It is resorted to because Koya girls are suffering from a feeling of insecurity originated from the Koya laws of inheritance of property. A Koya girl enjoys no right of inheritance of either her parents' or husband's property. She is entitled only to maintenance. The society has evolved a double standard for judging the identity of an unmarried Koya girl and a married Koya woman. In a family the future of one's son's wife is more secured than of one's own daughter whose maintenance is a socio-economic liability for the parents. The son's wife commands more respect than one's own daughter. The latter have become aware of their social disability and are drawing themselves closer to the public sphere of activities. Whatever they earn goes partly as a contribution to the parents in return for their maintenance and the rest goes in the form of savings. The traditional forms of investment of the earnings was building up of capital in the form of ornaments but now some of the Koya girls in Chatti have started saving with the Nagarjuna Grameen Bank. A number of Koya girls have acquired milch cattle with the help of the Grameen Bank and are running a *community dairy farm*. The Integrated Tribal Development Agency provides veterinary assistance to the *dairy farm*.

The sense of insecurity caused by the laws of inheritance of property is gnawing at the sensibilities of the Koya woman for whom marriage and domestic life have lost much of their meaning. Very few Koya widows are being looked after by the parents or the brothers of the deceased husband. The chances of widow remarriage are also very slim. The Koya widows, as said earlier, are not entitled to their husbands' property, hence the only alternative left for them is to stand on their own feet in order to maintain not only themselves but their children as well. A little saving serves as an insurance for bad days ahead since even wage labour opportunities are irregular.

There are clear indications that the Koya institutions of marriage and family are in peril. The average Koya family size stands at the precarious level of 4.42. The rate of irregular unions with non-Koya is on the increase. Also, there is an increasing aversion on the part of the Koya girl to lead a married and domestic life. The customary laws have lost effectiveness because of the increasing penetration of the Indian Penal Code in the Koya customary laws. The mechanism of ethnic boundary maintenance is crumbling fast. The crisis through which the tribe is passing cannot be sumounted unless the Koya woman is assured of security in future life, and the Koya boys compete with the non-Koya petty traders and lorry drivers in order to become attractive enough for the Koya girls. So long as the Koya girls are not protected from the lustful and treacherous luring tactics of the outsiders, the tribe has no future.

The customary laws of the Koya are no longer effective enough to impose any real measure of social control over the tribe in general and over the women in particular. As a result of these developments the social identity of the Koya woman is fast changing. The domestic sphere of their activities is shrinking whereas the sphere of their public activities is getting enlarged. As a result of the enlargement of public activities of the Koya women the traditional authority structure of the tribe is collapsing from familial level to the collective level of the *kulam* panchayat. On one the hand the customary laws are unable to hold the tribe together and on the other the tribe is unable to deal with the intricacies of the modern legal system of the State. The result is confusion. The *kulam* panchayat, as an agency responsible for the maintenance of Koya customary laws, has lost much of its authority and hard-punching social sanctions due to sweeping ecological, cultural and political changes in the region. However, one need not feel pessimistic about the weakening of the Koya customary laws giving rise to changes in the social identity of Koya women. The Koya society might be in for framing another set of customary norms more conducive to the existence and survival of Koya society as Pospisil (1972) feels that the law of preliterate societies is a part of "living law", created and carried on by the members of a society, a social phenomenon that is ever changing because of human action. It is, therefore, . . . a dynamic phenomenon and not a set of petrified or very slowly changing rules whose main role is to maintain the status quo.

We have first examined the pattern of family. It was earlier reported that a sense of permanent residence was absent among the Kadar and membership of the family also looked to be floating, because many people come and join a unit and leave after some time. There was no clear recognition of family or clan in an individual's name. The father seemed to be the head of the unit. While Thurston (1909) recorded the maternal uncle as the chief of a group, Ehrnfels (1952) maintained that he was neither absent nor strong. The basic trend that follows today almost resembles the earlier observations. Of course, there are some emerging patterns also. For example, among the Kadar of the developed area where they have some education and are employed in the forest, they use three names which stand for the Kadar group, their father and the individual concerned. The family unit apparently represents a nuclear type, specially in the Government-built Kadar colony. The notion of authority is attached to the father or any older male member of a family.

In dealing with marriage, Thurston maintained that marriage of boys with paternal relatives was banned and that with maternal uncle's daughter was preferred. Polyandry was indulged in by them Ehrnfels observed marriages with paternal cousins. He formulated that it was a matrilineal trend. It was also observed by him with regard to residence after marriage that more brides went to live in the bridegroom's place. Monogamy was predominant, though polyandry and polygyny also occurred. Brother-sister marriage was never met with. Marriage residence is very important for studying the local group. In the absence of a clan patri- or matrilocal residence he suggested to use virilocal or uxriolocal terms for it.

On the basis of the present observations it seems that these groups are so small and dispersed that they have no choice than to go for endogamous mating. The nature of their settlement and migration does not allow them to live far apart from each other in a settlement. Sometimes some families share the rock shelters together; so it is not always useful to emphasise upon the marriage residence. Even the preference or prohibition of kin marriage does not always occur according to their given statement. A great amount of fluidity pervades such a simple community life. In this way there are probabilities for them to lose track with their close kin. And there is no conscious effort to find out or recognise the kin as an absolute necessity. Multiple marriage for both male and female and frequent divorces were reported. No rigid rule exists for this. The children are sometimes taken care of either by father or mother or by both in succession. So, affection to children is not denied due to emotional attachment of the parents.

In the discussion of inheritance of property and succession to office it was observed by Thurston that sons as well as nephews could inherit and though matriarchal elements were present yet there was lack of direct succession through the female line. There was no firm authority established among them as also no codified inheritance laws. From the present observations also it is noticed that no systematic development has taken place in the case of inheritance of property or succession to office. The smallness of the group, its wandering nature and last possession of material belongings have weakened the development of rules for it. For succession to the office of the *muppan* and the *pujari* idea of patrilineal hereditary selection is reflected in the data. Whether hereditary or not these offices are generally assumed by the male members of the society, and there is no uniform response from them about who are really holding these posts at present. A new factor has emerged regarding the inheritance among the employed Kadar. In this case on the occasion of death of a Kadar employee his wife gets the money following the government rules.

The Kadar kinship system accommodates both father's and mother's relatives in its social structure and social activities. It looks like having a bilateral recognition in the community. This system approximates to the type of bifurcate merging. This also tends to follow the Iroqouis type suggested by Mukherjee (1973) found a general resemblance of these two types mentioned above among some matrilineal South Indian tribes.

The earlier reports, though not in detail, hinted that relatives from both father's and mother's sides used to participate in all social ceremonies. In the ceremonies recorded it is seen that there is an elaborate participation of various generations from both paternal and maternal sides. But the roles of all the kin are not distinctly specialised. The role of the elderly male becomes functionally conspicuous. In spite of a bilateral trend, patrilineal markers are dominant in the system.

The wandering Kadar groups being numerically weak, geographically dispersed and culturally disjointed have not yet developed rigid rules about the maintenance of their socio-economic or political life. Optimum interactions between member of a small group within a viable space limit have, perhaps, induced them to adopt this particular kind of social structure.

24

CONCEPT OF PROPERTY AND INHERITANCE AMONG THE IRULAS

S. N. MAHATO

The Irulas are not permitted to alienate any piece of non-patta land. No case of alienation of patta land was reported. The Forest Department has put several conditions on the lesee Irulas. One of the terms regarding land alienation reads as "any alienation of the leased area is prohibited". But some cases of alienation of land among the Irulas were reported.

Some of the Irulas have made their agricultural land more productive by clearing stones and weeds from the land. Sometimes the Irulas transfer their land to the non-Irulas but the whole transaction is kept secret. Manar area is in the midst of hills and under the reserved forest and as a result is not easily approachable from the plain area. There a local teacher (non-Irula) took a piece of land for two years by paying Rs. 400 to an Irular. The Irula was in need of money as he was wanting to buy some cloth and an ox.

Palamalai area is on the outskirts of the reserved forest. This is a relatively accessible area and the Irulas frequently come in contact with non-Irulas. Some non-tribals from a nearby village had taken possession of the Irula land. But during the "emergency" all these illegal transactions were scrutinised and all land belonging to the Irulas was returned to them.

Inheritance of Property and Customary Laws

The Irula society is patrilineal. Whatever an Irula possesses is equally distributed to male heirs, i.e. sons, excepting the hut where they live. Generally the question of division of property arises after the death of father. No case was noted where the property was partitioned during the lifetime of a father. There is a custom that, if the problem of division of property occurs during the lifetime of father, then an equal share would be given to his heir or heirs and father would retain one share. The youngest son or whosoever would look after the parents would get the parent's property after the death of father.

If a person does not have a male child, in that case the property would go to his brother or brother's son. The women are barred from any share from their father's property. Contrary to this if one has only one female child, then he can keep his son-in-law after the marriage of his daughter. During his lifetime he will call his son-in-law as *veedu-mapla*. Some instances are given below:

Case I: Since Gendai of Kunjurpathy had no male child he called his son-in-law Nanjan (30), living in Mallpaovi, about 7 miles to manage his land and cattle. After the death of Gendai his widow, Kaliammal (54), daughter Ramiamal (27) and Nanjan are living in the same house.

Case II: Ramaswamy (49) of Veerokkal hamlet in Monnar settlement has only one daughter Popthy (22) and no male issue. After her marriage, her husband Nagrajan (25) is living in this hamlet on the advice of his father-in-law, Ramaswamy. Nagrajan is now looking after the agricultural land, cattle, etc.

In the earlier records it is reported that the Irulas did not care much for land and hut. The Irulas were of nomadic habits and hence the idea of permanent residence did not strike them. Regarding their economy by the sale of the produce of forests, such as honey and bees wax or the fruit of their gardens, the Irulas were enabled to buy grain for their immediate sustenance, and for seed. but, as they never paid any attention to the land after it was sown, or indeed to its preparation further than by partially clearing it of the jungle, and turning it up with the hoe; or, what was more common, scratching it into furrows with a stick and scattering the grain indiscriminately, their crops are, of course, stunted and meagre. Thurston remarked, "when not engaged at work on estates or in the forest, the Irulas cultivate, for their own consumption" (1909B:376). This indicates that previously, land had less importance. In course of time some of them became cultivators.

Regarding inheritance in the recent past it is said, "They generally have little or no property to pass on to their heirs. Their property, real and personal, if any, is divided among the sons, with the exception of the dwelling house, which with the responsibility of the charge of the female, minors, go to the eldest son in addition to his share" (Nanjundayya & Iyer, LKA, 1930:389). Probably this customary rule of inheritance may be prevalent among the Irulas of Mysore. But this does not hold true in the case of the Irulas of Tamilnadu particularly where the present study was made. This may be possible due to long contact of the Irulas of this area with the Todas and Badagas. "Both these tribes comply with limited junior-right" (Lowie, 1921:239).

In the present situation the Irulas are putting much emphasis on agricultural activities. During the off season, they go far wage earning either in the forest or in tea or coffee estates. They also go for work as agricultural labourers. It is worth mentioning that Renga Mestin (50) of Manar Settlement was working as labour mate (Mestri) in Hollend coffee estate about five years back. He, however, accumulated approximately one thousand rupees in order to start horticulture and to do agriculture in a better way in his land. After coming back to Manar, he started to do so. In the meantime, people knew about his savings and since then he is known as *ayirankaran* (person having one thousand rupees) among the Irulas of the area.

Most of the Irulas at present demand to have patta land, i.e. full ownership right over the land instead of having usufructuary right. Besides, they have been representing to the government for the construction of a more pucca building for them to live in, and for an approach road to their hamlet. They desire to do cultivation on their land and hence demand seeds, ox and irrigation facilities.

It was observed that most of the Irulas have become good agriculturists. Idea of profit, property and the lust for money are gradually growing. This may lead them slowly to develop the notion of property and gradually to adopt some concrete rules of inheritance.

25

DISPUTE SETTLEMENT MECHANISM AMONG THE MALAI KUDI : A HILL TRIBE IN KARNATAKA

S. G. MORAB

A study on the customary law of the Malai Kudi tribe in Karnataka was undertaken. There is a mechanism of social control among the tribal people to deal with disputes of various nature when norms of the community are violated and also there are attempts to arrive at some settlement. It would be interesting to study the nature of disputes and their settlements, and the methods followed. Precisely, it will be this functional aspect of the law which forms the theme of the present paper.

The Malai Kudi in Karnataka are known by different names such as Kudiya/Mela Kudi of Coorg district; Malaye Kandi of South Kanara district; Malai Kudi and Maberu of Chikmagalore district. There are two dominant endogamous groups among them. Those who inhabit the four hills (*Nalu Malai*) are the Malai Kudi of the hills. The four hills where these tribals live are : 1. Banjar, 2. Ambate, 3. Ili, 4. Bari, in the south-eastern part of the Western Ghats in Belthangady taluk of South Kanara district in Karnataka. The Malai Kudi of the hills are patriarchal. They are mainly confined to the hilly and foot-hill areas. There were migrations by a few families to the hilly areas of Chikmagalore plateau long ago who are called by the name *Maleru*. Otherwise, the population is confined mainly to the hilly and foot-hills of Neriya village. The other group known also as the Malai Kudi in South Kanara district is ethnically different. They live in the plains villages and they have the avenuculate system of inheritance.

According to the 1961 Census the Malai Kudi in South Kanara district number 3,580 including the Malai Kudi of both the patriarchal and avenuculate groups. But the majority of them belong to the latter group who live in the plains villages. Both the groups speak Tulu, a language of the Dravidian family. For the purpose of studying the customary law of a tribe, the Malai Kudi of the four hills were selected.

Two tribal villages were selected for the study, and field work for one and a half months each was conducted there between March and June, 1977. One was the Banjar hill village, including Ambate hill which consisted of 26 families with a population of 92 persons. The other was in the Neriya village at the foot-hills with 10 families with 55 members.

Among the two tribal villages, the Banjar Hill was selected as "less exposed", since the tribal people there have relatively lesser contact with the outside world. The only outsiders they interact with are the non-tribal estate owners and their staff from Kerala. On the other hand, those who have settled down at Neriya village are "more exposed", as they frequently interact with the villagers belonging to many Hindu castes, Muslims and Christians. Among those who are considered as "more exposed" families are recent immigrants from the Banjar hills.

The houses of the Malai Kudi are dispersed in a vast area of their natural habitation. They live in nuclear families. Their traditional occupation was shifting cultivation (*kumbri*) earlier, but this was to be abandoned when the new landlords came into the picture, some 40 years ago. All the forest land, measuring about 5,000 to 6,000 acres was owned by the Hebbar of Neriya village. Except in the Ili hill, the Hebbar have lost control over the land at the present time. When other people bought the land from the Hebbars, they converted it into plantations. The Malai Kudi had no option but to take up the work of plantation labour. No tribal from the Banjar and Ambate hills owns any land.

A colony for the Malai Kudi was established for the Malai Kudi of the hills, about 10 years ago, but they did not occupy these colony houses. They preferred to stay in their traditional habitat except for some families.

The Mechanism of Social Control

The council of tribal elders is known as the panchayati or *sabha*. The panchayati is the institution to adjudicate disputes and to consider the issues which are referred to it. It is an institution of social control. In the matter of disputes, settlement is effected by the judicious decision of the adjudicating body, that is, the panchayati in this case. There was no question of dispute settlement among the parties concerned. The tribal jurisprudence comprises tribal norms and their violations. How far they are effectively dealt with or decided is a matter of detail which depend upon situations and the interests of various parties concerned.

In earlier days, the authority of the *gurikar* was respected and hence dispute-settlement was an easy task. The disputes which were of serious nature were referred to elders. On such occasions, the parties to litigation had the obligation to offer the local toddy of Bagine tree, and the guilty treated the members to a communal feast. This was an expensive affair and generally the garble litigants avoided disputes unless they were unavoidable.

The Malai Kudi had a certain code of conduct and violation by any- one was considered an offence. The tribal community being a small group and isolated from other cultures, the disputes were few. Since they did not own land in the forest, and they practised shifting cultivation in the vast tract of forest land, they had no disputes over any immovable property, such as land. No Malai Kudi could remember any dispute over land, as they had lost their traditional right over *Kumbri* land about 40 years ago. The tribals had the code of conduct, based on their customary law, violation of which was considered an offence, and as such it was dealt with according to their traditional norms.

Customary Laws Relating to Disputes

Quarrels : Quarrels between any persons were bound to arise due to someone abusing another. This used to happen when one was intoxicated with the toddy of the *bagine* tree. However, all quarrels were decided by the *gurikar*, making the parties to compromise by his mediation. Cases of physical assault are not reported.

Theft : Very rarely, theft of any article occurred. In such a case, the culprit, if proved by evidence, was fined and the fine money would be fixed by the panchayati according to the custom. Whenever a Malai Kudi man sets a trap in the jungle to catch a wild animal, he places a branch of a tree near the place, laying his claim for the trapped animal. In case, another person took the animal, it was regarded as theft and hence an offence. If the person who had set the trap could find out the culprit and if the guilty was proved, the *gurikar* and the panchayati would impose a heavy fine to the extent of Rs. 25 to 50.

Marriage and Divorce : A man can divorce his wife with the permission of the elders. If he deserts his wife for a long time, it was regarded as divorce. A divorcee can marry another unmarried woman in accordance with the usual rituals, with a Brahmin priest officiating as is done during the first marriage. However, the divorced woman can remarry (*kai pattavane*) only in the presence of the elders. It is not regarded as "marriage". A widowed woman has to remarry, but a widower can marry. The elders do not easily grant divorce. They start negotiations between the concerned parties and a decision will be given, if they failed in their attempt.

Usually, monogamous marriages are common. If anyone married another woman without the consent of the wife and the elders, such bigamous union was considered as an offence. In that case, a wife has the right to remarry and the husband will have no control over her. However, if the woman herself agreed to live with such a man, the community will have no objection for such bigamous unions.

Sexual Relationship : Sexual relationship is supposed to start after the marriage is solemnised. A day is fixed by the elders for the consummation of marriage, when husband and wife will begin their sex life. In case of violation of this norm, the elders take the matter seriously. Pre-marital sexual relationship among the members of their own community is not tolerated. In case a woman is found to have any pre-marital sex with a man of her tribe the latter shall marry the woman. If the man refuses, that woman is treated as married and divorced. She cannot then marry another, according to marriage rituals, but only remarry. In case the man belonged to another community, the woman is ex-communicated.

Extra-marital relations are taken seriously and the husband of a woman will divorce her. The tribal elders will not hesitate to grant divorce in such cases. More serious is the offence if a married woman had extra-marital relationship with a man of a different caste or community. And in such a situation, the guilty is boycotted by their community. Children belong to the community in the case of the woman having illicit sexual affair with a member of their own tribe. But the children of the woman begot by others are not accepted in their community.

In earlier days cases of the above nature used to come before the elders of the community for adjudication. An adult man from each family was invited to attend meetings of the panchayati or *sabha* whenever any dispute arose and deliberations were held.

In Banjar Hill, there are two leaders, one is the descendant of the traditional *gurikar,* and the other is a young man who assists the *gurikar* due to the latter's old age. Since the present *gurikar* has no male issue, the young man, who is the *gurikar*'s brother's son, will ultimately succeed the office.

The panchayati of Malai Kudi in Banjar Hill meets only when required. The venue of the panchayati is not fixed. It would be held in the place of the complainants usually and in the shrine at Ambate Hill of their community. The nature and types of disputes that were decided by their panchayati during the previous five years (1972-77) are given below. They will show the functioning of the panchayati in adjudicating the cases that came up before it.

A few of the cases that have come up before the elders of the tribe show that except the case involving sex offence, others are of not severe nature, though the disputes needed trial and adjudication. For instance, the following two cases dealing with quarrel among members of the community show that the issues raised are of a mild nature, if not trivial, but all the same, the tribal people were concerned about protecting the traditional norms, and about maintaining proper behaviour on the part of the disputants.

1. *Quarrel Between Husband and Wife*

L. Soma and his wife Lakṣmi living in "300 Acres Site" (now at Banjar Hill) used to quarrel among themselves frequently. Unable to bear, the woman left her husband's house for her father's brother's place (as she has no father) in the nearby Ambate Hill. Laksmi's father's brother G. Bairu is one of the leaders. At the initial stage, he tried to settle the dispute at the family level between Laksmi and her husband, but could not resolve the tangle. Then he took the matter to other leaders of Banjar Hill, including the head man. A meeting was held at Banjar Hill in the house of L. Soma. The girl was also called. There was discussion. The girl was not willing to go to her husband's house as her husband was harassing her and had not looked after her well when she was hospitalised at Belthangady in 1975. L. Soma also did not want to have his wife back as he was unable to adjust to her.

The panchayati advised the concerned parties not to take the case to extremes resulting in divorce, but to come to terms and live together peacefully. This had happened in 1976. Even after one year, the husband and wife had not reconciled and were seen living separately.

2. *Quarrel Over Hurling Abuse*

M. Soma of "300 Acres Site" is said to be an addict. On one occasion he had picked a quarrel with K. K. Soma of the same settlement and had abused the latter when he was in a drunken state. After a few weeks, K. K. Soma called some elders on a Sunday and made a complaint. Sunday is given as a holiday by the estate owners and it is convenient to hold meetings on that day. The case was discussed. The alleged offender denied having hurled abuses. The complainant insisted on a reprimand or a fine. But the elders decided that as it was not a case of deliberate act and as the offender had indulged in the alleged act when he was drunk, however, warned the alleged offender not to indulge in such acts in future. This case had occurred in 1977.

Prohibition of Marriage with Members of Other Group

A community would like to uphold the norms regarding marriage and any violation in this regard becomes a problem for the tribal elders.

Marriages in the Malai Kudis are supposed to take place strictly in one's own endogamous group. Whenever, there is any violation of the tribal code, the people are concerned over the matter. For instance, when K. Bairu's son K. Devu who works in Belthangady town decided to marry a girl belonging to a non-tribal group (Konkani-speaking peasant caste) four years ago, a panchayati was held in the 300 Acres (Banjar Hill) at the house of the *gurikar*. K. Bairu who stays at Neriya was called but he did not attend. K. Soma and K. K. Soma brought the matter before the panchayati, whether they could attend the marriage or not. K. Devu was their friend, besides working in a government department and having acquired some status. The headman did not approve of the marriage. There was the fear of their tutelary deity at Ambate hill taking revenge if they violated tribal norms. There was discussion. It was unanimously decided that none of their people from Banjar and Ambate hills would attend the marriage, which was against their tribal custom. It is of interest to note that some of the close kin of K. Bairu living in Banjar Hill (300 Acres) attended the marriage held at Belthangady town. Though the headman and some elders do not approve of such marriages, youngsters do not regard them as any serious breach of their custom. Changing situations, and movement of people to other areas, for work and employment, might make such marriages inevitable.

Sexual Offences Views Seriously

While the above cases may not be viewed so seriously in view of the nature of the disputes, those cases which involve any kind of sexual offences are treated very seriously by the tribals. The following case reveals how a case of this type was dealt with by the tribal people:

Pre-marital Sex Relationship

Marriage is held as a sacrament and it is conducted with various rituals by a Brahmin priest. A woman could marry only once and enjoy "married status". Any act of violation of this norm is regarded as a serious offence. It was alleged that the sister of Kunya at Neriya had indulged in pre-marital sex relationship with the brother-in-law of Kunya. The case was discussed at a meeting (*sabha*) held at Neriya village. Since there were hardly a few people, the meeting was a flop. However, the matter was pursued. The statutory panchayat Chairman of Neriya, a man of peasant caste, was invited to deal with the dispute. The latter had partly succeeded in stopping the sex affairs of the concerned parties by threatening the man to stop the illegal affair, lest he took the case to the police.

Kunya used to attend the rituals held at the shrine of their God of Ambate Hill. On one such occasion a few elders including the headman admonished Kunya to throw his sister out of the house, as she had violated the tribal norm and as such she was an offender. Their deities and spirits will not tolerate such behaviour. Kunya was helpless. He pleaded for mercy of gods to show a way out. He told the priest when the latter was in trance that he was suffering from a disease. He promised to turn his sister out of his house if his effort to marry her off to some man from the other area was not successful. The elders told Kunya that as they had no control over the parties concerned, they could not take any action but suggested to him to settle the issue without any adjudication. They feared that by making the issue public, their community was sure to get a bad name.

Monogamy not Bigamy

The tribal community follows the rule of monogamy and bigamy is not appreciated, unless the circumstances so demanded. A typical case given below illustrates this point amply:

Laksmi of Kottigere was married to Subba of the Banjar Hill settlement, when the latter was working as a plantation labourer in Kottigere. The couple had two children. Subba migrated to Kottigere area leaving behind his wife and children. There was no trace of him for about a year, and later he wanted to marry another woman from the Kottigere area. When Laksmi came to know about it, she complained to the headman. A meeting was held. Subba was invited but he did not attend the meeting. A prominent leader went to the place of Subba and persuaded the latter to desist from contracting marriage with another woman but all in vain. This case had happened in 1974. Even after the marriage, Subba meets his wife and children occasionally. The woman works as a plantation labourer and maintains herself, her old mother and the two children. Though bigamous unions are not allowed, as a tribal norm, in some cases, if the woman allows her husband to have another wife, the tribal elders do not interfere. When a woman decided to settle the disputes between herself and her husband, the tribal elders did not pursue the matter.

Observations and Discussion

As may be seen from the above description the disputes arise on various matters whenever there was violation of any code of conduct or tribal norm. Any breach of norm requires settlement, when such a breach was brought forward publicly. The Malai Kudi are a numerically small tribe, and as such there will be very few cases wherein the concerned parties would be willing to bring their grievances for adjudication. Many Malai Kudi elders would often ask as to where was the time for them to indulge in disputes as most of their time was spent in eking out their livelihood. Even then, occasionally certain disputes arise, and if there are any parties to voice their grievances over certain matter, the panchayati is there to deal with these matters.

During the five years, there were cases of quarrels between members, and other issues regarding bigamy, and pre-marital sexual relationship, which came up for the adjudication between the parties to the disputes before the tribal panchayati. The traditional institution of social control, the tribal panchayati, in this case, has lost its former power and as such any action the elders and the headman took was not all the time acceptable to one or both the parties concerned. Negotiation with a third party was always given a chance by the tribal panchayati in an attempt to adhere to tribal norms and, in one case, such as the quarrel among members for hurling abuse, such negotiation was useful in settling the dispute.

Tradition may have it that rules of conduct by members of a particular society may be obligatory, but this may not follow that they can invariably be obeyed for all time to come. It is possible they may be ignored, that they fall into disuse, or are amended or altered depending upon the circumstances. The will of the people is foremost in accepting or rejecting jural procedures of a community. Epstein observes: "Jurisprudence, it has been said, is a normative science; it is concerned with the realm not of the 'is' but of the ought and what ought to be is determined by a community's schemes or values, including concepts of equity and justice" (1967 : 207).

The Malai Kudi have their own code of conduct, as has been stated earlier, and the elders organise a panchayati to restore their code by conducting trial. The aim of such trials is to make people aware as to what "ought" to be the conduct of its members. but when serious cases like the pre-marital sex offences came up, the tribal code was violated more than being followed it. For this particular situation the instrument of social control, the panchayati, which has lost its authority to enforce jural actions against offenders had once again failed to negotiate as a third party. The reasons are obviously the lack of collective will and the individual approach to the issues. Exposure of the people to the alien cultures too has a bearing upon the behaviour pattern of members, who can withstand the punishments like ostracism. On ordinary issues where a small fine is imposed, the individuals readily accept it and go along with the tribal norm as far as practicable.

Concluding Remarks

The Malai Kudi who live in isolated areas of the Banjar and Ambate hills have been found to retain their traditional institution of social control in the form of panchayati. The *gurikar* convenes meetings whenever any case is referred to the panchayati involving violation of any tribal norm. There were five cases which had come to the panchayati during the period of five years for trial. Negotiations were hold in the presence of the third party, the headman and elders. Adjudication in the matter yielded some results but some disputes could not be resolved due to the inherent weakness in the institution. That is, it is not so powerful as it used to be earlier and hence, members could easily flout decisions.

Law consists of a body of rules, a set of procedures of inquiry and adjudication, and is an instrument of social control. But it also embodies values. In the case of the Malai Kudi, the aspect of value is a focal point. Since the time had come that they could take violation of any tribal norm as not irregular, the concerned parties in the premarital sex offence case allowed the dispute to linger on. The invocation of the divinity, their tribal tutelary God at Ambate, did not move forward the jural process. The inquiry into the dispute settlement mechanism was rather slow.

The approach of the *gurikar* as explained in the beginning has more relevance in the context of the dispute settlement mechanism of the Malai Kudi. The tribal jurisprudence, in the case of the Malai Kudi, relies on negotiations and adjudication with the presence of a third party. But Aubert's emphasis on dispute settlement among the concerned parties does not help in taking any jural action against the litigants without adjudication by a third party (Nadar, 1969).

For the enforcement of customary laws of a community, each community may devise ways and means like formulation of rules, procedures and conduct trials in case of violation by a jural authority embodied in institutions of social control, such as the panchayati, as in the case of the Malai Kudi. Normally, cases are not taken to statutory bodies like village panchayat or court, unless it was necessary. In one case, namely, Kunya's complaint, the chairman of the statutory village panchayat was asked to intercede but on a personal level and no other members of the village panchayat were apprised of the case. The obvious reason for it was the hoid of the Chairman on the offender, which the complainant and other tribal elders tried to take advantage of in settling the dispute. The jural authority, that is, the council of elders with the headman (panchayat) makes all-out efforts to protect the tribal norms and code of conduct, whenever there was any deviation, in a numerically small and isolated community.

Such attempts are all the more necessary for the very survival of the community. But the dispute settlements mechanism is complex and as such the sattlement of each case depends upon the will of members of a community, and the time and circumstances of issues, and interest taken by the headman and other members. A study of the disputes and their settlement among the Malai Kudi, therefore, shows that despite the dwindling authority of the traditional jural authority, an attempt by the tribal community is always made to preserve the sanctity of customary practices and traditional pattern of behaviour.

26

POLITICAL SYSTEM OF THE LAMBADI TRIBE OF ANDHRA PRADESH

T. SUBRAMANYAM NAIDU

The Lambadi area a semi-nomadic tribe residing in various states of India, having different names like Banjaras, Brinjaris, Lamans, Lambanis, Sugalis (Thurston, 1909). In the southern State of Andhra Pradesh where they are dominant they trace their origin from northern India, especially from Rajputana, which is supported by historical as well as linguistic evidence. They migrated from northern to southern India along with the great invading Mughal armies as carriers of grains and as suppliers.

The field work among the Lambadis of Andhra Pradesh was carried out from April, 1977 to July, 1977. Data were collected through interviews and schedules filled in with the help of the heads of households. Some relevant data pertaining to the two regions were collected from the police stations and judicial courts of Madanapalli, Punganun and Chittoor. Here I have concentrated my observation on the political system and its functioning among the Lambadi tribe.

The *naik* is the hereditary headman of the *thanda*. He is the richest person in the settlement and has considerable landed property. In the past Lambadis were wandering in groups with their pack bullocks, the *naik* exercised complete authority over his men and directed the movements of his group when travelling. As the days rolled on due to certain compelling circumstances they settled down in separate habitations known as *thandas* and the *naik* had control over his *thanda*. For the establishment of the institution of *naiks* the heads of all the *gotras* assembled in a place called "Konpolghad-badarbanda" and decided to keep the *thanda* under a hereditary leader called *naik*. To assist the *naik* in his religious and other business activities they also decided to have a *dhave* (sub-*naik*) and a

Karbari (secretary). In spite of this hierarchy of leadership, the people are at liberty to disqualify a particular person from holding any post if he does not enjoy the confidence of the majority. The *naik* exercises all the powers over their religious matters. His word is "law". While deciding their disputes, suggestions of other elderly people of the *thanda* are, however, generally given due weightage by the *naik* before he announces his decision.

Internal Organisations of the Tribal Thanda

The socio-religious organisation of the village has its independent set of office-bearers and functionaries as below:

Thana Naik

Thanda Naik (Head man of the village)
↓
Dhave (Organiser of the village council & rituals)
↓
Karbari (Cashier, fine collector for the village)
↓
Ghar Naiks (Head of the family)

FIG. 26.1: Intra-Thanda Tribal Council

The *thanda naik* is a pivotal figure in the *thanda* and wields great influence. He is always given a place of honour at all *thanda* ceremonies. Dhave is second to *naik* and also holds an important position in the organisation of tribal council. He receives the complaints and generally decides the cases after obtaining the formal approval of the *naik*. He arranges all the religious functions on time. Karbari collects the fines and donations from the *thandas*. The *thanda naik* is the constitutional head and the Dhave is the chief executive of the council.

Inter-Thanda Council (Sathandae Council)

For settling the disputes between *thandas* the Lambadis have their own inter-thanda council. At Punganun and Madanapalli each such council constitutes seven *thandas*. For all these seven *thandas* there is a Sathandae Moto *naik* (tribe headman). Each constituent *thanda* is the member of this council, although in practice other wealthy and influential as well as vocal and assertive persons also gradually come to occupy a place in it. Its functionaries are as follows:

1. Sathandae Moto *naik* (Tribal *naik*)
2. *Dhave* (organiser of the inter-village council and rituals)
3. *Karbari* (cashier)
4. *Thanda naiks* of all seven *thandas* (headman of each village acts as a member of the council)
5. Heads of family (heads of all the families of the seven *thandas* are the members in the council)

Serious breaches of the norms and traditions of the tribe as well as important intra-tribal disputes are heard and decided by these inter-*thanda* councils. Cases of divorce, failure to pay the promised bride-price, extra-marital relations, breaches of the rules of endogamy and exogamy, murder, suicide, theft and water right would be under the jurisdiction of this council. There is no clear-cut distinction between the powers and functions of the inter-*thanda* and intra-*thanda* councils when a serious case of incest is brought to the notice of any of these councils it takes action independently. Matters of primary local interest, abortions, adultery are brought to the intra-*thanda* council. While the cases related to specific tribal customs come under the jurisdiction of the inter-*thanda* council.

It is the duty of the head of the household to refer the nature of the case to the *dhave.* He, in consultation with the *naik*, fixes the date, time and place of the council meeting which is generally held in the *thanda* from which the case covers. The *dhave* informs all the *thandas* about the case which is going to be dealt with there. The parties involved in the dispute are asked to come fully prepared on the appointed day. Representatives from all the *thandas* attend the meeting. The Sathandae Moto *naik* occupies the high place, the *dhave* and *karbari* sit on either side of the *naik*. The *dhave* explains the purpose and briefs the people about the nature of the case and the names of the parties. If it is an appeal, the complainant is asked to state the case himself. In the case of a beach of the sexual taboo the *naik* briefs others about it. When the complaint has been heard and the accused admits his guilt, the council begins its deliberations on the nature of the punishment to be imposed. But if the accused pleads not guilty further examination is conducted. The *dhave* and *karbari* cross-examine both the parties thoroughly; witnesses may also be examined. Any head of the household can ask questions or seek clarifications from either party. Deliberations continue until unanimity is arrived at not only about the establishment of the guilt but also about the nature of punishment. The final verdict is delivered by the *naik* who also gives reasons for his decision. The verdict is binding on both parties; if a person disobeys the verdict he is liable to be excommunicated.

Given below are some of the specific cases which illustrate the kinds of cases brought before the council and settled.

Case No. 1 : Mudae Munasamy of Sugalimitta *thanda* fell in love with a married woman Nanki by name. One day Nanki and Munasamy eloped and got married at a temple. After three weeks they returned to the village. Nanki's husband brought this matter to the *thanda* panchayat. Before the panchayat Nanki refused to live with her husband.

Verdict : The council decided that Munasamy pay to the bride-price of Rs. 250 and marriage compensation of Rs. 750 to Nanki's husband. Munasamy paid the said amount and took Nanki as his second wife.

Case No. 2 : Sometimes it is difficult to try a case in a dispassionate way. In such cases the Lambadis take the help of political leaders to settle the case. Chinnappa *naik*, a businessman in Nakkaladinnal *thanda*, married an Yerukula girl Nagamma, in the Registrar's office. Chinnappa *naik*'s wife did not agree to stay in the same house. It was brought to the notice of the inter-tribal council. Deliberations continued for three days. The tribal verdict delivered by the tribal *naik* was not accepted by Chinnappa.

On June 26, 1977, the tribal *naik* and all the important members of all the *thandas* met Mr. Narasinga Rao, MLA Madanapalli, and requested him to settle the case. On the 27th council met in the *thanda*. After deliberations Mr. Narasinga Rao settled the case and asked Chinnappa to live with his wife only. He could keep Nagamma also but she must reside outside the village boundaries. He was also fined Rs. 200 for marrying a girl from another tribe. Chinnappa accepted the verdict.

Case No. 3 : The grounds of divorce must be distinguished from causes of divorce. Divorce can usually be related to non-fulfilment of rights or obligations assured at marriage. Some grounds for divorce involve non-fulfilment of the obligations of the housewife or householder. Adultery is common in this community.

Nanki, daughter of Narasimhulu *naik*, had extra-marital sexual relations with Munasamy. Nanki's husband Krishna *naik* used to quarrel with his wife for this. One night Nanki and Munasamy left the village and got married at Tirupati. After one month they returned to the *thanda*. Krishna *naik* brought this matter to the notice of *thanda* council. According to the tribal law the case was tried and it was decided that Munasamy pay the amount of bride-price and the marriage compensation to Krishna *naik*. Munasamy accepted the verdict and paid the amount. The marriage bonds were broken between Krishna *naik* and Nanki.

Case No. 4 : According to the Lambadi law and customs, going to court is taboo. They won't accept the judgment of the court. One Somili, wife of Ramji *naik*, filed her divorce case in the taluk magistrate's court at Rungamre. The case was taken seriously on both sides; nearly six months were taken to settle the case. Finally the judgment was given that Ramji *naik* pay Rs. 2,500 to his wife as "Jeevanartham". Ramji *naik* paid the amount, the marriage bonds were broken according to the state law.

The case was placed before the inter-tribal council. The council asked her to repay the bride-price and marriage compensation, failing which she would be ex-communicated. Somili returned the bride-price of Rs. 150 and marriage compensation of Rs. 500 and a fine of Rs. 75 to the tribal council.

Case No. 5 : Formerly Lambadis were notorious for committing crimes, robbery on the roadside, cattle-lifting, theft of grain or the property dacoity. The women also used to take a leading part in dacoities. The *naik* or the headman of the gang had an active role in the commission of crime. In the event of a gang or some of it being convicted, the other members of the gag had to take care of the families of the convicted.

On October 27, 1965, at 10 p.m. at Sujelmista, on the trunk road between Purgam and Madanapalli, 57 Lambadis of four villages stopped three lorries by placing stones on the road and committed theft of sugar and jaggery from the lorries. All the Lambadis were arrested. They were prosecuted. As a result 15 members were convicted under Section 595, IPC, and sentenced to rigorous imprisonment for two years. The remaining 42 members were acquitted and the bail bonds were cancelled.

In the light of the above judgment, the members of the intra-tribal council met on August 10, 1966. After a long discussion they unanimously decided that the remaining 42 members who had participated in the dacoity had to take care of the families whose members were convicted. The Gharili *naik* divided such families into 15 groups and each group had to take care of one such family in every respect, i.e., food, agriculture, etc.

Discussion

The Lambadis tribal council serves a useful purpose in exercising social control and its powers and decisions are not generally questioned. The representative character of the council has always been its strong feature. Mature and wise decisions given even without the aid of lawyers are beneficial to the people of a *thanda*. The *thanda* council is responsible for the administration of justice. The *thanda* is considered to be the supreme authority above all government bodies. This mechanism of social control being simple, efficient, expeditious and effective has continued to be in force for generations. The structure of the *thanda* and its internal organisation remained unaffected for a long time, despite the drastic political and economic upheavals that have brought about changes in the homebodies political organisation as a whole.

27

CUSTOMARY LAW AND DEVIANCE — A Study with Reference to Marriage and Family among the Yerukula

J. PARTHASARTHY

Apart from the works on law in pre-literate societies which were written by colonial administrators, missionaries, etc., there were scholars like Maine (1861), Malinowsi (1926), Hogbin (1934), who studied law in primitive societies from the anthropological perspective. Studies on primitive law developed from the collection of normative rules ("laws") and the observation of the application of such rules in different situations.

Of the two terms — custom and law — custom is of far earlier origin. In a broader view study of law which is the product of a rather complicated machinery of social and political organisation was unknown, at any rate in its present sense, in the primitive ages when society was not, as at present, a collection of individuals but an aggregation of families. There was no king or sovereign to frame rules or set "law" for these families. One family was independent of another and followed its own head, whose will or pleasure was "law" up to its own members. As families expanded into a community and the community into a tribe, rules and principles were established for the guidance of its members. It is not merely that "law" is of very recent origin but that, in most cases, it has been based upon custom and usage. This customary law is composed of a large body of rules, observed by the communities. Berndt while explaining the controversy on the use of the term "law" said "law centres in the main on the distinction between law and custom, between codified law and customary law, and oddly enough in view of the common derivation of the two words, between law and other 'legal' phenomena" (1962:13). While discussing the tribal customary law Epstein opines that "the recording of customary law is also important as a first step towards the systematic study of tribal system of law, and so provides the basis for further inquiry into the connection between legal ideas, concepts and categories and social structure and culture (1969:209).

Generally, all primitive societies have means by which the behaviour of their members can be channelised, either more or less successfully. Social control thus covers all the processes and groups to conform to the customary norms. They fall into various categories, some of them guarded by provisions or sanctions of either a positive or negative kind designed to counteract tendencies towards deviancy or disobedience. This paper attempts to examine the customary laws of the Yerukula community with special reference to the institutions of marriage and family and also evaluates how the behaviour is controlled by bringing the cases of deviation to their community council.

The Yerukula is one of the largest tribes of Andhra Pradesh numbering 1,62,560 (1971 Census). They are also found sparsely in Karnataka and Tamil Nadu States. According to the 1971 Census, the Yerukula who are classified as a Scheduled Tribe in 11 districts of Andhra Pradesh form 0.31 per cent of the total population of Andhra Pradesh and 9.81 per cent of the total scheduled tribe population of the state. It is found that 86.54 per cent of the Yerukula population live in rural areas, while 13.46 per cent are in urban areas.

The Yerukula derive their name from "Yeruka" which means "knowledge or acquaintance". The females of the tribe profess to be experts in fortune-telling, which they have adopted as a profession. They speak a dialect called "Yerkali basha", which appears to be a mixture of several Dravidian speeches. The Yerukula are divided into three large endogamous groups on the basis of their traditional occupations. They are Bidari Yerukula (trading), Dabba Yerukula (basket making) and Kunche Yerukula (fortune-telling and pig-rearing). The present study is mainly concerned with the Bidari Yerukula. The traditional occupation of the Bidari Yerukula is trading. They mostly trade in salt, tamarind, curry leaf (murrya koenigii) and pulses. They were once nomadic traders but now most of them have taken to agriculture in addition to their traditional trade. Besides agriculture and trade, they also make mats, ropes, twines, slings, etc.

Area of Study

The present paper is based on the data collected from two villages namely Erragudi and Kalagalla of Anantapur district in Andhra Pradesh in the year 1977.

Before going into the details of the marriage and family among the Yerukula, it is relevant to briefly discuss their traditional political organisation.

Kula Panchayat

The dominant feature of the Yerukula political organisation is its *kula* panchayat. In both Erragudi and Kalagalla villages they have their own *kula* panchayat. The members of the *kula* panchayat are usually elders who are called *peddamonushulu* and the head of the Yerukula settlement is called *berumonushya* meaning "big man". The *berumonushya* should be between 35 and 55 years of age and when he crosses the age of 55 he ceases to be the *berumonushya* though he may continue to command some influence on the *kula* panchayat. The *berumonushya* presides over all proceedings and is given an honourable position at all social functions. Cases of the following nature are taken up for arbitration in the *kula* panchayat : 1. Disputes relating to sex; 2. Disputes regarding property and loans; 3. Disputes regarding land; and 4. Quarrels between individuals or families. Usually they do not like their disputes to be discussed and decided by other castes and hence they try to settle all their disputes among themselves. The *kula* panchayat may decide a dispute in one sitting or adjourn for several sittings. When the facts are not available to identify the guilty person in spite of several adjournments in a particular case, then they try to determine the guilty through ordeals like both the parties dipping their fingers in boiling oil or lifting a red-hot crow-bar, in the presence of the *berumonushya* and the elders gathered for the purpose. The alleged culprit is expected to go through the ordeals without any pain or discomfort if he is innocent. The belief of the Yerukula behind these ordeals is that the divine power will protect the innocent and punish the guilty. Apart from solving disputes regarding theft and petty matters, the *kula* panchayat is also responsible for the maintenance of social order in the community as per the norms of the society. It found guilty one is suitably reprimanded and if the violation is serious he may be excommunicated from the community by the *kula* panchayat. Inter-dining or even serving water to the ex-communicated person can be permitted only after he admits his quilt and has taken oath in front of Berumonushya that in future he will not indulge in any such activities. For re-admission the ex-communicated man must undergo purificatory ceremonies.

According to Yerukula, life is meaningless without marriage and it is parents' moral duty to arrange marriage for sons and daughters. The majority of legal disputes which are brought before the *kula* panchayat concern with matters arising out of marriage, claims to a share in bride-price or a return of bride-price on the occasion of re-marriage. Before discussing the disputes concerning marriage let me discuss the types of marriage contracted among them.

Types of Marriage

It appears that negotiated marriage is preferred particularly when one weds for the first time. Generally the father takes the initiative in finding a suitable bride for his son. The marriage is performed at the bride's residence. Marriage by service or elopement is rare among them. A man may keep several women as his wives provided he has the capacity to maintain them but polyandry is prohibited in the Yerukula community. In Kalagalla village there are three cases of polygyny marriages and in Erragudi one. Generally all the wives live in a common house with their husband.

Bride-Price

Bride-price known as *sulla ponnu* is common. After fixing the date the bridegroom's father pays a fixed amount of Rs. 48 in cash as bride-price to the bride's father. Generally, the recipient of the bride-price is the bride's mother's brother. The bride-price must be given to the brother even if the marriage is with the maternal uncle or with his son.

In case the groom's parents are very poor, at least half of the fixed bride-price must be paid before the ceremony, to enable the girl's father to pay off her maternal uncle's share and to make wedding preparations. The balance may be cleared after marriage either in lump sum or instalments. The bride-price is non-refundable in the case of divorce or death. In a *maganali* case (without divorce) woman accepting and living with another man as his wife, the second husband has to give the amount of *sulla* i.e. Rs. 24 along with marriage expenditure to her first husband.

For example, in the year 1971 at Kalagalla village, Lanjipolla Chowdappa had developed extra-marital relations with Venkatamma, wife of Nallaba Doddappa. This case was brought before the *kula* panchayat by Nallaba Doddappa. The *kula* panchayat was convened and it decided that Lanjipolla Chowdappa pay Rs. 24 to Doddappa. Lanjipolla Chowdappa paid the amount to Doddappa.

Marriage Laws

An account of Yerukula marriage laws would not be complete without the mention of the laws of endogamy and exogamy. Generally, the breaches of the rules of exogamy and incestuous extra-marital relations are the subject of dispute brought before the Yerukula *kula* panchayat.

The Yerukula are divided into three large endogamous groups on the basis of their traditional occupation. They are : Bidari Yerukula, Dabba Yerukula and Kunche Yerukula. These groups do not marry among them. The Yerukula observe strict endogamous rules regarding their marriage. Their clans and lines are exogamous. The laws of exogamy extend farther than this and include persons who are closely related by marriage; persons related by blood; and finally, persons standing in a particular social relationship to each other. Here it is essential to note about the Yerukula *gotramu* (clan) and *intiperu* (family name) to understand the rules and restrictions of their marriages.

Gotramu (Clan)

The Yerukula are divided into three exogamous divisions, as *gotramulu* which are unilateral groups of relatives, multilocal in settlement, the members of which are determined by unilateral descent.

These exogamous divisions clearly show that the Yerukula obtained their *gotra* names from the particular religious services offered to their beloved god. According to Thurston (1909 : 449): "The members of the first two divisions are pure Koravas (Yerukulas), the legitimate descendants of Koravas who have never married outside the caste, whereas the third division represents and includes the mixed marriages and the offspring thereof." Thus it is understood that the Kavadi and Sathpadi clans of Yerukula community consider the people who belong to Mendragutti or Menapadi as lower in social hierarchy.

Intiperu (Family Name) : The *intiperu* is characteristic of the Yerukula family. It acts as an exogamous unit. The *intiperu* is attached as a prefix to a boy's family name. Since the Yerukula society is patrilineal, the intiperu of a boy remains the some throughout his life, but a girl changes her family name when she marries and it becomes that of her husband's family name. Those who are having the same intiperu also constitute the pollution group and hence it is a patronymic grouping of agnates.

Gotramu and Intiperu : Both the intiperu and gotra are regulating factors in the choice of mate. Each gotra consists of a number of intiperu. A person who belongs to one intiperu of a clan cannot make alliance with the other intiperu of the same clan. He is allowed to marry a girl of another intiperu of another clan. Any sexual intercourse between the members of the same gotramu (clan) is tabooed. Further, a Yerukula should not have any alliance with women of lower castes like Chakali (washerman), Mangali (barber), Mala and Madiga (scheduled castes).

To draw the attention specifically to the function of rules and restrictions of their marriage let me present a few deviant cases.

Case 1 : In Yerukula community an alliance between the *intiperu* of Pabburay and Munga cannot be established either by legal or illegal means, because both these intiperu come under the same clan, i.e., Kavadi. Therefore, they consider themselves as one family and the members should treat each other as brothers and sisters.

Two persons belonging to the Kavadi clan developed extramarital relations among themselves. The husband of the girl reported the matter to the *kula* panchayat. Which found them guilty and excommunicated both of them. The people of their community in the village and neighbouring villages were informed of the decision taken by the *kula* panchayat and also were warned that none should give or take anything from them, or give any shelter to them or enter into any kind of relation with them. Because of these restrictions, they suffered a lot for two days. They went to a nearby village where they took food and water at the house of a Mala. The Yerukula consider people of the Mala caste to be inferior to them. As both of them were not able to bear their hardships, they returned to the village and begged for mercy from *berumonushya.* The *kula* panchayat was convened. It decided to re-admit them after the ritual purification. On one Saturday morning, after taking bath and performing puja in Anjaneya Swamy temple, the tongues of both were touched by a piece of hot gold by *berumonushya.* Then both took oath in front of elders that in future they will behave towards each other as brother and sister. The man then gave a feast to the elders of *kula* panchayat at his expense, which demonstrated that he had been purified and accepted by his people.

Case 2 : In 1977, in Kalagalla village F had extra-marital relations with G of Madiga (cobbler) caste. According to their customary law, a man should not have any alliance with a woman of lower caste. The case was reported to *kula* panchayat where it was decided to ex-communicate F from their community. After six days he pleaded for mercy to the *kula* panchayat. His request was accepted and he was re-admitted into the community after ritual purificatory ceremony. He served special meals to *kula* panchayat elders.

Prescriptive and Preferential Marriage

In Yerukula community, marriage with an elder sister's daughter is allowed but the daughter of a younger sister should not be taken as wife. Junior sororate system is existing among them. A man may marry two sisters but not after the has worried the younger sister. He cannot marry the older sister either in regular marriage, or in *seere-kettinchu* ceremony, on the ground that the relationship with wife's elder sister is looked upon as equivalent to relationship with of a mother.

At Kalagalla village, Pubburay Jellappa married his first wife Sunkamma's younger sister Nagama, because his first wife was suffering from asthma. Mote Balappa of Erragudi married his first wife Sunkammo's younger sister Uligithi Papomma because his first wife suffered a serious attack of paralysis. In Yerukula community senior and junior levirate system is in existence. Generally two sisters may be married to two brothers. There is no objection to the exchange of daughters between two families in marriage.

Remarriage

In Yerukula community, widow marriage is allowed and a woman can marry several times, provided at the time of every subsequent marriage, her previous husband should not be alive or she has been granted separation from her husband by the *kula* panchayat.

A Yerukula, who wishes to marry a widow, purchases new clothes for himself and a saree for her. The *berumonushya* is invited along with other elders of the village for the marriage. On the day fixed for marriage, in the presence of all the invitees in the evening, he presents her a new saree in front of her house. This simple ceremony is known as *seere-kettinchu*. On this occasion he has to pay Rs. 24 as bride-price to the former father-in-law of his would-be wife. If the widow has any children they are left in the care of the relatives of the former husband. If she has children below the age of two years, she takes them along with her to her second husband's house. After two or three years she sends them back to her former husband's house or to his relatives.

Case : Mota Sunkanna of Erragudi village married Pannara Remake in the year 1969. She gave birth to two male children who died soon after birth. On account of this he decided to divorce her and took the case to the *kula* panchayat, where the decision was given in favour of him. Then in the year 1973 he married a widow by performing *seere-kettinchu* ceremony, in the presence of *berumonushe* and other village elders at Erragudi. The two children of his second wife were sent back to the house of the relatives of the first husband. The divorced first wife Remake also got married, again by performing *seere-kettinchu* ceremony.

The laws of regular marriage hold good for the children who are born after re-marriage. A widow gets the status of a married woman in the community after re-marriage. She participates in all festivals, religious functions and other important occasions, which take place in her house and in the village like any other woman.

Divorce

Divorce is known as "Rookha perku Kodthutu". The divorcees are allowed to marry again. But there could be dispute on the grounds for divorce. Marriage implies a stable relationship between the husband and his kinsmen on the one hand, and the wife and her kinsmen on the other. This relationship is maintained by a complex system of reciprocal obligations, duties and conventional pattern of behaviour. Between the married couple there are errors, breaches of good behaviour or recognised rights which the Yerukula will quote as the usual causes of divorce. A Yerukula man may demand divorce from his wife for the following reasons:

Barrenness : If his wife fails to produce children at all, a divorce will usually by demanded by the husband. Barrenness amounts to failure of the woman to fulfil the procreative obligations to which here husband has a legal right.

Laziness : A Yerukula has a right to extract domestic and any other work from his wife, and he may call for divorce if she is lazy and does not listen to his commands.

Adultery : A man may ask for divorce if he discovers that his wife has committed adultery.

Desertion : If a wife runs away to live with another man her husband is more likely to seek a divorce.

Incurable Disease : A Yerukula may claim a divorce if his wife gets an incurable disease.

The grounds for divorce which will receive the support of a married woman's natal family are as follows:

Impotence or Sterility of the Husband : A Yerukula woman may divorce her husband if she bears no children and it is known that her husband is importe. In such circumstances, her family will usually acknowledge her plea for a divorce and allow her to marry else-where.

Failure to Support Wife : If the husband fails to fulfil his economic duties towards his wife and children, if he is too lazy to do work, her family may seek a divorce.

Cruel Treatment : A Yerukula woman may demand a divorce and receive the support of her family if her husband persistently ill-treats her or beats her without reason.

Process of Divorce

If a person wants to give divorce to his wife on some grounds mentioned above, he should so inform the *kula* panchayat of the village. One day the Berumonushe invites other Peddamonushulu and conducts the proceedings of the *kula* panchayat. Both parents of husband and wife are invited and in front of all, the husband has to give a pot of toddy with five sets of betel leaves and supari nuts along with a "rooka" (coin) of 25 paise to his wife. After the acceptance of this the Berumonushe declares that the husband and wife are formally separated from each other. There is no necessity of repayment of bride-price or any other compensation, if both desired for divorce. But if the divorce is on account of wife's adultery or desertion, the divorced woman may marry her paramour, and the latter has to pay half of the amount of bride-price and the complete expenditure of marriage to the previous husband.

Case : In Kalagalla village Venkatamma, wife of Nallaba Doddappa had extra-marital relations with Lanjipolla Doddappa. This affair came to the notice of her husband Doddappa and he reported the matter to Berumonushe and on this ground he desired to give divorce to his wife. The *kula* panchayat was convened and in the meeting, the husband Doddappa gave a pot of toddy along with 25 paise "rooka" and betel leaves to his wife. Then *kula* panchayat announced that Doddappa had divorced Venkatamma and it is decided that Lanjipolla Daddappa, her paramour, has to marry Venkatamma and he has to pay Rs. 900 to Doddappa as the expenditure of his marriage.

Family

"In all human societies, the workshop, so to speak, of social reproduction is the domestic group. It is this group which must remain in operation over a stretch of time long enough to rear offspring to the stage of physical and social reproductivity of a society to maintain itself" (Fortes : 1962 : 2). This is the justification for a particular society may comprise two or three successive generations. The family in Yerukula community at Erragudi and Kallagalla villages can be considered to be the smallest basic kin unit in active operation. The Yerukula family acquires membership through marriage, birth and adoption. Being a patriarchal and patrilineal society, the mode of residence among them is patrilocal. Generally in the Yerukula community, the elderly male member of the family is the locus of authority. In case of his death, his wife, if she is elder to his brothers, becomes the head of the household.

A family custom is defined to be "the usages of a family transmitted successively (from father to son) according to law". It generally relates to matters affecting the members of a family in their relationship to each other and to the family as a unit. Amongst the members of a family it has an obligatory force and distinguishes the family by its rules from other families. These rules chiefly concern adoption, marriage and mode of inheritance of property. As we have already discussed about marriage, it is now necessary to understand the customary process of adoption and mode of inheritance among them.

Adoption

Adoption, known as *Dachu Aasukondu* in the Yerkali dialect, exists in the Yerukula community. When a person has no children or is without a male child, he may adopt a boy, preferably the son of his brother or one belonging to the same exogamous division. Yerukulas also permit adoption boys from other tribes like Voddar, Sugali, etc., but not from Muslim, Chakali (washerman), Mala and Madiga (Scheduled Castes). There is no ceremony observed for adoption of a child in this community except that of taking off the old waist-thread of the boy and putting on a new one which is called *Malatadu Marchu*, and giving a dinner to the tribesmen to announce the fact. The duties of an adopted child are similar to those of a natural child and he is the successor of the property of his adopted parents.

An essential part of adoption in the Yerukula community is the publicity of the relationship and of the intentions of the adoptive parents. The natural parents of an adopted child have generally no right to reclaim the child from its adopted parents so long as the child desires to remain with them. But if the child consents to return to its own parents, it should be restored to them. In such cases the adoptive parents are entitled to recover from the natural parents compensation for the expenses they incurred in bringing up the child. When the adoptive parents refuse to maintain their adopted child, they cannot claim from the natural parents any expenses incurred by them in bringing up the child. In Erragudi village Mota Chinnappa adopted Venkatesulu, aged 12 years, son of his younger brother, after the *Malat Maradchu* function. Mota Chinnappa had only one daughter with a large property. Since he did not have a male child, the circumstances made him to go in for adoption. The following two cases reveal how the *kula* panchayat deals with the deviant cases pertaining to adoption.

Case 1 : In the year 1970 in Kalagalla village B had adopted a child, aged 9 years, son of C and asked C to stop the adopted child's coming to his house, but C argued that it was the boy who wanted to come to his house and do some work in his house. He further told B that in future he would not come to his house. Then B became angry and reported the matter to the *kula* panchayat. The *kula* panchayat was convened and the opinions of the two concerned parties were heard and then the *berumonushe* announced that after adopting the child, B has incurred some expenditure in bringing up the child for one year so B should get Rs. 500 from C. The *kula* panchayat also ordered that C pay Rs. 50 towards the expenditure of the invitees of the panchayat. C paid Rs. 50 to the panchayat immediately after the decision was taken and to B in two years.

Case 2 : In the year 1969 in Erragudi village, A refused to bring up his adopted child due to loss of his property and he sent the boy to his natural parents' home after bringing up that child for one and a half years. A had to abide by the decision of the *kula* panchayat.

Inheritance

In the Yerukula community the mode of inheritance is patrilineal. The property is equally divided among all the children. Primogeniture is not recognised among the Yerukula. When the father dies leaving behind his sons and unmarried daughters, the sons exclude the married daughters in the division of property. Ultimogeniture and usufractuary modes of inheritance are not in existence among them. If there is more than one wife, the property is equally shared between them on the death of their husband. In Errugudi village in the year 1976, after the death of A, the *kula* panchayat allotted half of the property to A's second wife, after ruling out the objection raised by A's first wife's eldest son.

The children of the divorced wife are entitled to have a share in the property of their deceased father because in Yerukula community even after divorce, the children live in their father's house. Division of property of F was brought to the *kula* panchayat. In the year 1958 F had given divorce to his first wife J on the grounds of desertion and married H. On the death of F, H refused to give a share of F's property to her husband's divorced first wife's children. This matter was brought to the notice of the *kula* panchayat. It decided that the first wife's children should get half of F's property and, accordingly, the property division took place before the *pedda monushulu*.

An adopted child ordinarily forfeits all claim to inheritance of the property of his natural parents. A daughter's right to the ancestral property of her father is recognised when there is no male lineal discendant, nor a widow nor a mother of the deceased. Unmarried daughters were excluded from inheritance and they must be maintained out of the property of the deceased father. They are permitted to remain in possession of their father's property till their marriage.

The systematic and integrated unwritten law channelises the deviant behaviour of the Yerukula people especially with reference to the institutions of marriage and family. The Yerukula council called *kula* panchayat is a strong and functional organisation and is responsible for the maintenance of social order in the community.

According to them, life is meaningless without marriage and it is the parents moral duty to arrange marriage for their grown-up children. They maintain exogamy, which can be seen by strict obedience of the customary rules and restrictions of marriage by them. Being a patrilocal and patrilineal society the mode of residence among them is patrilocal. Regarding the rules and regulations of marriage, divorce, adoption, inheritance, etc., generally forms an opinion about any community on the basis of these rules and regulations which reflect ideal motivation. But if we focus our attention on the functioning of the normative rules and restrictions in the Yerukula society, we can say that reality is not exactly the same as ideal.

Caste/tribal councils all over the country have lost their original importance. In some places they organise social reforms and recreational facilities for their members. Even the use of the *kula* panchayat for settlement of local disputes seems in most villages to be almost a minor one. But among the Yerukula the *kula* panchayat was, and is, used as an effective instrument for the control of the deviant behaviour of the members. It is noticed in the Yerukula community that authority is not centralised. Each Yerukula settlement has its own *kula* panchayat, the *benmonushe* and *pedda monushulu*, and cases of each settlement are locally settled. All can aspire to become *pedda monushulu* some time or the other and this may indirectly satisfy the ego of the aspiring ones.

At present, in the Yerukula community, ordeals or severe punishment for culprits is no more practised. Apology is generally granted soon after the individuals ask for it and undergo the specific rituals. The Yerukula men have perhaps rightly guessed that going to courts needs more money and to settle their problems through courts also requires much time. The Yerukula understand the importance of maintaining their solidarity in present atmosphere of modern politics. And to maintain that solidarity, they perhaps are wiser to accept the ruling of their *kula* panchayats.

28

CUSTOMARY LAW AND POLITICS — A CASE STUDY OF THE BAGATA AND RELATED TRIBES OF ANDHRA PRADESH

N.V. KAMESWARA RAO

In the present paper an attempt is made to portray the persistence of political significance of the British policy of indirect rule in the tribal areas of Vishakhapatnam district in the present state of Andhra Pradesh through tribal chiefs called *muttadaras* who were mostly from the Bagata tribe and its consequent impact on the modern political situation of these tribal areas. The field work for this study was conducted in the Paderu taluk of the agency area of Vishakhapatnam district. This taluk has a population of 1,83,090 persons and its area is 1,199 sq. miles. It was constituted in 1959 and the significant feature of this taluk is that it contains a number of tribal groups like Bagata, Konda Dora or Konda Kapu, Porja, Valmiki, Kotiya, Kodu or Samante, Nooka Dora and Konda Kammara who live in multi-tribal villages.

According to the system introduced by the above Act of 1839 and again the Scheduled Districts Act XIV of 1874 each agency was placed under an Agent (Collector). Under each Agent were appointed some Assistant Agents, each in charge of a division, and under each Assistant Agent were appointed several sub-magistrstes — Munsifs.

The important feature of these rules is that they have always empowered the Agents and their subordinates with civil, criminal and revenue jurisdiction. Regarding administration of justice, the Agents and their subordinates were required in criminal matters to follow the Criminal Procedure Code, but in civil matters they were required to follow a set of simple rules framed for their guidance and Sections 36 to 43 of the Civil Procedure Code relating to the execution of decrees. While, therefore, in criminal cases there is an appeal from the decision of the Agents to the High Court, in civil cases there is no appeal from their decisions to any higher authority.

In the agency portions of the Zamidari areas the British followed a dual policy. While the Zamidars were made responsible for the collection of revenue, the British Government reserved the powers to administer these areas with regard to justice and other matters. At the same time they made use of the existing *muttadari* system for the maintenance of peace and tranquillity in these areas. The *muttadar* became responsible to the Government for maintaining law and order in his *mutta* (group of villages) and continued to be responsible to the Zamidar for collection of the revenue due to the estate. Thus the *muttadars* in Zamidari areas had two overlords.

Further, the *muttadars* held the *muttas* on service tenure subject to the fulfilment of the obligations laid down in the *sanads* granted by the Government and the Zamidar. They had no proprietary rights over the lands in their *mutta* and could not alienate in any way. So long as they held the *muttas* it rested with them to distribute the arable land among the tribals to collect rents from them. They had proprietary rights to the forests in their *muttas* but they did not claim any. The *muttadars* naturally appropriated to themselves large extents of land and kept them in their own possession enjoying them rent-free. but for the remaining land in the *mutta* they were merely agents of the Government.

Traditional Councils

Along with the abovementioned State-imposed law machinery, there were four types of traditional councils dealing with both intra-tribal and inter-tribal disputes and other matters in which customary laws of the tribal society occupy a prominent place in dispensing justice and for awarding punishments.

Foremost among these traditional councils was the *mutta kattu* or *mutta* council which was presided over by the *muttadar*. It was inter-tribal and inter-village in nature. Cases which the other councils in a *mutta* (group of villages) village by the *pettandar* (village headman) and other elders were brought to this council.

Gramakula panchayat or village tribal council was intra-tribal and intra village in character. The affairs of a single tribe in a village were usually discussed in the deliberations of this council. It was presided over by the tribal leader known as *kula pedda* for that particular tribe.

The regional tribal council known as *gumpu kattu* was inter village intra-tribal council. It was presided over by the *purushakari*, a tribal head in religious matters and other pertaining to each of the different tribes.

Lastly, the village council or *grama peddala* panchayat which was intra-village and inter-tribal in nature used to settle disputes in which persons belonging to different tribes were involved. In a *muttadar's* native village he used to preside over this council also.

Out of the above councils, the *mutta* council or *mutta kattu* presided over by the *muttadar* used to settle disputes and matters pertaining to all the villages in the *mutta* irrespective of tribe.

Gramakula panchayat or intra-tribal council of a tribe in a village was having jurisdiction over cases like eating with forbidden tribes, speaking with a person of an inferior tribe in the case of women, committing adultery with an inferior tribe person and eating prohibited food.

Functions of the Council

The regional intra-tribal council or *gumpu kattu* of a tribe used to settle *maganali* cases i.e. compensation to the husband of a woman who eloped with another person and divorce cases.

The duties of the village elder council or *grama peddala* panchayat consisted of arbitrating over a number of disputes and quarrels arising assaults where the injuries were not of a serious nature, thefts, failure to repay loans, property disputes were trespass, witchcraft and sorcery and finally seducing women. Usually the proceedings of a village elder council were being dominated by a *pettandar* or village headman who was a Bagata. Whenever there was any serious breach of the peace, the *muttadar* was informed of it and he used to award punishment to the offenders.

Besides the above councils, the Bagata and other tribals had religious gurus who were either Vaishnavite Brahmins or Jangams (Saivite) from the plains. Periodically they used to visit the villages in the tribal areas and were conduct expiation ceremonies for those who were outcasted from their tribal groups as a result of certain ritual offences pertaining to each tribe and falling under the jurisdiction of the Grama Kula panchayats or intra-tribal councils.

Muttadars and Pettandors Dominate

At the same time the *muttadars* and *pettandars* used to dominate these councils as a result of their official positions in the Government as custodians of law and order. Their word was law to the ordinary tribals. The only course left to the other tribals to deal with a difficult and cruel *muttadar* in those days was resorting to witchcraft. There were instances where *muttadars* were supposed to have been killed by witchcraft by the Konda Kapus and other tribals. The *samantha* tribals are known to be expert in witchcraft. In course of time the Bagata came to be the dominant tribals in this area. As already stated the *muttadars* and *pettandars* were from the Bagata tribe, so they distributed most of the land in the valleys to the Bagatas. This made them a dominant land-owning group in the tribal areas of Vishakhapatnam district. Their former hold on the official positions can be inferred from the titles like Naidu, Dora, Majji, Padalu and Patrudu which they use at the end of their names. Soon the Bagatas claimed themselves as Kshatriyas and started wearing the sacred thread and having Vaishnavite priests from the plains as their religious mentors. In the multi-tribal villages of this region the Bagata, due to their hold on the cultivable land and their position in the Government, were able to dominate the village affairs. This gave them a kind of status ranking corresponding roughly to that of the caste system of the neighbouring plains. The Bagata came to be at the top of this hierarchy while the Valmikis who were considered to be untouchables and leather workers by occupation stood at the bottom. All the other tribal groups found themselves in the intermediate positions in the hierarchy according to their status vis-a-vis the Bagata and Valmiki so far as drinking and commercial relations were considered. The Bagata also avoid beef-eating while the tribes like Konda Kapu and Valmiki have taken to it.

The land holding position of the Bagata also made the other tribals either dependent on them as the former's farm servants or to take up *podu* cultivation exclusively like the Samanthas who live on the hill-tops for the purpose. In the multi-tribal village a kind of *jajmani* system came into vogue with the Bagata as the patrons. The Konda Kammara, another tribal group, supply iron implements necessary for the agricultural operations. The Ghasis rear pigs. The Nooka Dora work as agricultural and forest labourers.

As Reddy (1973 : 161) points only during the times of hunting also "there are distinct roles prescribed for different tribal groups. According to their traditional rules, a hunter who first strikes the animal gets a bigger share in the meat. But the division of labour between the groups is such that a member of the lower section scarcely gets a chance to strike". Again the members of the lower or inferior tribes should not touch the game even if they strike it first. Only the Bagata and other tribals belonging to the top rank like Kotiya, Nooka Dora, etc., could cut the animal and distribute it to others.

The same type of rules operated and are still operating in other spheres also. For instance, the offences which come under the purview of the intra-village and intra-tribal council of each tribe also reflect the above status ranking. These offences are : 1. Eating with forbidden tribes, 2. Marriage with forbidden tribes, 3. Speaking with a person of inferior tribe in the case of a woman. 4. Committing adultery with an inferior tribe person and 5. Eating prohibited food. According to the customary laws of the tribals in this region all the above offences were and are punishable with either excommunication or fines depending on the nature of the offence. Thus if a Bagata married another tribal woman he would be excommunicated from his tribe. If a Valmiki married a Bagata woman, then that woman would be permanently excommunicated from the tribe. In the case of a Bagata who married an inferior tribal woman he would be taken back only if he pays *tappu* or fine and undergoes a purification ceremony conducted by the *purushakari* of his tribe. This must be accompanied by leaving that woman also.

The Bagata were also dominating all the traditional councils in a village due to their dominance over other tribals. Thus the ultimate deciding authority in a village was and is the one dominated by the Bagatas, i.e. the *grama peddala* panchayat or village elder council, which was inter-tribal in nature. The other tribals due to their poverty and as their tribal leaders were living in different villages usually approached the village elder council dominated by the Bagatas in matters of intra-tribal nature also. As Reddy, aptly (1972 : 35) remarks "the rules of social distance are also connected with the seating arrangement of the village council constituting the village headman, the chief of the tribes, the representatives of the tribes and the priests in the village which settles the disputes of the village members. The members in the council sit a little apart from each other according to their rank in the tribal hierarchy".

Bagata in Post-Independence Period

The impact of Independence on the tribal population was considerable. The Congress Party which came into power exempted the scheduled tribes from the various codes of law that were enacted from time to time. In the tribal areas of Vishakhapatnam the tribals like the Bagata have adapted themselves well to the modern political set up. During the decade 1951-1961 the tribals went to the polling booths to elect their representatives to the panchayat and State Legislatures. At the same time they were loyal to the *rajas* and *muttadars* who once ruled them. In the 1967 General Election some of the Rajas contested from reserved constituencies. The Yuva Rani of Jeypore (Orissa) was elected as member of the legislature from the Madugula tribal constituency in Vishakhapatnam district. The same was the case with the former Bagata *muttadars* who succeeded in getting themselves elected as Panchayat Sarpanchs, Samiti Presidents and members of the legislature. For instance, in the 1962, 1967 and 1972 elections a Bagta who was from a *muttadar* family was elected as member of the Legislative Assembly. In the 1978 elections an influential Bagata who contested as a Janata candidate replaced him. Out of the 55 panchayats in Paderu taluk 28 panchayats are having Bagatas as Sarpanchs, out of the six Panchayat Samithis in Paderu taluk five Panchayat Samitis have Bagatas as presidents.

Why Bagatas are Dominant

How does the customary law enter into this type of political system? What are the factors that made the Bagatas dominant at the village level as well as at the higher levels of power? These are some of the pertinent questions at this stage.

As stated earlier the Bagatas were the *muttadars* under the local non-tribal Rajas and the British administration. Thus after the administration arrival the right to the and came to be validated by allegiance to the *muttadar* in the first instance (who used to distribute and collect rent) and ultimately to the Government. Since many of the *muttadars* were Bagatas, and since the Bagatas in general were much closer to the administration and the *rajas* and since they were able to exploit the political power vested in them, the political superiority they achieved began to resemble that of a dominant caste in the neighbouring plains. This was also aided by the numerical preponderance of the Bagatas which helped them in the struggle for power in the modern democratic system and institutions. Thus in brief the main political alignment for a tribal in this region had been clan, later the *mutta* under the rule of a *muttadar* in the former days and recently the "tribe" in its modern incarnation as a political category and emergent pressure group.

The onset of the democratic institutions and the abolition of the traditional *muttadari* system brought some changes in the mode of dominance of the Bagatas over as other tribals. There is an increasing competition now at all levels of political activity from the other hitherto dominated tribals.

Regarding the Kond politician Bailey, (1970 : 146) observes : "Even in such an apparently simple case as that of the Konds of Orissa the successful Kond politician has to exploit the caste-like structure of relationships between himself and his Oriya overlords; the rules of the bureaucracy and, increasingly, the rules of the modern democracy at the State level, at the newly established level of local self-government and to a very slight extent at the national level."

Similarly the Bagata leader has to exploit his relationships with other tribals living in a village. Most of the Bagata leaders as already stated are from the former *muttadar* families. In contrast to their former counterparts, i.e. the *muttadars*, they have to employ rather in a subtle manner the traditional loyalties and resources in order to win over their followers. At the same time they still use to a considerable extent the village panchayat and other institutions connected with dispensing justice to coerce their opponents and to protect their own followers. For instance, a Bagata leader nowadays protects his own followers in the following manner :

1. To see that a needy follower gets a wife by paying he minimum *oli* (bride-price) or *maganeli* (compensation).
2. To allow a follower to use the "waste" land in the village for cultivation which in ordinarily belongs to the whole village.
3. To allow only the followers to utilise the "communal trees" and other natural resources depriving others.

These are apart from the other benefits he provides them as a result of his position in the Panchayat Raj institutions. At the some time he can coax his followers into submission by awarding the fines and other punishments if they are caught in unlawful activities and other criminal offences which come under the purview of the village.

Other customary rules which come in handy are the custom of "bond friendship", etc. Thus a Bagata will enter into this type of friendship with another tribal and exploit his relationship not only for economic gains but also for political ends. Thus there are instances where a Bagata leader stepped down in favour of his "bond friends" who is also a Bagata in a political contest over a panchayat election. Another important aspect of the relationship between the modern political and the traditional system is that there are instances where the customary rules are transgressed by influential political leaders. This is in the field of inter-tribal marriages. There are instances where Bagata leaders married women of inferior tribal groups in order to win over those tribal groups. In ordinary cases these men would have been excommunicated from their tribe, but due to their knowledge of the modern law and also due to their political superiority they are able to manipulate the system to suit their needs. Further, one of the factors arising out of the new system of political institutions is that of the dichotomy of "self-interest" on the one side and "group loyalty" on the other. Under the present political system an aspiring and ambitious Bagata is swayed between these two contradicting loyalties.

Customary Laws Abused

From the above discussion it is evident that the institution of customary laws is closely related to the modern political process in the Bagata region, i.e. Vishakhapatnam agency. It is also seen how the Bagata due to their control over economic resources command the obedience of one and all in the multi-tribal villages and use both informal and formal panchayats for tightening their grip over their followers and also for controlling rebellious elements. Thus the Bagata are controlling two leadership positions — one, the formal government instituted status of sarpanch and members of the statutory panchayat and the other that of an ex-*muttadar* or priest of the village (*pujari*) which is that of an informal traditional leader. As sarpanchs they play present the day broker's role (as Bailey: 1970 puts it) mediating between villagers and development officials in which role they can grab the advantages of the development programmes. In the role of the informal traditional leader a Bagata continues to fulfil many of the traditional obligations of a wealthy and powerful patron. He protects his servants, arbitrates serious disputes and helps in other affairs. The total effect of this situation is that the customary laws or the mechanisms of social control have become a handy tool for an ambitious Bagata to seize power at the village level as well as for furthering his own interests in the political field while the poorer sections of the tribals can do nothing but to oblige and succumb to the machinations of the powerful Bagata elite. The situation described here compares well with the situation elsewhere. For instance Beidelman (1961, 1966) describes the use of locally-run Government courts in the Ukaguru chiefdoms of Tanzania and shows how the judgements of these courts were used to further Kagaru political aims at the expense of four minority tribal groups living in the same area. He also states that the vindictiveness of the Kagaru against members of minority tribes was mitigated by the intervention of a Kagaru patron, or by special relationships between the defendant and the Kagaru headman or court holders, but without this aid the non-Kagaru evidently did not stand a chance against a Kagaru in a court. Beidelman makes use of the Kagaru situation to show the effect of the policy of indirect rule at the local level. The same is true with regard to the tribal areas of India where in the absence of legal codes the courts have been empowered to decide disputes, after ascertaining the prevailing custom. This has given scope for many abuses. Influential tribals are able to produce before courts concocted evidence about the customary law which go in their favour or that of their followers thus depriving their less influential tribal brethren of justice. The Bagata region is not an exception to this unfortunate development and this calls for a proper codification of the customary laws so that they may not be abused for making political capital.

PART V

WESTERN INDIA

29

TRIBAL CUSTOMS AND LAWS OF WESTERN INDIA — AN INTERPRETATION

R.S. MANN

Five tribes, both big and small, have been covered for the study of tribal customary laws in western India. The Bhil, the largest and the most widely scattered tribe, was covered by two researchers in two different and distant settings. In all, four Bhil villages, two in Rajasthan and two in Gujarat, were studied. Other tribes, studied in respect of customary laws, include Mina and Garasia of Rajasthan and Gamit and Dubla of Gujarat. Out of the 12 villages covered, six were comparatively more exposed to alien influences. The Bhils of Rajasthan were studied in Jegeewar and Kanba villages of Udaipur and Dungarpur districts respectively. In Gujarat, they were studied in Jamunbihir and Jeket villages of Dang and Panchmahal districts respectively. Malwas village of Jaipur and Manipura of Sawai Madhopur were studied for Minas; Gegrood and Talwaron-ka-Naka villages of Sirohi district for Garasia; Mahuwas village of Bulsar and Nani Chikli of Surat for Gamit; and Nogama village of Bulsar and Rayam of Surat for Dublas.

The acculturative influences made an impact on some of the tribal customs and laws in two ways. First, there is some sort of infraction of the laws concerning a particular customary behaviour. Secondly, and this involves circumvention, the tribals bypass their customary laws and do not adhere to the standardised norms. This phenomenon is met with within smaller as well as bigger tribes, as also in the case of the more as well as less exposed sections of the same tribe. The infraction and circumvention are generally at the level of individuals rather than at the level of tribe or section barring the *bhagat* or Christian sections. The Christian Bhils or Garasias do not adhere to many customarily prescribed practices. The superstitious rituals involving rain-making, for example, are not subscribed to by them in material as well as in an ideological sense. Likewise, the preference for polygyny and the practices of bride-price (*dapa*) and re-marriage (*natra*) are denounced by the Christian families. Their attitude to many other customs and practices has also undergone change. Many among the Bharat (devotee) Bhils, Garasias and even Gamits have drifted into a certain new way of living, away from customary prescriptions. For instance, they refrain from participation in animal sacrifices (say, of goat or cock) made on certain occasions by their non-*bhagat* tribesmen, from taking meat or alcohol under the influence of *bhagatism.* They are also different in respect of their dress, worship pattern, etc. As separate social identities, the *bhagats* among the Bhils, Garasia or Gamit distinguish themselves at the level of role playing which involves avoidance of many of the customary prescriptions. They have emerged as endogamous units within the framework of devotion to the different *gurus* and have been helped in this by their being puritans and teetotallers with consequent implications in traditional life-style of the Bhils, Garasias and Gamits.

Three Categories of Laws

Three different categories of laws are reported to exist in the tribal areas. First, that which exclusively supports tribal customs and associated ways of life. Second, that wheet maintains the social order of various castes living with tribes or in the vicinity of tribal habitations. Third, that which is constituted by formal laws or the State legal system. The procedures involved differ in the case of these categories. Similarity between certain tribes and caste groups, in the matter under reference, is çertainly not ruled out. This holds specially true in the case of the tribals who have lived with caste Hindus for long and in fairly close proximity. In the light of simultaneous existence of two or three categories of laws, in certain areas, a measure of adjustment became unavoidable. At some places, the arrangement of this kind is smooth. Tribals, by and large, remained unconcerned about caste customary laws so long as they were not involved in the process of Sanskritisation. The practice of bride-price in the case of the Bhil, Garasia, Gamit and partly Dubla is in distinct from dowry among the castes. Likewise, marriage by elopement, so popular among the Bhils and Garasias, is not approved by neighbouring castes or by formal laws. The formal system of law provides for punishment in the event of elopement. The Minas would not be satisfied with the penalty imposed for some offences by the formal laws and would try the offender in their caste councils which are strong not only at village but also at regional level. It may be mentioned that the Minas and Dublas have coexisted with castes for over centuries. The Minas even equate themselves with the Rajput, Jat, Gujjar and Ahir castes of their region, share many a culture trait with them. Likewise, the Dublas have centuries old relationship with the Patels and other castes of the area. Unlike the Minas, they are involved in the relationship of *hali-dhaniama* (bondage) with the Patels. They serve their land-owning masters under this system pledging individuals as well families in the service of their masters (*dhaniamas*). In such an age-old interaction, the Dublas, too, have picked up many traits of caste system. The Minas and Dublas have relaxed certain rigidities of their respective tribal customary laws. *zhagra* (chiefly pertaining to compensation) system among the Bhils, Minas and Garasias is rooted in the tribal social order. The same holds true for *nukta* (death feast) of the Minas. Following restrictions on guests, under the Guest Control order in 1976-77, there was a conflict between the Minas and police. The Minas invite people to the death feast according to their social status. When people more than the prescribed limit under the formal laws were invited in a village of Sawai Madhopur, the police intervened. A few of the latter's party were killed during the intervention.

The effectiveness of the native law is revealed when an individual is tried afresh for his fault, even when he or she has already undergone punishment or penalty under the State laws, for committing the offence. This specially pertains to the Minas and partly to the Bhils and Garasias. They consider their traditional mechanism of social control superior to others. There are two explanations for such a recourse. Firstly, the tribals are not satisfied with the punishment given under the State laws. Secondly, the State laws are not accepted and recognised as their own or as governing them. Cases are not wanting where persons, for the same charge, have been tried twice; first, under the State legal system and its procedure, and secondly, by the tribal council after the person returns to his native place. The community remains unsatisfied unless the person is penalised according to the local procedure. Such a situation demands that the importance of native law cannot be undermined, and it may be worthwhile to give them their due place in the formal system of social control.

Normally the majority of people submit to the customary laws. For instance, bride-price is paid in marriage. Simultaneously, there is some relaxation in its ideological and operational rigidity. This is specially noted in those cases where an alternative relief mechanism exists. The bride price must be given, but then a boy can work in the prospective father-in-law's house for some period to compensate for bride-price, which he otherwise, cannot arrange in cash or in any other form. But the condition of bride-price in marriage cannot be ignored or avoided, except in the case of the Minas, who are moving towards the dowry system.

Every tribe has its own customary laws. However, in the case of Zamindar Mina and Chowkidar Mina, as also in the case of the Kalia Bhil and Palia Bhil, or the *bhagat* and non-*bhagat* Gamit, there are many common elements in the customary laws of different tribes. Say, a better status is given to tribal women. Uniformity and difference in the customary laws of a tribe, living in two settings, is influenced by a number of factors. The same holds true when the customary laws of one tribe are viewed in the light of those of others. In addition to the influence of traits of alien culture, a phenomenon that occurs through contact, the other relevant contributing factors include the nature of economy, ecology, religion and to some extent the force of social organisation.

Male the LOCUS of Authority

In a family, the eldest male member forms the locus of authority, and this is a common feature among all the tribes. The succession of authority, descent and inheritance of property are all in the male line for all the five tribes. The pattern of residence is patrilocal. Thus, the tribal society of western India is run on patriarchal lines. However, the tribal women enjoy freedom of movement, mate selection (exception being the Minas), pre-marital sex relations (except the Minas) etc. The age at marriage is high in the case of the Bhil, Garasia, Dubla and Gamit.

Pressure, as an element in the mechanism of social control, does work, especially with the headman of a council, though all the tribes cultivate democratic ways in general. In this aspect the headman is regarded as a privileged person. A woman never heads a traditional tribal council in any of the five tribes. The authority of an individual or a council is defined within the dimensions of the customary law. It has undergone some change after the emergence of an alternative infrastructure of Panchayati Raj bodies. There is a general decline in the recognition of authority of the traditional heads.

A social offence is outright condemned, as people consider it sinful or immoral. But the fact may be condoned by calling upon the offender to pay fine, say, or throw a feast or to reach an agreement, without any implication of spending or physical hardship. This preserves tribal solidarity. A socially ostracised person is readmitted into the group, and the committing of a heinous crime can even be pardoned. This holds true for all tribes. However, imposition of punishment by State interferes with old punishment procedures and rituals, religious sentiments, socio-psychological feelings and other kinds of relations. But this has not shattered people's faith in their customs and norms.

The concept of the "Customary law" sounds clear when viewed in the case of the tribe which lives in relative isolation (say, Palia Bhil, Chowkidar Mina, Gamit, Bhil, Garasia, etc.) or in case of those where culture contact has been very nascent. Otherwise, the concept needs to be reviewed for the tribes whose history of culture contact with others is centuries old and has been intimate (say, Dubla, Zamindar Mina, Bhil, Rajput, Garasia, etc.). Where the isolation has long been broken, the customs and the supporting laws are fast changing. Some culture traits (say, *dapa, nukta, natra, zhagra*, etc.) remain; others are partially changed, and there are others (say, pollution norms), which are totally alien but have been absorbed by the tribals for a long time and now appear to have become customary with them. In the same tribe the original, the borrowed and the imposed practices are met with.

30

MECHANISM OF SOCIAL CONTROL AMONG THE MINAS

S.H.M. RIZVI

The Minas are among the oldest inhabitants of Rajasthan and are one of the aboriginal tribes of the country. They claim a noble descent from "Matsya" or "Minavatar", the incarnation of Lord Vishnu in the disguise of a fish. The bulk of the tribe is concentrated in Jaipur, Sawai Madhopur, Udaipur and Alwar districts of Rajasthan. In view of their occupation the Minas are mainly divided into two major groups, (a) Khetor Mina or Zamindar Mina or Purana Basil and (b) the Chor Mina, or Chowkidar Mina or Nayabasi. The former were employed as guards in the forts and palaces and their main occupation is settled agriculture, while the latter are notorious for their anti-social activities. The Minas were considered to be the members of criminal society during the pre-Independence period and were subjected to daily attendance at the nearest police station under the Criminal Tribes Act (1924).

The group under study being numerically big and spread over a large area, two villages — Malwas and Manipura — were selected. This was to facilitate the study of the tribe in two situations, one at traditional habitat and the other at a place where they have come in contact with other communities and are exposed to agents of change. Malwas, in Dausa tehsil, is one of the earliest settlements of the Minas and has a major concentration of the Mina households. It is 23 kms away from the urban-industrial complex and is not connected by any road, thus the impact of ideas and values brought in by an improvement in the communication and developmental activities is of a minimal magnitude. But as it is difficult to describe and analyse a society on a static level, changes and influences, affecting them have been noticed as they came up in the course of study. To enlarge the scene owing to social change and acculturation data were collected from another village. Manipura village of district Sawai Madhopur was selected taking these factors into consideration. It is a non-traditional habitat of the Minas. It is ethnically heterogeneous where the Minas live and interact with other non-tribal communities. It has a sizable population of the Minas and is situated at a distance of 9 kms from the big industrial complex manufacturing cement and allied products. It is connected with the nearest-urban centre (Sawai Madhopur town) through a State highway. The village was also exposed to SITE programmes conducted by the Space Application Centre, Ahmedabad.

Unique Family Pattern

The Mina villages show a unique family pattern. Firstly, it lacks nuclear type of family. The Minas live in patrilocal residential units i.e. household families which are also the smallest economic group in the community. The *ghar* is characterised by a common monetary pool and after the father's death the sons may or may not divide the property and have a common or separate monetary pool. The Minas further recognise a larger family unit including all the living male consanguine. This group is referred to as *kutumb*. It consists of at least three generations of male consanguine, their spouses and children. Tradition prescribes that the *kutumb* should maintain the divorced, widows and orphans of its male members, and provision is also made for the support of deserted daughters of the family and their children.

Thok and Got

A smaller unilinear unit is *thok* or lineage, patrilinage to be precise, of varying generation depth. Its members are geneologically related and describe themselves as *thok bhaya* (lineage brother). Each village has one or several *thoks* residing together which group themselves under a legendary figure and refer to this group as *got*. A *got* is strictly exogamous.

The *got* among the Mina consists of several clusters of *thok* dispersed over a wide area. There is no classification of the *got*. They are all of the same status, and members of different *gots* are free to marry each other except where a union is considered incestuous due to an already existing relationship.

Levels and Mechanism of Social Control

Two important elements are discerned in the Mina tribal council. *panch patel*, and the other *patel* (the headman of the *thok*). The tribal council though an informal body plays a significant role in their life. The *patel* is the representative spokesman of one *thok* and belongs to the oldest *thok* of the village. The office of the *patel* is hereditary. Succession to the "Patelship" is by birth, i.e. the first-born male child of the first wife. If the first wife has no male issue then the first-born male child of the second wife in succession becomes the *patel.* But if he is not survived by a son his younger brother succeeds him to the office. In case the *patel* is survived only by a minor son, his brother takes over with the understanding that when the minor comes of age he will vacate the office in his favour.

During the pre-Independence period the authority of the *patel* had legal sanction from the then rulers. He had certain duties (like revenue collection from the village) and if he carried them out with utmost honesty and sincerity the State did not interfere in the affairs of his community. For these services the State some honorarium. At present most of the Mina villages are inhabited by a number of different *gots*. It is, however, generally agreed that a village must have been inhabited at its early stage of growth by the members of one *thok* belonging to a particular *got*. Members of other *gots* must have come later. Early settlers were regarded as *thuns* (owners) of the village and hence the senior member of the senior *thok* of the early settlers enjoyed the special status of being the *patel* of his settlement. In the unexposed village the members of Baiphlawat *got* are generally regarded as the oldest inhabitants.

These five *patels* form *panch patel* or the tribal council at village level. The exposed village had two *thoks* of Kankarwad and Bannawad *got*. Members of other 11 *gots* came later after seeking permission of the early settlers to whom they were probably related as affines or cognates and in certain cases they were unrelated. Hence there are about 10 *patels* of 10 *thoks* who form the *panch patel* of an exposed village. The *patel* is not only the spokesman of his *thok* but is also vested with all the ritual power. For example, during the birth of a male child in the family when the local midwife cuts the umbilical cord of the newborn baby and buries it in a pit the *patel* decides the amount (*honal*) to be paid to the newborn's father's younger brother. While constructing a new house or well the *patel* has the honourable role of placing the first stone (*nechak'*) and during marriage the *patel* is vested with all the disbursing power to pay the money to the bridegroom's father (*hathlewa*) and his associates (*baratis*). *Panch patel* as stated earlier settles all disputes concerning Mina inhabitants of the village. There is no written constitution but oral traditions are there which conform to the existence of such councils since time immemorial.

Besides the village-level tribal council one finds an informal group of village elders including non-Mina individuals who settle disputes between a Mina and non-Mina within the village. This informal group is called *panch mahajan*. The number of members of *panch mahajan* varies from five to seven in which four to five *patels* of Mina *thoks* and one or two heads of Brahmin and Mahajan households of the village would be invited to settle the dispute. This informal grouping does not have power of physical coercion. In case charges are proved against a particular individual the decision is generally brought to the notice of the Gram panchayat, a statutory body which implements the decision in view of the existing rules and laws. There is a strong link between the *panch mahajan* and the statutory panchayat.

On viewing these two councils at village level described above, it becomes evident that the *panch patel*, distinctively, stands out in its structure, function and legal sanction from the other existing councils of the village, like the *panch mahajan* and Gram panchayat. The intra-Mina disputes are generally expected to be settled within the *panch patel* which is an authorised body to deal with the socio-religio-legal aspects of Minas, the latter having faith and confidence in the decision taken by the council. However, when cases and disputes are not settled to the satisfaction of the contending parties, legal help is sought from the existing Government judiciary. Such cases being rare, *panch patel* functions as a mechanism of social control, a system complete by itself.

In contrast we find that the *panch mahajan*, the body constituted to settle disputes arising between the Mina and non-Mina communities of the village, has its powers greatly reduced. This may be attributed firstly to the numerical dominance of the Minas who usually prefer decisions in their own favour. Secondly the existence of the formal statutory panchayat which came into existence in 1954 after the State Government passed the Rajasthan Panchayat Act, 1953. The Act vested statutory panchayats with both executive and judicial powers (*Government of Rajasthan*, 1964, p. 9-10, 106). However it is interesting to note that the villages under study being tribal in nature apparently also see to the interests of the non-tribal residents and give them a fair deal.

Kheda Panchayat

Mina villages situated within the radius of five miles recognise the representative tribal council called *kheda* panchayat which settles inter-village disputes involving Mina inhabitants. This council is constituted by representative *patels* belonging to the oldest *thoks* of the respective villages. During the field work it was observed that the *kheda* panchayat mainly dealt with cases concerning disputes over marriage, *nata*, divorce, adultery, seduction and sometimes theft. The contending parties approach their respective *patels* the later inform the other members of the *kheda* panchayat through a *rajbalai* to meet at a convenient village and suitable time for hearing the dispute. All the proceedings are carried out at a central place in the village in the presence of the public. The *kheda* panchayat like *panch patel* has the religiously sanctioned right over physical coercion, punishment and fine.

Samaj Panchayat

The *samaj* panchayat is constituted of representative *patels* of Mina villages lying within the radius of 10 to 15 miles. This council is empowered not only for physical coercion, punishment and fine but also with the right to excommunicate and accept the accused in the community after certain ritual expiation. Moreover it can impose a fine of up to Rs. 500. Thus offences considered most "heinous" by the tribal community are brought to the notice of the *samaj* panchayat.

Pargana Panchayat or Gadhatpeshi

The Pargana panchayat or *gadhat peshi* comprises representative *patels* of all the Mina villages lying within a *pal*, territorial division of Min Desh (meaning the country of the Minas). This council is empowered not only to excommunicate but also to accept back the accused in the community. It also has the right to change or alter Mina customary laws within their full socio-cultural context. It also looks after the welfare and socio-economic development of Minas living in the *pal*.

Religious Sanction

The sacred area (rectangular raised platform under a banyan tree) where the tribal council convenes is always the chosen site next to the central Mina shrine of Sita Ram, who is believed to preside supernaturally over the court whenever it is in session. The *patels* choose one of them to preside over the deliberations and concensus judgement is sought from of the *patels*.

These tribal councils not only utilise their coercive powers to reconcile disputing parties and to award compensation to the innocent, they also attempt to bring along "razinama" (agreement on mutual understanding) between contestants after which normal social relations are expected to be resumed. The councils rely indirectly upon the diffused moral sanctions embodied in kinship, *thok* and *got* relationships to support its efforts to restore peace and harmony in the society.

To understand the functions of these councils at various levels an attempt is made to analyse the cases dealt by them. The abovementioned infrastructure of these councils throws light on their operation and function within the framework of social control. As discussed earlier the three-tier structure of the tribal council at village, subregional and regional levels has also a significant bearing on the social control of a wider group, by restoring peace, harmony and goodwill among the individuals living in their jurisdiction.

Eldest Male Locus of Authority

Within the family the locus of authority lies on the eldest male member. The sphere of his authority is limited within the following areas: family, economy, decisions regarding marriage of the members of the household, mobility of a women members to their in-laws' house and their natal home, and gifts to be given to certain category of relatives at the time of marriage and death. A son or younger brother has to seek his permission before establishing an independent cooking hearth. Lastly, and most importantly, he is the chief disbursing authority of grains and money. This entire authority structure is symbolically represented in the tribe by the customs of tying the headgear (*pagri baudina*) which is a 5-6 metre peice of cloth tied around the head.

After the father's death during the performance of death rites (*nukta*) the *patel* of the *thok* ties the deceased's pagri on his son's head ceremoniously in the presence of heirs, relatives and friends. However, it is noteworthy that the major decisions taken by the eldest male always have to be approved by the *thok's patel*.

Nata Marriage

Nata marriages are frequent in the Minas and an accepted form of marriage. In this, a married woman with living husband and offspring can remarry another married man – her second husband, paying cash compensation called *jhagre ka paisa* to her former husband. In many a case the woman in question may be deserted, widowed or divorced. If the woman is widowed or divorced the compensation money is paid to the living male guardian of the woman both the women's father and her in-laws claim the money. It was noted during the field work that a widowed woman after the 10-day ritual mourning resumes her duties as a married woman in the household. Her deceased husband's brothers (elder and younger included) are entitled to cohabit with her and the children born out of such unions are legally recognised by the entire household and get the share of their mother's deceased husband's property.

Divorce Permitted

Amongst the Minas divorce is referred to as *chorna* literally meaning (to leave). The tribal society permits both its men and women to seek divorce. The men mainly seek divorce on the grounds of adultery, barrenness and incurable diseases and neglect of duties towards children and husband. The woman can seek divorce on the grounds of impotency, incapability to provide maintenance for the household, cruelty, criminality and insanity. The legal aspects of divorce are very clear-cut amongst the Minas. A divorced woman, irrespective of whether her husband divorced her or she divorced him, has to forgo the rights over her children and jewellery which she received at the time of marriage from her in-laws. In case, a child is lactating then she is allowed to bring up the child till the age of five years and then to return it to his father. In case the woman in question remarries in the meantime and her second husband adopts the child (if the child is male) then he has to pay cash compensation for the child to the wife's first husband. If the woman is not remarried, after her divorce she becomes the liability in her father's household. This may be one of many reasons for the rarity of divorce cases where women seek divorce. Irrespective of the mother's marital status the children continue to live with their fathers and are entitled to their father's property. Male children may be adopted under the Mina customary law. A male-childless couple can take on heir from within the *ghar*, and *kutumb*. There are three necessary conditions for a valid adoption.

(a) Both sets of parents must agree,
(b) The child should be a legitimate offspring of the patrilateral uterine relative.
(c) The matter must receive full family publicity.

The adopted child also gets an equal share in his father's property along with the other sibs.

Property Inheritance and Succession

Agricultural techniques made possible the continuous exploitation of the same fields. Thus the Minas largely remained for generations agriculturaists by cultivating the soil which satisfied their basic need, i.e., food. Conceptions of property are constantly changing with the development of technology and change in moral ideals. The widespread concept of property is expressed by the Minas in terms *Jagjagati* and *Khetibari*.

During the course of interviews special focus was given to questions pertaining to the ownership of a piece of land and the kind of right the person holds on the land. The following points emerged from the intensive interviews collected in the two villages:

(i) Till the mid fifties the ownership of land vested in the individual thoks, the representative patels seeing to the equal distribution of the produce from the fields among the cultivators.

(ii) Many aged informants still remember referring to the land as belonging to their *thok*.

(iii) It is only after the abolition of the Zamindari system that land was distributed among the individuals of the village and this was the beginning of the individual ownership of land.

Traditionally in the unexposed village the total land of the village was divided among five *thoks* while the land of the exposed village was originally divided among two *thoks,* namely, Kankarwad and Barmawad, but later migration of some other *gots* in the village necessitated division of land among 10 *thoks*. However, at present a Mina can and does claim his ownership right over a piece of land (*khetibari*) in the village and the idea of *thok* and kin-concreted ownership of cultivable land is totally lacking in both the villages under study. Except for the fact that as yet, under customary laws a Mina cannot dispose of his land to a non-Mina without the consent of his *thok*'s *patel*. This is perhaps the remnant of the age-old traditional ownership pattern of the property. This customary law has also saved to some extent most of the contemporary Mina villages from encroachment by other tribes and communities. Hence it is evident that the tribe tries to hold the rights of the land of the village. In extreme cases where cash is needed by a Mina family the land is mortgaged to another Mina.

The inheritance law allows an equal distribution of the property of the deceased father among his sons. Daughters are not entitled to any share. The principle of the division of land is that the sons shall inherit enough land to provide them and their families with a livelihood. If the father's land cannot maintain more than one family then the younger brothers are entitled to receive a nominal share in its produce. If any heir who wishes to sell his share wholly or in part he has to offer it for sale first to his co-heirs and then if they refuse to buy it, he is at liberty to dispose it of to any Mina bidder.

Crops in the field and in store are inherited in equal shares. Wells in the fields or rear residential land are equally inherited by the heirs. For example, if there are four brothers the water would be drawn by all of these equally, i.e. for irrigation purposes. Livestock, money, tools, clothes, carts, etc. (*jagiagats*) are owned by the family and rarely by individuals.

Repayment of Debts

During the *nukta* (a death rite) ceremony the entire amount of debt is calculated and publicly announced and to clear this the eldest son gets the major share of his deceased father's property.

A woman owns only the ornaments given to her as gift at the time of her marriage by her father-in-law. Till she continues to live with her in-laws, she has the right over the ornaments but the moment she leaves the house and remarries (*nata*) she is expected to return all the ornaments to her in-laws which become the property of her first husband. These ornaments are again used as gifts to the bride when her husband remarries.

According to Mina customary law before the abolition of the Zamidari system the grazing land (*chak charaka*) was restricted by allocating some grazing area (*nasht*) to each *thok* which used to pay a nominal fee of rupee one per year to the ruler. After the abolition of Zamidari system, since all the pasture land belongs to the nation, there no restricted grazing areas.

Thus it is evident that the principal means of acquiring land under the traditional tenure is inheritance. Mina's being a patrilineal society the authority transfers to the eldest son. It is true that since the period of British rule and promulgation of the Rajasthan Land Reforms and Resumption of Jagirs Act (1952) the process of change from group to individual rights of ownership has continued unabated even though legally the right was no longer the right to full ownership, but only a right to occupancy. Due to this the individual became increasingly important in every respect. This whole process of individualisation coupled with the similar ideas affected the customary laws pertaining to the holding of land. Offences were by the tribal council.

Murder Compensation

Whenever a case of murder comes to the tribal council it assesses the amount due in compensation to the murdered man's family. The accused undergoes a purification ritual by bathing in the Holy Ganges, and gives a feast to the Brahmins.

Killing of Cow and Peacock a Crime

Killing of a cow or peacock is a crime of a high degree and the punishment for such offences if proved is to undergo a ritual purification by bathing in the Holy Ganges and by feeding a particular amount of grain to birds, as decided by tribal council.

Marriage with a Non-Tribal an Offence

Marriage with a non-tribal is an offence which other punishment but excommunication from the tribal society. However if the marriage alliances are with a clean caste like the Brahmin, Rajput, Mahajan, Gujjar and Jat the tribal council imposes a heavy money fine as punishment and after going through ritual expiation (Ganga nahaye) the accused can be taken back in the society.

Theft

In case of a theft the thiefs is ordered to return the stolen property or its value and in addition to pay some compensation as decided by the tribal council. If the thief himself has no property or he is unable to pay, his consanguineous are asked to pay.

Criminal and Common Assault

The tribals make a clear distinction between criminal and common assault. The beating of wife or son by a man, though a physical assault, is not considered unlawful. The physical assault, caused by a dispute between villages, is redressable. The sole redress or punishment for such an offense is compensation assessed according to the severity of the injury.

Adultery Prevalent but Punished

Extra-marital relations, maintained clandestinely, are widely prevalent amongst the Minas. In case it is reported then it is punishable as adultery and a fine is imposed and compensation ordered be paid to the husband. The amount of the fine and compensation does not depend on the circumstances of the case but on the economic status of the convicted man. He is also reprimanded (*paabendi*) by the tribal council and worked not to commit such as act in the future.

An adultress in the Mina community faces very trying punishment. The woman is barred from carrying on her clandestine meetings. At night she is chained with *naud*, an iron anklet with chain. During the day efforts are made not to send her out from the women's quarters for work but if need be she is sent to the field under the watchful eyes of some family elder.

Rape a Rare Phenomenon

Rape is a rare phenomenon amongst the Minas and when committed compensation is paid and in addition a fine is also imposed on the guilty.

Collision of Two Legal Systems

The following case recorded in exposed village (the first case in the history of the village where complaint is made to the State Government authorities to seek justice) would give an idea how two legal systems (traditional and local government) collide:

Time (1962) Case of Illegal Pressurisation and Mortgage of Land

Ramsingh Mina of exposed village mortgaged his land to Varpal *patel* for a sum of Rs. 500 to perform the death rites of his father. This happened sometime in 1959. The amount with interest went up to Rs. 881 and Varpal asked Ramsingh to pay the amount. Ramsingh agreed to sell the mortgaged land for Rs. 2,065 to Varpal and asked for the balance sum after deducting his debt. Varpal refused to purchase the land at such exorbitant price and continued the use of the mortgaged land. Ramsingh was again in need of money for his remarriage. To meet the expenditure he sold his two other plots of land, with the mortgaged plot, to Moriya Mina. While Moriya wanted the possession, Varpal refused to give and when Moriya forcibly asserted his claim on the disputed plot he and his kinsmen were beaten up by Varpal and his kinsmen. This was the first violent clash between two *gots* and relations became strained. The *panch patel* was approached by Ramsingh and Moinya who gave the judgement that Varpal should not claim his ownership on the plot owned by Ramsingh when Ramsingh agrees to return the borrowed money. Varpal refused to abide by decision and was accordingly fined Rs. 500. It was decided that till that fine is paid, no Mina of the village will have commensal relationship with Varpal and his family. Varpal remained firm in his arguments. But before his son's marriage he paid the money to the *panch patel* and only then could perform the marriage with pomp and show. Ramsingh, advised by Moriya and his kinsmen, took the dispute to the *kheda* panchayat which agreed with the decision of the *panch patel.* But Varpal again refused to agree. So the dispute was brought to the notice of the *gadhat peshi* which was convened in a nearby village *ajnouti* under the presidentship of Shri Mohjiram.

A summons was issued to Varpal but he refused to appear before the tribal council on the apprehension that there may be a clash. He wanted that the council must give in writing the guarantee of his life and then only he would appear. Consequently the *gadhat peshi* took the responsibility and sent Ram Niwas to call Varpal with a note of guarantee. Even then Varpal did not appear, and asked for another convenient date. The *gadhat peshi* agreed and decided to meet again. Varpal in spite of receiving a summon from Phulji (Rajbalai) appear before it. So the *gadhat peshi* met on January 23, 1968, and looking into the misbehaviour and attitude of disrespect shown by Varpal passed judgement. Varpal was fined for contempt of the council and was declared excommunicated from the tribe. It was further decided that if the accused paid the fine on or before February 23, 1968, he would be permitted the membership of the tribe. This decision was printed in a local printing press and distributed in all the villages of the *pal*. Varpal paid the fine before the expiry of the last date. Thus the main dispute remained unsettled because of Varpal's absence. Varpal in the meantime filed a suit against Ramsingh and his associates in the local court and received the permission to cultivate the disputed land till a verdict was given. When Ramsingh and Moriya came to know about this they in return filed a case of illegal possession by Varpal in the local court. Sometimes in 1969 and since then many violent clashes have taken place between the two *gots* in which two human lives have been lost. Consequently a large number of (around 16) civil and criminal suits are filed with the local court and police, without any result. Varpal continues with the cultivation of the land under dispute.

This case particularly throws light on a *patel*'s behaviour which brought down the respect for a *patel* in the eyes of the villagers and Varpal being a *patel* does not enjoy the due respect any more. The case has more bearing on the conflicting situation before the customary laws in dealing such cases of disrespect shown towards the tribal council.

Concluding Remarks

Compatibility and Conflict

The preceding discussions have dealt with the customary laws of the Mina tribe in the context of the socio-cultural matrix of contemporary Mina society. After a careful analysis of the cases dealt with by the tribal councils it can be seen that throughout there appears to be an apparent harmony between the people and the customary laws as perfect instruments for social control: an undercurrent of gradual erosion of faith in the tribal council and its decreasing authority is strongly felt by the people. This feeling gets strengthened by the approachable offices of the State Government and the idea of police protection which gives a momentum to the unrest in the people's mind regarding the integrity of the *patel* and sanctity of the role of *panch patels*.

Deviations from the normative pattern, though rare, suggest that the Minas in general still repose their faith in their traditional customary councils. In the past the Mina State comprised several smaller States (referred to as "pals") and this holds good even today. All these States settle most of their disputes without referring to the Local Government authorities. The State *pradhan* acts as the chief spokesmen of the people and has direct contact with the State authorities seeing to the development and welfare of the tribe. Throughout the field work a single *thok* was observed as a group and the prevalence and practice of the customary law studied. It was found that the *thok*'s *patel* has the authority to administer and implement the various tribal laws. In conclusion the compatibility and conflict, in other words, the changes in the tribal customary laws, would be viewed through the change in the authority and the role of the *patel*.

The tribal customary laws are based upon experiences and are altered from time to time with the changing circumstances. Thus a new step in social development or evolution affects the existing tribal customary laws. Since judgement demands that the law should fit the changing situation, it will be checked whether the people revert to the legal policy of the State or they still prefer to continue with the customary laws and the tribal councils. As has been found, the changes in the customary laws are mainly due to the changing conditions of tribal life, caused by the outside influence which sometimes creates new legal possibilities in the cases like divorce and remarriage without the payment of *jhagre ke paise*. In the cases dealt with here it is observed that there is practically no change or modification in the traditional customary laws, they still exist on their traditional pattern. The modern legal code on the other hand acts as a supplement to the traditional jurisprudence. Even that is in a very limited manner, only serving the people, where the judgement has been passed against them by the tribal council. Moreover, it is felt by the people themselves that the modern legal authorities only help in causing delay in giving the final judgement (the standing example being the "stay orders" obtained in the few cases which were brought to the court), as against the prompt action taken by the tribal council. Not only that, involvement in the law courts involves spending money on the court personnel and lawyers the latter showing no personal interest or involvement with the party, rather they are very impersonal and objective in their approach and are extremely bureaucratic. Since this situation involved a lot of money and time, it becomes totally impracticable for the tribal farmer to stay in town and pursue a case. This has led the tribals to realise the positive aspects of their own customary laws and council chiefs. But with the existing situation, the burning problem equally felt by the people and their council is the authority of the latter which is put in total jeopardy due to the existence of the State law courts. Hence, the outcome of all these endogenous and exogenous forces acting on the legal pattern of the tribal society is the presence and applicability of the tribal legal pattern as well as the modern State legal pattern. Of course, the intensity of popularity of one over the other being different, the tribal society continues to exhibit complete harmony and does not show any structural change within their legal framework.

Educated go to Law Courts

In the two villâges studied for this problem it was found that the people go to the State law courts for the most serious matters like homicide and suicide which are of rare occurrence. In such cases it is the *patel* who goes and reports the matter. However, in the exposed village it has become usual in the last few years for the young educated men to revert to the law courts. This is mainly due to the fact that they have maximum interaction with the town dwellers. This situation is clearly evident from the case study of the exposed village. The case of land mortgage involving Varpal, the *patel* and his two sons, holding clerical posts in the local government office, did not submit themselves before the decision taken either by the *panch patel* or *ghat peshi* Pargana panchayat. They lodged many complaints of assault and threat against Ramsingh in the local police station. During the period of ten years the dispute was before the panch patel, about 13 complaints had been registered by Varpal and a same number of complaints is reported against Varpal by the opposite party of Ramsingh. The case became the talk of the entire area. The people are not only indignant at Varpal's action but equally at the action taken by the police, which kept Ramsingh and his other associates behind the bars for about 10 days after the violence between Varpal and Ramsingh's parties. According to the conscious model of the respondents two legal patterns collide here. They feel that Varpal should have shown more deference towards the Gadhat Peshi's decision taken in favour or Ramsingh. Varpal should not have got Ramsingh and his party comprising *patels* imprisoned. Moreover, the interference of police and court in the judgement of the tribal council and the delay of total 10 years, in giving a judgement is also being criticised by the people. Hence, it is beyond the comprehension of the people as to why some men resort to court, since the non-acceptance of the tribal council's decision entails incurring the disfavour of the entire tribe and excommunication. For reinstallation in the tribe they have to pay a heavy fine to the tribal council. The probable explanation given by the educated section of the village is that "only the 'detribalised' go to the police and courts". Besides their deference towards the tribal council, these people have a deep-rooted faith in their local deities and the tribal council always holds court near the shrine of a deity and while investigating a case the witnesses are made to vow in the name of the deity and speak the truth regarding the case. The people fully believe that in case they do not keep the vow and lie then they would incur the deity's wrath. Thus, when a party knows that they are in the wrong they never like to take the case to the tribal court. In the Ramsingh-Varpal case both the parties felt that they were beaten up undeservedly by the opposite party. Thus, Varpal's courage and guts to flout the tradition and seek the help of modern jurisprudence can be attributed to this sons' long association with the town court. For long years the two educated young men had witnessed several such cases being adjudicated in court. And the judgement given by the tribal council holds little meaning to them. Thus they became instrumental in inducing their father to bring the case to court and not to submit to the judgement given by the tribal council. Therefore in the exposed village this case opens up an avenue for the other people to file their cases in the local courts and in, fact, following this case several other cases had been field. In contrast, in the unexposed village we find only one case field in the local court.

Varpal being a *patel* himself brings down the esteem of *patels* in the eyes of the villagers by his association with the State court, indirectly affecting his authority as the *patel* of the *thok.* Hence, Varpal's action becomes instrumental in weakening the confidence of the people in the council *patels,* the practice of the tribal customary law.

Another important aspect which emerges from this study of the tribal customary law is that the existence of the State law court and its strict discipline specially regarding punishment (imprisonment and police detention) creates fear in the minds of the people and they, therefore, uphold and subscribe to their tribal council's verdict. A standing example of this is the rape cases. For this offence the *panch patel* imposes heavy fives as compensation which varies for Rs. 1,000 to 5,000. Though this is considered to be a "heinous crime" yet, the *panch patels* have no means to physically coerce the convict and force him to pay. It is only now that they threaten to inform the police if the man refuses to pay the compensation money. Fearing imprisonment and detention under police custody, the convict submits to the judgement of the tribal council, thus strengthening the very base of the institution, the tribal council.

On reviewing the present state of the Mina customary laws it can be stated that certainly the authority of the *patels* is on the decline partly due to the maintenance of law and order by the police who are vested with authority and the *patel* is in capable of inflicting physical coercion as punishment. Hence, the authority of the *patel* is restricted to imposing monetary punishment and ritual expiation. Thus the people who wrong can conveniently stay away from the village due to the shift in their economic system and education. Coming to the people who are directly affected by the two judiciaries — State and tribal — they have carved a way out for themselves. They neither deny their customary law nor reject the State law and have the best of both which favour and protect their interests.

31

CUSTOMARY LAW OF THE DUBLA

N.K. SINHA

Out of the 27 tribes in Gujarat, the Dubla occupy the second position in terms of numerical strength. Their population, according to 1971 Census, is 3,88,589. They are concentrated in the districts of Surat, Vulsad, Broach and Baroda. Some of them are also settled in Khaira, Panchmahal, Sabarkantha, Ahmedabad and Dang districts. They live in mixed villages with the caste Hindus.

While the statutory council looks after the problems which affect the village community as a whole, the Dubla *jati panch* of the village attends to the problems of the Dublas alone. The tribal council of the Dublas differs from other tribes from a specific angle — they have been economically dependent on the higher caste landlords. Though the Dublas, in Rayam, are numerically dominant, but due to their economic dependence on the landlords they considerably bank on the higher castes even in taking decisions in various matters. Before Indian Independence, the tribal villages were isolated from the point of view of political matters. The headman was in charge of maintaining the law and order. Before the enforcement of the Panchayati Raj, in 1954, the village headman was nominated by the District Collector and was called Police Patel. His tenure of office was for five years. The position of the Police Patel was not, in all cases, hereditary. The two villages under study have their own tribal councils, called *jati panch*. The Dubla *panch* is a selected body of the elders of the Dubla tribe. A Dubla *panch* becomes most effective at the time of divorce. Sometimes, an informal sanction of elders is sought when an engagement is confirmed. And, therefore, a divorce also necessitates the sanction of the tribe elders. Besides, the *panch* settles disputes involving various families of the tribe. Such disputes may arise out of abuse, pre-marital sex relation, witchcraft, etc.

The disputes are generally settled after a long discussion in which both sides are given due hearing. When a party is found guilty, it is punished by the imposition of a fine appropriate to the offence. In most cases the fine is imposed in cash. The whole amount of fine is not given as compensation — a part is spent on drinking or giving a feast to the members of the *jati panch*.

Jati Panch at Three Levels

The *jati panch* of the Dublas can be seen at three levels.

(i) *Faliya Panch* (hamlet council),
(ii) *Jati Panch* (village council),
(iii) *Chaura* (a Dubla regional council).

Faliya Panch

The *faliya panch* consists of only one member called *faliyas patel.* He is selected by the elderly members of a hamlet. The main qualification for becoming a *patel* are honesty and maturity. The *Faliya Patel* acts as arbitrator in disputes regarding division of ancestral property. In settling betrothals, especially the items of dowry to be given by the bride father, the *faliya patel* has a say. The bride-price is also fixed in consultation with them.

Jati Panch

The *jati panch* of the Dublas consists of all the *faliya patels* and a chief who is called *jati patel.* He is also selected from among the elders of the village. His selection is governed not only by the consideration of age and experience but also by the status and influence of a person. The inter-hamlet and inter-tribal or tribal caste disputes are to be settled in consultation with each *faliya patel.* The *jati patel* is not a hereditary post. The incumbent changes every year. A *jati patel* is considered the wisest man of the Dubla community, and his advice, on various matters, is usually followed.

The ceremony of selecting a *patel* is called *pagadi-pandhabi* (tying the turban). In case the Dubla *patel,* is ignored he does not bother for the problems of the villagers.

Chaura

A council represented by 12 to 20 villages is called *chaura*. Its meeting is requisitioned to solve intra- and inter-tribe disputes for fixation of bride-price and to take some important decisions like removal of a bad or harmful custom prevailing in the Dubla community. The *chaura* is represented at least by five members, including the *jati patel* from each village. The *chaura* has also made the Dubla community realise the advantages and privileges sanctioned by the Government for the Scheduled Castes and Scheduled Tribes. This organisation also directs social reform to be undertaken for the community with the help of organisations like Halpati Seva-Sangh, Halpati Sangthan and Rani Praja Seva Sangh. Generally, the members of the *chaura* are between the age of 42 and 50 years. During my stay in Rayam it was reported that the last *chaura* of the region was called in 1952 in Rayam itself to raise the amount of bride-price which was then Rs. 12.25. In the *chaura* meeting the bride-price was raised to Rs. 40.25 paise. This *chaura* meeting was followed by another in September, 1972, in Haripur village near Khadod in Bardoli taluka.

But representatives from two villages turned up and it resulted in the cancellation of the meeting. The purpose of this meeting was to raise the bride-price and to fix the fee for divorce. Lately the divorce fee has been fixed at Rs. 51. In case a wife seeks divorce, she has to pay Rs. 12.25 paise.

Police Patel the Alternative

If the statutory panchayat fails to decide a case the persons involved may approach the Police Patel whose position continues to be recognised since the British days. He has been a village-level officer whose main duties, at one time, were (i) to protect the village from decoits, (ii) to maintain peace and order in the village, (iii) to communicate to the Taluka office any event disturbing the peace and order in the village and to ask for immediate police aid, if necessary; and to help the village accountant in revenue collection. For all this he received from the Government, i.e. Taluka office, a fixed amount the ranging from Rs.40 to Rs. 70. In the British regime, Police Patels were given land as a part of their allowance. This position was nominated one, though approved by the landlords. A Police Patel could not become a member of the statutory village panchayat. Only the members of the landlord class have been nominated as Police Patels.

The statutory village panchayat has the power to impose a fine. In British India, the Police Patel exercised this power. In case of a serious offence, say, adultery and inter-caste marriage, the Dubla *jati panch* exercises the right to excommunicate the offender. But when an offender realises his or her folly and seeks apology, he is liable to be excused. No incident of excommunication took place in both the villages. The excommunication is only for an hour till the ordeal continues. One is readmitted the community after he pays Rs. 5 to Rs. 10 to the *jati patel*. He also serves liquor. There has been no physical punishment. Only a feast is to be given to the members of the *jati panch* and to the community members who pleaded in his or her favour. It was reported in Rayam and Nogama that no Dubla ever approached the court of law, at Vulsad or Surat, for seeking solution to a dispute. The Dubla informants were proud to inform that the *jati patel* is never disobeyed by them.

The young Dublas of Rayam have gone in for a bigger organisation of the community living in Bardoli taluka. The organisation, Halpati-Sangthan, was formed in 1975 at Surat under the leadership of Sri Jashwant Chauhan, a political figure. Every village has a branch of their institution and is headed by an *agyawan* (Initiator). The *agyawans* of Rayam and Nogama villages are Natwar Bhai Manga Bhai, who is also the *faliya patel,* and Ranchor Bhai Gopal Bhai. An *agyawan* collects a sum of Rs. 3, each quarter, from every member of the community, and finally deposits it in the main office at Surat. This amount meets the expenditure on the publication of their magazine, *Jagte Raho*, and on meetings of the Union.

Rights of Children

If a man marries a widow and does not agree to keep the children, born of the deceased husband, they generally go to live with their maternal grandfather or maternal uncle. The agnate relatives look after the children. This happens in the case of the widow as well as divorce. The widow who remarries and is subsequently divorced has no right to claim maintenance from her former husband's relatives. It was also reported, by some, that a divorced woman or widow carries her children, born of previous husband, to her second husband. Where the children would live, after divorce, is decided by the *jati panch* when the *panch* is called for separation or remarriage. The social position and legal rights of children, born of remarriage, are considered as in case of those born of the first marriage. But this is not always true.

Rights to Divorce

Chuta-chedi is the local term for divorce. *Far-gati*, another local word, too, is often used to signify disagreement or dissociation between a husband and a wife. It is also used when a wife leaves her husband and goes to her father, expecting that her husband will follow her and she would eventually return.

Right of divorce is granted to man as well as woman. The contract of marriage can be dissolved by the mutual consent of the persons concerned without any interference of a formal court. However, the Jati Panch cannot be ignored. Divorce is granted by an assembly of Panchas of both the sides. It is ascertained from the husband and wife whether they are willing to continue to live together or are agreeable divorce. While granting divorce, a certificate is prepared, in duplicate, and is signed by the husband and wife. *jati panchas* of both the sides remain its witness.

Generally, the Dublas do not interfere in husband-wife relationship. If one desires to get a divorce, he or she requests some of the consanguineal relatives. Both the parties fix specific date and place for requisitioning a meeting of the *panchas*. On the fixed date, the husband or the wife comes with two or three members of his or her village *jati panch*. In all cases, where the divorce is granted in favour of wife, the bride-price amount must be returned.

It was reported that in most of the cases divorce is desired by the wife. Cases of men divorcing wives are not many. The divorce fee of Rs. 51 (including the bride-price) is to be repaid to the husband. If some serious allegation is proved against any of the spouse, the *panch* has the right to ask for more amount as fine. If a wife desires divorce and the husband is bent upon keeping her, and if allegations are proved against the wife, she has to pay more amount, up to Rs. 101, as decided by the *panch*. Divorce for a husband is easier as he has to pay less than what a wife has at least, in simple cases, as compensation.

Grounds for Divorce

Though separation for man and woman is easy, so long as it is not sanctioned by the *jati panch,* it involves certain disabilities. The *panch* never takes the initiative nor does it advise or suggest divorce. But it has to act if the parties seek official sanction. The usual grounds for divorce, among the Dubla, are as follows:

i. Sterility of the wife
ii. Sexual unchastity of either spouse
iii. Quarrelsome nature
iv. Laziness, resulting in the neglect of household responsibilities
v. Frequent absence from home without sufficient reason

Variations mark the process of securing separation. It is usually considered more difficult for a man to get rid of his wife than it is for the wife to get rid of her husband. Both the husband and the wife blame each other before the *panch.* Generally, a husband charges his wife with adultery, neglect of duties, contagious disease, etc. If a wife charges her husband with cruelty, impotence, neglect of maintenance and incurable disease, say, leprosy, the divorce is granted easily.

The infact of divorce is mainly on the husband and children than the wife. To make it more clear, I may discuss the position of a Dubla woman in the community. Among the Dublas a woman occupies the position of superiority in several aspects of the social life of the community. The cause of this high position is her steadiness and efficiency as compared to the man. Another factor is economic. She is more active, thoughtful, and takes greater care of the family than what the husband does. A Dubla woman is generally considered more clever than the man. There are more charming specimens of womanhood than of manhood. Other than woman, the children are also affected in the event of a divorce. Social position of the children born of the previous husband is equal to others in the community. The father has the right over the children, born of his wife, when the latter is divorced. At times this *jati panch* throws the responsibility of children on the mother, after a divorce is declared. If the woman remarries, and the second husband is not willing to help the children born of the first husband, then the children stay with her agnate relatives. The maternal grandfather or the maternal uncle takes their responsibility. In this case the children neither get the affection of the mother nor of the father. Such children become *gori* the cowboy, and thus maintain themselves.

Family Types

The Dubla family is patrilineal and patrilocal. It may, at times, be matrilocal. The membership of a domestic group, among the Dublas, is sanctioned by more than one criteria. A person, born in the family or domestic group, automatically inherits its membership. A girl, married to a man of a domestic group, acquires membership of her husband's family. Girls lose the membership of their parent group when they get married.

In Dubla society, which emphasises patrilineal principle in matters connected with descent, inheritance, naming, authority, residence after marriage, etc., persons other than the patrilineal kins do not have an important place in the family. An extension of family, through daughters, is generally possible when the son-in-law is picked up as *ghar-jamai*. It may also occur when a divorced or widowed daughter, with one or more unmarried children, comes to live with her parents.

Adoption not Widely Prevalent

A person may be admitted to a family through adoption. The adoption, however, is not widely prevalent among the Dublas. It is rare that a man is issueless — if a wife is barren, she can be divorced and the man may remarry another girl. If a man has daughters alone, he may choose such bride-groom who may be willing to stay in his own family after one of the daughters is married to him. It is only when a man has no child, due to his physical inability, and when he has enough property, including land, house, cattle, etc., he likes to adopt a son.

For adoption a man usually selects a boy from his own clan. This is done with the consent of the boy's father or guardian. No special ceremony or ritual is performed. Brother's son is preferred for adoption. A few relatives and members of the *jati panch* are invited and served with liquor. This is to make known to the public that the boy has been adopted. The real father has no claim over his son after the adoption is publicly announced. The adopted boy takes the name of the adopting father and his family. The adopted son is taken as the legal heir by the Dubla community.

Children of Unmarried Woman

An unmarried woman's child is taken as illegitimate. The regularisation of such illegitimacy is done only after the marriage of those involved in the sexual union. Sexual relations are not permitted without marriage. Pre-marital sex is discouraged. But it was also reported by some that pre-marital sex relations are not taken serious note of. The young boys and girls are simply asked to get married. This is done by the *jati panch*. If a girl gets pregnant, prior to her marriage, the seducer is forced to marry her. But a married woman, found involved in extra-marital sex relations, is excommunicated. According to Dublas, such an immoral woman lowers the prestige and does not deserve to be a community member. The laws of morality are, thus, more strictly applicable to woman than man.

Pre-marital sex relations exist more among the Dublas, as they work together especially in the field. Intimacy leads to the act when the two go out to respond to nature's call. The birth of an illegitimate child is a rare phenomenon. If, it occurs, however, the child is accepted as the child of the man who marries the female. Identity of the father is confirmed by the mother. Sometimes the seducer leaves the village, leaving behind the girl in pregnancy.

In such a case the *jati panch* helps her in getting married. In this type of marriage a lesser amount of bride-price is given. Now the man who marries her becomes the father of the illegitimate child. If the seducer returns, after the marriage of the seduced girl, the *jati patel* asks him for a feast as penalty. If he fails or refuses, he is excommunicated.

Kinship Obligation

As part of kinship obligation, the brothers should extend mutual cooperation in all walks of life. And the brothers, when they begin to grow, follow the required social norms of behaviour. After the death of father, the eldest brother is responsible for the care of his younger brothers. Even if they do not continue to live in the same house, as is true in many cases, the solidarity between the brothers is traditionally emphasised.

Kinship obligations have their own place in brother-sister relationship. This involves many aspects of life. He helps in her marriage. If a divorce takes place and if the divorced sister remarries, the children are looked after by her brothers. A brother plays the part of *vastario* (mediator) between the two parties on the occasion of marriage of the sister's son. The elder sister acts next to a mother towards the younger brother or sister. She is responsible to take care of her younger brother and sister. There is another interesting customary obligation whereunder a sister's husband acts as *anvario*, one who follows, in the marriage of her brothers. The *anvario* has to carry the bride-groom on his shoulders up to a point where the marriage ceremonies are held.

Birth-to-Death Poverty

An average Dubla does not own much property. The Dublas that they are born in poverty and die in poverty. The birth of a child is an occasion of rejoicing in the family. But the birth ceremonies are performed after borrowing money from some non-Dubla. Thus, the birth of the child itself brings in economic hardship. Children go without proper clothing and nourishment. They begin the married life with debts on them. They die almost penniless and the death ceremonies, too, are performed with borrowed money. Poverty is, thus, the very breath of Dubla life.

The movable property, held by the Dublas, includes clothes, cooking utensils, tools and a few ornaments. Some Dublas own a limited acreage of land which is treated as immovable property. It was reported that the land, in reality, is owned by the landlords, on which the Dubla houses and huts are built. Lately, the Government of Gujarat has transferred the residential land in the names of the Dublas themselves. The Dublas take even their huts as movable property. Their huts made of straw and reed, do not cost much. They are unfit for dwelling in the rainy season, unless heavily repaired every year. The whole hut can be pulled down and removed to a distant place in a few hours.

Traditionally the Dublas were provided land, for residential purpose, by the landowners whom they serve. The relationship between a Dubla and a landlord has been termed as *hali-dhaniyama* (agricultural labour and landlord). A *hali* is a labourer for the landlord and one who has taken a loan from the landlord and pledged himself to serve him as his master for a number of years. For cultivation, the landlords need labour. They have been using the Dublas for this purpose and procured their services even from other villages. Landlords pay the conventional wages including the residential land. Almost every Koli, Kanbi, Patidar and Vaniya family, in both the villages, maintain at least one family of Dublas as *Hali*.

A few Dublas own small-pieces of arable land. The produce is quite insufficient for their survival. Whatever land a few Dublas now possess (two cases in Rayam and one in Nogama) was given to them by the then British Government in recognition of their services. The land was too small to support them. They had to ultimately sell or mortgage the land to someone for ready cash for their immediate needs. As a result, most of it was mortgaged. A common method of securing loan is by mortgaging the land in favour of the creditor. Initially, the possession of land is taken by the creditor for a fixed number of years. But subsequently when one fails to repay the loan, the land gets adjusted against the interest on the loan advanced.

The livestock, kept by the Dublas, also forms part of the movable property. Most of the Dubla families keep poultry birds in their houses. This is, however, never run on commercial lines, and is chiefly for domestic use. A chicken may occasionally be sold to someone needy.

The Dublas have no customary right over the natural resources. It is only lately that the Government of Gujarat has provided public grazing land. Its use is open to all. A cattle owner, *hali* or *dhaniyama,* may graze his cattle. Free grazing is not confined to the tribals, the non-tribals too have equal rights over it.

The villages depend on running water for the use of cattle. This, however, does not mean that the other sources cannot be used. De facto, the right covers only that place where the area is dominated by the tribals.

Inheritance Rules

Among the Dublas, ultimogeniture is the rule of inheritance in case of the residential house. If there is any agricultural land it is equally shared by all the sons of a Dubla after their father's death. As stated earlier, most of the Dublas are landless; their property chiefly consists of residential land, ornaments and household articles. Silver necklaces are the main ornaments of a Dubla woman. The residential land is inherited by the youngest son who continues to live with the parents. The elder son(s) establish their own houses. The ornaments are inherited by the daughter-in-law and, in her absence, by the daughter. In general we can say that a woman inherits some property from her mother-in-law or mother. But if we look in broader sense, the ornaments remain the property of the father or sons who really paid for those ornaments. After the death of mother, the youngest son takes the ornaments and keeps them to his marriage. These are gifted to his bride. In case of divorce, the boy gets back the ornaments from his wife. After the death of father, the mother keeps her ornaments and later gives them in her daughter's or son's marriage. A divorced woman retains the property which was gifted to her by her parents or any other kinsman at the time of marriage. This property consists of ornaments, utensils, clothing, etc., and when she leaves his house, either on divorce or after quarrel, she still remains its owner. Keeping it thus in her name and under her control is security to her in case of need. After her death, such property is supposed to be returned to her father's brother or other heirs by the *jati panch*. In a family having *ghar-jamai*, the property is inherited by the daughter if a Dubla does not have any son. In case of more than one daughter, the mode of female ultimogeniture is applicable. The property of an unmarried man is inherited by the nearest primary relative. The mode remains patrilineal. In case of no inheritor, the residential land or the hut is transferred to any person according to the last wish of the owner, in consultation with the *jati panch*. It may be mentioned that as the sons inherit father's property, they are liable to inherit his debts too. A Dubla hardly has any property to give to his sons. Rather, it is the burden of debt which they inherit from the father. The eldest son of a Dubla gets married, and makes his new house and may also enter into *hali-dhaniyama* relationship of another *dhaniyama*, his father's *dhaniyama* often allows it, with the consideration that other sons of his *hali* still live with the father and the youngest of them is to inherit the land on which the house stands. And since the land belongs to *dhaniyama* there is every chance that the youngest son would repay the debt of his father and get into the relationship with the father's creditor, that is *dhaniyama*. This handing down of indebtedness and burden, from one generation to another, has an important implication, specially in the context of the *hali-dhaniyama* system prevailing in south Gujarat.

Succession not Hereditary

Like other tribes, the Dublas have their own tribal organisation called *jati panch*. A *jati patel* or *panch* is a selected body of the elders of the Dublas. Anybody can become *patel*.

The Dublas do not have an official priest. They believe in magic. The white magic is practised by the *bhagat*, the white magician. Anybody can become a *bhagat*. It was reported, from both the villages, that not a single office of the *bhagat* running as hereditary.

The Dublas suffer from a sense of inferiority if there is a woman in the *jati panch*. It was reported from both the villages that no woman was ever selected as member of the *jati panch*. Otherwise a Dubla woman enjoys equality among the sexes. The women do not keep themselves in seclusion (*parda*), and are generally free to go about for various purposes. In some aspects of social life the Dubla women rather occupy a position of superiority. They have steadiness and efficiency. Two factors, among others, may be considered as responsible for the superior position. First is demographic, that is, women are less than men; second is the economic factor that is, women are more active and take greater care of the family than the husband. But, in the offices of the tribal councils, women are avoided.

Contract Service to the Landlord

Permissive use of property is not prevalent. Only a few Dublas are owning small pieces arable lands on which they can hardly grow enough for their existence. The only contract marking out Dublas is concerned with their service to the landlords. And this is reflected in the *hali-dhaniyama* system in the villages of south Gujarat. The services of the *hali* and his entire family are at the disposal of *dhaniyama*. As a *hali* he has to serve his master until the debt is repaid. A *hali* works from morning to evening, with a little break for meals around noon. During the peak agricultural season, that is, at the time of sowing, transplanting of paddy and cutting of grass, a *hali* starts working early in the morning, before sunshine, and continues till late in the evening, with the usual break for meals. As a *hali*'s hut is close to that of the *dhaniyama*, he is called, if necessary, even during the night to attend to some urgent work. Besides the usual agricultural work he, at times, is required to work elsewhere. He drives the *dhaniyama*'s bullock-cart to some nearby village or town. His wife works in *dhaniyama*'s house, attending to various kinds of domestic duties. His son(s) look after the cattle. Grown-up sons and daughters help their parents to lighten their burden. The son who serves as *gori* or grazier takes the *dhaniyama*'s cattle, every morning, to the grazing land and returns only before sunset. To him, a *dhaniyama* occasionally entrusts some other work in or outside the house.

The annual cash wages of a *hali* vary from Rs. 24 to 30. He is also issued a daily ration of four seers of rice and one seer of barley (or two meals) and 25 paise for tobacco. A skilled *hali,* who knows how to drive a tractor in the fields or use the electrically operated irrigation pumps, is paid Rs. 125 to 150 per month. This is in addition to his daily meals. But such *halis* are very few (one in village Nogama and four in village Rayam). Besides this, a *hali* occasionally borrows money to meet the expenses incurred on guests, in extending hospitality, for making payment to different functionaries at the time of birth of a child and on observing certain rituals after death of a member of the family. He also gets clothes on festive occasions like Diwali and-or at the beginning of the monsoon. Besides this, he is also given a small sum of money occasionally. This payment is known as *pini* and consists of a rupee or so, specially used to drink toddy. A small amount of money is also given on the festive occasion of Holi. A *hali*'s wife is given part meals, twice a day, and one or two rupees per month for her services. If a *dhaniyama* engages a *hali*'s wife, *haliyani*, for the whole day, she is given full meals, twice a day, and half a seer of barley in addition to one or two rupees per month. His son, the grazier, is given food once a day, in addition to 25 paise per day. It may be mentioned that a *hali* lives with his family in a hut which is usually built on the *dhaniyama*'s land. A *dhaniyama* lends money for purchase of ornaments to be gifted to a daughter or daughter-in-law, or for payment of bride-price, as the case may be.

The remuneration, explained above, is not paid in cash, but is credited and adjusted towards the repayment of the debt which a Dubla *hali* owes to his master. Such a system might have perpetuated and persisted over generations without any major change therein. This is because a Dubla boy starts serving his father's *dhaniyama* right from his childhood. At the time of his father's death, he is fully aware that his father owed a sum to his *dhaniyama* which he has to repay.

Extent of Deviation from Customary Laws

Marriage

The impact of urban culture on the institution of marriage is clearly observed. There has been a great deal of simplification of rituals.

Marriage ceremonies, which once ran for three days, have now become a one-night affair. Moreover, a far less number of relatives and tribesmen now attend it. It was observed in both the villages that the duration between the *nani-tadi*, betrothal, to the departure of the bride for the bridegroom's house has considerably shortened in course of time. Three marriages in Rayam and one in Nogama were observed during the course of field the work. The inclusion of a Hindu custom, *satpadi*, of marriage and engaging a Brahmin to perform the marriage ceremony are later additions among the Dublas. Similarly, in dress, diet as well as other standard of living, the Dublas have been influenced by the urban ways.

The way of acquiring a mate is changing. The young Dublas are inclined to self-arranged marriages. This is specially true for Rayam. In such marriages, no third party is involved and no rituals are performed. The girl simply comes and stays with the boy. The parents concerned and other villagers reconcile after a little fuss. This is, otherwise, regarded as an irregular form of marriage. The union is not regarded complete unless the boy makes some payment to the girl's parent and gives a feast to the *jati panch*. The young Dublas of Rayam have increasingly taken to this mode.

The marriage by elopement usually occurs when the parents of the boys and girls are not in favour of the marriage between the two.

Babli daughter of Chitu Bhai of village Rayam, was engaged to Soma, son of Chana Bhai of village Timba in Kamril taluka of Surat district. This happened in 1976. But Babli had a love affair with Babu Bhai, son of Narsi Bhai of village Rayam itself. Babli was not in favour of getting married to Soma. But her parents were not happy with the affair of Babli and Babu Bhai. One night Babli and Babu Bhai left the village and disappeared. Babu took Babli to his maternal uncle's house in Tundi village of Palsana taluka in, Surat district. Both started living as husband and wife. Later on the parents of Babli and Babu persuaded them to come back to Rayam. They also gave their consent for the marriage. But the father of Babu Bhai had to pay the bride-price to Babli's father. Immediately after the marriage of Babli, Chana Bhai, father of Soma, with whom the betrothal had taken place earlier, approached Babli's father and asked for the return of bride-price. The *jati patel* was called for a compromise. Chitu Bhai had to pay Rs. 25 excluding the return of bride-price. This was as per the judgement of the *jati panch*.

There is yet another way of acquiring a mate. and the same can be explained through the following case history.

Kanji Bhai, son of Vyar Jetha, resident of village Rayam got married with Somi, daughter of Bhana Bhai, a resident of Chikhali in Kamraj taluka. This happened in 1957. After about 10 years of married life, separation took place between the couple. Somi suspected extra-marital relations of Kanji with some other woman. Kanji transported female labourers from the farms to the village by the tractor which he drove. His extra-marital relations started in 1966 and they caused tension in the family which continued for four to five years. Somi left Kanji Bhai's house, along with her four children in July, 1967. She returned to her village, Chikhali. Kanji Bhai persuaded his wife to return. She refused and instead asked for separation from Kanji. The separation took place in 1970. During the proceedings for separation allegations and counter-allegations were made by the *panchas* of both the parties. The discussion continued for three hours and ultimately ended in favour of Somi who appealed for separation. The allegation against Kanji was proved and he had to pay Rs. 101 to Somi for her having charge of the four children. After a period of three years, Kanji fell in love with Amba, daughter of Chitu of village Rayam itself. He brought her in his house in 1973. Since then the two have been living as husband and wife, without any formal marriage. He did not pay the bride-price. Kanji looks after his wife's younger sister and the mother-in-law.

Pre-marital Sex Relations

Pre-marital relations are reported among the Dublas which mostly result in marriage. It was also observed, specially in Rayam, that the adolescent Dubla boys and girls get plenty of opportunities to go to the fields either for grazing cattle or for collecting wood for fuel or for labour and to respond to the call of nature. Thus girls and boys come close which leads to pre-marital sexual affairs. Of course, lately such marriages are encouraged as they save considerable expenditure on various ceremonies and rituals. Formerly, the cases, regarding pre-marital sex, were penalised through excommunication of the person concerned. Pre-marital sex relations are not seriously viewed among the Dublas. But if a girl gets pregnant, the seducer is forced to marry her. This is managed by the *jati patel* under threat of a heavy fine or excommunication as alternative. Sometimes the seducer leaves the village. But when a woman is found to have sex relations with a man from another caste or tribe, she is excommunicated. According to Dubla notion, such an immoral woman degrades the prestige of the community and does not deserve to be its member. The laws of morality are thus applied more strictly to women than to men.

Narration of a case of pre-marital sex relations seems to be important to justify the above statement. Manu, daughter of Chana Nathu, resident of Sagariya *faliya* in Nogama village, fell in love with Shoma, son of Bhana of the same *faliya*. Mention may be made that though the Dublas do not have any dormitory, the unmarried boys and girls mix freely at work and play. In due course the love affair led to sex relations which led to Manu's pregnancy. Shoma did not marry Manu. He, instead, left the village and went to Surat. Chana Nathu, Manu's father and once the *jati patel* of the village, met the *jati patel* and sought a remedy. The *jati patel* assured him of all help in getting Manu married. He contacted Nathyo, resident of Manikpur village, some 9 kms south-east of Nogama. Notwithstanding the knowledge fact that Manu was carrying, Nathyo married her. Manu delivered a female baby some 20 days before the marriage. Of course Nathyo did not pay any bride-price. Now the two live happily with the daughter born of Shoma. When Shoma returned, after Manu's marriage, he was excommunicated by the *jati patel*. He, thus, faced all disabilities for three months. Lastly, he confessed his guilt to the *jati patel* and was subsequently expiated after a feast to the community members of Sagaria *faliya* and the *jati panch*.

Group Marriages

The system of group marriage was introduced by the Halpati Seva Sangh, as recent as in the current decade. Group marriages are organised by the Sangh once a year. This form of marriage was introduced to save wasteful expenditure. There is no provision of bride-price in it. Exchange of gifts does occur for this type of marriage, parents from both sides as also the relatives assemble and witness the marriage ceremony.

It has been observed in Rayam that priests from other ethnic groups in the village also serve the Dublas. A Kanbi *patel*, who has learnt some Sanskrit verses recited at the time of the wedding ritual, acts as priest. It may be pointed out that the Kanbi *patel*, who acts as priest in Rayam, does not possess as much knowledge as a Brahmin priest does. But he can serve the purpose. For the Dublas, the accuracy of rites does not matter much. But what is important is the presence of a Brahmin priest at the time of marriage. Moreover, the Dublas have been observed making use of some of the sacred things, including *kumkum* (red powder), *nada-chhadi* (sacred coloured thread of hard spun yarn), rice and coconut at the time of wedding. After the marriage ceremony is over, the couple visit the village temples housing Hindu deities. They bow to them and seek their blessings.

Basic Family Unit

The basic unit among the Dublas is joint-family. But separation in the family occurs at an early age. From a boy, around 10, to a *hali,* of sixty years of age all get engaged for an independent earning. A *gori*, the cow boy, after becoming *hali* tries to establish a separate unit even before marriage. After the marriage of a boy, tension marks the family, especially after the coming of the bride. Two causes which prompt a man for separation from his joint family are his marriage and his separate source of income.

Social Offences

A Dubla is frank, simple, faithful and honest. He is fond of liquor. He does not steal. It was observed in both the villages that the Dublas have no criminal behaviour. Deviations mostly concern quarrels over women. Some can be attributed to intoxication. Those engaged as *hali, haliyani* or house servants are trustworthy, and money entrusted to them is not misappropriated. In Rayam, a case or two of theft from the landlord's orchards were reported. But they are rare.

The Dublas, however, take a more relaxed view of chastity and sex life, personal freedom in marriage, social concomitants of marital life, etc.

Violation of tribal endogamy and breach of other marriage restrictions constitute social offences in Dubla society. While writing on marriage rules and restrictions, it was made clear that marriage between parallel cousins and cross-cousins is taboo; the boy and the girl should not be related to each other through four descending generations from the mother and father sides. Dubla society regards incest with horror and punishes the offender with excommunication. A Dubla boy and girl are permitted to marry if the girl conceives as a consequence of premarital sex relation with the boy. But if such a situation arises between relations of the prohibited degree as mentioned above, the marriage is not permitted. Rather the boy is excommunicated. A case may be cited in support.

Shankar, son of Soma Bhai, a resident of Nava Faliya of Rayam fell in love with his cousin sister Dalita, daughter of Mani Bhai of the same *faliya*. It was in 1975 that they committed sexual intercourse. In due course Lalita got pregnant. The matter came to the notice of *faliya* members who communicated it to the *faliya patel,* Raoji Bhai. In the meantime, Shankar conveyed his consent to Lalita's father to marry her. But as the relationship between him and Lalita was in the prohibited degree, they were not permitted to marry. Shankar approached the *faliya patel* to seek his help. But the *patel* too did not approve of his marriage to Lalita. In course of time Lalita delivered a female baby. It happened during my stay in village Rayam. Shankar was very keen to keep Lalita and his daughter with him. For this, he even approached the *jati panch* who also did not approve of the move. He was excommunicated. Lalita's father was called by the *jati patel* and was asked to get Lalita married to some other boy. As per the situation of the case, during my stay, Shankar was staying alone. Nobody was cooperating with him in any way. Lalita was staying, along with her daughter, with her parents.

In the second line of social offence comes adultery. It is regarded by the Dublas as a form of theft, and the adulterer is fined. In adultery, post-marital relation is taken more seriously than pre-marital. The Dublas allow the adulterer to marry the woman provided the husband grants her divorce. But then the adulterer must pay the fine, including the bride-price.

A case of post-marital sex relation was reported from Nogama. It seems relevant for discussion. Gulab Behan, daughter of Khala Bhai, from village Kukeri, Chikhali taluka, got married to Bhagu, son of Ganda Bhai of Nogama. This was in February, 1972. After about a year of marriage some conflict arose between husband and wife. The cause for conflict was extra marital relations of Bhagu with his elder brother's wife, Dhani. Gulab Behan returned to her parents five times, and was taken back, by Bhagu, after some confession. But Gulab insisted on divorce as she was no more willing to stay with Bhagu. The date, fixed for divorce, was April 14, 1977. She came to Nogama with her parents, paternal and maternal uncles and the *faliya patel.* Bhagu was accompanied by his father, elder brother as *panch* and the *falia patel*. Apart from the *panch*, other elderly members from both sides joined the ordeal. The arguments continued for two hours and allegations counter allegations were made. Lastly, the two parties selected five persons, two from Gulab's side and three Bhagu's side. The discussion again continued for about an hour resulting in favour of divorce. The allegation against Bhagu was proved. He had to pay Rs. 105.25 paise as fine. All the utensils, given to Gulab Behan in marriage, were returned to her. Gulab returned the ornaments.

If a women deserts her husband and stays with another man, without proper divorce, she is excommunicated so long as she does not have marital approval from the *jati panch*. The case below supports the statement.

Makan Manji, son of Manji Bora of Kundal *faliya* got married to Mani, daughter of Govan Bhai, in 1961. This was Mankan's third marriage. His two wives had died earlier. Mankan had three daughters and two sons from the earlier wives. After 15 years of married life Mani, his wife, deserted him and went to stay as a keep with Nathu, son of Gulab Sukra. Interestingly enough, Mani was some 13 years older than Nathu. Makan complained to the *faliya patel*. The *faliya patel* called for the *panch* and Mani and Nathu. During the *panch* sitting, Mani and Nathu remained absent twice. As such, nothing could be decided. The second sitting of the *panch* was requisitioned by the *jati patel*. But again Mani and Nathu did not come for *jati patel*. Both sought divorce. It is through the latter that Makan was entitled to get back the amount of bride-price. He approached the Sarpanch of the statutory panchayat and sought a decision against Mani's adultery. Kush Bhai Patel, the then Sarpanch of Nogama, called on Mani and Nathu on April 3, 1977. He did so after consultation with elderly members of the village. The allegation against Mani and Nathu was proved. Both of them consented to living together. During the ordeal, Mani paid back the bride-price to Mankan. A *dharma vibah*, marriage without any payment of bride-price, was agreed upon by the ordeal and thus Mani and Nathu were announced as husband and wife. It took 14 hours to come to the final decision. Initially, the *panchas* tried to reconcile the two parties, but when attempts failed, and when they were satisfied with the grounds for divorce, they declared the marriage dissolved.

Witchcraft

Cases of witchcraft are not dealt with by the *jati panch*. It was reported that if a Dubla suspected an act of witchcraft, he would abuse and beat the concerned woman. It is the accused woman who approaches the Police Patel or the statutory panchayat for justice. In all, the Police Patel reported 13 cases. One of these cases, recorded from the Police Patel, is as under.

Pali Behan, a widow of Nogama, was charged with committing an act of witchcraft. This was done by her ex-husband's younger brother, Rawla Besta. Rawala's son developed high temperature and could not get relief for a long time. Pali Behan was held responsible. She resided just behind his house. He alleged that it is because of her black magic that the boy was not getting cured. Rawla often abused her, and one day she was severely beaten by him. Pali complained to Bhagu Bhai Lalu Bhai, the then Police Patel of Nogama, against the offence. He helped to reach a compromise between the two. Some fine was imposed on Rawala and the case was finally settled by the Police Patel and Kush Bhai, the then Sarpanch. It happened in year 1977.

Generally a Dubla feels shy of pointing out a witch or black magician. The above case history was, therefore, recorded from the Police Patel.

Other offences like assault, injury and deliberate destruction of property are dealt with by the village statutory panchayat. Among the minor offences are included abusing, under intoxication, and petty conflicts among family members over property.

32

IMPACT OF PANCHAYATI RAJ ON SUCCESSION OF THE BHILS

S.P. LALA

The Bhils are a large tribe which ranks third in size on the tribal map of India. The 1971 Census put their number at 52,51,086. The bulk of the Bhil population is concentrated in the contiguous areas of Rajasthan, Gujarat, Maharashtra and Madhya Pradesh and accounts for about 99 per cent of the total Bhil population.

The word Bhil is believed to have been derived from a Dravidian word, *"vil"* or *"bil"* meaning a bow or a bowman. Perhaps this etymology is appropriate to the Bhils as until recently they were seldom found without this weapon.

Owing to the wide distribution of the Bhils in different States and regions they show regional variations in their languages, habits, customs and so on. Often mention is made of "Bhili" as the dialect of the Bhils which belongs to the Indo-Aryan linguistic family.

The present paper is based on the study of the Bhils of Dangs only. The Dangs is the smallest district of Gujarat, mainly inhabited by the tribal people like Bhils, Kunbis or Koknas, Warlis and Gamits. It is a one-taluka district consisting of over 312 villages.

The Dangs as a whole are a large and almost unbroken forest. Its thickly forested region covers an area of 656.59 square miles. The protected forests account for an area of 302.64 square miles and the remaining 853.64 square miles are reserved forests.

From the oral tradition of the local people it appears that the Bhils are the aboriginals of Dangs. The others like the Kunbis or Koknas, Warlis, Gamits, etc., are comparatively late settlers in the region.

The Dangs was the only area where the Bhils had been able to retain their royal position till 1947. It is perhaps the geographical situation and cultural isolation which might have helped them to retain their age-old tradition in Dangs to a great extent.

From the District Gazetteers and from some stray references it appears that there were 14 petty estates in Dangs in the earlier period (at the time of arrival of the Britishers). All the estates were held and headed by the Bhil chiefs. Five of them claimed the title of Raja, the others were styled as Naiks, Pradhans or Panwars. All were practically independent though a formal superiority was ascribed by the British Government to the Raja of Ghadvi, under whose banner the rest were bound to serve at the time of war. According to one agreement reached in 1905 the then government took lease of the forest from the Bhil rajas to exploit the forest products. The Bhil chiefs retained certain powers over the Bhils and other communities of the area such as Kunbis or Koknas and Warlis. However, the Bhil rajas had to rule under the overlordship of the then Government of India. These rajas and chiefs enjoyed full freedom in their respective States and had the rights and privileges like the other Princely States of the then India. Their States had been annexed to the Government of India in 1947. But all of them still receive an annual political pension from the Government of India. Although rajas and Naiks had a considerable degree of influence, yet, the public opinion could make itself felt through a council of elders. The Ghadvi Raja acted as an overlord of 40 hereditary officials many of royal descent, known as *kunwars*, who functioned in the community festivals and other matters of importance. Each chief also had his own councillors appointed by him from among the old men of the village. Further down the hierarchy, there was a headman of each village which was also a position hereditary by nature. Every headman had his councillors selected from the elders of the village and at the grassroots level, there was an informal democratic set-up run by the direct participation of adult men of the village.

In the Dangs area, there was a judicial system, functioning through a hierarchy of courts. There one could go in appeal from the court of the sub-chief to the chief and from that to the royal court. Witnesses were brought by each contender in case the chief summoned up and gave the judgement. The function of is tribal judiciary system appeared to be lessen social tension by a balanced verdict, so that both the parties, aggrieved and accused, may return to their normal relationship after some time. Thus compensation to the aggrieved person rather than punishment to the guilty was preferred while settling any dispute. Informal courts often brought the disputants together and sometimes made an amicable settlement. The attempt of both the informal and formal courts was to be impartial in their judgement and often verdict was more guided by the customary laws rather than an objective evaluation of the case. In general, there was flexibility in the legal interpretation and emphasis was on the spirit rather than the matter of law.

Although there was great emphasis on differences in the status of the people in the political hierarchy the life-style of all of them was almost the same. If a chief could amass large herds of cattle, through his successful raids on the Kunbis or neighbouring non-tribal people, he did not use them for his own interest only. He distributed most of them to his subjects. The raja, chiefs and sub-chiefs too lived in bamboo huts, like the commoners. Only in recent times some of the rajas have constructed modern pucca houses with several windows and doors.

Mutual Inter Dependence

The relationship of the Bhil rajas and their subjects was not based on the relationship of exploitation but of mutual interdependence. The Bhils were exempted from paying revenue to the raja which the Kunbis and Warlis had to pay. It was expected by the rajas that the Bhils, Kunbis and Warlis could stand by him in any encounter with the outside enemy. For this kind of act it was obligatory on the part of the rajas to pay them in kind mostly in the form of food and cattle.

A sort of reciprocity of obligations existed and helped to maintain a social equilibrium in the Bhil society. Authority and power were always dispensed with generosity, which was reciprocated by the other side with humble submission. When the raja received gifts, from the kings of other native States, he shared them with his followers. It has already been mentioned that there was no significant difference in the style of life of the rajas and the commoners but they had differential status in society. In the tribal society of Dangs the high-ranked personalities wield power over people and access to desirable goods. The formal etiquette and ritual behaviour associated with status emphasised the social distance between those who had power and those without it. The Bhils, Kunbis and Warlis were cautious and careful about their behaviour with the high-ranking persons of society. This had implicit and explicit reflection over their day-to-day interaction. For instance, no villagers would like to attempt to see the face of the raja's wife or wives. Even today this etiquette is observed with equal respect. Thus, the political hierarchy starting from the raja down to the common man had a firm base in the political structure of Dangs.

Now the situation has changed to a large extent. The Bhil rajas and chiefs have been divested of all power. They lament over the development which seems to be favourable for the progressive populations like the agricultural Kunbis.

Democratic System Brings

The statutory panchayat had been introduced in the district of Dangs for the first time in 1972. With this new change, the structural pattern of the village council had not been altered in any significant way. But certainly at the district level this change opened up an avenue through which the political power has reached the Kunbis. The Kunbis were perhaps waiting for such an opportunity for generations. Prior to the introduction of the statutory panchayat in Dangs, the village councils in the district were represented mostly by the Bhil rajas and *nayeks* in their own territories. With the new panchayati system the Bhils have lost their hereditary positions in the village political structure to a great extent. The village councils are now represented by the elected members from the village. The democratic system based on adult franchise brought an end to the age-old tradition of the Bhils in Dangs. The Kunbis did not miss the opportunity to replace the Bhils in the village councils in the areas where they are numerically dominant.

Even after the introduction of the statutory panchayat the traditional village council, known as *gaon panch,* consisting of three members, is still very much functional. It is headed by the Police Patel and he is assisted by two members, viz. *karbari* and *jagle.* All the offices of the *gaon panch* were represented mostly by the Bhils. Now along with the traditional *gaon panch,* the statutory village panchayat named gram panchayat is also prevalent in the villages. It is consisting of nine elected members and is headed by the *sarpanch.* The tenure of the gram panchayat is five years. It is mainly responsible for the development work of the village while the Police Patel is responsible for the maintenance of law and order in the village.

With the awakening of a new democratic consciousness the

people were not happy with the Bhil supremacy in the power structure of the area. So the Kunbis instantly grasped the idea of the democratic principle for having a drastic change in the authority structure. They could put pressure on the old system to yield to the new democratic set-up. Thus, now all the members of the *gaon panch* including the Police Patel are elected by the majority vote. Previously the Police Patel was nominated by the Government. Now in most of the villages his hereditary position is lost for ever though in a few villages it still continues. Here people got elected by virtue of their own merit and not for their past position.

As the people of Dangs could mould the old system into a new pattern they do not feel the necessity of the statutory village panchayat. It exists as a formal institution but is not very effective in the changed village situation. But its apparent ineffectiveness does not minimise its significance at a greater level. Rather the Kunbis use it as a stepping stone to have a wider control over the regional politics. However, in the village, the *gaon panch* is doing all the duties entrusted to the gram panchayat. Though the Police Patel is mainly responsible for the maintenance of law and order. he keeps constant vigilance over all the affairs of the village. He acts as the media between his people and local administration. Hence it is his duty to look after the matters which are referred to him by the local administration. For settling a dispute, brought to his notice, he arranges an informal gathering with the help of his associate Jagle. Traditional guidelines like reasoning direct evidence in giving his final verdict. For an offence like theft, minor physical assault, causing harm to any one's property, illicit relation with a woman, the Police Patel may impose a fine of up to Rs. 12 on a person/s who is/are involved in such an activity.

The members of the *gaon panch* are still paid some honorarium/remuneration as it was in the olden days. The Police Patel receives a sum of Rs.37 per annum while karbari receives Rs. 27 for a year. The remuneration of *jagle* as he works as a messenger is Rs. 50 per month paid quarterly. These remunerations are paid by the government. It is interesting to note here that the people of Dangs have made a synthesis in this regard too. In the pre-Independence days the Bhil chiefs used to assemble in a congregation called *darbar* held during the Holi festival at the District Headquarters, Ahwa. There the raja used to receive the royalty of forest in the form of honorarium from the then British Government. The

Police Patels were given red turbans and brass vessels which were considered as token of prestige. Now also, the payment is made to the rajas and other functionaries in the same fashion but in a different name only. The *darbar* is still held and has the same lustre. The only significant change is that the practice of giving of red turban had been stopped since Independence and also the amount of honorarium to the rajas, now considered a political pension, has been reduced to per cent of the earlier amount. So, nowadays during the *darbar* rajas cannot spend as lavishly as they could in the earlier days.

Previously all the offices of the *gaon panch* ran in family line for generations thus concentrating power in a few lineages, But now the power has been decentralised as the tenure of the traditional council has also been fixed for five years. This is an important contribution of the Panchayati Raj system which could give a new dimension to the traditional authority structure of Dangs.

Age-old Customs Change

Introduction of the panchayati system has affected many age-old customs prevalent in the area. Some examples are given below.

(i) Marriages are now settled in the presence of the Police Patel of the village council and not in front of the Bhil chiefs of the locality.
(ii) The Bhil chiefs had a customary right to secure Rs. 7 as *kargut* which was actually a kind of tax to be paid by the parents of a boy to the Bhil chief of another jurisdiction from where they were going to receive a girl for marriage with their son. The said *kargut* is now being secured by the Police Patels.
(iii) The community festivals are now being inaugurated by the Police Patel as the village chief in place of the Bhil rajas and Nayeks in their own jurisdictions.

The Bhils are now mostly cultivators or agricultural labourers. Agriculture forms the chief basis of their economy. The Bhils are still found occupying portions of land in the valleys and on the hillocks in certain states. Usually, they grow on land which is not sufficiently fertile to provide enough food all the year round. The Bhils live from hand to mouth.

To a Bhil, *bhuin* (agricultural land) is the most important piece of property. The bullocks which are used for cultivation of land also form a most useful item of property of a Bhil. Shelter being a primary need, a Bhil is always keen to erect one which may serve his purpose. He makes all efforts to equip it as per his capacity as a Bhil social fabric is essentially linked to his hut. Many Bhils did not hesitate to opine that their huts form the most valuable property to them. The Bhils also keep some livestock which is of help in scarcity situations. As a source of meat supply, to perform some of his social and religious functions and also as a source of good income, a Bhil family knows the utility of raising the livestock. The latter include cows, buffaloes, goats and fowls which are considered as part of property. A Bhil possesses some metallic utensils and ornaments. These also bear his traditional sentiment. These are his valuable property. The ornaments are usually made of brass, copper, zinc and bell metal. Silver ornaments are rarely found.

As a principle of inheritance of property, all the sons, by the same father, equally share their parental property. There may be some differences depending on the relations among the brothers, as also with their sisters, where the quantity of share may vary by mutual understanding. Cases are not uncommon where the eldest brother was allowed to get a bigger share.This is granted in the traditional of way sharing parental property.

In the absence of a son there is no bar to transpiring the property of a deceased to his daughter. In the absence of son and daughter the property of the deceased goes to his brothers or to the brother's sons. This holds good for landed property too. If there is no living claimant, the property of a deceased is taken by the village panchayat. It ultimately goes under the control of the local administrative body.

Mention may be made that in Bhil society the system of child adoption is in vogue. And as per their customary law, an adopted child can inherit the property of his foster father.

Succession to office to always is from father to the eldest son. The different positions of Bhil chiefs of Dangs (designated as rajas, *nayeks, pradhans* or *panwars*) were always hereditary by tradition. Primogeniture was the rule not only for inheritance of property, but also for succession of chair related to political power in the Bhil society of Dangs.

In the family sphere also the Bhils of Dangs follow the principle that after the death of the family head, the eldest son of the deceased (if he is adult) should take the position of the head of the family. The

Bhils follow patriarchal principle and patrilineal system.

After Independence all the Bhil chiefs were divested of their political power in Dangs. This was done by the new government. Still the tradition continued. However, the end came in 1972, when the statutory panchayat system i.e. was introduced. Now, succession to office in the political councils of the district by way of inheritance has been stopped. In the family sphere, of course, the tradition is still being continued with its earlier pattern of behaviour.

SECTION VI

NORTH-WESTERN INDIA

33

TRIBAL CUSTOMARY LAW IN NORTH WEST INDIA

J.C. DAS

The study of customary law in north-west India goes back to the colonial rule when administrators, lawyers and scholars wrote about the Hindus of this region (Boulnois and Rattigan: 1878, Tuper: 1881, Roe and Rattigan: 1895, Raturi: 1918, Stowell: 1919 & n.d., Lall: 1920, Joshi 1929). One objective of these works was to highlight variations in regional Hindu customs and usages and help the British Indian judiciary in dispensing local litigation satisfactorily within the frame of "Common Hindu Law". There is an often-cited case (Special Civil Appeal No. 49 of 1915) which exemplifies the inapplicability of Mitakshara law (Common Hindu Law based on Sanskrit scriptures) to the local Khasiya Hindus of Garhwal and Kumaon divisions. Briefly, the case is like this:

"Fateh Singh was the son of Daulat Singh by Mst. Maina. The facts proved were that a brideprice of Rs. 200 was paid to Maina's father; that she was brought to Daulat Singh's house in a *dooly*, that the *biradari* was feasted and that a ceremony known as Ganeshpuja was performed. Fateh Singh sued to set aside a sale deed and a deed of gift executed by his step-mother in favour of Gobar Singh... (but) the legitimacy of Fateh Singh was challenged (under Mitakshara). In all the three local courts of Kumaon Fateh Singh was successful.... (as) officers with experience of local conditions knew that Mst. Maina was lawfully married.... The conditions however were changed when the case went before the judges at Allahabad. They looked to the record for evidence of .... Saptapadi and Phera Bhaura ceremonies ordinarily considered essential... and were not satisfied. When the case went back to the Kumaon courts, Fateh Singh failed apparently on his inability to establish in a court of law a custom which derogated from Hindu law" (Josh : 1929 : 40).

In fact, judgements for want of such feedback in those days generated a good deal of controversy among the local people and in some cases, the judges themselves remained dissatisfied with their judgements. This can be noticed in the following remarks of the then Commissioner, Kumaon Division, in Fateh Singh versus Gobar Singh case (cited above) in a decision which was "disapproved throughout Garhwal" (Lal 1920).

> "The persons are residents of northern Garhwal and probably have never heard of Mitakshara Law. However, calling themselves Hindus, they have to abide by it when they come to court... Were this the ultimate court of appeal, I would not hesitate to hold, what is no doubt held locally, that the son of Daulat Singh is quite legitimate enough to succeed his father's farm. As, however, the directions given me are so drawn up, it is impossible for courts of Kumaon to do so" (Stowell, n.d.)

The Scheduled Tribes of the region have not been adequately researched in terms of their customary laws. Except for a few para, dealing with the Bhotia, the Bhokas and the Tharu (Lal: 1920), we have no information on other tribes. We, therefore, highlight the features of the region's tribal customary laws, particularly centring around the aspects of inheritance and succession.

Although the north-west region covers roughly one-third of the country's total area and covers five States (Jammu and Kashmir, Punjab, Himachal Pradesh, Haryana and Uttar Pradesh) and two Union Territories (Delhi and Chandigarh), it is the least populous zone in terms of tribal population (1981). The region has three distinct ecological zones: (i) Himalayan zone comprising Jammu and Kashmir, Himachal Pradesh and larger hilly area under Garhwal and Kumaon Divisions of Uttar Pradesh. This eco-zone is further delineated into two sub-zones, viz. (a) the high altitudes characterised by rugged terrain, semi-arid to arid climate, little or no vegetation, heavy snowfall during winter and so on; and (b) the middle and lower altitudes represented by friendlier topography, moderate to high rainfall to medium to dense forest, no snowfall, etc. which are conducive, agriculture, (ii) the swampy, malaria-prone foothills zone, famous by the term *terai*, which comprises southernly low lands of Kumaon Division, the districts of Lakhimpur Kheri,

Gonda, Bahraich, Gorakhpur, etc., under Uttar Pradesh. (iii) the flat alluvial plains of Uttar Pradesh, Punjab and Haryana. The Union Territories of Delhi and Chandigarh fall in this zone.

Of the three eco-zones, tribal concentration is restricted to the first two zones spread over Jammu and Kashmir, Himachal Pradesh and Uttar Pradesh. The tribes are : the Bhotia, Boksa, Jaunsari, Tharu and Raji in Uttar Pradesh; Bodh, Gaddi, Gujjar, Jad (inclusive of Lamba and Khampa). Kinnaura, Lahaula, Pangwala and Swangla in Himachal Pradesh; Bodh, Balti, Drokpa, Mon, Beda, Gara, Changpa and Purigpa in Jammu and Kashmir. In this list, those living in Jammu and Kashmir have acquired "Scheduled Tribe" status in 1989 only and hence 1981 census does not include them. In the present discussion also, these groups do not figure much, except for occasional references.

The population data of 1981 census shows that the largest tribe of the north-west region is the Tharu (95,542) of Uttar Pradesh who are located in the *terai*. However, the large tribal populations in Himalayan zones are the Gaddi (76,860), Jaunsari (68,348), Kinnaura (47,913), Bhotia (32,311) Gujjar (28,121) to name a few as per the 1981 census. Tribes with small populations are Raji (1,087) and Swangla (165) as per the 1981 census. However, according to a survey, the population of the Raji, who are found in Pithoragarh district only, was only 371. While the Himalayas account for 66.2 per cent, the *terai* zone shares 33.8 per cent (comprising Tharu and Bhoksa), of the region's tribal population.

The Himalayan tribes of the region share interesting socio-economic and socio-cultural characteristics in contradistinction to those in the *terai* who are settled cultivators. At least three Himalayan tribes, viz., Bhotia, Gaddi and Gujjar, follow transhumance (seasonal migration) while the Raji, who are now being vigorously persuaded to settle down by the Government, led full-fledged nomadic hunter-gatherer life until about two decades ago. Although found settled and pursuing agriculture today, the Raji have not yet abandoned their earlier nomadic habits and still many Raji families revert to gathering and nomadism.

At a general level, the Himalayan tribes of this region may be categorised into following groups in terms of their economic activities: (i) The northern highlanders like the Bhotia (U.P.), the Jad, the Bodh, the Kinnaura, the Lahaula (Himachal Pradesh) who are located along the international border with Tibet. These communities' traditional economy was once based on trade (non-existent now) with Tibet. They now rear sheep and goat and practise pastoralism, supplemented by agriculture, horticulture and also cash-earning occupation of gathering of medicinal and aromatic herbs, mainly. This is particularly true of the Bhotia of the U.P. Hills, (ii) Communities like the Gaddi and Gujjar primarily subsist on pastoralism. Their involvement with agriculture is marginal. Of these two, the Gaddi are sheep and goat pastoralists while the Gujjar are buffalo herders, (iii) The erstwhile nomadic Raji, who are incipient agriculturists now, depend on a variety of occupations like labour, tree-felling and sawing (*chiran*) in forest, including gathering, (iv) The terrace cultivators are mainly represented by the Jaunsari who also participate in pastoralism (sheep, goat, cattle) but not in the same way as communities under the first two categories do.

In the socio-cultural sphere, the Himalayan tribes reflect both variations and commonalties. While the Jaunsari, Kinnaura and Gaddi societies are stratified along caste lines having a caste system of sorts among them the other tribes lack it. Still there are a few, e.g. Bhotia and Raji, who claim Rajput status (Das : 1983 : 161-3, Das & Raha : 1981). In fact, some Bhotia sub-groups, viz. Johari and Nitwal, are highly acculturated and Hinduised. Another important attribute is polyandry which is prevalent among the Jaunsari, Kinnaura, Bodh and Lahaula mainly. In spite of these variations, these tribes exhibit an overall similarity with respect to their being patriarchal and their sharing several marriage norms, flexibility with regard to women's freedom and their status and so on, which have an important bearing on their customary laws.

Custom and Law

Anthropologists have often been accused of describing "custom" in detail while neglecting "law" when they deal with "customary law". It is difficult to draw a sharp line between "custom" and "customary law" as the latter arises from the premises of the former which explains the social context. As Sapir says, "the formulation of custom in the sphere of rights and duties of individuals in their manifold relations lead to law. Custom becomes law when it is recognised in some ways as governing a class of relations segregated as juridical" (1967 : 661-62). We shall now try to understand the tribal customary law of north-west India in three aspects, viz., paternity, wifehood and sonship, since they notionally and empirically vary from the law and practices in common Hindu law as well as the Anglo-Saxon jurisprudence.

Paternity, Wifehood and Sonship

To appreciate the meaning of paternity, wifehood and sonship as prevalent among the tribes of this region, we are required to understand the many types of man-woman sex relationships which exist and are considered valid by these tribes, though not all such relationships exactly fit into the conventional definition of marriage. Socio-economic expediency, together with ecological compulsions, had been a contributory factor in social sanctions of these relationships. Tribal marriages in these parts are essentially a contract with little or no sacerdotal meaning associated with them. Payment of fixed or mutually agreed amount of bride-price is a must which is followed by a community feast. Though a good number of rituals and ceremonies are observed in marriage, they are, strictly from customary legal viewpoint, not indispensable nor do they carry weight unless the conditions of bride-price payment and community feast have been met. Before going into the questions of paternity, wifehood and sonship, a brief discussion on man-woman sex-based relation is necessary. Three types of conjugal relations are recognised as valid or legitimate:

(a) Marriage between a man and an unmarried woman who is marrying for the first time. Such a girl is referred to as *byati* in the Kumaon hills and hence this type of marriage is called *byati bya*. Among the Bhotia this marriage entails payment of bride-price (*lei/yerh)* and price of milk (*nutung*) paid to the bride's mother. Corresponding terms used by the Tharu are *tek* (bride price) and *doodh ka dam* (price of milk). Other tribes follow the same principle though they have different terms for it.

(b) Marriage with a married woman who is either a widow or a divorcee or simply a paramour, not legally divorced from her husband, alive or dead. The elder brother's widow sometimes starts living as "wife" of her deceased husband's younger brother for which neither payment of bride-price nor throwing of a community feast is required. But conjugal relation with a widow of another man, or with a divorcee or a non-divorced paramour attracts payment of bride-price and (or) compensation by the new husband, after which the relation acquires legitimacy. This form of marriage is popularly known by terms like *dhanti*, *dogharia*, *kolti* among the Bhotia, and by *radivivah* among the Tharu.

(c) Another type of relation is that between a supportless widow and a man who works as a ploughman (*haliya*) and has sexual relations with his widow-employer. Such a man is referred to as *tekwa* or *kathala* in U.P. hills, who is a servant-husband and who has no *locus standi* but whose offspring are legitimate. The Bhotia, however, is said to be unaware of this practice. But the Tharu recognise this relationship and call it *odhara* or *ghar baitha* or *Chutkata*. Such relations exist among the Raji, though very infrequently met with.

The above-mentioned relationships are regarded legitimate provided they have not infringed the norms of clan/patrilineage exogamy, and observed prohibited kinship degrees, and avoided incest.

In the light of conjugal relations described above, the issues of paternity and wifehood may be discussed as follows:

1. The notion of paternity is not necessarily based on biological procreation. In other words, legal paternity is not synonymous with biological paternity in these societies. The case of *tekwa* or *gharbaitha* is suggestive in this regard as the children begotten by them are recognised as heir to their mother's property which, in fact, is owned not by their progenitor father but by the previous husband of their mother. It may, however, be stated that this custom is very rare now as under the impact of acculturation it has largely disappeared.
2. The abovementioned notion of paternity more explicit in the case of polyandrous union is more pronounced than actual biological fatherhood, as upheld by *duster ul anl* or the record of custom for Jaunsar Bawar, as well as the empirical data. The children, born of common wife/wives in a polyandrous family, bear the name of the eldest brother only and are not claimed by brothers, no matter who the actual progenitor may be. The same practice exists among the polyandrous Kinnaura and Lahula.
3. Under the Tharu custom, *sikari*, the unmarried pregnant girl, if not later married to the man responsible for her pregnancy, is given in marriage to a needy Tharu without any bride-price

on condition that the latter would accept the paternity of the child.

On the question of wifehood, i.e. who can be lawful wife, it may be stated that apart from the formally married wife, the other categories of wife are follows:

(a) A woman who was abandoned or widowed but who subsequently became the wife of her paramour or her deceased husband's younger brother, without going through any ritual. This category is recognised by all tribes by terms such as *kolti* by Bhotia, *radi* by Tharu, etc. Except levirate, this form of union requires to be finalised by payment of bride-price and/or compensation to the woman's former husband (if alive) or to his family (if dead). Among the Bhotia, she would be regarded as *kolti* as long as compensation amount remains due, and her offspring are called the *telia* or *re-abnoe* (meaning one who is removed by the payment of compensation to the former husband. It may, however, be noted that *telia* are, regarded as the legitimate heir of their father's property.

(b) Another category is *odhari* or *gharbaithi* as the Tharu call her. Though she is not considered as lawful wife yet her offspring by the man are legal heirs of the latter's property. Her status is paradoxical, a concubine at one level but a mother of "legal heirs" of her man at another level.

In the light of the foregoing discussion, the sons among the tribals of this area are of four categories:

(a) The real son, referred to as *asal*, born out of *byati* wife.
(b) The *kam asal*, i.e. the sons begotten by a man of his lawful wife who was either a widow or an abandoned wife of another man.
(c) Sons from *tekwa* or *gharbaitha*, that is, servant-husband.
(d) *Jhantela* or step-son born of wife's earlier marriage. Such sons among the Bhotia are entitled to succeed to their step-father's property equally with their step-brothers.

The custom of adoption is recognised by these tribes. The adopted sons, described as *dharamputra*, are, however, few.

34

SOME ASPECTS OF TRIBAL CUSTOMARY LAW AMONG THE GADDI

R. SARKAR & V. SARKAR

The Gaddi is a generic term which includes within its fold Brahmans, Rajputs, Khatris among the ritually pure communities and Hali, Sippi, Rihara etc. among the ritually impure communities. It is a transhumant population inhabiting the tract between the Dhaula Dhar and Pir-Panjal ranges in the Brahmaur sub-tehsil of Chamba district, Himachal Pradesh. Their territory is known as Gaderan and they number 76,860 souls according to 1981 census.

The Gaddis historically are not an indigenous population of the State. While the Brahmans believe to have been brought here from Delhi by Raja Ajai Varman during 780-800 A.D. the Gaddi Khatris and Rajputs believe to have fled from Lahore, to this part of the remote hills, to escape persecution at the hands of Aurangzeb. For over 1000 years they have been living in the Gaderan, with their herd of sheep and goat, moving from high hills of Brahmaur valley down to the plains of Kangra and Punjab in the winter months crossing the Dhaula Dhar and ascending back to their summer encampments in the high hills during summer months.

With years of residence in the area, they have been subjected to various influences both biotic and abiotic, which have shaped their cultural pattern, for adaptation to the environment, and it is with these in view that we propose to look at customary rights among these people.

Among the Gaddis the two sides of the family are reckoned with not only in vocabulary but in customary law, definite functions being associated with definite type of relationship. The family is patrilineal, the wife and the children belong to the father's clan. The importance of paternal kindred is well established in their society. The movable and immovable properties descend from father to son and it is the father's relatives who perform the funeral rites.

Both parents are recognised; first by virtue of the sentimental bond, connecting them with their children and second because the husband and wife, together with their children form an economic and productive unit. A man among the Gaddis marries primarily because he needs a woman to manage his house, to look after the cattle and fodder, to bring grass and firewood, and to help him in the agricultural activities.

Quite contrary to the prevailing practices in the adjoining areas of polyandry, Gaddis are monogamous, probably in continuance of age old practice, before the their immigration to this area.

The intensity of obligation with the kin group varies with the proximity of kinship. Though a number of paternal uncle and father's cousins may be addressed by the same term as that of the father, it is the father that provides his wife and children with such necessities as ought to be provided by him in accordance with the customs. Though a man's cousin is called brother, it is his own brother that inherits the widow through the levirate and only in the absence of brothers does a more remote kinsman functions as a substitute.

Marriage is considered to be an important institution among the Gaddis, for it is considered as a sacred duty of the parents to see the child married in order to achieve salvation. For achieving this end, often the parents married their children at a tender age, but this practice has been replaced now-a-days by adult marriages.

Gaddis are largely monogamous, however, polygyny is permitted if the wife is barren or suffers from some incurable disease or mental disorder, the occurrence of which is rare.

Marriages are preferred from among the community. The Brahman, Rajput and the Khatri sections among the ritually clean communities freely intermarry, without any inhibitions of their caste affiliations. Similarly the ritually unclean communities marry among themselves as a rule. A person of ritually clean caste marrying a girl of unclean caste is ostracized by the community, and there is no provision of readmittance in the community fold even by paying punitive fines as is the custom elsewhere. Cross and parallel cousin marriages are not allowed and so are the members of the same *anderla gotra* not allowed to marry. They exclude certain generations of relations both on the father's side and mother's side before entering into matrimony.

The rules of residence also exert influence on the life of the Gaddis. A Gaddi looks for a mate in some other village, other than his own and as a rule takes his wife to his own village. Thus, while the males lived all their life in the same village, the females spend most of their life away from the natal village. Exceptions being marriage by service wherein, the boy in order to pay the bride price comes to work and stays in his prospective father-in-law's house, but once the amount is paid, he marries the girl and returns to his village with his wife.

Divorce and widow remarriage is permissible. A woman who does not want to stay with her husband returns to his native place and in that event the bride-wealth received by the father is realised with penalty by the groom's side for breach of marriage. Similarly if a woman wishes to marry another man or simply elopes with him, he is expected to compensate her husband before seeking her hand. However, if a man deserts his wife without any tangible reasons, the bride price is forfeited. After divorce, the children are the liability of the father. Both surrogate (senior and junior) are accepted forms of marriage, but it is not obligatory for either of the partners.

The existence of these practices also governs their inheritance law. Ordinarily, the courts follows the Mitakshara law of inheritance, but the local customs among the Gaddis have their own law of inheritance called the Mundaband and Chundaband law of inheritance. Munda means son i.e. in the Mundaband law of inheritance the property is divided by the rule of male equigenture and Chunda means wife i.e. the property is divided per stripes and not per capita. The respective shares of the wives are further sub-divided equally according to their number of sons. while the former mode is resorted to in case of monogamous unions, the latter being resorted to in the event of polygynous unions.

If a man dies without any male issue, the property would be equally divided amongst his wives, who have only a life interest in it., and have no authority to dispose off the immovable property. On their death, its assess on to the nearest collaterals. In case she remarries she loses her interest in it. If she forms an illicit connection with someone while under the roof of her husband and a child is born, the posthumous child called *chakandu,* is treated as a legitimate child of the deceased, though born years after his death, and shall have the right of inheritance.

Gaddis hold the view, that as long as a widow continues to live at her husband's house she is entitled to his property, but the moment she gives up her house to live with some one else, she forfeits her right of inheritance. Persons taking widow as his wife, who is at that time in the family way, and born subsequently is reckoned as his child.

II

The Gaddis are the traditional herder of sheep and goat, which is known as *dhan* among them. It is primarily because of this wealth that they have to move down to their winter encampments, as the area remains covered for part of the year under a thick blanket of snow, as a result of which grass or pasture lands are not available to them during the winter months. Even during the days of the princely states, they enjoyed *haquqs* (customary rights) given to them by the erstwhile rulers, in the forest areas, where they grazed their flock in the pasture land called *tarkals.* This was free of any charge and they enjoyed these rights by way of their being early settlers. Their rights were not only restricted to the use of *tarkals,* but they also enjoyed rights for collection of leaves as fodder, dry fallen branches of leaves as fuel, wood for construction of houses etc. With the abolition of princely state and the forest areas passing into the hands of forest departments, the facilities which they traditionally enjoyed has been curtailed to a large extent and Gaddis have no longer free access to it.

However, in recognition of their customary rights they still continue to have certain rights and privileges. The pastures (*tarkal*) are allotted direct of the Gaddis on payment of nominal tax per hundred sheep and goats which is paid twice a year to the Forest Department. it is interesting to note that each shepherd has his own fixed land (*dhar*), which only he can use as pasture lands for his flock. Besides, they also continue to have the privilege of collecting fallen branches as firewood, and long beams of wood for construction or repair of their houses is given at a highly subsidized rates or it would be better to say that they are charged only a taken amount, whereas, those who do not have the customary rights over the forested areas, can avail of these facilities at the prevalent market rates.

Besides being the herder of sheep and goats they are also agriculturists but they are not considered good at it, for reasons of scarcity of agricultural land and small land holdings, and a short season for agricultural activity. As a result of all this, coupled with indigenous technology, Gaddis have developed a system of mutual cooperation in agricultural activities. Often the cultivation is done jointly, but when the crop is ripe, they harvest their own patch separately. This accelerates the sowing of crops and the excess of manpower required is met with indigenously, so that they move down to lower hills before the snow blocks their movements.

III

The traditional system by which the Gaddi arranges the mutual exchange of labour, whenever a need for cooperative venture arises is called as *bartandari* or *birton* rights.

If a man wants to build a house an invitation is sent to each and every household who are expected to provide an adult male member to assist the man who intends to build a house. In return the host is obliged to provide free meals and liquor to all those who have assisted him in the work. Likewise in agricultural activities especially those which are labour intensive, as also when the boundary walls of the terraced fields have to be strengthened or repaired, people are willing to work together in spirit of total cooperation. Even small children are seen doing the job of bringing pebbles or whatever little is well within in their capacity. Even in social functions such as marriages, feasts etc people provide free labour. There is invariably a strict compliance of these norms; failure of which will not only bring social ridicule to the person not sending the help, but will also not receive help, when required by that family. Even in the observance of *chehi,* a collective collection of fuel for marriage, a member from each house in the village joins in the enterprise.

The other mode of *birton* commonly called as *kamanbirton,* is also existent among them and is customarily regulated. As the name 'kaman' suggests it is the relationship existing out of work on various social and economic fronts between the land owning and the serving communities, and is also referred to as patron-client relationship. The serving castes render their specialised services, when required, and are compensated for it at harvest times by payment in food grains. The social services are rendered by serving castes on various occasions of life cycle rituals, like birth, marriage and death. For instance, the purohit is obliged to perform the rituals for worshipping Kailu to prevent any miscarriage or abortion of the mother-to-be in their clients house. Similarly, he is also to forecast the future of the child after birth by preparing the horoscope and also to advise his client for pacifying the effects of the constellation of evil star if any, and also to officiate at marriage and death rituals. Not only he officiates at rituals of ritually clean castes but also performs marriage and other rites of the Sippis and Reharas who are considered ritually unclean. From them, the Gaddi Brahman accepts *dakshina*, but not food, unless cooked by a person of clean caste. Sippis are also considered as best *chelas*, and officiate as priest at Shiv temples, and at the time of trance even a Brahman consults a Sippi *chela*.

IV

Thus, one can see various occasions of interaction between different caste constituents governed by their customary law. It not only influences the individual in all walks of life but lends a distinct colour and identity to their society. It is rather paradoxical that man makes these regulations to eventually put a check to his freedom. Yet, he submits to it not out of any compulsion but more out of reverence. In the words of Malinowski. "He obeys them 'slavishly', 'unwittingly', spontaneously through mental inertia combined with fear of public opinion or of supernatural punishment or again through a pervading group sentiment if not group instinct', (1926)".

35

SOCIO-ECONOMIC CONTEXT OF THE CUSTOMARY LAW AMONG THE BHOTIA

J.C. DAS

Every society has its own ways to maintain order and coherence among its members on the one hand and to keep frictions and arbitrations to the minimum on the other. The Bhotias of Kumaon Himalayas are no exception to this rule. Throughout Kumaon, the Bhotias were famous for their erstwhile trade with Tibet in which they maintained an enviable monopoly. On account of their fabulous trade they emerged as economically the most prosperous community of their region and had been able to amass enough wealth and property. With the stoppage of trade in the sixties, the Bhotias have diversified their economic activities and, under changing circumstances agriculture, horticulture, animal husbandry, business and service have become important sources of subsistence. Agriculture, which during their days of large-scale involvement in trade, played a secondary role, has now become an important prop of thier domestic economy.

The property *(jaijat)* of the Bhotias can be of two kinds : movable *(chal)* and immovable *(achal)*. The movable property includes ornaments, clothings, grains, agricultural implements, animal wealth like cow, yak, sheep, goats etc. The immovable property consists of land, dwelling house, orchard, watermill and so on.

Of all the immovable property, land is the most valuable. Broadly, two main categories of land are found — land owned by an individual household and land owned by the village community. The latter category is described as the *gaon sanjayati* land. The first category comprises practically all cultivated areas (including few patches of fallow land occasionally) orchard, house sites, and areas used for making water-mills. *gaon sanjayati* lands usually comprise extensive stretches of uncultivated lands, portions of which offer grazing to the domestic animals of the village. It may be noted here that sometimes one may find a third category of holding jointly owned by the members of the same lineage (*rath*).

Property Inheritance and Succession

Since the Bhotia society is patrilineal, the rights of inheritance descend through the male line only. All sons, including those from the *kolti* wife, get an equal share in their deceased father's property. Although the issue from the *kolti* wife are looked down upon yet this cannot prevent their getting an equal share in the property, and no discrimination, on this account, can be permitted against them. Customarily, during partition of property the eldest brother is given a plot or two more than his share of land as a token of respect which is known as *jetho-ban*. However, this *jetho-ban* is not a matter of right at all because if the co-sharers wish so may do not to give any extra plot to their eldest brother who has no means to acquire that.

In the past when *sautia-bant* was prevalent among the Bhotias, the division of property used to take place as per the number of wives a person had, and not as per the number of sons. But the practice has ceased to operate for long and the sharing is now done as per the number of sons and not as per the number of wives. Daughters cannot inherit property. When a person does not have any male child, his property ultimately passes on to his collaterals who are *waris* (heir, e.g. brother, brother's sons). But so long the deceased man's widow is alive she may hold the property but she is not expected to release any part of her late husband's property by way of gift nor is she expected to sell any portion of it under normal conditions. Only in an emergency she may sell a part of the property which may not be subjected to questioning by her *waris*.

The property of dead father is held by a daughter (if there is no male heir) till she gets married. But even after her marriage if she choses to remain in the father's house keeping her husband there she will continue to possess the property.

In the absence of any heir or *waris*, the property of a deceased person is inherited by the village community but such instances are not common. Mostly in such situations, a person, before his death, resorts to the system of adoption, locally termed as *chachyam*. There is no particular ceremony prescribed to make the adoption operative.

Usually a feast is arranged to celebrate the occasion, attended by friends and relations which may be deemed as public announcement. Usually the son of a near relation is chosen for adoption. A case of adoption in Dar village reflects this.

Lati, sister of Jaspal Singh of Go village, was married to Pahri Singh of Dar village and remained issueless. Lati desired to adopt her brother's son, Gandhu (son of Jaspal) as, *dharamputra*. Gandhu thus became their adopted son and inherited their movable and immovable property but consequently lost all rights to his parental property at Go village. Gandhu also performed the last rite (*sradha*) of his adoptive parents.

A person having no son may bring his married daughter and her husband to stay with him as *ghar jawain*. Through the act of *byenama* (registration), the *ghar jawain* may be given the status of a heir of his property and before doing this the person is required to get the approval from his *waris* without whose consent he may not be able to do it. In earlier days *byenama* was done in favour of *ghar jawain* but at present the same is done in favour of one's daughter, so that if the *ghar jawain* divorces her later on she has no difficulty and is self-supporting.

Finally, it is interesting to note among the Bhotia that re-partition of property may take place should the father acquire sons after the partition has been effected. For example, A begets X and Y after the property was distributed in three shares among him and his previous sons M and N. But after the birth of X and Y, re-partition would take place in order to maintain an equal share too all sons.

Petua Banṭ

During the time of partition of property among brothers, the standing crop in the field as well as the amount of stored grain, reserved for domestic consumption (excluding seeds reserved for sowing purpose) will be divided as per the number of *pet* (belly) equally. However, a child who has not cut teeth would not be considered in such a case.

The distribution of seeds for sowing would be done equally as per the number of co-sharers. Cow, sheep and goats and other domesticated animals are distributed equally. It may be pointed out here that in case there is only one animal and there are more than one co-sharers then the person who would keep the animal would have to give each of the co-sharers the share of cost of the animal.

Natural resources like forest, grazing grounds, etc., are the property of the village community and everyone in the village has a natural right to use those to the extent up to which the village community's interest is not felt endangered by the individual user's narrow motivated self-interest.

Socio-economic Offences

The disposal of cases in their traditional manner is very simple. On receiving a complaint a panchayat meeting is held in order to pass judgement. It may be noted in this reference that for the same kind of offence by different individuals, the amount of fine may not be the same. Mostly, the variation of the fine is due to the background of the offender which the panchayat takes note of. If the general view of the people about the offender is not adverse then he may not be as severely fined as the one who has earned the bad reputation of being wicked. In most of the cases, the usual way of settling a case is to impose a fine on the offender. Severe forms of punishments like socio-economic boycott and excommunication are rarely awarded and these are effected only in grave cases like detection of incestuous relations etc., which tend to disrupt the socio-cultural health.

In the following paragraphs, the offences that usually occur in the Bhotia society are discussed along with the method of settlements. It may be mentioned that records, regarding cases, were not maintained in the panchayat. Hence the cases given here were collected from the informants who could narrate them from their memories.

Broadly we put the offences under two categories, viz. economic and social.

Economic Offences

1. In the event of theft, the case is generally not referred to panchayat if the suspect's identity is not clear enough. In such a situation, usually the family, which has incurred loss from theft, will collect some rice from each family of the village to offer the entire amount of rice thus collected to *ista devta* (presiding deity) or *gaon devta* (village deity) and solicit judgement from these supernatural powers. The Bhotias claim that this is enough to frighten the guilty person as according to the local belief severe misfortune will descend

on the offender subsequently due to the wrath of the deity. On account of this, the offender usually returns the article quite stealthily, for fear of supernatural punishment.

But, in case the identity of the thief is clear and that can be proved, then the case is referred to the panchayat. The panchayat would ask the offender to return the stolen article to its actual owner.

2. In case a person has illegally tilled another's land, taking the advantage of the latter's ignorance or absence from the village, the same is deemed as an offence — an encroachment on other's property. The owner may file a suit to this effect in the panchayat. The panchayat would direct the tiller to vacate the land after the standing crop's harvest is over. Besides the offender has to give half the crop to the owner of the land.

3. When a domestic animal belonging to one family causes damage to the crop of another's field, the latter may bring the incident to the notice of the panchayat. In this case the panchayat members would inspect the field and assess the amount of damage and may ask the guilty to pay this amount to the complainant family.

Social Offences

Example 1: It has been mentioned earlier that the acceptance of *binti chakti* by the girl, party is taken as a promise to marry the boy from whose side the same has been offered. And neither of the party is expected to cancel the deal later on. In case the betrothed girl elopes with another person then the boy's party may take the issue to the panchayat to get double the amount (in cash) spent on account of *binti chakti* by them earlier. Sometimes such issues are resolved amicably without the intervention of the panchayat. For instance Chander Singh's daughter Nathma of Dar village was betrothed to Gyan Singh of Dugta and the latter had also offered *binti chakti* to Chander Singh. But before the actual marriage took place, Nathma eloped with Dewan Singh of the same village and married him. Chander Singh himself went to Dugta village and amicably settled the problem. Gyan Singh voluntarily withdrew the offer and the case thus ended.

Example 2: Mangal Singh of Dar village eloped with Shin of Go village who had already taken Rs. 100 *tama* from another man of Go village with the promise to marry him. But her eloping with Mangal Singh meant breach of promise to marry. A panchayat meeting was held in Go village in this connection and Mangal Singh paid Rs. 200 (double of the initial sum) as fine and acquired Shinu as his wife.

2. For all social offences, excepting a breach of clan exogamy, cash fine of different ranges are generally imposed on the offenders. The Bhotia of Dar village say that they have never come across a rape case. In case of adultery and other sexual offences a fine ranging from Rs. 20 to 100 or above is always imposed by the panchayat. For instance, during my field work in Dar village a case of seduction of a widow was brought before the panchayat. The panchayat imposed a fine of Rs. 10 on the offender which surprisingly was a very small sum.

In the case of defamation of an individual by another the offender has to pay *pati* (damage charge) as fine.

36

THE JAUNSARI OF UTTAR PRADESH

SEM TOPNO and N.K. GHATAK

The old inhabitants of Jaunsar-Bawar pargana of tahsil of Chakrata in the district of Dehradun of Uttar Pradesh are known as Jaunsari. The name is derived from the region and so it does not denote a specific ethnic group. The region is of multi-ethnic nature with the Khasa and Koli now known as Kolta sharing socio-cultural tradition. Ethnically, Jaunsaris belong to the same groups of Khasas and Kolis that form the predominant population of the Himalayan region of Uttar Pradesh and Himachal Pradesh. Politically, Jaunsar-Bawar has been a distinct since historical times when it formed a part of the Sirmur estate. Immigration of people to Jaunsar-Bawar and Rawain Jaunpur (now in Uttar Kashi) has mostly taken place from Simla Hills of the present Himachal Pradesh. So Jaunsaris have common socio-cultural traditions with the neighbouring people of Sirmur, Mahasu, Jubbal Taroch and Rawain-Jaunpur. There is no restriction on marriage alliance among these people. Though ethnically the people of these areas belong to the same group, they are not regarded as Jaunsaris who are now scheduled as a tribe. The Jaunsaris are found exclusively in the Jaunsar-Bawar region. They were declared a Scheduled Tribe for the first time in 1967, and so no census record is available about the tribe prior to the 1971 census. In 1971 census there were 56,699 Jaunsaris in a total population of 79,128 in Chakrata tehsil of Dehra Dun.

The Jaunsaris are settled agriculturists. Bullocks and buffaloes are an inseparable part of the agricultural operation, for cultivation is carried out through plough technology and it is only on the steep slopes, in narrow valleys and on rolling land that hoe technology is practised. They also domesticate animals for milk and manure. Sheep and goats are reared in considerable number for meat and wool. Buffaloes and goats are also important for ceremonial occasions as they are sacrificed to the local deities but buffalo sacrifice has now been discontinued. Fowls and pigs are also reared by the lower classes in Jaunsar-Bawar but pigs are not domesticated in the Bawar area nor is pork taken.

Good quality of land is found only in valleys. The cultivable lands are widely scattered in the hills and valleys. A lot of time is spent on the preparation and maintenance of fields, in the busy agricultural season, and in looking after the cattle.

Rain Dependent Agriculture

Agriculture is wholly dependent on rainfall except in the valleys where water is available for irrigation. Sometimes water is taken to a considerable distance through channels.

Two crops are grown in the year — Kharif and Rabi. The Kharif crop is sown during the rains in June and reaped by October, though there are local differences in the season according to altitude. Rice, *mandua,* maize, potato, ginger, *choulai, gagli* and tobacco are the principal Kharif crops while wheat, barley, mustard oil and pulses are the Rabi crops which are sown in October and November and reaped in April and May. The grains produced in Jaunsar-Bawar are generally locally consumed. Potato is a cash crop and is generally exported to the plains. Some quantities of ginger, turmeric, chillies, tomato, poppy, etc., are also produced and exported. Horticulture has recently been introduced in the area. Among the fruit trees are walnut, apricot, peach, pear and apple.

Hunting is done individually but fishing is always carried out communally during a festival known as "Yaan". There is no marketplace nor are weekly markets held in the area. Prior to the establishment of a military cantonment and tehsils headquarters at Chakrata, people used to visit Dehra Dun for their requirements such as salt, gur and spices. They had also an internal arrangement in which things and services were exchanged.

The clothes of the people are made from homespun wool. Cotton is imported from the plains but it is now available at Chakrata, Tiuni, Sahiya, Kalsi, Lakhamandal, etc. Men wear cotton trousers and shirts in summer but in winter woollen trousers and woollen coats are worn. The usual dress of women consists of a *ghagra* (a sort of petticoat) and jacket called *kurti*. The headgear, known as *dhantu*, is a small piece of coloured or black cloth and is tied round the head like the border chief.

Jaunsari women are very fond of ornaments. Ornaments are made of gold and silver. Formerly Kolta women were forbidden to wear gold ornaments. Ornaments are made locally, by the lower castes and are of different patterns and sizes. They include necklaces, ear-rings and tops, nose-rings, head chains, bracelets and belts and rings for the fingers and toes.

Jaunsari houses are generally double-storeyed. The wall of the ground floor is made of stone and mud plaster with alternate layers of Deodar beams. It is reserved for animals, sheep, goat and cattle. The upper storey is made with slate stone slabs while in Bawar the roof is covered with square and rectangular wooden boards and some roofs are also covered with stone slabs. Granary is generally made outside the main house. Cattleshed known as *chhani* is built close to their cultivated land.

The usual food of the Jaunsaris consists of rice and bread with pulse, some vegetables, *ghee* and *matha*. During marriage and festivals special kind of food is prepared. On these occasions goat's meat is also taken. Local variety of liquor is also prepared for these occasions.

The Jaunsaris celebrate a number of festivals including Besco, Dewali, Magh, etc. Mahasu is the supreme deity of the Jaunsaris whose temple is of Hanane in Bawar. People believe in spirits, omens, oaths and ordeals. There are among the Jaunsari those who are consulted when there is theft in someone's house, who also diagnose diseases and are also called witch doctors. The seer or *baki* is always from the Khasas and never from Kolta and Bajgi.

Multi-caste Villages

Villages of Jaunsar-Bawar are of a multi-caste nature. The most prominent castes of the region are Khasas (who are identified as Brahman and Rajput) and Koli or Koltas who are found in almost all villages. In the hierarchical order the Khasas occupy an upper rung. They are the traditional land-owners and cultivators. The Koltas are placed of the lowest rung of the ladder, who are associated with agricultural labour work and leather work. The intermediate group consists of artisan castes — Sonar, Lohar, Barhai, Bajgi (drummers) and Nath Jogi (religious servicemen and mendicants). The Chandal and Dom are assigned the lowest place along with the Koltas who are also associated with the Chamar and Mochi of the plains. The village community is socio-politically and economically dominated by the Khasas. They also occupy the highest ritual position. In Birnat Bartil, the village under study, the Khasas (Rajput) are numerically dominant. The other castes in the village are Kolta, Bajgi, Chandal and Nath-Jogra-Jogi. Almost all communities of the village are land-owners and cultivators.

Levels and Mechanisms of Social Control

Traditional Council, Forms and Functions

Villages in Jaunsar-Bawar are well organised under its two institutions — *sayana* and *khumri*. *Sayana* is the village headman. He usually belongs to the family which is settled in the village for generations. *Sayana* comes from the oldest branch of the family of the founder of the village. The other leaders are also members of well-established families in the village. To understand the village organisation, we have to know first of all its lineage organisation. Lineage is an extended family of the collaterals which is known as *aal*. It is a patrilineal group. The members of an *aal* are believed to be the descendants of a common forefather, who was an early settler of the village. Although this cannot be traced genealogically, all member families of the *aal* claim their common pedigree through the *bhera,* a subdivision of the *aal*, consists, of one or more families established on the division of an earlier family. In this way, one's consanguineal relationship to the correct generation is traced. The leadership in the *aal* is centred in the *aal sayana* who is a senior member of the senior branch among all member families or *bheras* of the same *aal*. He attains this position by seniority and as a matter of hereditary right. He is, on the one hand, a conventional leader and representative of the whole *aal* in dealing with other *aals* and other castes in the village, and on the other he has the authority to settle intra-*aal* disputes. He is an important figure in the village meeting (*khumri*) where he represents the interests of his *aal* members at various levels. There is also a *bhera sayana* in each sub-lineage. *Bhera* is a more intimate kin group, so he has less authority than the *aal sayana*. In a village meeting he represents his *bhera*.

Village meetings are conducted by the village council under the leadership of *aal* or *gaon sayana*. A village meeting or *khumri* is invariably monopolised by the dominant caste, i.e. the Khasas, whereas the component *aals* of the caste are the contending parties in the meetings. As a rule *aal* families cooperate under the leadership of the *aal sayana*, in the interest of all members of their *aal*. In the village *khumri* it is the *aal sayana* and *bhera* that take a leading part in the discussions. So the village *khumri* is, more or less, the meeting place of all members.

Above the *gaon sayana* is the headman of the *khat* (unit of the group of villages) who is known as *sadar sayana*. In the whole of Jaunsar-Bawar, there were 39 *khats* each having a *sadar sayana*. In the olden days, however, there was also a superior group of *sadar sayanas*. These *sadar sayanas* held a position more powerful and higher than the ordinary *sadar sayanas* and were known as *chauntras*.

The traditional *sayana chari* system, with regard to the affairs of the village and area, consisted of three main stages — village level, *khat* level and all Jaunsar-Bawar level — the leaders of these three levels were known respectively as *gaon sayana*, *sadar sayana* and *chauntra*. In some cases, there were more than one *gaon sayana* in one village, or more than one *sadar sayana* in one *khat*, and sometimes there were *sadar sayanas* of the Khog or a sub-division of the *khat*.

Gaon sayana was the head of the village community. It is, as a rule, the *gaon sayana* or one of the more distinguished *gaon sayanas* who presides over the meeting (*khumri*) of the village council. He is the final authority in general. He also represents the whole village in the inter-village matters and deals with outsiders in general. He is responsible for the management of the village temple, and he sees that the *puja* is performed regularly. He receives quests, visitors and officials coming to the village and arranges for their accommodation and meals, and looks after the law and order in general. He collects land revenue according to the allotment. The post of the *gaon sayana* is hereditary and is regulated according to the rule of primogeniture.

But it was the *sadar sayana* who held the key position in the traditional local government of Jaunsar-Bawar. It was he who was the real and supreme controller of all matters within the *khat*. He was subordinate to the *chauntras* and had to coilect the land revenue according to the allotment given to him by the *chauntras*. After the abolition of the office *chauntra* the *sadar sayana*'s position was more consolidated. He not only had the sanction of local tradition, but also enjoyed official recognition to exercise his administrative and judicial powers over the *khat* with the help of *khumri* of which he was the president. On the death of a *sayana* his eldest son succeeds, if he is unfit or minor he still holds the title, but a relative does the duties of the office. A *sayana* may resign in favour of his eldest son; if he dies without issue his brother succeeds; a woman cannot be a *sayana*. The succession to the post by his brother requires the confirmation of the Government and he is also subject to removal in extreme cases.

There were two *sadar sayanas* in Bawar the region. One of the was the forefather of the present *sayana* of village Birnad.

This was the traditional council of administration of the village and *khat.* There were four influential *sadar sayanas* who controlled the whole of Jaunsar-Bawar. Their council was known as *chauntra.* Their judicial powers were unlimited, having been given for their allegiance to the previous rajas, whereas their functions as revenue collectors were indispensable to the British Government. However, all the four *chauntras* were relieved of their functions and finally their council abolished by the British Government in 1849 when a new settlement was made. With this settlement their powers and duties were abolished altogether, and the management of each *khat* through its *sadar sayana* was established. When the statutory gram panchayat was established, the *sayanachari* system was also abolished.

Khumri was the council of *gaon sayanas* and *sadar sayanas*. It had manifold functions. Generally speaking, *khumri* functioned both as a judicial body to decide cases and disputes among the villagers, and as an administrative organ to manage various sorts of public matters. According to the traditional concepts of law and order among the Jaunsaris, the criminal and civil offences respectively were:

(a) Theft, sexual offences, witchcraft and caste behavior.
(b) land, pasture, division of family and divorce.

Theft is regarded as a serious crime because it directly involves someone's property. It is very rarely committed. With regard to sexual offences these are decided keeping in view the status of the woman. It is only with *rheyanti* that sexual indulgence is prohibited and such offences are severely punished. Witchcraft is also a serious crime. The punishment imposed by the *khumri* on the guilty party is usually a fine and social boycott. The weight given to the importance of the civil cases listed above has social and economic implications.

Statutory Council

The traditional *khumri* has been replaced with the statutory council. The traditional institution handled both judicial and administrative functions but when the statutory panchayat system was introduced they were separated. The judicial functions are performed by the *nyay* panchayat and the administrative functions by the gram sabha or the gram panchayat. The members of these sections of the panchayat are elected through adult franchise.

The gram sabha has administrative duties and powers to deal with the public affairs which were usually taken up by the traditional *khumri* including management of public organisations and public property, celebration of festivals, keeping of community funds and levying of certain taxes and the development measures introduced by the Government with regard to the communities in the villages such as public sanitation and keeping of population registers. The *nyay* panchayat, on the other hand, is purely a judicial body with powers to maintain law and order, to try cases, and to levy fines up to Rs. 100.

Panchayats are assisted by a panchayat secretary in their functioning. He is a government servant, His duties are to help the village panchayat carry out their duties in conformity with the regulations.

Since the introduction of the panchayat system the powers and activities of the traditional *khumri* were curtailed to a certain extent. However, the traditional panchayat, at village level, is still functioning. In the traditional section the judicial and administrative functions were performed by the same body, i.e., village or *khat khumri* which was the final authority the for deciding all matters. While in the new system the functions of the two bodies are clearly demarcated. In this case, the old system was more efficient because the cases were solved without any delay. There are some practical difficulties in following the new system. The new units are multi-village organisations but a local problem is often a concern of only one or two villages but the whole unit is to be mobilised and thus is wasted much labour and time. This is a big problem for a member has to walk a long distance to attend the meeting. This is why attendance at the meeting often is poor.

Among the important reasons which retard the popularity of the *nyay* panchayat is the incompatibility between the new regulation and the old traditions with regard to the divine witness. As the people here believe Mahasu Deota to be the supreme and omnipotent and omnipresent authority, the decisions made in the judicial cases almost invariably are based on an oath taken in the name of the deity. This is a procedure which a modern panchayat *adalat* could never allow and this would probably remain as one of the reasons why the panchayat cannot replace the traditional *khumri*.

The long procedure which takes much time for a case to be solved is another reason for low popularity of the panchayat. This is why in the *nyay* panchayat of Birnad only two or three cases have been reported so far and on these cases too no judgement could be given and sent to the court.

It is the higher caste which does not take much interest in the new system of panchayat. Since the *khumris* are fully dominated by the high caste people, the abolition of *khumris* would mean liquidation of their power. But the low caste, particularly the Koltas, favour and welcome the new panchayat. They find that their cases are judged with fairness in the panchayat than in *khumri*. Moreover, they get representation in the new panchayat while in the *khumri* their presence was not required. Now prior to the decision of cases no Bistara (court fee) is required in the new panchayat while in the old it was essential to deposit this money which varied from Rs. 5 to 10 or more and sometimes the *panches* were entertained to a feast. These are now no longer in practice.

Customary Laws Regarding Marriage, Family and Kinship

Types of Marriage

Polyandry is traditional to the Jaunsaris. Fraternal polyandry is now found only among the Khasas. All men of each generation who are brothers marry together with one, or as is usually the case, more than one wife. In this form of marriage, as a rule, the eldest brother takes a wife or wives, and it is through him that his brothers have access to the common wife. Formerly, when there was no custom of consulting the almanac before marriage the eldest brother was married to the selected woman, but now the almanac is consulted. Accordingly each brother's stars are matched with the woman's, and who ever's stars tally with her's, he marries her and the other brothers automatically join him. In polyandry the fraternal brothers alone marry a single wife, but generally more than one wife is taken by the brothers. This form of marriage is known as polyandry. Monogamous marriage is not unknown among the Jaunsaris and in recent times this form of marriage is on the increase. Polygynous marriage is also in practice among the people. In this form of marriage a man, who has no brothers, takes more than one wife. In the 46 households in village Birnad Bastil, there are 10 cases of polygyny and one of polyandry. The rest are monogamous marriages.

Residence after Marriage

Residence after marriage is patrilocal among the Jaunsari. The brothers who go for polyandry and polygyny live with the fathers. In case there are only girls in a family a son-in-law is kept as *ghar jawain.* In case of an inter-community marriage, such as with the Gurkhas who come to the area to seek job as labourers, they settle anywhere according to convenience. In village Birnad Bastil a Gurkhas has settled and married a Jaunsari woman of village Chousal. So the Jaunsaris are exclusively patrilocal in residence after marriage.

Bride-Price

In reality there is no custom of payment of bride-price among the Jaunsari but Mazumdar has stated that it exists (1960 : 124). For the marriage of a boy the bridegroom's party finds out a suitable girl for him. After negotiation when the girl's father accepts the proposal of marriage for his daughter he is given Re. one which is known as *fadar.* After receiving this money he cannot give word to any other prospective bridegroom. But he can refuse to give his daughter in marriage if something wrong is proved against the boy, and in that case he refunds the money. If the bridegroom's party itself refuses to take the girl subsequently, they cannot demand this money lack from the girl's parents. After the marriage, when the newly married couple visits the girl's parent's house for the first time the bridegroom presents gifts in the form of cloth to the parents. He also gives something to her younger brothers and sisters. The parents in return also give him whatever they like. This is merely an exchange of gifts and cannot be said to be the bride-price.

Rules and Restrictions or Marriage

The Jaunsaris are a patrilineal people. In the absence of any clan or gotra, lineage plays a great role and functions as an exogamous group. The local term for lineage is *aal* though it has also a subdivision which is known as *bhera*. All the *aals* generally reside within a village. An *aal* member has also territorial relations with its members in other villages. These are known as *dai* brothers. This patrilineal group of *dai* are exogamous for marital relations. No marriage can take place within a village because in a village members of only one *aal* are found. Marriage within the *dai* members is taken as incest and it is a serious offence. Marriage cannot take place in the consanguineal group. It can take place only with the *saga* or affinal kin who have no relationship at all with one's own *dai*. In terms of kinship and marriage Jaunsari individuals recognise three groups of people — *dai* or *agnates, saga* or affinal relative and non-related caste men — who may become his *saga* when a marriage relation is established with them. The Jaunsaris avoid marriage with father's sister's daughter. In other words among cross-causins and maternal parallel cousins there can be no marriage relations as they use the same term as used for one's own brothers and sisters. Marriage cannot take place with mother's sister's daughter with the ego because she is more intimate with the ego's mother. But now some cases are reported of such marriages.

There is no prescriptive marriage among the Jaunsaris but they prefer to marry with *saga* relatives because their conduct and behaviour are well known to them. This is why if a man wants to take a second wife he prefers to marry his wife's sister because she is well known to him.

Levirate and Sororate

As the Jaunsari society is polyandrous no cases of levirate marriage are reported. Because in that case if one brother dies the other brother remains as husband of the woman. Among the Jaunsaris there are monogamous marriages also and in case one brother dies without an issue the woman can marry her husband's brother if unmarried. In short, levirate is not prohibited by the Jaunsari. Sororate marriage is quite common among the Jaunsari. Because in a polyandrous marriage wife's sister can become a co-wife and a number of cases are reported in the Jaunsari society of such marriage relations. Exchange marriage is also found among the Jaunsari and a few cases are reported.

Divorce

There is a large incidence of divorce and it can be initiated by either party. Women as well as men are free to divorce and remarry without much difficulty. A woman can have several husbands without losing her prestige. No procedure is prescribed for divorce, all that a woman has to do is to get a man who is willing to marry her and pay *chhoot* (divorce) money to release her. If a woman has to divorce her husband she visits her parental house a number of times in a year and stays there for a longer time. At this moment some prospective husband or husbands who too either have been divorced or widowed approach the girl's father. The latter goes to her husband's house to settle the terms of *kheet* or *chhoot* money. If the prospective husband or husbands are willing to pay the amount the divorce is settled. Unless the girl's first husband is paid what he demands or what will be settled through arbitration the girl cannot marry elsewhere because if she does, the case will be brought to the *khumri*. But with the establishment of the gram panchayat the authority and privilege of settling disputes even of the social nature through the *khumri* now no longer exists. And it is due to this inactivity of the *khumri* that Kolia Kolta of village Birnad could receive nothing when his wife was married away to another man by her parents.

Jaunsari men rarely divorce their wives, however intolerable their relationship may be. She is not divorced by the husband or husbands on ground of adultery, desertion, neglect of duties, diseases, insanity, barrenness, crime, witchcraft practice, etc. The wife has an economic role and procreative function. Extra-marital relation is no ground for divorce. It is the wife who generally initiates for divorce and on a very trivial ground a wife may leave her husband because of the constant pressure of work or if she is not provided the dress and ornaments required by her, or if she finds it difficult to adjust in the husband's family. Distance from the parental home also sometimes becomes the ground for leaving the husband's house.

Family

Jaunsari family follows the principle of patrilocal varience, patrilineal descent, patronymic designation and patriarchal authority. It also has extended family relations which include all male members of living generations in the patrilineal line of descent along with their wives and unmarried sisters and daughters. Often there are also married sisters and daughters who remain in the family before the consummation of marriage or after divorce or on being widowed. Child marriage is common but the female remains at her father's home till puberty. The Jaunsari have basically polyandrous families. Nuclear families among the Jaunsari exist due to compulsion. If a man has no brother, he has no alternative but to have a nuclear family. But a man can marry as many wives as he can, so polygynous family is also not rare. The Jaunsari practise fraternal polyandry but they are allowed to add as many wives as they want to the number of wives. So, among the Jaunsari a combination of family forms is found these are both polyandry and polygyny which is termed as a polygynandrous family.

Adoption

When a family has no issue or if there are only female children a male child, from among the *aal* or *dai* brothers, is adopted in the family with the consultation of lineage members and *gaon sayana*. No child from outside these specific groups can be adopted. But this, too, is not a hard and fast rule and varies from village to village. For instance, in village Kanda (Bawar) a Rajput adopted a Gurkha boy, but consent was required of the *sayana* of the village. Adoption of a child must be sanctioned by the *aal* members. Otherwise the adopted son has to face a number of difficulties. If no person is willing to give a child to be adopted by a family a child from outside the *aal* can be taken but sanction of *aal* members is absolutely necessary. If a family has only female children a son-in-law (*ghar jawain*) can be adopted with the consultation and sanction of *aal* members and the *sayana*.

If there is an issue through extra-marital relations of a wife, it belongs to the husband and is considered as legal.

Kinship Obligation

Kinship obligation among the Jaunsaris can be considered in terms of consanguineal kinship group and affinal kinship group. *Dai* is the broad kinship group among the Jaunsari-Bawar. An ego can trace actual geo-ecological relations with the *dai* brothers. *Aal* and *dai* in the absence of any clan or gotra also functions as an exogamous unit. *Aal* also functions as a pivot of the caste in all affairs personal, family and village, concerning their day-to-day life and subsistence. *Aal* members are obliged to help one another. The mutual obligations are binding on social and ritual occasions. During marriage and death *aal* members work as a team. When a daughter is married all the *aal* members participate in the marriage ceremony and go with her to perform the ceremony at the bridegroom's house. A daughter in her native village (mother's village) is *dheyanti* not only to her parents but to all *aal* members and to the village as a whole. Similarly when a son is married all *aal* members assist the family. If a sister dies at her parent's house and her husband cannot come to attend her funeral ceremony, the brother performs the last rite in the absence of the husband.

Customary Laws Regarding Property Inheritance and Succession

Concept of Property

Property consists of objects which are useful in life and which are rare and take time and energy to procure. Thus movable as well as immovable types of objects are included in property. The Jaunsari idea of property is not very different. But what is more important is the social relationship of the people with respect to ownership and utilisation of objects. The important movable property for the Jaunsaris are cattle and sheep clothes and ornaments, and many other household goods, agricultural implements, grain, etc. These movable property are acquired through barter, sale, purchase, service and labour. Immovable property consists of the house, land and trees (particularly fruit trees).

Formerly, low caste had no customary right to own landed property. This right was only for the Khasas.. There were two kinds of cultivators — *mouroosee* (owner cultivator) and *gair mouroosee* (non-owner cultivator). Owner cultivators belonged to the Khasa community and they had no right to dispose of their land. The non-owner cultivators had no such rights. The owner cultivator's right over his land is permanent and he cannot lose this right even if he runs away from the village. He can claim that land whenever he returns.

There are two types of land among the Jaunsaris, with respect to authority. The first is called *sibal.* Its ownership is on the basis of individual right. An individual and his family and the owner-cultivator of this land they will enjoy all the produce from this land individually.

The second category of land is the community land of the village. It is fallow land of the village on which the forest grows. It is known as *sanjoyat* and is a grazing ground of the villagers. No one but the owner is allowed to collect grass or send cattle to the *sibal* land, while the *sanjoyat* land is open for all. But people who are not members of the village are not allowed to tend their cattle on this land. Shepherds from the high Himalayas, particularly Gaddi and Gujjar, generally pass through the area during winters but they have to seek prior permission of the village headman or the *khat sayana*. They are charged for it and the value varies according to the number and species of the cattle.

Collection of firewood from the trees standing on the *sanjoyat* land is allowed to the villagers. But now the Forest Department has taken control of much of the areas of *sanjoyat* land and no one is allowed to cut the trees, particularly the green ones without prior permission of the Divisional Forest Officer of the area. If a tree falls down and becomes dry, only its branches can be taken away for firewood. No one can cut down trees which stand on the *sibal* land. He can cut the branches but not the top portion.

The villagers of Jaunsar-Bawar are annually allotted trees from the reserved forest for construction and repairing of house, making plough, etc. They have the right to collect produce of medicinal importance. No land owner can cultivate any barren land, which has not been included in any check, without permission of the Collector. The government has the right of selling and letting that land to whomsoever it likes. No one can collect wood which comes down the current, the river. It belongs to the government. If a person makes and erects *gharat* (water-mill) on the river which falls within the jurisdiction of the reserved forest area, the owner of the *gharat* has to pay a tax. People can tend cattle in the Forest Department area only when they possess a pass. Also, fishing in the river which falls in the jurisdiction of the Forest Department is not allowed without a pass.

Pattern of Inheritance, Succession and Contract

The system of inheritance of property is patrilineal and the brothers inherit the property. No female can inherit the property. The post of the *sayana* is also hereditary. On the death of a *sayana* his eldest son succeeds but if he is under-age or otherwise unfit, the title of the *sayana* continues in his name. His brother or any other son of the deceased does the work for him as his deputy, as *naib* and if the *sayana* wishes he can make his eldest son *sayana* during his lifetime, but his brothers have no claim to the *sayana* because they are landowners. The *sayana* can, if he chooses, allow them to receive a portion of the *bisouta*. In case of division of property the *sayanachari* is not distributed though all other property is. A younger son cannot take the title of *sayana*. If the eldest son should die and have children such children can claim the title but no one else. When a *sayana* dies without an issue his wife cannot claim the title of *sayana*, the deceased's brother succeeds to the post.

Land is given to the landless or to persons who have small pieces of land given by the Zamindar on the basis of rent or share-cropping. The share-cropping rate is 50 : 50. The landowner provides seeds and the person who takes the share provides manure to the land. He has to work in it too. He takes care of the crops and after harvest cleans the seed for division. There is no fixed period for it.

If a Zamindar wishes to sell any portion of the land he has under cultivation, he must first through the *sayana* get the permission of the share holders of his village and also of the Zamindars of the *khat*. When a person of that *khat* wishes to buy it he cannot sell or mortgage it to a resident of another *khat*.

Formerly a purchaser of land was responsible for the payment of revenue. Now in case of a mortgage or sale the person in possession is responsible for the revenue. But the deed of mortgage must contain a condition that only the Zamindar rights are mortgaged and not the land itself. But when the mortgager takes possession he is only entitled to it till his claim has been satisfied or till the expiry of period agreed on at the time of the mortgage. The mortgager is also responsible for the revenue. With regard to mortgage it can only be executed by permission of the *sayana*. No period is fixed for the duration of the mortgage, and no fees are paid, and the *sayana* receives four annas for writing the deed, the mortgage must be recorded by the *karkoon*.

If anyone sells or mortgages anything to two persons, and the first purchaser takes possession and the money is returned to the second, the seller is considered dishonest. Ornaments are also mortgaged at the rate of Rs. 2 per day and remain in the possession of the mortgager until the owner takes back.

The debtor has to give the creditor eight pucca *seers* of corn at each harvest for each rupee, until the original sum is paid up, and if anyone is unable to pay interest and becomes insolvent, the creditor takes his original amount in the presence of four arbitrators and if the eight *seers* paid annually remain due, he forgoes it. If a debtor cannot pay his interest to the creditor and has to give much grain, then the creditor makes him pay his interest to the creditor and has to give much grain, then the creditor makes him pay double the original. The custom with regard to grain is as follows — that for the span of one year, the original quantity is increased by 50 per cent, and in the second year the accumulated amount or that which remains after a part is paid back is again increased to by 50 per cent. If the debtor has not paid any interest and becomes poor and insolvent, under these circumstances, the debtor mostly Kolta work at the creditor's home to pay back the amount and become bonded labour in course of time.

Extent of Deviation of Customary Laws

The traditional customs of polyandrous and polygynandrous marriage are being replaced by monogamous marriages, though still polygynous marriages are also held. Child marriage has long been discontinued but stray cases are also reported of this form of marriage. Though arranged marriage is still the custom boys and girls have ample opportunities to decide their future. It is due to child marriage that the frequency of divorce was high. With the increase in the age of marriage, it is less so.

According to the forms of marriage the family also was polyandrous or polygynandrous as the case may be. With the increase in monogamous marriages the number of nuclear families are increasing and polyandrous and polygynandrous families are now dissolving to giving way to nuclear families due to the influence of the plains people. There is no change in the structure and organisation of kinship system. There is the lineage of *bhera aal* and *dai* and consanguineal and affinal kinship relations are still maintained in the traditional pattern. There are still the headmen of *bhera* and *aal* who are respected as earlier but their privileges have been taken away. They have the same duty today as they performed in the olden days. And very often village *sayanas* call upon a *khumri* to decide the matters pertaining to the welfare of the society and village community.

Inheritance of property is patrilineal. And it is the male issue only who inherits the property; females are excluded from it. The brothers jointly inherit the property of the deceased. With respect to division of property all have the equal share. *Jethong* and *kanchhag* have been discontinued. The dependants have the same rights and privileges, when the brothers separate.

As the statutory gram panchayat has taken over the functions of the traditional village institution the election of the members to the new panchayat is made on the basis of adult franchise. The traditional leaders, *sayanas*, have no place in the new administrative organ and there is no question of succession to their post. But still the descendants of the *sayanas* are honorifically addressed as *sayanas*. The post of the *pradhan* is through election and not through succession.

Now all the local people of Jaunsar-Bawar, irrespective of caste and community, have been distributed land and given ownership right of. Now there are no Zamindars and tenants. Now all are tenants of the Government. The sale and mortgage of property are now registered in the Tehsildar's court and the *sayana* has no function at all. Lands are classified into three categories, according to the ownership right — *sibal, sanjoyat* and land of the Forest Department. *Sibal* is owner-cultivators' land and *sanjoyat* is village community land. The fallow land under the Forest Department is not allowed for Mautor. If the river water which comes under the jurisdiction of the Forest Department for irrigation, it is charged Rs. 5 annually. The space is also given for making gharat at an annual rent of Rs. 40 per gharat. There is no restriction on collecting dry wood, but no one is allowed to cut down the standing one. It is strictly prohibited to collect stone from the forest areas and a canal cannot be led through the area which comes under the Forest Department. No one is allowed to tend his cattle in the forest area unless he possesses a pass from the Forest Department. If one wants a pass then he has to deposit money according to the number of the species of cattle — sheep and goat Re. 1, cow and bullock Rs. 3 and buffaloes Rs. 5. For honey collection and medicinal plant collection a lease can be taken out by the contractors. Mines, etc., are Government property.

Social Offences

Social offences in respect of traditional customs are never reported to the statutory panchayat but are decided through the traditional system. Cases of beating, fighting, divorce, etc., are settled in the village itself. Offences are committed very rarely. The cases which generally go out from the traditional *khumri* are related to theft, land and pasture. Theft also is not committed against fellow villagers and against property which is under individual possession. Most of the cases which have come to light are related to forest trees. In year 1977 some trees of the Forest Department were found in a ditch. It was a case of theft and the person responsible was fined Rs. 250 by the Forest Department.

Conclusion

As stated, social offences are settled in the village itself and never come to the panchayat. It is the offences with regard to property that come to the *nyay* panchayat. The people raise no objection if the traditional custom is thus restricted by the government. The people are reluctant to change their customary behaviour but they seldom oppose the State laws. The people are slowly giving up taking *chhoot* (divorce money which the government prohibits). Child marriage is not in practice now a days and people like to give their daughters in marriage at the age not lower than 15 years. Buffalo sacrifice has recently been abandoned.

A vice which has crept into the region concerns sending women into brothels in the plains areas. This practice is strongly opposed by the Government with the help of local people. The Adimjati Sewak Sangh and Nehru Yuvak Kendra are discouraging the practice and all the agents have been caught and punished by the Government. With the passing of the Bonded Labour (Abolition) Act, all the Koltas and lower castes who were under this system have been released and settled after providing them with land and jobs. The social injustice from which they were suffering is no longer in existence generally but as the people are too much tradition-oriented and money-minded it still persists among the Koltas.

The importance of traditional leaders is still felt as the gram panchayat has not been able to replace the traditional social control institution.

The status of women in Jaunsari-Bawar is still low. The *rheyanti* has no right to control family property of her husband. The *dheyanti* too has absolutely no rights in the family of her father as she is no longer a member of her father's family after her first marriage, which an unmarried *dheynati* is entitled to under the arrangement of her marriage by her father or brothers. Among the Jaunsaris no discrimination is reported in regard to the education of boys and girls. Women are still fond of ornaments which are provided by their parents or husbands.

The traditional rule with regard to transfer of land has considerably been amended. Mortgage and sale are now duly recorded by the *patwari* and are registered. The custom of working at creditors and landowners' house by the debtors and tenants has been discontinued with the passing of the Bonded Labour (Abolition) Act.

SECTION VII

ANDAMAN AND NICOBAR ISLANDS

37

TRIBAL CUSTOMARY LAWS IN ANDAMAN AND NICOBAR ISLANDS

T.N. PANDIT

There are two key words in the term "customary law" — custom and law. Custom has been defined as "a socially prescribed mode of behaviour, carried by tradition and enforced by social disapproval of its violation" (Kamarovsky). And law, according to the well-known definition of Pound, is "social control through the systematic application of the force of politically organised society". It is further explained that "a social norm is legal if its neglect or infraction is regularly met, . . . by the application of physical force by an individual or group possessing the socially recognised privilege of so acting". However, some authors have used the term law to include most, if not all, processes of social control. Again, according to Pound, sociology of law has to be concerned with three things :

(i) "the legal order, i.e. a regime of adjusting relations and ordering conduct by the systematic application of the force of the politically organised society.

(ii) "the authoritative principles and guides to the determination of disputes in society, a code of precepts. . . .

(iii) "the judicial process and administrative process."

Thus the study of law and legal process whether in preliterate or more complex societies is a subject of very wide implications where morals, religion, social values, etc., have to be brought in.

For our present purposes it may be useful, at this stage, to use the term customary law somewhat loosely and include most forms of regulatory social processes under its scope.

Tribes Covered

Included in this project are the following tribal communities:

1. Great Andamanese of Strait Island
2. Onge of Little Andaman
3. Nicobarese of Nicobar Archipelago

    (a) Northern Group
    (b) Central Group
    (c) Southern Group

4. Shompen of Great Nicobar

Wherever the size of the tribal community is small the entire tribe was covered for field work (Great Andamanese and Onge). But in the case of the Nicobarese, coverage was effected through selective village studies in various Islands in different geographical/cultural zones.

Brief Description of Tribes

Andaman Islands

Great Andamanese

Originally 10 tribes spread out in the Andaman Islands with distinctive geographic and cultural identities and a population of several thousand (4,000 to 8,000) in 1858. The decades following contact with "civilisation" led to a sharp demographic decline. The surviving community of 24 souls at the Strait Island represents five of the original tribes. There had reached a state of anomie almost and seem to be slowly regaining some social cohesion. They have been studied at length by Man and Radcliffe-Brown in the late 19th and early 20th centuries. Recently they have been studied by Chakraborty.

Originally hunters and food-gatherers the Great Andamanese have now changed in many ways.

Onge

Originally a large population but today only 106 souls survive in Little Andaman, their original home. They have been in close contact with civilisation for about 90 years. Today they share their Island with several thousand settlers.

Though originally hunters and gatherers, they have been subject to some changes in the recent decades. The Onge have been studied by Portman (19th century), Cupriani (1952-53) and recently by Bose.

Nicobar Islands

Nicobarese

A large population of nearly 18,000 (1971 Census), the Nicobarese are spread out rather unevenly in 12 Islands of the Nicobar archipelago. The archipelago is divided into three geographical/ cultural zones — Northern, Central and Southern. About 12,000 of the population is concentrated in the northernmost island of Car Nicobar (area 49 sq. miles) and the rest 5,000 are spread out in 11 other Islands.

Traditionally horticulturists who grow coconut, arecanut, etc., and herders who rear pigs the Nicobarese live in settled villages along the sea coast.

But they have been open to many modern influences and have had extensive contact with outsiders, i.e. traders, church, government agencies, etc., during the last century particularly. Cash and market economy have been introduced by the private trader by buying surplus local products (coconuts, arecanuts) and selling a variety of recently introduced consumer goods.

Shompen

The Shompen are an inland tribe inhabiting the forests of the Great Nicobar Island. Unlike the other Nicobarese they are semi-nomadic and live in very small settlements. However, they do gardening but do not keep large herds of pig. They hunt game (pig, etc.) and collect forest products.

Tribal Customary Law: Andaman Tribes

Social Control Mechanisms

The Great Andamanese and Onge societies have traditionally been among the simplest tribal societies in the world. The political authority is of a minimal kind and by no means institutionalised.

The social order is largely dependent on "the influence of the more prominent men and women". The influential men and women are elderly and experienced persons and are wise, generous and helpful towards others. Such people intervene in all situations threatening social order. However, they act individually and not as a body. There is no punishment for recognised offences whether against individuals or society. The only deterrent is "loss of public esteem" to which most people are highly sensitive. Guilty people may also indulge in temporary self-exile or be subject to retaliatory action by the aggrieved party.

The commonly accepted anti-social acts are murder (extremely rare), injury, adultery, theft and wilful damage to property, violation of ritual and social prohibitions, sorcery (very rare), laziness, lack of respect and courtesy to elders and others, mean and bad tempered behaviour, etc. It is clear some of these concern only individuals while others are of general concern to society. Quarrels between local groups which may last for years are settled by collective action by the respective members of the concerned local groups. Beyond the family the significant social/economic/political unit is the local group. Several local groups together constitute the tribe. Each local group has its own territory or hunting grounds. Membership of a local group can be lost by migration and acquired with the consent of other members.

Marriage and Family

Monogamy is the rule. The wife goes to live with the husband in a new hut. Presents are received by the couple at marriage but there is no bride-price. Marriage between "lood-kin" is prohibited though limits of prohibition are not clearly defined and known. However, in practice marriage between close, recognisable consanguineous relations is strictly forbidden, and will amount to incest. One can marry within or outside one's local groups. Remarriage of widows and widowers is allowed. A widow may preferably marry another man within her husband's local group. Divorce, though rare, is possible. Men and women bearing same names cannot marry. Adoption of children by families and of adults by local groups is common and popular. However, with the sharp decline in numbers, many of the rules and prohibitions have been diluted as an adjustment to changing social conditions, especially so among the Great Andamanese. These days a wife may even discreetly be shared by the husband with his wifeless friends but earlier strict fidelity was expected between a married couple. Earlier reports do not mention children born out of wedlock but these days, among the Great Andamanese, where lots of crossing with outsiders has taken place during the last century, biological fatherhood is not given too much importance. All children even the "illegitimate" ones are gladly accepted and cared for normally. But among the Onge old rules still persist and adultery even among themselves is frowned upon, with outsiders it is highly resented (complaints have on some occasions gone to police and courts of attempted assault, etc.). But love affairs between youth are accepted as these lead to marriage.

Husband and wife, brothers and sisters and parents and children are closely bound to each other by life-long duties and obligations and sentiments that go beyond death. Parents take interest in their children even when they have been given for adoption. A local group consists of a series of families which may or may not be closely related but a special bond of kinship is accepted among and obligations. All food, for instance, in a local group is shared among members irrespective of who hunts the game and who collects the items. They also stand by each other in all situations concerning their common vital interests.

Property

The resource area consisting of forest and sea coast belong to a local group collectively. Others can hunt, fish and collect only with prior permission of the members otherwise quarrels will ensue. This is the immovable property of the local group as also is the communal hut shared by the individual families. Maintenance of the allotted portions of the hut is done by the families but roof, etc., is made and maintained by joint effort. The smaller huts are owned and maintained by individual families. The ornaments, tools, weapons and utensils are individually owned and disposed by being given as presents, etc., to anybody. Offspring have a right over the property of the parents and these rights may extend to other close consanguineous kin.

The eldest surviving members, male or female, can succeed to the position of head of the household depending on his/her personal qualities, health and reputation. By virtue of the good and desirable qualities a person can acquire a position of influence within the local group and the tribe as well.

Ever since the contact with the outsiders and the superior political authority, represented by the latter, sometimes some individuals have received special recognition and titles also signifying political status, such as *Raja,* etc. Wherever such recognition was given to persons already respected by their community, it enhanced their position further. But otherwise this did not prove very important for internal affairs of the tribe. Such people usually could converse with the outsiders in the latter's language and acted as interpreters betweens their own and outside communities or agencies.

In recent years, for instance, Loka (an old man) of Great Andamanese and later Tambolai (a young man) of the Onge were successively appointed member of the Chief Commissioner's Advisory Committee and, as such, were consulted on many matters concerning their tribes. Their already important position was thus boosted further.

Customary Laws : Nicobarese and Shompen

Social Control Mechanisms

Among the Nicobarese the political authority is properly institutionalised through a pyramidally arranged levels of social control authorities. At the base of the pyramid is the entire tribal community of an Island or adjoining Islands and at its apex is the chief headman or chief captain.

In every island there are a series of permanent villages built generally close to the coast. In each island live several families (mikoon) each having a head to organise and to look after its interests. A number of families together constitute a lineage/ramage (*linem*) with a head. A village has a number of ramages. The ramage heads together constitute the *village council (kambhoka)* and they elect a head/captain from among themselves with one or two vice-captains. The village captains together constitute the "Island Council" and they elect a chief captain and a vice chief captain. When ladies are elected to the post they are called *rani.* Both captain and *rani* are borrowed terms and there are no Nicobarese equivalents for them.

The various chief captains/*ranis* together form an informal tribal council to look after the interests of the entire tribe vis-a-vis the outside agencies and to maintain internal order and unity. Until recently there was a kind of supreme leader of the Nicobarese in the person of Bishop John Richardson, a father figure though he did not, of late, hold any formal office.

The various political councils and positions have the active recognition of the Andaman and Nicobar Administration which is governed as a Union Territory. Captains at various levels act on the basis of their personal good qualities, i.e. experience and age, wealth, education, wisdom and capacity to negotiate and understand and defend local interests, etc. But the authority of the councils and captains is not exercised despotically but they always keep their ears to the ground and take into account the public opinion about a matter. It may be the question of giving judgement on disputes, offences, or deciding about respective contributions for a festival and feast.

Tribal leaders also sit as members on the Chief Commissioner's and Home Ministry's Advisory Committees to represent their viewpoint.

The common offences are theft, damage to property, adultery, murder (very rare), pre-marital relations leading to pregnancy, etc.

Among the Shompen also village heads/captains and councils are reported to perform the same duties and functions as in a Nicobarese village. They also take care of matters involving relations with other Nicobarese, the settlement and the government agencies in Great Nicobars. But there is no evidence of any island council operating there. In fact, some Shompen group do not see eye to eye with each other, besides, their population is barely 150 distributed over a dozen settlements or so.

Marriage and Family

Marriage is strictly monogamous. Residence after marriage can be either at husband's or wife's place depending upon where more workers are needed. Marriages are almost always preceded by romantic and even sexual relations which are socially accepted things provided no complications arise. The lineage/ramage is treated as an exogamous unit as all members are blood-kin and cannot marry among themselves as that would amount to incest. Earlier, marriages were preferred within the village but nowadays marriages outside the village are also frequent. Marriage with wife's younger sister does take place sometimes though this is not obligatory, for adultery and desertion, etc.

Divorce is allowed and remarriage can follow for both partners. Widowed partners can also marry. Lack of children can be taken care of by adoption. Any children born out of wedlock or as a result of incestuous unions are adopted by the mother's parents. Adopted children of all kinds enjoy the same status and privileges within the extended family and ramage as do other children.

Property

Property (both movable and immovable) is owned at three levels.

(a) That owned by the ramage includes forest land, plantations, fresh water sources, fishing rights in these waters also belong here. Pigs also belong to the ramage.
(b) Domestic belongings are owned by individual families and include pots and pans, weapons and tools, canoes, etc.
(c) Personal belongings include things of purely personal use such as clothing, fancy goods, special tools and weapons owned by an individual.

Damage, misuses, and theft of all kinds of property are punishable offences under their customary laws. Property is inherited and managed at the levels at which they are owned by the elders with fairness and taking into account the needs of all.

Among the Shompen the plantation and domestic pigs and tools, weapons and utensils are owned by individual families. Rights over hunting and collecting area are also exercised by the local groups to the extent possible. Property is inherited by the near kin who constitute the members of the surviving family and the new head manages it.

Conclusion

The tribes of Andamans and Nicobars represent two levels of growth and development of customary laws. This is understandable as they have different cultural, historical and ethnic backgrounds. Andaman Tribes have traditionally been hunters and gatherers and the

Nicobarese and the Shompen horticulturists and herders. During the last century and more they have been subjected to different historical and demographic experiences causing irreversible changes in their outlook and worldview — Andaman tribes fighting for basic survival as populations and societies and the Nicobarese grappling with the problems of population growth and modern influences on their culture and life and seeking means of adjustment to these. In case of, Andaman tribes some would argue, "laws" do not exist whereas among the Nicobarese there is an elaborate and well crystallised judicial legal framework built within the traditional social structure. However, social life is regulated by various custom norms, usages, sanctions and values existing within each society.

The Great Andamanese traditionally follow monogamy, but in view of their biological extinction and in some cases and, due to lesser number of females, the wife sleeps with her husband's friend in his absence with his consent. Marriages are arranged by the older man and woman. When the parents of a youth who is of suitable age to be married perceive that he has formed an attachment with a girl, they take it upon themselves to arrange marriage. Earlier they had a rule of avoidance between the parents of the bride and bridegroom but nowadays as they are not having a good number of population so they have modified the practice. The father of the bridegroom avoids talking with the mother of the bride and vice versa.

When a marriage has finally been arranged an evening is fixed for the ceremony. Though they had some simpler function, like the elder's advice for a happy family, nowadays that simplest form of marriage has become more simple. After all of them are entertained in a hut mainly bride's father's, in the evening elderly ladies ask the bride to arrange a bed for sleeping. With the consent of the elder members of the group the bride and bridegroom sleep together, and from this the boy and girl are taken as husband and wife. The next day the bride comes with the bridegroom to a new hut near the bridegroom's father's.

They do not have the practice of bride-price but in practice the friends and well-wishers of the new couple in order to help establish a new family present some articles like *birball* (dancing ornament for waist), *ka* (bow), *laich* (arrow), etc.

Marriage between persons belonging to the same local group was the custom in former times, but with the changing situation they now marry from other local groups too. Marriage was forbidden between near consanguines and also they had a restriction on marriage between a boy and a girl who bore the same name though they were not blood related. In the present demographic position due to less number of females the Great Andamanese are now forced to disobey the traditional rules. Widow marriage is approved by the society, remarriage is common. Almost all of the present Great Andamanese are married more than once. Levirate and sororate marriage is also practised. Divorce is not uncommon. Both male and female can divorce. The divorced lady takes the children with her if she wishes.

Adoption was common and it was a matter of pride for those who adopted a child. Almost every family adopts a child as a chain system. They love children very much so they never hate an illegitimate child. To them there is nothing wrong with the birth of a child before marriage and they don't look down upon the boy and the girl for their illegal intercourse. In the present situation we can see that almost all the children are born due to the mixing of Great Andamanese women with the outside, and till social fathers love these children they are brought up in their laps. Their argument now is that as we are very less in number, these children at least will increase the number of persons who will speak their tongue, and represent them after their death, moreover with them around playing they would not feel lonely.

The Great Andamanese child is always given a name before he is born. The nearest kin or the friend of husband gives his name to the newcomer when he or she is in the mother's womb. That is why in the Great Andamanese society more than one person bears the same name and they do not have sex discrimination and both male and female have the same name. To utter the elder person's name is improper in the Great Andamanese society so they have a practice of using nick-name. The person who gave the name to the baby has some obligation to the mother of the baby before and after birth. He collects the seasonal varieties of fruits, tubers, fishes and other food materials and gives them to the mother so that she nourishes the baby. After birth he collects articles for the baby for his good growth.

The local group was the land-owning group and each member had the right of hunting on their country forest. They did not have the ideas of immovable property. But nowadays the government has constructed huts and allotted them a plantation which is now the only immovable property of the Great Andamanese family. Hunting and fishing implements made by them are one of their important properties. Shell necklace, waist belt, and other dancing ornaments are also their important property. A canoe is owned by the person who first selected the suitable tree for it in the forest. But the drumming board is the common property of the society. Modern utensils and cloth are now available to every house.

The property is inherited by the persons (male or female) bearing the same name of the deceased. If more then one boy and girl bear the name of the deceased the younger girl inherits the property to the exclusion of the own zones and daughters.

According to a Great Andamanese rule the eldest members get the best things of their choice and they have the right to distribute to the members according to their need. Though the present members of the tribe are aware of money but still they usually exchange their collected articles with the required articles with their known persons.

All these people are at much the same level of legal development. Settlement of disputes was through the court of arbitration which performed the ritual to sanctify the settlement reached. The judges ware only advisers who formally declared decisions reached by general agreement between all the parties concerned. There was, however, penalising of a habitual wrongdoer or a person who was a danger to the whole community. Such a man could be publicly outlawed by the community and put to death. There was no redress for adultery other than by fighting. Feuds are said to have been settled by direct negotiation between the parties concerned.

The recent changes in the social life of the Great Andamanese render it difficult to determine what was the former practice.

38

MECHANISM OF SOCIAL CONTROL AND RESOLUTION CONFLICT AMONG THE ONGE OF LITTLE ANDAMAN

D.K. BOSE

The Onge inhabit Little Andaman island which is about 66 nautical miles south of Port Blair, capital of the Andaman and Nicobar islands. The Little Andaman has the graticules of 10° 30′ to 10° 50′ North and 92° 15′ to 92° 30′ East. The area of the island is about 290 sq. miles.

An investigation was made in 1977 of the principles underlying the Onge customary law. The social control mechanism of the Onge is concerned with the establishment and maintenance of internal cooperation which implies some form of regulating relations between members of the band and the clan living in a territory. The Onge descent is patrilineal and residence patrilocal. There are exogamous patrilineal clans located in a particular territory. Monogamy is the rule and polygamy is not permitted. Among the Onge we find two distinct social groupings, the first of these is the grouping through kinship — it contains the family and clan; the second grouping has a territorial basis. The traditional authority structure that we recorded in the Onge is still dominant and operates within its existing normative framework. In them there is a clear-cut distinction between secular and sacred institutions. The band head acts as the chief of the band and the priest is the religious head, rarely there are conflicts between the two.

There is a common belief that the Onge live in a state of anarchy, but if we go deep into their style of life it will be observed that they have a coherent social control mechanism which binds them together and there is some degree of compulsion as they all the time cannot do exactly as they like. The Onge of the Little Andaman are divided into six territorially based unilineal descents and a number of bands claiming mutual descent from a distant ancestor, again in the male line, constitute an *onokologa* (clan). According to the Onge system the *onokologa* holds a specific area or territory in which all its band houses are built. The *onokologa* is exogamous and has a name, viz. Ami, Amiya, Chulinga, Gaya and Maya. Members of an *onokologa* believe in a common ancestor, usually thought of as some generation ago, sometimes within historical time, sometimes long before that. In every band a senior man plays an arbitrative and advisory role in group affairs, besides this there is no specifically political authority. Still when the chief (*eichoba*) or the senior man says something concerning the maintenance of social order the members of the band acknowledged his authority. The chief when he acts as leader, his office is called *enata* in the Onge dialect. We have not recorded any further grouping of any kind above this level. However in taking some decisions in the matters relating to territory and clan all the band chiefs, moving in a particular territory, assemble and decide matters of common interest. The band leadership might have evolved through dependency between individuals and band for subsistence, shelter, etc. Thus he plays a crucial role in the Onge social control mechanism.

No Escape from Punishment

They believe that none can ever escape the consequances of unexpiated breach of their customary law which their ancestors laid down for the well-being of the community. It is the moral obligation of an individual to follow in the footsteps of their ancestors. If by chance they fail to do so, calamities may fall upon then. The Onge feel that if anyone disregards the social customs, it is not only injurious to the culprits but to any band sheltering the guilty person. The fundamental idea of community responsibility brings them together to live in compact groups and maintain social order. The customary laws that regulate the Onge way of life are reflected in almost every sphere of their social life and any sort of deviant behaviour in any of the subsystem is not tolerated and is brought before the notice of the chief. In Onge society band is the primary social unit concerned with the enforcement of social control. There is no recognised territorial council among them.

The office of the *eichoba* (chief) of a band is always hereditary. His eldest son is always supposed to be the chief, if he is capable of running the office effectively, otherwise the chief is selected by the band members to look after their affairs. If the primogeniture system does not materialise then the title or right goes to another person through formal selection by the band members. The Onge put emphasis on certain special qualifications of the man who acts as their chief: (1) He must be an elderly person within a particular band. (ii) He should have a thorough knowledge of the ecology of the territory and natural boundaries of the group. (iii) His contacts with other bands and other territorial groups must be very cordial. (iv) He must be well versed regarding Onge customs and traditions. (v) He must be a married man with wife living with him in a particular band territory, — widowers and women do not qualify for the chief's post

Eichoba's Three Main Functions

The *eichoba* (chief) performs three important functions: (a) administrative (b) executive and (c) judicial. The priest (*koira*) of the band performs the religious function and the sorcerer (*touora*) does the function of the magician in the group. The primary purpose of the chief in a particular band is to maintain peace and harmony among the respective members who comprise the band and at the same time to guard the Onge customs particularly in respect of social and economic matters against breaches. The chief sits in the communal hut with all the members of the band for the redressal of grievances. In case of a complaint he summons the members of the band in an informal way and before the litigants open the subject for discussion or hearing. After hearing from both the parties, the chief reviews the points raised and announces his judgment to the band members. He decides cases of quarrel, abuse, illicit sexual relationship, divorce, trespass upon other's land, damage of property, theft of particular possession, etc. In the event of a dispute involving persons from two or more bands representatives of all the bands concerned take part in a discussion which is generally held in the area of the defendant. When the chief tries any case the members who attend the court are not supposed to use any weapon or arm and physical violence is not tolerated. Onge women are also permitted to attend the meeting of the chief when any case is in progress. They believe that *Tojawalanga*, the supreme deity of the Onge, is always supporting the chief and sits with him when any such meeting is in progress. Thus his decision is always taken as the decision of their supreme deity. So an Onge cannot escape from the effect of a breach of a tribal custom and once the decision of the chief is announced the offender is to abide by the decision. The chief of a band generally considers only serious breaches of the Onge customary laws. There is a general belief among them that automatic supernatural punishment for some ordinary breaches of various social customs is bound to come to the offender, thus the chief does not take much initiative to settle disputes or punish the offenders in such matters.

An Isolated Pygmy of Asia

If we need to know the problem of culture contact with the outside population among the Onge we need to study the change situation in historical depth. The Onge may be considered to represent the most characteristic group of the isolated pygmy population of Asia and Oceania during the course of some millennia it has remained separated from the continent and without external contacts. The Onge are not much influenced in their traditional customary law although contacts between the Onge and non-tribals data back to latter half of the 18th century. It was only during the British period that interaction between the two was little intensified. Of course the British administration were much interested in friendly relations with the tribe and were never interested in imposing any political organisation on them. During the pre-British period there are written references that the Onge had regular interaction with Chinese and Burmese traders who occasionally used to visit their territory and barter goods them for birds' nests (*hawabil*), *ambarage*, shell, etc. They might be giving them tea, tobacco, etc., to get above mentioned items. In this period the dogs were introduced in the Onge culture by the Burmese which became part and parcel of their life. The early impact of these outside agencies can easily be found in their socio-economic life.

Apart from this the growing need of barter with alien people has given rise to some type of leadership which does not exist in their ideal culture. To protect them from the exploitation of outsiders in late 1972 a social worker was posted at Hutbay to look after the Onge welfare. Under the advice of the social worker, an Onge named Sri Lacchu was formally chosen as representative of the Onge tribe and declared as *raja*. The result was chaotic as Sri Lacchu although chosen as chief among the Onge had no idea who was expected to take orders in all sorts of matters from him, whom the Onge had known all their life not as an intra-tribal authority but simply as the chief of one of the bands. Of course after one year this was understood and this experiment was abandoned. After the death of Lacchu some of the Onge realised that he was respected by almost all Government officials and outsiders for being declared as *raja* of the Onge community and became interested to get that post and a competition was recorded among the band chiefs living in six clan territories. Where little is to be gained by being the chief, there is seldom if ever competition for the office, but where it carries great material advantage and prestige dispute about the leadership and conspiracies against an incumbent often occur. Thus the band chiefs also tried to influence the Tahsildar posted for Onge welfare in 1975-76 to get their names recommended as the intra-tribal chief or *raja* to the Chief Commissioner of the Andaman and Nicobar islands.

The youths who were a little advanced among the Onge became interested to get that post. Thus an Onge named Sri Tambolai ultimately became successful in convincing the Tahsildar and on August 20, 1976, he was announced as the intra-tribal leader as far as the Dugong Creek group is concerned. Sri Tambolai knows Hindi well and proved to be a good medium to explain the views of the Government as well as of private organisations for the welfare of the Onge. The Andaman administration started thinking seriously about the welfare of the Onge and several welfare schemes were taken up during 1975-76 thus a lot of welfare activities are going on at the Little Andaman mainly at the Dugong Creek. Establishment of hospital, school, power house, free rationing, etc., for the benefit of the Onge are under way. Altogether a new settlement for the Onge at the Dugong Creek came up where provision is being made to provide wooden houses for the Onge living in and around the Dugong creek area. But a conflict started when other band chiefs mainly the band chiefs of the Amiya and Gaya clans did not agree with the decision of the Andaman Administration about the selection of Sri Tambolai as the intra-tribal chief who belonged to the Ami clan and did not have any right over any territory as he belonged to a group which lost their territory due to the settlement of Bengali refugees in their area. The Onge living in the Dugong Creek settlement started a non-cooperation movement with the administrators posted there in connection with Onge welfare programmes. Ultimately the Chief Commissioner, Andaman and Nicobar islands, was approached and he had to announce the name of Sri Napikotai, a band chief of the Gaya clan as one more *raja* or intra-tribal chief. This of course did not solve the problem as other Onge who live in the Dugong Creek area and do not belong to the Gaya or Ami clan were not happy with this decision. They often show dissatisfaction and always consult their band chiefs in matters relating to their welfare. This conflicting situation gave rise to dissatisfaction among the Onge and the idea of an intra-tribal chief may collapse at any moment.

The introduction of an intra-tribal chief among the Onge, i.e. *raja* system of government and authority, has reduced the powers of the band chief to some extent but they continue to be influential. The introduction of the new system had led to confusing situations in some cases. This happened as the Onge were unable to grasp the idea and structure of the new system. In Onge customary laws formerly decisions used to be taken either by the band chief or by consensus, but the introduction of the new system had tended to replace consensus by majority decision.

39

PROPERTY AND INHERITANCE AMONG THE NICOBARESE AND SHOMPEN

T. LAL

Among tribal communities the customary laws determine the status of each member of the community. The social, economic, legal and religious expects of the Nicobarese and Shompen were recorded noted during the year 1975 and 1977 at the Great Nicobar island.

The Great Nicobar island is situated in the south-eastern portion of the Bay of Bengal and is the largest in area among the Nicobar group of islands. Its area is about 865 sq. km. Its southern tip, the Pygmalion Point, is hardly 145 km. north of the Acheen Head, the northern tip of Sumatra

The Great Nicobar island is hilly and densely forested. The tropical climate of this island is more uniform than in the Andamans. There is good rainfall throughout the year, but scanty rain during February and March. It is the only island of the Nicobar group which has rivers. The virgin soil, enriched by years of addition of organic matter due to decay of vegetation, is extraordinarily fertile and favours lush growth. There is, however, very little commercial timber in the island, though there is a large quantity of cane bamboo. It has more variety of fauna than any other island of the Nicobar group. The rivers Galathea, Alexandra, Dagmar and Jubilee are the prominent ones and are full of crocodile, turtle and fish. The reptiles like snake and lizard, mammals like monkey and pig, birds like Magapod and pigeon, insects like caterpillar are not absent.

The population of the island is very scanty. The island is also remarkable for being the only island of the Nicobar group which has people of two tribes — Nicobarese and Shompen. The Nicobarese are about 219 in number and live in the coastal area. They are horticulturists. They maintain coconut plantations. In the past there were quite a few villages on the east coast also, but at present all of them have been deserted.

The Shompen are very backward people found in the Great Nicobar island only. They mostly live in the interior though some of them are also found in the coastal area. Due to the lack of adequate contacts with them their exact number is not known, but during my field survey I contacted 81 Shompens while the other Shompens were living somewhere in the interior not yet visited. According to my Nicobarese informants and other various reliable sources I noted that the total population of the Shompens was 162, while the coastal Nicobarese numbered 219. The Nicobarese have more children than the Shompens. The Shompens are a semi-nomadic tribe of the Great Nicobar island who mostly depend on natural resources.

Remarkable Spirit of Unity

The Nicobarese society is characterised by a remarkable spirit of unity, feeling of brotherhood and a sense of belonging to one community in which individual desires and interests are subordinated to those of the community. It has two apparently contradictory features of social hierarchy and equality of rights. The people work under the command of the village headman, head of the family and other elders and in fact all important matters of the village are decided by these few persons. Rights of all villagers are safeguarded and there is no question of any person exercising special privilege to the detriment of the rights of others. Indeed, to the Nicobarese the whole community is a sort of big family and the individuals are united to each other by bonds of attachment and sympathy such as found between members of one particular family. All people mix freely on the social plane.

There is an extreme type of joint family system among the Nicobarese and the family is the unit of all social life. The composition of the Nicobarese family is very different from that of the Shompen society. Among the Nicobarese not only the wife, children, brothers, sisters, etc., are included in the family, but many distant relatives such as collaterals, cousins, etc., form part of the family. The Nicobarese joint family is controlled by the head of the family and all the other members work under his command. The qualifications of the head of the family include age, qualities of leadership, intelligence and above all capacity to control and command.

Shompen and Nicobarese Different Entities

The Shompen society is distinct from the Nicobarese although it is believed by some that the Shompen and Nicobarese belonged to the same ethnic stock but the Shompens lost contact with the outside world and their way of life remained as it was many centuries ago. It is difficult to say how far this is true, because it seems the Shompens are different from the Nicobarese and they also speak a different language. During my field observation I came across the Shompens and their settlements. They live in small groups and the members of the group are related to one another by blood or by affinity. The social groups of the Shompens are based on tradition, kinship and locality. The Shompens maintain a very small sized family. It consists of husband and wife and their unmarried children who live in the same hut. The Shompen son of each particular group and family makes a separate hut after marriage for himself and his wife. It is also observed that he may go to his wife's village and stay with her. The residence pattern is both matrilocal and patrilocal as I observed among both Shompens and Nicobarese. I could not trace any marriage ceremony among the Shompens. I came across three cases of polygyny out of which in two both the wives are still alive. The Shompen couples have great affection and love for each other and both are extremely fond of their children. The Shompen society is neither patrilineal nor matrilineal. It is bilateral which means the existence of father's line as well as the mother's line of descent.

In the very small sized family of the Shompen the husband is considered the head of the family. He is controls the family and all the other members (wife and unmarried children) work under his command. The Captain of the Shompen village and the head of the family decide all the important matters of the village. The Captain in a Shompen village is responsible for the welfare and maintenance of all the members of the group.

Concept of Property

The concept of property collective or individual is marked among the Nicobarese and Shompen tribes. The rights of property among these tribes are determined by the tribal customary law. The Nicobarese are having their property on both collective and individual pattern. During my own observation I noted that each head of the family among the Nicobarese controlled his individual property including movable and immovable. But as regards the property the Shompens are very much poorer than the Nicobarese. The Shompens live in small groups and they are mostly having collective property except for some articles. The property of the Nicobarese and Shompens will be described under the three heads of movable property, immovable property and natural resources of the island as well as the sea shore.

Movable Property

The Nicobarese tribes are well advanced regarding the posession and availability of movable property in their society. The Nicobarese have livestock like pigs, chicken, dogs as their property. During my second visit in 1977 among the Nicobarese I observed that the headman of a Nicobarese village Pulobeth had goats among his livestock. This practice of keeping goat started about two years back due to very close contact with the settlers of the Great Nicobar island. Other things like clothes, ornaments, utensils, hunting and fishing equipments, musical instruments and transistors, cultivation implements and equipments used for making their canoe as well as the implements used by them for cutting wood and construction of their huts are considered the movable property of the Nicobarese.

The Shompens' movable property is comparatively not so rich, as they are mostly dependent on the natural resources. Their movable property consists of traditional clothes, ornaments, utensils, hunting and fishing equipments, wooden sticks from particular woods to make fire, cultivation implements, implements for cutting wood and to construct their huts, glass and plastic bottles (collected from sea shore) to keep honey, livestock like pigs, chicken among some of the Shompens group but specially the dogs are their major movable property among the livestock. The Shompen groups inhabiting the interior on the west coast don't have as good livestock as the Shompens on the east coast although the Shompens of the west coast have very close contact with their neighbours, the coastal Nicoberese.

Immovable Property

The immovable property of the Great Nicobar island relates to agricultural resources. The people depend upon the produce of their plantations and forest wealth. There are no industries and the few items of handicrafts of the people cannot be taken to be any the products of organised cottage industry.

As regards the immovable property of the Nicobarese it is better organised and more advanced than that of the Shompens. The Nicobarese people are well equipped for their plantation. The major immovable property among the Nicobarese consist of the coconut trees and their products. Each head of the family among the Nicobarese has his individual plantation of coconut and arecanut trees. Regular maintenance of their plantation and well-equipped method for its cultivation help derive good production.

As regards the immovable property of the Shompens, they keep gardens depending upon the availability of suitable land at an approachable distance from their settlements. Generally the Shompens maintain at least one garden very close to their settlement. Their other gardens come within the radius of 2/3 km. from the settlement. Their gardens are generally along the plains of the river banks or on the gradual slopes of the hills.

The Shompens maintain their gardens themselves. The major product of their garden is the pandanus fruit. The pulp of pandanus is used as a food. They also produce coconut in their garden only for personal consumption as food. It is because of the little production that sometimes the Shompens feel the shortage themselves. Thus the question of the Shompens selling their product does not arise.

The Shompens have no individual garden for each family. They have the garden property in the collective form among each group of a particular settlement. The maintenance of the garden is controlled by the captain in a Shompen village with the help of the head of the family. All other members work under his command. The Shompens of the east coast are more or less coastal inhabitants. The non-availability of flat land for better coconut plantation as in the case of the Shompens of west coast has resulted in the poor plantation of coconut trees. This differentiation exists from village to village among the Shompens.

Customary Rights over Natural Resources

As the Great Nicobar island is very close to the equator and its climate is tropical, there is thick luxuriant growth of vegetation. The vegetation varies from place to place according to the soil and distance from the sea. At the outer edge of the island there are coconut trees and beach forests. In the interior of the island are thick tropical forests full of natural wealth.

Although the Nicobarese and Shompens are inhabitants of the same Island, there are distinct territorial regions for their settlements as well as natural resources. There are different customary rights and laws regarding the centre and utilisation of the natural resources among the Nicobarese and Shompen.

The location of the Shompen village as well as the Nicobarese has also a regional dimension in the same Island. The Shompens live in the interior while the Nicobarese live in the coastal area. Some of the east coast Shompens are also coastal inhabitant while the east coast of the island is deserted by the Nicobarese. Regarding the natural resources as the property of these tribes they are described separately for each tribe — Nicobarese and Shompens — as under:

The Nicobarese tribes inhabit the territorial region from south to north of west coast of the Island. It consists of the coastal area of the west coast from the Nicobarese village Pulobaba to Rehehong, a total belt of the coastal region occupied by the Nicobarese. Besides their coconut plantation each head of the family has access to the forest wealth individually such as the timber for construction of huts, various varieties of cane bamboo, wild fruits like pandanus, pineapple, arecapalm, and some other kinds of fruits which are used by the Nicobarese. Hunting of wild pigs is also an economic activity of these people. They are experts in hunting. They take dogs with them to hound the wild pigs and also have the spears to kill the wild animals. With the help of their dogs they kill the wild pigs very easily. They never enter the Shompen territory for hunting purposes.

Fishing Major Economic Activity

Fishing is a major economic activity of the Nicobarese who have various types of spears for fishing and to hunt the turtles, etc. They kill crocodiles in the creeks and tortoise in the sea by canoe. The variety of fish in the sea is a natural gift for these people. According to their rights and customary laws the Nicobarese utilise their natural resources and they never interfere with their neighbours, the Shompens. Entering the Shompens territory to secure natural resource is strictly prohibited by each headman of the Nicobarese village. During my own observation I observed the Nicobarese natural resources with the help of my Nicobarese informant. At present each family of the Nicobarese has in its possession the natural resources individually.

A remarkable practice among the Nicobarese that I observed was the hunting of wild pig which they roast in fire with wooden sticks. After roasting it all the hunters take its flesh. It is strictly prohibited to talk to one another. Except the hunters nobody is allowed to take a share in it. The day on which they take the flesh of the wild pig, they will not take any other kind of food from their houses. They are not allowed to talk with other members of the family after taking the flesh of that pig.

As the hunting, fishing and food-gathering are major economic activities of the Shompens, these people mostly depend upon the natural resources. The Shompens have the definite territorial rights and privileges for hunting wild animals like wild pigs, etc., and fishing activities. Food gathering includes wild fruits pandanus, arecapalm, and tubers of some particular plants, eggs like megapod and caterpillar; honey is collected for bartering as the local administration fixed the price at Rs. 10 for each bottle of honey and payment to these people not in cash but in kind as they require. The Shompen also collect the timber wood, cane and bamboo for the construction of their huts, the special type of bark of a particular tree to make their traditional cloth specially used for women. These all economic activities of the Shompens related to natural resources. All these territorial rights and privileges among the Shompens are determined by traditional customs and the tribal customary laws.

Patterns of Inheritance

Now we turn to the pattern of inheritance, that is, to get property as heir or to possess property by transmission from the past generation.

Among the Nicobarese the pattern of inheritance of property is matrilineal. Mostly the girl of the original family among the Nicobarese is considered heir to the property by transmission from the past generation. This is known as matrilineal pattern of inheritance of property. But once the girl leaves her original family to live with her husband, the head of her new family becomes responsible for looking after her and treats her with the same affection and consideration as shown to any other member of family. On leaving his original family the rights of the boy in the property of the original family are terminated according to the traditional customs among the society of these people.

Thus both the patterns of inheritance have been observed among the Nicobarese. But the matrilineal pattern of inheritance is dominant.

As regards the pattern of inheritance among the Shompens it is neither patrilineal nor matrilineal, it is bilateral, which means the social affiliation of the children is to both the father and the mother. If a Shompen boy lives with his father after getting married, he has the right to get his father's property and accordingly the property will be inherited by him as heir. In case the boy leaves his original family to live with his wife, the rights of the boy in the property of the original family are terminated. In this manner the property will be inherited by the girl (wife) as heir from her mother's side.

Thus both patterns of inheritance among these people are governed by the tribal customary law among the Shompens.

Role of Contracts

The Shompens have barter contracts on fixed terms with the Nicobarese for their natural produce like honey, arecanut, betel leaf, cane strips etc. In exchange they take from the Nicobarese articles as required by them. This contract has been made by the Shompens of the west coast who live in the interior and are very close to the Nicobarese. The other groups of the Shompens from the east coast of the island are having contracts on fixed rates for their a produce like honey and lemons. The local administration has fixed the rate of each bottle of honey at Rs. 10 and of each lemon at 25 paise only. The Shompens get the prices of their articles in kind as per their requirements.

The Nicobarese have sale contracts with Gujarati private traders known as Nancowrie Mercantile Company for copra and betelnut on fixed terms. These traders have opened consumer cooperative societies in all the major islands of the Nicobar group. From these cooperative societies the Nicobarese get payment in cash against supplies of copra and betelnut. The Nicobarese also purchase consumer goods such as rice, sugar, tinned food, tea, cigarettes, cloth, knives, crockery, utensils, shoes, toilet articles, etc., in cash or credit which is adjusted against their accounts of copra and arecanut sales.

Conclusion

The property relations among the Shompens and the Nicobarese depend upon the produce of their gardens and plantations, their access to forest wealth as well as the size of their livestock, their economic hunting of wild animals, fishing and food-gathering. All activities of these tribes are related to their traditions and customs which determine the rights and duties among them.

As regards the administration, the Assistant Commissioner, whose headquarters is at Campbell Bay, is the seniormost administrator of the area for both non-tribal and tribal populations. He is the principal officer responsible for the administration and welfare of these tribal people and development in the island. The special responsibilities of the local administration include protection of the interests of the Nicobarese and Shompens as well as the development of these communities. Thus these tribes are developing their resources as well as conducting thier economic activities with the help of the local Government. But the Shompen community will take more time to develop than the Nicobarese. Between the two tribes of this island the Nicobarese being more advanced have benefited more from development programmes.

40

MARRIAGE, ADOPTION AND INHERITANCE AMONG THE CENTRAL NICOBARESE

G.C. MANDAL

All islands in the Nicobar region are inhabited by the Nicobarese. On the basis of cultural and linguistic characteristics of the Nicobarese, the Nicobar islands have been divided into six distinct divisions: (1) Car Nicobar, (2) Chowra, (3) Teressa and Bompoka, (4) Katchal, Camorta, Nancowry and Trinket, (5) Little Nicobar, Kondul, Pulo-Milo and Great Nicobar, (6) Shompen area of Great Nicobar. But on the basis of geographical distribution the islands have been divided into three groups: (1) Northern Group comprising Car Nicobar, Chowra, Teressa and Bompoka, (2) Central Group comprising Katchal, Camorta, Nancowry and Trinket, (3) Southern Group comprising Little Nicobar, Kondul, Pulo-Milo and Great Nicobar as per the 1921 census.

During my field work in the Central Nicobars I visited three islands, namely, Katchal, Camorta and Nancowry. I conducted my study in two villages, namely, Chotoinak in Camorta island and Kapanga in Katchal island. Apart from this, I also visited the West Bay Katchal, Ghula, Jansin and Hakon-hale villages in the Katchal island for short periods. The Nicobarese of these islands are identified as "Yolohua".

The Nicobarese are horticulturists and grow gardens of coconut, arecanut, banana, yam and pandanus. Besides the plantation works, they also practise fishing and hunting. However, in the Central Group of Nicobar Islands the plantation work and fishing are still considered to be the main occupation of the people. The copra and arecanuts are the only products which they sell to the cooperative societies to earn money. Besides selling this the Nicobarese of the

Central Nicobars are earning money by doing work in Nancowry Mercantile Company as labourers, salesmen, drivers in the launch, and few are employed in the Government offices as peons, chowkidars, policemen, etc. In Camorta Island, Dawood of Kakana village practises agriculture and produces paddy in the fields. In Katchal Island, Harry Saul of the West Bay Katchal village also cultivates paddy in the fields. Both of them have cows and bullocks and they have employed Ranchi labourers for this work.

Marriage Rules

Among the Nicobarese of the Central Group of Nicobar Islands, namely, Katchal, Camorta, Nancowry and Trinket marriage is called *kaman-she* or *mihiteak-she*. Nowadays monogamy, the socially accepted norm, is followed strictly. It is said that polygamy was once in practice. Among the Nicobarese of these islands when the boys and girls attain puberty they are considered to be of marriageable age. The boys attain maturity at the age of 14–16 years and the girl attain the marriage age at 12-13 years generally. When a girl attains the marriage age she is called *holian*.

The traditional type of the marriage among the Central Nicobarese may be termed as marriage by courtship as both the girl and the boy love each other and afterwards they marry. During this time if the boy and girl have any difficulties among themselves or have any difference of opinion, they leave each other and may find other partners. The boy and girl have every right to choose their partners and generally she has a greater say in this respect. When the boy and girl like each other they inform their parents and ask for arranging marriage. There is no elaborate marriage ceremony among the Nicobarese. The parents of the boy or girl inform the captain of the village or the chief captain of the island and all gather at a place and discuss the matter and approve. A feast is arranged by the boy's and the girl's parents. After this feast the boy and the girl live together either with the boy's parents or with the girl's parents. However, it depends on the boy and the girl but generally the family with less men folk is preferred to work in the garden. It is said that in most of the cases in the past the boy used to go to live with the wife's parents. This system is called *ong-dring* or *goolam*.

The Nicobarese do not marry close blood relatives. Cross-cousin or parallel-cousin marriage is not permitted. However, such a marriage after a three-generation gap is not prohibited. Incest, i.e. sexual relationship with mother, father, sister, brother, father's sister, mother's sister, mother's brother is strictly prohibited. But they can marry husband's brother or wife's sister even though the levirate or sororate is not the rule. Children from such marriages have the same status and rights as the children of the common type of marriage.

Divorce (*yange*) is common among the people and is socially approved. Generally the girls have the upper hand in divorce. If it is found after marriage that either the husband or wife is not cooperative, helpful or adjusting or is inactive and lazy or impotent, they divorce and remarry. The husband can divorce his wife if he finds that she is not cooperative and helpful or she is attracted to other men or she does not work properly. Generally, the grounds for divorce are as follows:

1. Adultery ... *Kumlong oto*
2. Incompatibility of temperament ... *Hat-yahicho*
3. Barrenness ... *Mibo*
4. Cruelty ... *Insenyo*
5. Impotence ... *Hat-mikaya*

The children of the divorced couple go either to live with the mother's or the father's parents and sometimes the mother also takes the children with her to her new home. The children get equal status and rights in their society like others. Children of unmarried girls are generally kept by the girl's parents and they live with full status and rights. There is no social stigma attached to them in their society.

Family : (Kaman-she)

In the Central Group of Nicobar Islands both the joint and simple types of families are found. In the village of Chotonak in Camorta island out of a total of eight households three are joint families and five are simple families. The Nicobarese family includes the husband, wife, children, brothers, sisters, mothers, fathers, distant relatives and sometimes the servants who live with them for a long time and become members of the family by marrying somebody.

The family is controlled by the head of the family called *omyaa* in all in respect of social, religious, economic matters of the family. Both male and female can be the head of the family which depends upon the qualities of the person and the decision of the previous head of the family. The elder or younger member of the family can be the next head of the family after the death or retirement of the present head. They consider the following criteria : good behaviour and politeness, leadership quality, intelligence and capacity for hardwork.

Acquisition of Membership Adoption (Ireuhala)

In the Central Nicobars adoption (*ireuhala*) is very common but there are no specific rules. The couple can adopt any boy or girl from their relative's family or from any village family. The adoption is considered one of the noble deeds in their society. The couple who do not have any child may adopt any child of their brothers or sisters or of any person who has more children than he is able to feed. Sometime the sons and daughters of an unmarried son or daughter are adopted in the family.

The adopted children are socially and legally accepted by the Nicobarese society. The adopted sons and daughters are considered as their own brothers or sisters by the children or the family. The adopted boys or girls have all the rights in the family and he or she can e : be the head of the family and can also inherit the property if she or he has got all the necessary qualities and is liked by the head of the family. They do not approve of the marriage of an adopted boy or girl with the children of his/her own. It is considered illegal and incestuous.

Children of Unmarried Parents

The Nicobarese are permissive and almost boys and girls indulge in premarital sex. Sometimes before marriage they also have children. If the couple marry, these children live with them but if they do not marry and find another person to marry then the children rarely go with them. They generally live with the girl's parents or sometimes with the boy's parents. These children are adopted in their family.

Rights and Obligations of Family Members

In the Central Nicobars the head of the family is all in all and he/she has all responsibility towards his/her relatives and kin. The brothers. sisters, father, mother, etc., are looked after properly by him/her and they get all attention, respect and love from each other. The elder brother or sister or the head of the family take care of other sisters and brothers and always tries to keep them happy. The juniors respect their elders and are always obedient to them. In their society the old people enjoy high prestige and all the juniors in the family obey and respect them. The old man or woman advises the head of the family in all respects. The head of the family has the obligation for younger sisters or brothers marriages, and to look after their children like his/her own children. The other members of the family are very cooperative with each other and they help the head of the family in all work. The husband gives the wife a proper role in his house and life so that she is happy and on her part the wife helps her husband in his plantation work and keeps the house properly. The younger sisters and brothers respect and obey their elder brothers and sisters and help them in doing various jobs at home or in the plantations. However, it is all the responsibility of the elders to look after the youngsters.

Inheritance of Property

Concept of Property (Tanolsiyon)

(i) *Movable:* In the Nicobarese society in the central group of the Nicobar islands pigs, fowls, canoes, spears, pots, baskets, ornaments, etc., constitute movable property. The head of the family is the owner of all this property and has all the rights over it to sell or distribute it to others. The other members cannot sell or dispose of it without his/her permission. They can use it for themselves but have no right to give it to anybody. The head of the family is all in all in this respect.

(ii) *Immovable:* The land (coconut, arecanuts, pandanus, banana) forest, etc., are considered immovable property by them. All of these are owned by the respective heads of families. The other members can use it for family consumption but cannot sell or dispose of it without the head of the family's approval.

(iii) *Rights Over Economic Resources:* Streams in the forest are owned by the different families of the village. Each family has its own area where it exercises its rights to utilise it according to its needs and choice. If anybody from another village or family wants to utilise it he/she has to take permission from the owner of the place. However, for collecting drinking water, the permission is not necessary but for fishing it is a must. For collecting fire wood, or fruits, tubers, etc., in the forest nobody can enter an area without the permission of the owner. The forest products like timber, wild and edible fruits are not owned by individual families and all the villagers can collect. They are not already demarcated by others. In the forest produce all of them have equal rights.

In the Nicobarese society they do not have any written document regarding their ownership (*mahachia*). The property can be owned by anybody irrespective of sex. The head of the family inherits all the property from the previous head and he/she looks after it and has all the rights over it.

Pattern of Inheritance (Makalani)

The head of the family owns all the property and it depends upon him or her whom he will give his/her property after his/her death. Generally, the head of the family selects a suitable person from his/her family members as his/her heir to be. He or she also becomes the head of the family and all the responsibilities go to him/her for the family. In their society there is no restriction on a female to be the head of the family or owner of the property. They have equal rights over all the property. After marriage if the boy or the girl goes to live with the parents-in-law he/she loses any claim over the property but if he or she comes back to live with the parental family she is supposed to get the share if it is divided. Generally the property is not divided among the brothers and sisters but if it is due to a quarrel or any dispute the head of the family has every right to divide it according to his/her discretion.

Land Tenure

The plantation land or residential land or open land all belong to the head of the family. He can give it to anybody for making a hut or growing a plantation but there is no written document and the land ownership rights rest with the head of the family. The person who takes the land for temporary use can utilise it for producing anything he likes and can get all benefits out of it but he cannot be recognised as an owner.

Recent Trends

In the Central Group of the Nicobar islands marriage in the past was very simple but nowadays most of them after adopting Christianity, resort to the Christian way of marriage. There is a growing trend towards establishing elementary families as against the extended ones. The reason being the economic independence. Some of them have independent incomes from employment offices, etc. but regarding inheritance of property the traditional system is still followed.

ANNEXURE I

TRIBAL CUSTOMARY LAW : GUIDELINES

1. Each Regional Officer should take up at least six tribes. They should be so selected as to represent the main sub-regions and the major and minor tribes, the more exposed and the less exposed ones.
2. Each tribe should be studied at two places : one in the traditional habitat and the other at a place where they have come in contact with other tribes/communities, etc.
3. Special study should be made of the cases disposed of in courts.
4. Each tribe should be studied for three months in the filed, one and a half month at each place.
5. All changes in the customary law should be carefully recorded in their proper context.
6. Each regional station should make proper arrangement for taking photographs for visual documentation of the work.
7. The field worker should collect carefully evidence and records from traditional the Tribal Council or Panchayats and Government offices.
8. Cases should be collected on the basis of geealogies.
9. Information on demography, basic economic life and social environment in which a tribe is living should be collected.
10. Part I of the Cyclostyled Scheduled should be read carefully.

PART I

These project will cover the traditional and normative rules governing and regulating the customs of the tribes. Observance of these rules is indispensable for the maintenance of social order and continuity of culture. As these are inseparable from the context of the culture, a brief account of culture is necessary to understand customary laws. The cultural areas of operation of these rules, particularly in the dispensation of civil and criminal justice, need also to be identified. The legal, social and supernatural sanctions which make these rules effective are also to be understood.

Owing to social change and acculturation, infractions of these rules may be anticipated. Apart from recording the operative rules, and their mechanisms, specific cases should also be studied on the basis of genealogies. The opinion and attitude towards these operative rules and the circumstances in which their violation is tolerated are also important to note.

PART II

Guidelines for Collection of Data

1. Levels and Mechanism of Social Control

1.1 Form and functions of tribal council both at village and regional levels (including the informal groupings like the group of village elders who sometimes settle the dispute within the hamlet)
1.2 Constitution — types of functionaries, mode of recruitment, kinship base-hereditary, selection and government nomination, etc., range of choice in selection of headman and other members
1.3 Spheres of social control, nature of cases deal
1.4 Other activities
1.5 Its authority to impose fine (amount), or inflict physical punishment and other means adopted like vilification and excommunication.

2. Family

2.1 Locus of authority
2.2 Types of family.

3. Marriage

3.1 Age of marriage
3.2 Pre-puberty marriage
3.3 Marriage of younger daughters before elder daughters and marriage of younger sons before elder sons

3.4 Bride-price

3.4.1 Amount of bride-price (cash, kind)
3.4.2 Nature of its payment
3.4.3 Recipient of bride-price
3.4.4 Who share it — father, mother or any other relatives
3.4.5 Conditions for the refund of bride-price (in case of divorce, death, etc.).

3.5 Forms of marriage (modes of acquiring a mate)

3.5.1 Local terms

3.6 Types of marriage

3.6.1 Polygyny/polyandry
3.6.2 Different types of polygyny/polyandry
3.6.3 Number of spouses
3.6.4 Time and circumstances in which each marriage took place
3.6.5 Do all the wives/husbands live together?

3.7 Rules and restrictions of marriage

3.7.1 Endogamy and other rules
3.7.2 Exogamy — clan, village, etc.
3.7.3 Incest rule
3.7.4 Prohibited consanguineous kin like grand-mother, mother, daughter, grand-daughter, brother's daughter, sister's daughter, etc.
3.7.5 Prohibited affinal kin like wife's mother, wife's elder sister, wife's sister's or brother's daughter, etc.

3.8 Prescriptive and preferential marriage — breach of prescriptions.
3.9 Levirate — senior and junior
3.10 Sororate — senior and junior
3.11 Residence after marriage — patrilocal, matrilocal (in terms of domestic group, lineage, village, etc), matri-patrilocal avanculocal, etc.

3.12 Remarriage and social rules regulating

3.12.1 Remarriage of widows and divorced women with children or without.
3.12.2 Where do the children born of previous marriage reside?
3.12.3 Social position and the legal rights of children born of remarriage.
3.12.4 Marital right over widows as spouse.

4. Divorce

4.1 Is divorce permissible in the society? How it is affected — local name, notion towards it.
4.2 Grounds of divorce for a husband : viz. adultery, desertion, neglect of duties, contagious disease, barrenness, incompatibility of temperament.
4.3 Grounds of divorce for a wife, viz. cruelty, impotence, neglect of maintenance, adultery.
4.4 Other grounds, viz. witchcraft, sorcery, crime, etc.
4.5 Whether divorce is granted in the case of insanity or incurable disease of one of the spouses
4.6 Legal effects of divorce
4.7 Repayment of bride-price or any other compensation
4.8 Social and legal position of the children

5. Adoption

5.1 Rules and specific kin
5.2 Position of adopted son as heir or successor

6. Children of unmarried women

6.1 Legitimacy of child — mechanism and process of legitimisation of illegitimacy
6.2 Identification of father and his duties and obligations towards such child.
6.3 Social stigma

7. **Kinship** obligation towards brother, sister, widow, mother etc.

8. Concept of Property

8.1 Different types of property

8.1.1 Land and land tenure

8.1.1.1 Residential land — rights and nature of ownership, basis of right.

8.1.1.2 Arable land — distribution and demarcation, rights and nature of ownership.

8.1.2 Livestock

8.1.3 Produce-agricultural or non-agricultural

8.1.4 Other movable property and right over it and basis of right.

9. Inheritance

9.1 Modes of inheritance of landed property of married man/woman, unmarried man/woman

9.2 Principal heir-primogeniture, ultimogeniture, etc.

9.3 Woman as heir

10. Customary rights over natural resources

10.1 Grazing right

10.2 Water right

10.3 Right over jungle for hunting, gathering, etc.

11. Succession

11.1 Transmission of office like chieftainship, headmanship, priesthood, etc.

11.2 Eligibility of women for these office

12. Succession

12.1 Transfer of property by gift, barter or sale

12.2 Permissive use of property

12.3 Service

13. Categorisation of social offences

13.1 Wrongs against the person (defamation, abuse, assault, etc.)
13.2 Wrongs against family (education of women, adultery, etc.)

13.2.1 Differential treatment of adultery for men and women.
13.2.2 Responsibility among the adulterers.
13.2.3 Exception and permissiveness in respect of certain kin in regard to pre- and extra-marital sex relation.

13.3 Wrongs against property (trespass upon other's land, damage of crops, theft of livestock, etc.)
13.4 Other social offences like murder, homicide, rape, infanticide abortion, etc.
13.5 Attitude towards these offences
13.6 Punishment for such offences
13.7 Ritual expiation of an offender

Case Records

14. Records of cases (as many as possible but not less than two of each type) from village and regional council or any other court.

Note: Most of the data should be collected through genealogical and case history methods. While collecting case records details of type of offence, the parties involved, month and year, decision, punishment, time taken for settling the case, etc., should be noted.

PART III

Explanatory notes on the technical terms used in the Tribal Customary Laws Schedule.

Normative Rules	:	Standard customary norms and rules prevalent in the society.
Civil Justice	:	In respect of ordinary cases of disputes between different persons concerning violation of social

		and moral codes, etc.
Criminal Justice	:	In respect of offence related to physical torture, assault, murder etc.
Acculturation	:	Broadly culture change and particularly change in cultural practices.
Adultery	:	Voluntary sexual relations between two persons of opposite sex other than own spouse.
Customary Obligations	:	Binding of customs
Usufructuary	:	Right of enjoying the use and advance of another's property.
Primogeniture	:	Right of inheritance and succession of the first born.
Ultimogeniture	:	Inheritance by the youngest son/daughter only, e.g. in Khasi society the youngest daughter inherits the major share. In Lushai society the youngest son inherits the property.
Concept of Property	:	Idea of a class of assets included as property that can be acquired and inherited.
Alienation	:	Transfer of a title or right to another person, e.g. alienation of land means transfer of the ownership of land to another person by sale and occupation.
Social Evaluation	:	Proper assessment of social phenomena or events made by the members of a society. Principles or elements taken into consideration for assessing the nature of offence as immoral, moral, etc.
Circumvention	:	Non-adherence to the standard rules of the society; rather by-passing them by ways not approved by the members of the society.
Social Control	:	Maintenance of social order in the community; exercise of control over the members by a council/headman, etc.
Vilification	:	Defaming others by public ridicule, or speaking ill of a person for an anti-social act.
Preferential Marriage	:	Preference in selection of marriage mate. Example: cross-cousin marriage, preference for mother's brother's daughter instead of father's

		sister's daughter.
Prescribed marriage	:	Customary and obligatory rule of the society to marry a particular kin, like mother's brother's daughter, when a suitable person is available.
Polyandry	:	A form of marriage in which a woman marries two or more men (may be also brother either at a time or one after another).
Incest Taboo	:	Sexual relation among near kin like members of a family, close consanguineal kin, agnates, etc.
Incest Taboo	:	Taboo or restriction on sexual relations among near kin.
Marital Right	:	The rights acquired by respective spouses after getting married. These are for sexual relations, economic cooperation, educating the children, etc.
Mode of Inheritance	:	Transmission or passing of property from parents to children. If a man's property passes to his son, it is known as patrilineal; if a woman's it is known as matrilineal; when a man's property passes to his sister's son, it is also a case of matrilineal inheritance.
Permissive use of Property	:	Right to use a property — land, pond, etc. If the owner permits another to do so. It does not give right to sell or appropriate the property for good.
Ex communication-	:	Expulsion or turning out a person from a community for a grave social offence.
Polygyny-	:	A form of marriage in which a man marries two or more women at a time or one after another while one wife is alive
Locus of Authority	:	The person responsible for exercising the authority in the society. He is either village headman, chief or any other person (Locus — place, seat).
Legitimisation	:	How an immoral or illegal act and illegitimacy normalised or regularised by the subsequent approval of the society or through religious observances.
Expiation	:	Amends for sinful or immoral act through ritual performance, payments or fines providing feast

		to members of the society or to the authority.
Compatibility	:	Agreement, consistance and coexistence, not conflicting.
Emic	:	View and perception of the tribe
Matri-patrilocal	:	Both matrilocal and patrilocal residence
Avunculocal	:	Residence in mother's brother's place

CHAPTERISATION SCHEME

I. Introduction
   a. A brief note on tribal customary law
   b. Need for studying customary law — general and with specific reference to India.
   c. Scope of the present project
   d. Methodology

II. A brief description of the tribe
   a. Distribution and numerical strength, etc.
   b. Ethnographic detail of the tribe with particular reference to village, specify notable differences.
      i. Socio-economic and ritual position of the tribe vis-a-vis other tribes and castes in the villages.

III. Levels and mechanisms of social control — forms and functions of:
   a. Traditional council
   b. Statutory council
   c. Any other

IV. Customary laws regarding marriage, family and kinship.
   a. Marriage
      i. Types of marriage
      ii. Residence after marriage
      iii. Bride-price
      iv. Rules and restrictions of marriage
      v. Prescriptive and preferential marriage
      vi. Levirate
      vii. Sororate
      viii. Remarriage
      ix. Divorce

b. Family
   i. Adoption
   ii. Children of unmarried couple
c. Kinship obligations

V. Customary laws regarding property, inheritance and succession.
   a. Concept of property
      i. Movable
      ii. Immovable
      iii. Customary rights over natural resources
   b. Pattern of inheritance
   c. Succession
   d. Contract

VI. Extent of deviation of customary laws
   a. Marriage, family, kinship
   b. Property, inheritance and succession

VII. Social offences, their categorisation and redressal, substantiate with case histories

VIII. Concluding remarks
   a. With particular reference to compatibility and conflict between customary laws and State laws.
   b. Trends of change in the customary laws

ANNEXURE II

CORRESPONDENCE

Professor Upendra Baxi
Dean
Dear Dr. Singh:

I am very sorry that my reply to your kind letter No. KS-2/76 dated January 10, 1977, should have been so delayed. This proved inevitable in view of somewhat ruthless pressure of work.

I am extremely delighted that you are planning a sophisticated research programme on tribal customary laws. This is a field in which much needs too be done on a sustained basis. I will be happy to cooperate with you in every manner with the successful completion of the programme.

I think that your note on the project (see Annexure I) is fairly comprehensive. I remain, however, a little anxious concerning the use of certain categories of Anglo-Indian law in the project note. For example, the note refers to "theft", "homicide", "murder", "ownership", "usufructuary right", "property" right, etc. The use of these categories, howsoever handled, is likely to create a systematic bias in the understanding of the tribal law. For one thing, we seem to presume that identical or even similar conceptions such as these exist in the tribal law; and for another that these categories could really be useful in either understanding, describing, or evaluating the structure of tribal society and its legal systems. It is, therefore, very essential, in my opinion, not to use these categories of the Anglo-Indian law but instead to classify the conduct in question as accurately as possible in terms of the nature of claims involved between parties and protected or sacrificed by the state of tribal law. I have suggested a rough division of this kind of framework in a study of the Lok Adalat at Rangpur. I enclose a copy of the tentative version of the paper.

You might also find the general framework adopted in this paper somewhat useful. For example it may be very worthwhile, in addition to the study of the disputed matters, the type of sanctions, the process of dispute handling, the manifest and latent functions of the conflict-resolution procedure.

As regards the relationship of tribal law with the State legal system, perhaps the framework I suggest in my enclosed paper might be a convenient one. I think that the interaction between the tribal law and the legal change immanent in this interaction, may be the primary focus of this aspect of your project. Of course, there are other ways of going about the same task as is illustrated by the works of Max Gluckmann, Paul Bohnan, and more generally by Richard Abel, mentioned in my enclosed paper.

My renewed apologies for this delay. I hope there will still be some time for you to incorporate the ideas arising out of these materials in your research, if not at the field work stage, at least at the stage of interpretation and evaluation.

Please feel free to write to me on any matter connected with the project. I assure you of a much more prompt response in the future.

With best regards,

Yours sincerely,
(Upendra Baxi)

Dr. K.S. Singh
Director
Anthropological Survey of India
Government of India
27 Jawaharlal Nehru Marg
Calcutta-16
Encl: As stated above

Extracts from the paper "From Takrar to Karar"

Disputes coming before the Lok Adalat can, first, be typed by reference to the scope of the subject-matter. By "scope" we mean the range of parties or the "units" involved or affected. From this standpoint the following classification results:

(i) disputes involving parties from Gramdani and non-Gramdani villages (inter-village);

(ii) disputes involving two or more Gramdani villages (inter-village);

(iii) disputes involving two or more non-Gramdani villages (intra-villages);

(iv) disputes involving any of the three preceding elements on the one hand and agents of the national (state) legal system on the other (intra-systematic);

(v) disputes involving two parties from the same village (intra-village);

(vi) disputes involving the Ashram, its centres or other policy-making units/administrative units and villages (sub-systematic);

(vii) disputes involving two or more Ashram units (individuals, or Karvakarta and Ashram units, i.e. sub-systematic).

Second, disputes can also be classified by reference to the nature of the subject matter. From these standpoints the following categories can be discovered in disputes brought before the Lok Adalat:

(i) disputes involving the contention that the physical integrity of a person is threatened or injured by us of physical force (ordinarily, in our parlance, "adjuction", "grievous hurt". "attempt to murder", "murder", but also beating, child-bashing etc.);

(ii) disputes involving the same contention about the physical integrity of a person with the difference that the force used is supernatural (and not physical) force (typically witchcraft, for which the official system has no counterpart);

(iii) disputes involving credit transactions;

(iv) disputes involving "ownership" or rights of cultivation in land;

(v) disputes involving one's alleged rights of use and enjoyment of certain resources such as animals, crops, ploughs or dahej ("bride-price") "property" disputes. However, we should avoid imposing our conceptions of "property" in this realm pending further study;

(vi) disputes involving the contention that one's honour or reputation is impugned by given behaviour (such as the new disputes now coming before the Lok-Adalat where anonymous love letters give rise to marital discord);

(vii) disputes involving marital discord and ultimately terminating the marital tie;

(viii) disputes involving the contention that an individual is harmed (in any of the abovementioned ways) by a Karyakarta (worker) or the Ashram.

Of course, there is some overlapping in disputes classified on the two axes of scope and subject-matter, but this is necessarily due to the fact that the classification concerns the same phenomenon. Also, more categories can be added in each range; we claim no exhaustiveness for our identification of categories. The principal point is that the range of social interaction leading to dispute behaviour is more clearly visible in this complexity through use of this kind of analytical framework than through any kind of "gross" and lateral classification of disputes.

It is also important to note that we came across disputes which illustrate each one of these categories in our research even though it was merely exploratory. In the section which follows, we organise available information in a more general and descriptive manner, as that is the only option presently available to us.

The relation between the Lok-Adalat system and the state legal system is undoubtedly many-sided and complex as seen thus far, and calls for sustained investigation. Broadly, there are four patterns of relationships:

(i) complementary;
(ii) symbiotic;
(iii) exclusive;
(iv) antagonistic.

The complementarity relation between the Lok Adalat system and the state legal system has already been stressed so far (see part IV). In some matters, clearly, the relationship pattern is clearly symbiotic; this is mainly in relation to intra-Ashram disputes, matrimonial disputes and some petty disputes, where the State legal system does not relate itself in any significant manner with the Lok Adalat system and vice versa — whether this be in terms of norms, techniques or processes.

The exclusivity pattern is further complex. Generally serious criminal matters like homicide are strictly left to the processes of the State legal system, although in the early stages of the Lok Adalat there were instances where the perritent offender "murderer" was "punished" by way of rehabilitation to look after the widow, children and land of the victim for a term of years under close community supervision. The State legal system penology would have in those situations affected adversely both the families — those of the offender and the victim — whereas the Lok Adalat's penal and rehabilitative sanctions are certainly far more advanced. But probably such actions by the Lok-Adalat are matters of past. We were told, for example, that a couple of days prior to our visit, a corpse floating near the Ashram river was promptly handed over to the police for prompt investigation.

Dr. K.S. Singh,
Director

Anthropological Survey of India
27 Jawaharlal Nehru Marg,
Calcutta-700 016.

March 8, 1977

Dear

I enclose a copy of the letter from Prof. U. Baxi of the Faculty of Law, University of Delhi, who has made a study of the indigenous legal system in a tribal area of Gujarat, together with the extracts from his paper entitled "From Takrar to Korar". He has described the relationship between the State Legal System and tribal system of settling disputes and enforcing sanctions.

Secondly, he has asked us to underline the conceptual difference between the formulation of various terms like "theft", "homicide", "murder", "ownership" and "usufructuary right", "property right", etc. largely conditioned by the English Law and tribals' own understanding of their customary law, their indigenous hereafter.

I will, therefore, urge that the terms which we have mentioned in our schedule guidelines and the context of the conceptions that exist among the tribes should be examined. The investigators should find out the cultural and ethnographic context of the terms in the tribal legal system while analysing concrete cases.

Kindly bring the points I have mentioned to the notice of all research workers of your station engaged in the project on Tribal Customary Law.

Yours sincerely,

(K.S. Singh)

Encl: Extract
copy of letter

To all Regional Officers of the Anthropological Survey of India.

SELECT BIBLIOGRAPHY

Abel, R.P. 'A Comparative Theory of Dispute Institutions in Society'. *Law and Society Review*, 8, 1973, p. 217.

Abraham, C.M. 'The Custom of Polyandry as Practised in Travancore'. *Eastern Anthropologist*, 12, 1958-1959, pp. 107-18.

Acland, T. *Popular Account of the Manners and Customs of India*. London: John Murray, 1847, p. 186.

Adam, Leonard. 'The Social Organization and Customary Law of the Nepalese Tribes'. *American Anthropologist*, 38, 1936, pp. 533-47.

———. 'Criminal Law and Procedure in Nepal a Century Ago'. *Far Eastern Quarterly*, 9, 1950, pp. 146-68.

Agarwal, P.K. 'Legal System of a Tribal Village'. *Administrator*, 22, 1977, pp. 49-55.

Aier, L. Imti. 'Ao Naga Social and Customary Genealogy.' *Mokokchung*, 1969, pp. 8-9.

Aiyappan, A. 'Marriage by Elopement Among the Paniyans of Wynad'. *Man in India*, 16, 1936, pp. 27-37.

Aiyar, K.S. Sankara. 'The Impact of the West on Indian Society and Law'. *Bull. of the Inst. of Traditional Cultures*, Madras, 1959, pp. 10-46.

Alexeyev, Sergei. *Socialism and Law, Law in Society*, 1990, Moscow: Progress Publishers.

Ao, Tajenyuba. 'Ao Naga Customary Laws'. *Mokokchung*, Tarapkaba Ao, Govt. H.E. School, 1957, p. 101.

Archer, W.G. 'The Forcible Marriage'. *Man in India*, 25, 1945, pp. 29-42.

———. 'The Illegitimate Child in Santal Society'. *Man in India*, 24, 1944, pp. 154-69.

———. *Tribal Law and Justice, A Report on the Santal*. Delhi: Concept Publishing Company, 1984.

Aubert, V. 'Law as a Way of Resolving Conflicts : The Case of a Small Industrialized Society' in L. Nader (ed.), *Law in Culture and Society*. 1969.

Avadh Prasad. *Lok Adalat : A Probe into its Organization and Working Process*. 1976 (mimeo).

Bailey, F.G. *Tribe, Caste and Nation : A Study of Political Activity and Political Change in High Land Orissa*. Bombay: Oxford University Press, 1960.

———. *Strategems and Spoils : A Social Anthropology of Politics*. Oxford: Blackwell, 1970.

Bainbridge, R.B. 'The Saorias of the Rajmahal Hills'. *Memoirs of the Asiatic Society of Bengal*, II: IV, 1907, pp. 43-84.

Baldwin, C.D. *Garo Law*, 1933, pp. 1-6.

Banerjee, S.P. 'Crimes in Tribal Areas'. *Bull. of the Tribal Research Inst.*, Chhindwara, 1:2, 1961, pp. 4-8.

Barma, H.C. *Notes on the Marriage Systems of the People of Assam*. Sibsagar, Assam: Anand Ram Barma, 1908, pp. 60.

Barna, K.L. 'Human Sacrifice in Assam'. *J. of the Assam Research Society*, 6, 1968, pp. 4-11.

Barnes, J.A. 'Law as Politically Active : An Anthropological View'. in G. Sewar, ed. *Studies in the Sociology of Law*, Canberra: Australian National University, 1961, pp. 167-96.

Barpujari, H.K. 'Early Judicial Panchyats in Assam'. *J I H*, 42, Aug. 1964, pp. 343-49.

Bartia, P. 'Crime and Witchcraft Among the Tribals of Madhya Pradesh'. *Bull. of the Tribal Reaserch Inst.*, Chhindwara, 3:2, 1963, pp. 21-9.

Baruah, Tapan K. *The Idu Mishmis*. Shillong: The Adviser to the Governor of Assam, 1960, pp. 55-66.

Basu, N.B. 'Position of a Tribal Village Headman' in The Changing Tribes of Madhya Pradesh. *Bull. of the Tribal Research Inst.*, Chhindwara, 2:4 & 3:1, 1959.

———. 'Tribal Village Headman'. in Naik, ed. *The Changing Tribes of Madhya Pradesh*. Indore: Government Regional Press, 1961, pp. 1-5.

Baxi, U. *Indigenous Dispute Settlement and Socio-Legal Change in Law and Development in India; Themes, Problems, Literature; Law and Development*, New York: International Legal Centre, 1973, 1976 : forthcoming.

———. 'From Takrar to Karar : The Lok Adalat at Rangpur-A preliminary study' *Journal of Constitutional and Parliamentary Studies*, 10, 1976.

———. *Socio-Legal Research in India : A Program* - Schrifts Occasional monographs, No. 12, The Indian Council of Social Science Research, 1975.

Beals, Alan Robin. *Culture Change and Social Conflict in a South Indian Village*. Dissertation. Univ. of California, 1954.

Beidelman, T.O. 'Intertribal Tensions in Some Local Government Courts in Colonial Tanganyika'. *J. Afr. Law*, 10 (2), 1966, pp. 118-30 and 11 (1), 1961, pp. 27-45.

Berndt, M.R. *Excess and Restraint—Social Control Among a New Guinea Mountain People*. Chicago: The Chicago University Press, 1962.

Betts, U. 'The Village Duel in Apa Tani Society'. *Man in India*, 28, 1948, pp. 163-69.

Bhattacharya, Ashutosh. 'Death-rites, Funeral Ceremonies and Idea of Life and Death Among the Hill Saora of Orissa. *Bull. of the Dept. of Anthropology*, 1 : 2, 1952, pp. 1-16.

Bhattacharyya, M. *Gazetteer of India*, Manipur, 1961.

Bhattacharya, Ranjit. 'Evolution of Conceptual Pattern for Field Work Among the Peasants of West Bengal'. *Journal of the Indian Anthropological Society*, 9: 1, 1974, pp. 9-16.

Bhowmik, P.K. 'Lodha Marriage Custom'. *Man in India*, 34, 1954, pp. 105-11.

———. 'Further Notes on Lodha Marriage'. *Man in India*, 34, 1964, pp. 301-314.

Bihar. *Special Laws Applicable to the Santal Parganas*. Patna: Secretariat Press, 1965, pp. 155.

Biswas, P.C. 'Primitive Religion, Social Organization, Law and Government Amongst the Santals'. *J. of the Department of Letters*. Univ. of Calcutta, 36, 1935, pp. 1-84.

———. *The Ex-Criminal Tribes of Delhi State*. Delhi: Department of Anthropology, Univ. of Delhi, 1960, p. 154.

Bohannan, P. *Justice and Judgement among the Tiu*. 1957.

Bonington, C.J. 'The Bhantus : A Criminal Tribe of India'. in J.H. Hutton, ed. *Census of India, 1931*, Vol. 1, Part 3B, Simla: Government of India Press, 1935.

Borang, Koton. 'Traditional and Customary Laws of Adis : How to Preserve Them'. *Arunachal News*, 10: 3, April-May 1981, pp. 25-28.

Borton, R.F. 'Ifugo Law'. *American Archaeology and Ethnology*. California: University of California, 15:1, 1919.

Bose, J.K. 'The Garo Law of Inheritance'. *Anthropological Papers*. Univ. of Calcutta, 6, 1941, pp. 81-150.

Bose, J.K. 'The Nokram System of the Garos of Assam'. *Man*, 36:54, 1936, pp. 44-6.

Boulneis, Charles and W.H. Ratigan. *Notes on the Customary Law as Administered in the Courts of the Punjab*. Government Press, 1878.

Bradley Birt, F.B. *The Story of an Indian Upland*. London: Smith Elder & Co., 1905.

Brown, R. *Statistical Account of Manipur*, 1873.

Burling, Robins. *Garo Marriage and Matrilineal Descent*. Dissertation, Harvard University, 1958.

Burridge, K.O.L. 'Disputing in Tangu'. *American Anthropologist*, 59:5, 1957, pp. 763-80.

Busia, K.A. *The Position of the Chief in the Modern Political System of Ashanti : A Study of the Influence of Contemporary Social Changes on Ashanti Political Institutions*. London, and New York: Oxford University Press for the International African institute, 1951.

Cain, John. 'Native Customs in the Godavari District'. *Indian Antiquary*, 4, 1875, pp. 197-98.

Calvert, H. 'Notes on Custom and Beliefs in Spiti'. *Indian Antiquary*, 38, 1909, pp. 49-51.

Campbell, A. 'Rules of Succession and Partition of Property as Observed by the Santals'. *J. Bihar & Orissa Res. Soc.*, 1905, pp. 21-25.

Cantlie, Keith. *Notes on Khasi Law*. Aberdecu: Henry Munro Ltd., 1974, pp. 192.

Carrey, William. *The Garo Jungle Book or The Mission to the Garos of Assam*. Philadelphia, Boston: The Juden Press, 1919.

Carstairs, G. Morris. 'The Case of Thakar Khuman Singh : A Culture Conditlional Crime'. *British Journal of Delinquency*, 4, 1953, pp. 14-25.

Census of India, 1961. *Uttar Pradesh : Village Survey Monograph of Rajderwa Tharu, 46*. Census of India, 1961, Vol. 15, Pt. 6. Monograph series No.1, Delhi: Manager of Publications, 1964.

Census of India, 1961. *Uttar Pradesh : Village Survey of Darkot, 30*. Census of India, 1961, Vol.15, Pt. 6. Monograph Series No. 9. Delhi: Manager of Publications, 1965.

Census of India, 1961. *Uttar Pradesh: Village Survey Monograph of Gharpatta Malla, 14*. Census of India, 1961, Vol. 15, Pt. 6. Monograph Series No. 10. Delhi: Manager of Publications, 1965.

Census of India, 1961. *Uttar Pradesh: Village Survey Monograph of Bankati, 14*. Census of India, 1961, Vol.15, Pt. 6. Monograph Series No. 11. Delhi: Manager of Publications, 1965.

Census of India, 1961. *Uttar Pradesh: Village Survey Monograph of Chapny, 21*. Census of India, 1961, Vol.15, Pt.6. Monograph Series No.24. Delhi: Manager of Publications, 1965.

Census of India, 1961. *Special Tables for Scheduled Castes and Tribes*. Vol, XI. Part V-A.

Census of India, 1961. *Village Survey Monographs, Bhatbanga*. Superintendent of Census Operations, Bihar.

Census of India, 1971. *Scheduled Castes and Scheduled Tribes*. Table C-VIII, Parts A & B. New Delhi: Government of India.

Census of India, 1971. *Scheduled Castes and Scheduled Tribes*. Series 1.

Chakraborty, Chintabarau. 'The Custom of Privileged Theft in India'. *Indian Culture*, 2, 1935, pp. 366-70.

Chanda, Sudhendu. 'Political and Judicial System Among the Terassa Islanders'. *Khadi Gramodyog*, 17:9, June, 1971, pp. 572-79.

Chari, B.R. *Census of India, 1971. Scheduled Castes and Scheduled Tribes of Orissa*, 1975.

Chatterjee, B.K. 'The Marriage Ceremonies of the Bathuria of Mayurbhanj State'. *Man in India*, 9, 1929, pp. 293.

Chattopadhyay, K.P. 'Khasi Kinship and Social Organization'. *Anthropological papers*, Univ. of Calcutta, No. 6, 1941, pp. 1-39.

Chattopadhyay, K.P. 'The Cultural Basis of Rules of Inheritance'. *Science and Culture*, 9, 1943-1944, pp. 56-62.

Chattopadhyay, K.P. 'Khasi Land Ownership and Sale'. *Eastern Anthropologist*, 2, 1948-1949, pp. 133-37.

———. 'Khasi Land Ownership and Sale'. *Eastern Anthropoligist*, 2, 1949, pp. 155-124

Chattopadhyaya, S.K. (ed.). *Tribal Institutions of Meghalaya*. Gauhati: Spectram Publications, 1984.

Chaudhury, B.N. 'Judicial Administration of Assam, 1845-58'. *J. Univ. Gauhati*, 11:1, 1960, pp. 1-16.

Chauhan, Brij Raj and Brij Behari Swaroop. 'Nyaya Panchayats and Leadership Opportunities in Tribal Areas of Rajasthan'. *Eastern Anthropologist*, 28:4, 1975, pp. 359-65.

Chowdhury, Bhagirathi. 'Bathudi'. *Adivasi*, 3, 1963-1964.

Costa, Guilio. 'The Garo Code of Laws'. *Anthropos*, 49, 1954, pp. 1047-50.

Crawford, C.G. *Handbook of Kuki Custom*. Imphal: Directorate for Development of Tribals and Backward Classes, Government of Manipur, 1984 (Reprint).

Cressy, Paul F. 'Criminal Tribes of India'. *Sociology and Social Research*, 20, 1935-1936, pp. 503-11.

Crooke, William. *The Tribes and Castes of the North-Western India*. Vol. I & II, Delhi: Cosmo Publications, 1974.

Crooke, W. *The Tribes and Castes of North-Western Provinces and Oudh*, Vol. I-III. Calcutta: Government Printing Press, 1896, Delhi: Cosmo Publications (Reprint, 1974)

Dalton, E.T. *Descriptive Ethnology of Bengal*. Calcutta: Office of the Superintendent of Government Press, 1872, pp. 219-28.

Damaut, G.H. 'Succession of the Sister's son'. *Indian Antiquary*, 8, 1879, pp. 205-06.

Danda, Ajit Kumar. 'Cultural Patterns Regulating Laws of Inheritance of the Santals'. *The Modern Review*, 112:4, 1962, pp. 306-10.

Danda, Dipali, G. *Among the Dimasa of Assam: An Ethnographic Study*. New Delhi: Sterling, 1978, pp. 107-11, 149-64.

Das, A.K. & M.K. Raha. *The Rabhas of West Bengal*. Calcutta: Government of West Bengal, 1967.

Das, J.C. *The Raji of the Himalayas : An Ethnographic Study*. Calcutta: Anthropological Survey of India. 1983, (Unpublished).

Das, J.C. and M.K. Raha. 'Divergent Trends of Transformation Among the Kumaon Bhotia', ed. Christoph Von Furer Haimendorf, *Asian Highland Societies*, Delhi: Sterling, 1981.

Das, J.K. 'The Tribes of Orissa'. *Census of India, 1961, Report on Scheduled Tribes of Orissa.*

Das, J.N. *An Introduction to the Land Laws of Assam*. Gauhati: Lawyers Book Stall, 1973.

Das, Tarakchandra. *The Purums* Calcutta: Calcutta University, 1945, pp. 172-85.

Das, Veena. 'Sociology of Law in India : A Trend Report' in *A Survey of Research in Sociology and Social Anthropology in India, Vol. II.* Indian Council of Social Science Research, Bombay: Popular Prakashan, 1974, pp. 367-400.

Datta, Bhupendra Nath. *Hindu Law of Inheritance: An Anthropological Study*. Calcutta: Nababharat, 1957, p. 246.

Dehon, P. 'The Religion and Customs of the Oraons'. *Memoirs of the Asiatic Society of Bengal*, 1:9, 1906, pp. 121-81.

Derret, J. Duncan M. *Religion, Law and the State in India*. London: Faber and Faber Ltd., 1968.

Desai, I.P. 'Crime, Primitive Law and Some Social Anthropologists'. *Sociological Bulletin*, 3:1, 1954, pp. 28-41.

Dhaganwar, Vasudha. 'Tenancy Laws and Bhils Woes'. *Times of India*, 7 Sept, 1975, 9 : 1.

Dhar, Niranjan. 'The Rule of Law and the Indian Tradition'. *Quest*, 58, July-Sept., 1968, pp. 37-41.

Dikshit, J.C. 'Criminality amongst Bhil Adivasis of Jhalwa District'. *Indian Sociologist*, Meerut, 4:5, 1963, pp. 1-5.

Doley, Birochan. 'Law of Tribal Belts and Blocks.' *The Assam Tribune*, 28 June, 1986, pp. 5-7.

Doshi, Sambhu Lal. *Bhile*. New Delhi: Sterling Publishers (P) Ltd., 1971, pp. 284.

Douber, William. 'Some Observations on the Manners, Customs and Religious Opencus of the Larka Coles (Kols, Chota Nagpur)'. *J. Asiatic Society of G.B. & Ireland*, 18, 1861, pp. 370-77.

D'Souza, N.S. 'Mother-Right in Traeltico'. *Sociological Bulletin*, 2:8, 1953, pp. 132-42.

Dube, S.C. 'Inter-Tribal Relations : A Study'. *Man in India*, 30, 1950, pp. 73-80.

Dubois, J.A. *Hindu Manners, Customs and Ceremonies*. Translated from the author's later Frencho M.S. and edited with notes, corrections and Bibliography by Henry K. Beauchamp. Oxford: Clarendon Press, 1936, p. 741.

Dutta, Parul *The Tangoans of the Namchik and Tirap Valleys*. Shillong: N.E.F.A., 1959, pp. 63-64.

Ehrenfels, U.R. Von and Velayudhan, P.V. 'Legislation Against Matriliny'. *The Anthropologist*, 3:1-2, 1956, pp. 35-47.

Ehrenfels, U.R. *Kadar of Cochin*. Madras: University of Madras, 1952.

Elwin, Verrier. *Maria Murder and Suicide*. London: Oxford University Press, 1943, pp. 260.

———. 'Two Bodo Murderers'. *Man in India*, 25, 1945, pp. 56-65.

———. 'A Police Report on a Case of Witchraft in Mandla District in 1937'. *Man in India*, 27, 1947, pp. 180-83.

———. *Democracy in NEFA*. Shillong: NEFA Admn., 1965.

———. *The Nagas in the Nineteenth Century*. London: Oxford University Press, 1969, pp. 522.

Endle, Sidney. *The Kacharis*. London: Macmillan & Co., 1911, pp. 24-32.

———. 'The Case Method in the Field of Law,' A.L. Epstein, ed. *The Craft of Social Anthropology*. London: Tavistock Publications, 1967.

Enthoven, R.E. *The Tribes and Castes of Bombay*, Vols. I-III. Bombay: Government Central Press, 1920 and 1922.

Epstein, A.L. *Matupit : Land, Politics and Change Among the Tolai of New Britain*. Berkeley: University of California Press, 1969.

Esme. 'The Garo, Their Customs and Mythology'. *Calcutta Review*, 18, 1885, pp. 47-71.

———. 'A Garo's revenge'. *Calcutta Review*, 84, 1887, pp. 11-71.

Eswariah, G. Land Transfer Regulations in Scheduled areas of Andhra Pradesh – In appraical. *J. Ind Authopol. Soc.* 13:1, Mar. 1978: 41-45.

Fallers, L.A. *Law Without Precedent : Legal Ideas in Action in the Courts of Colonial Busoga*. Chicago: Chicago University Press, 1969.

Fershit, A.I. 'The Evolution of Primitive Norm'. *Current Anthropology*, 18:3, pp. 409-13.

Foning, A.R. 'Some Customary Laws of Our Lepcha Tribe. *Bull. Cul. Res. India*, 14:1-2, 1980, pp. 17-21.

Fortes, Meyer. 'Introduction' to J. Goody, ed. *The Developmental Cycle in Domestic Groups*. Cambridge: Cambridge University Press, 1958.

Fox, Robin. *Kinship and Marriage*. London: Penguin Books Ltd., 1967.

Frederick, Drew. 'Notes on the Castes and Certain Customs of the Dards'. *Transactions of the Second Session of the International Congress of Orientalist*, London, 1874, pp. 400-04.

Friend-Pereira, J.E. *Census of Assam, 1911*. Vol. III, Pt. 1.

Furer-Haimendorf, Christoph Von. 'Beliefs Concerning Human Sacrifice Among the Hill Reddis'. *Man in India*, 24, 1944, pp. 11-28.

———. 'Notes on Tribal Justice Among the Apa Tanis'. *Man in India*, 26, 1946, pp. 181-95.

———. 'Hereditary Friendships and Inter-Tribal Sex Relations Between Todas and Mudugas'. *Man*, 54:24, 1954.

———. 'Changes in the Authority System of a Deccan Tribe'. *Wiener Volkerkundliche Mittellungen*, 3, 1955, pp. 1-8.

———. *The Apa Tanis and Their Neighbours*. London: Routledge and Kegan Paul, 1962, pp. 100-20.

———. *The Konyak Nagas*. New York: Holt and Rinehart and Winston, 1969. pp. 40-63.

———. *South Asian Society - A Study of Values and Social Controls Land*. East-West Pub, 1979, 7, pp. 239.

———. *Moral and Merits : A Study of Values and Social Control in South Asian Societies*. Weidenfeld and Nicolson, 1967.

———. *The Reddis of the Bison Hills : A Study in Acculturation*. London: Macmillan and Co., 1945.

Galanter, Maro. 'The Displacement of Traditional Law in Modern India'. *Journal of Social Issues*, Oct. 1968, pp. 65-91.

———. 'The Aborted Restoration of Indigenous Law in India'. *Comp. Stud. Soc. & Hist.*, 14:1, 1972, pp. 53-70.

———. 'Indian Law as an Indigenous Conceptual System'. *Items*, 32:3-4, 1978, pp. 42-6.

Gandhi, J.S. *Sociology of Legal Profession, Law and Legal System : The Indian Setting*. Delhi: Gyan Publishing House, 1987.

Ganguly, P. and Pal, A. 'Some Aspects of the Judicial System in Chowra Island'. *Folklore*, 2, 1961, pp. 153-60.

Ghafur, Muhammed Abdul. *Complete Dictionary of the Terms Used by Criminal Tribes in the Punjab Together with a Short History of Each Tribe and the Names and Places of Residence of Individual Members.* Lahore: Central Jail Press, 1879, p. 164.

Ghosh, A. 'Antiquarian Laws of India'. *Cultural Forum*, 4, Dec. 1961, pp. 59-61.

Ghurye, G.S. *The Scheduled Tribes*. Bombay: Popular Prakashan, 1963.

Girtler, Roland. 'The Dichotomy of the "Legal" and the "Traditional" Panchayat - An Indian Dilemma'. *Bulletin of the International Committee on Urgent Anthropological and Ethnological Research*, 18, 1976, pp. 35-43.

Glucklich, A. '*Karma* and Social Justice in the Criminal Code of Manu'. *Contributions to Indian Sociology*, 16:1, 1982, pp. 59-78.

Gluckman, M. *Politics, Law and Ritual in Tribal Society*. Chicago: Aldine Publishing Company, 1965.

———. *The Judicial Process Among the Baretso of Northern Rhodesia*. 1955.

Gokhale Institute of Politics and Economic Change. *Law and the Adivasis : A Study of the Peasants of Akkalkuwa of Dhulin.*

Gough, E. Kathleen. *The Effects of Recent Legislation on the Matrilineal System in Malabar*. Dissertation. Univ. of Cambridge, 1950.

Gould J., and W.I. Kolb, ed. *A Dictionary of Social Sciences*. 1964, pp. 298-99.

Goyal, N. *The Ideas of Baretse Jurisprudence (1967), Cultural Revolution in a Tribal Belt*, 1968.

Griffiths, W.G. *The Kol Tribes of Central India*. Calcutta: The Royal Asiatic Society of Bengal, 1946, p. 333.

Guha, B.S. *'Introduction' to W.G. Griffiths's The Kol Tribe of Central India*. Calcutta: Royal Asiatic Society of Bengal, 1946.

Gullio, Costa. 'The Garo Code of Law'. *Anthropos*, 49, 1954, pp. 1041-66.

Gulliver, P.H. *Social Control in an African Society: A Study of the Arusha, Agricultural Masai of Northern Tanganyika*. Boston: Boston University Press, 1963.

———. 'Case Studies of Law in Non-Western Societies' in Nader, L. (ed.) *Law in Culture and Society*. Chicago, Aldine Publishing Company, 1969.

———. 'Introduction' to Case Studies of Law in Non-Western Societies Nader, L., ed. *Law in Cultural Society*, Chicago: Aldine Publishing Company, 1969.

Gurdon, P.R.T. *The Khanes*. London: Macmillan & Co., 1914, pp. 62-5.

Hankins, Frane. H. 'Adaptation' in *Encyclopaedia of Social Sciences*, New York, 1954.

Hasan, Amir. *The Kola of Patha*. Allahabad: Kitab Mahal, 1972, pp. 128-35.

Hitchcock, John T. 'Surat Singh, Head Judge'. Joseph B. Casagrande, ed. *In the Company of Man. Twenty Portraits by Anthropologists*. New York: Harper & Brothers, 1960, pp. 233-72.

Hodgaon, Brian Houghton. 'On the Laws and Legal Practice of Nepal as Regards Familar Intercourse Between a Hindu and an Outcaste'. *J. OF The Royal Asiatic Society of G.B. and Ireland*, 1, 1834, pp. 45-56.

Hodson, T.C. 'Mortuary Ritual and Eschstological Beliefs Among the Hill Tribes of Assam'. *Archive Fur Religiouswi Swissen Schaft*, 12, 1909, pp. 447-59.

———. 'Some Naga Customs and Superstitions'. *Folklore*, 21, 1910, pp. 296-312.

———. 'The Some Garo and Khasi Marriage Systems Contrasted'. *Man in India*, 1, 1921, pp. 106-27.

———. *The Naga Tribes of Manipur*. Delhi: B.R. Publishing Corporation, 1974, pp. 70-115.

Hoebel, A.E. *The Law of the Primitive Man*, 1954.

Hoebel, E.A. 'The Political Organisation and Law-Ways of the Comanche Indians'. *American Anthropological Association Memoir no. 54*, Contributions from the Santa Fe Laboratory of Anthropology, Vol. 4., 1940.

Hoffman, J. 'Principles of Succession and Inheritance Among the Mundas'. *J. Bihar and Orissa Research Society*, 1, 1915, pp. 5-10.

———. 'Principles of Succession and Inheritance Among the Mundas. *Man in India*, 41, 1961, pp. 53-68.

Hogbin, J.I. *Law and Order in Polyensia: A Study of Primitive Legal Institutions*, London: Christophers, 1934.

Horam, M. *Social and Cultural Life of the Nagas*, 1977.

Hosten, H. 'Paharia Burial Custom'. *Anthropos*, 4, 1909, pp. 669-83.

Howell, P.P. *A Manual of Nuer Law : Being an Account of Customary Law, its Evolution and Development in the Courts Established by the Sudan Government.* London, New York and Toronto: Oxford University Press, 1954.

Hungyo, P. 'Village Administration of Tangkhul Nagas.' *Proceedings of the Seminar on Social and Political Institutions of the Hill People of North East India*, Shillong, 1977.

Husain, Syed Khaja Mahboob. 'Tribal Inheritance'. *Man in India*, 31, 1951, pp. 84-97.

Hutton, J.H. 'The Sema Nagas'. London, Macmillan & Co., 1921, pp. 119-88.

———. 'On the Connection of Different Nagas and Other Tribes in Assam, Their Origins and Certain Customs', in *Census of India, 1921, Vol. 3 Assam, Part 1, Report,* Appendix C. xvii- xix, Shillong: Govt. Press.

———. *The Angami Nagas*. London: Oxford University Press, 1969, pp. 107-174.

ICSSR (Indian Council of Social Science Research). *A Survey of Research in Sociology and Social Anthropology*, Vols. I-II. Bombay, Popular Prakashan, 1972.

India, Government. *The Santal Parganas Manual, 1911*. Patna: Secretariat Press, 1964. (Third edition).

Indigenous Law in India. *Comp. Stud. Soc. Hist.*, 14:1, Jan. 1972, pp. 53-125.

Ishwaran, K. 'Customary Law in Village India'. *International Journal of Comparative Sociology*, 5, 1964, pp. 228-43.

Iyer, L.K. Ananthakrishna, 'Comparative Study of the Marriage Customs of the Cochin Castes'. *J. Asiatic Society of Bengal*, 10, 1914, pp. 295-315.

Iyer, L.A. Krishna. 'Inheritance Among the Primitive People of Travancore'. *Man in India*, 6. 1926, pp. 194-96.

———. *The Travancore Tribes and Castes*, Trivandrum: Supdt., Govt. Press, 1939, pp. 341, 2 v.

Jagannathan, R. *District Census Hand Book, Jabalpur.* Bhopal, 1964.

Jay, Edward. 'A Case of Absence of Conflict: The Hill Maria Gonds of Bastar'. *Man In India*, 45:4, 1965.

Jolly, Julius. *Hindu Law and Custom*, Translated by Balakrishna Ghosh. Calcutta: Greater Indian Society, 1928, p. 341.

Joshi, L.D. *The Khasa Family Law*. Allahabad: Government Press, 1929.

———. *Tribal People of the Himalayas, A Study of the Khasas*, 1984, New Delhi: Mittal Publications.

Kaberry, P.M. 'Law and Political Organisation in the Abelam Tribe, New Guinea'. *Oceania*, 12:1, 1941-42, pp. 79-95; 3, pp. 209-55; 4, pp. 331-63.

Kanal, U.R. *Customs and Manners of Central Punjab* Dissertation, Univ. of Bombay, 1947.

Kane, Pandurang Vaman. *Hindu Customs and Modern Law*. Bombay: Univ. of Bombay, 1950, p. 122.

Kantowaky, Detlef. 'Indiache Laiengerichte; die Panchayata in Uttar Pradesh'. *Verfassung Und Recht in Ubersee*, 1, 1968, pp. 140-61.

Kapadia, K.M. 'The Criminal Tribes of India'. *Sociological Bulletin*, 1:2, 1952, pp. 99-125.

Karan, Mahendra Nath. *Short History and Ethnology of the Cultivating Poda: An Exposition of the Origin of the Cultivating Poda, Their Status, Ways of Life and Social Manners and Customs*. Diamond Harbour: Rai Charan Sardar for All Bengal Bhatya Kshatriya Samiti, 1919.

Karandikar, S.V. *Hindu Exogamy*. Bombay: D.B. Tarapore Vala & Sons, 1929, p. 308.

Karve, Irawati. *Kinship Organisation in India*. Poona: Deccan College Monograph Series, 1965 (Second edition).

Khairwal, C.S. 'Customs and Traditions in Jaunsar - Bawar' *JR. L.B. Shastri National Academy of Administration*, 20:2, Summer 1975, pp. 909-19.

Khare, R.S. 'Indigenous Culture and Lawyer's Law in India' *Comp. Stud. Soc. Hist.*, 14:1, 1972, pp. 71-96.

Khasi Customs. *Calcutta Review*, 1905, pp. 261-269.

Kirkpatrik, W. 'Oaths and Ordeals of the Goharas: Kanjars of the Delhi Dist.'. *J. of the Asiatic Society of Bengal*, 7, 1911, pp. 753-56.

Knowles, J. Hintox. 'Social Customs : Death in Kashmir'. *Indian Antiquary*, 18, 1889, p. 287.

Krishna Iyer, V.R. *Law and Social Change: An Indian Overview*. Chandigarh: Panjab Univ., 1978.

Kroeber, A.L. 'Classificatory Systems of Relationship'. *Journal of the Royal Anthropological Institute*, Vol. XXXIX, 1909, pp. 77-84.

Kurian, George. *Changing Patterns of Family Structure and Customary Law in Hindu Society*.

Kusum, K. and Bakshi P.M. *Customary Law and Justice in the Tribal Areas of Meghalaya*. Bombay: N.M. Tripathi, 1982, xiii, pp. 192-94.

Laeeuddin, Mohammed. *Census of Mayurbhanj State, 1931. Vol. 1,* Calcutta.

Lal, Hira. 'Human Sacrifice in Central India'. *Man in India*, 1, 1921, pp. 57-66.

Lal, Panna. *Kumaon Local Customs* (in Hindi). Allahabad: Government Press, 1920.

———. 'An Enquiry into the Birth and Marriage Customs of the Khasiyas and Bhutiyas of Almora District'. *Indian Anriquary*, 40, 1911, pp. 190-99.

Law Research Institute (The). Eastern Region, Gauhati High Court, Gauhati, *Customary Law and Justice in the Tribal Areas of Meghalaya*. Bombay: N.M. Tripathi Pvt. Ltd. 1982.

———. *A Study of Administration of Justice Among the Tribes and Areas of North-Eastern Region*, 1987.

———. *Customary Law and Practies of the Garo of Meghalaya*. 1982, Cyclostyled.

———. *The Customary Laws and Practices of the Apatanis of Arunachal Pradesh*. 1985.

———. *Mizo Customaty Laws and Practices*. unpublished.

———. *The Customary Laws of the Dimesa of Assam*. 1986.

———. *The Customary Laws and Practices of the Wancho of Arunachal Pradesh*. unpublished.

———. *The Customary Laws and Practices of the Angami Nagas of Nagaland*. 1985.
———. *The Customary Laws and Practice of the Riang of Tripura*. unpublished.
———. *The Customary Laws of the Tripuri of Tripura*. 1986.
———. *The Customary Laws and Practices of the Tangkhul of Manipur*. unpublished.
———. *The Customary Laws and Practice of the Ao of Nagaland*. unpublished.
———. *The Customary Laws and Practices of the Pati Rabha of Assam*.
———. *The Customary Laws and Practices of the Thodoukulis of Manipur*, 1986.
Leitner, G.W. 'Manners and Customs of the Dards: Amusements, Beverages, Birth Ceremonies, Marriages, Funerals. *Indian Antiquary*, 1, 1872, pp. 7-14.
———. 'Dard Forms of Government'. *Indian Antiquary*, 1, 1872, pp. 187-88.
———. *Dardistan in 1888 and 1893, Being An Account of the History, Religions, Customs, Legends, Fables and Songs of Gilgit, Chilas, Kandia (Gabrial), Yasin, Chitral, Hunza, Nagyr and Other Parts of the Hindukush*, as Also A Supplement to the Second Edition of Hunza & Nagr Hand Book. Printed as Pt. III Working Oriental Univ. Institute, 1889.
Lowid, R.F. 'Note on the Ownership of Land in the Nicobar Islands'. in *Census of India, 1911, Vol. 2. The Andaman and Nicobar Island*. Calcutta: Supdt., Government Printing Press, pp. 121-22.
Lowie, R.H.. *Primitive Society*. New York: Liveright Publishing Corporation, 1921, Fifth impression, 1960.
Luiz, A.A.D. *Tribes of Kerala*. New Delhi: Adimjati Sevak Sangh, 1960, p. 257.
Lyall, Charles J. *The Meitheis*. London: David Mutt, 1908, pp. 58-94.
Mahato, P.P. 'The Continuum of a Performing Art Form of Jharkhand Region Chho Dance of Purulia. *Folklore*, 22:3, 1981.
Maine, H.S. 1861. *Ancient Law : Its Connection with the Early History of Society and its Relation to Modern Ideas*. London, Boston: John Murray, 1963.
Majumdar, D.N. *The Fortunes of Premitive Tribes*. Lucknow: The Universal Publishers Ltd., 1964, pp. 1-64.
———. 'The Criminal Tribes of Nothern India'. *Eastern Anthropologist*, 1:2, 1947-1948, pp. 33-40.
———. *The Garos: An account of the Garos of the Present Day*. Gauhati: Law Year's Book Stall, 1956, pp. 20-21.
———. *Himalayan Polyandry*. Bombay: Asia Publishing House, 1960, pp. 163-78.
Majumdar, Nabendu Dutta. *The Santal : A Study in Culture Change*, Memoir No. 2, Calcutta: Deptt. of Anthroplogy, Government of India, 1959.
Malinowski, Bronislaw. *Crime and Custom in Savage Society*. London, 1926.
Maogregor, C.R. 'Rough Notes on the Traditions, Customs, etc., of the Singphos and Khamptis. *Babylonian and Oriental Record*, 7, 1894, pp. 172-76.
Marshall, Mckim. 'Village Structure and the Punjab Government'. *American Antropoloigist*, 55, 1953, pp. 137-43.
Marshall, William E. *A Phrenologist Amongst the Todas or the Study of a Primitive Tribe in South India: History, Character, Customs, Religion, Infanticide, Polyandry, Language*. London: Longmans, Green & Co., 1873, p. 26.
Mathur, Asha. 'Religious Practices, Customs and Superstitions'. *J. L.B. Shastri National Academy of Administration*, 20:2, Summer 1975, pp. 899-908.
Mazumdar, S.N. *Ao Nagas*. Calcutta: S. Majumdar, 1925, pp. 48-49.

Merton, R.K. *Social Theory and Social Structure*. New York: The Free Press-Collier Macmillan, 1957; Indian Edition, New Delhi, Amerind Publishing Company, 1972.

Mills, J.P. *The Lotha Nagas*. London: Macmillan & Co. Ltd., 1922, pp. 87-112.

———. *The Rengma Nagas*. London: Macmillan & Co. Ltd., 1937, pp. 128-63.

———. 'The Custom of Temporary Marriage Among the Eastern Angami Nagas', *Man*, 37:156, 1937.

———. 'A Note on Head Hunting Among the Mishmis of the Lohit Velley, Assam'. *Man in India*, 27, 1947, pp. 74-5.

———. 'The Sacred Chiefs of Assam'. *Man in India*, 28, 1948, pp. 149-51.

———. *The Ao Nagas*. Delhi: Oxford University Press, 1973, pp. 162-214.

Misra, P.K.. 'Jenu Kuruba'. *Bulletin, Anthropological Survey of India*, Vol. XVIII:3, 1969.

Mitra, K.P. 'Customs and Taboos observed by a West Bengal Woman from Pregnancy to Child Birth'. *Man in India*, 4, 1924, pp. 174-92.

Mitra, Sarat Chandra. 'The Custom of Life-giving Charity in Orissa'. *J. of the Anthropological Society of Bombay*, 13, 1924-1928, pp. 583-90.

———. 'A Note on Human Sacrifice Among the Santals'. *J. Bihar and Orissa Reasearch Society*, 12, 1926, pp. 153-57.

———. 'Further Note on Human Sacrifice Among the Santals. *J. Bihar and Orissa Reasearch Society*'. 14, 1928, p. 278.

———. 'Note on the Prevalence of Cannibalism Among the Birhors of Chota Nagpur'. *J. of the Anthropological Society of Bombay*, 14, 1928-1932. pp. 479-80.

———. 'A Note on the Human Sacrifice Among the Birhors of Chota Nagpur'. *J. Bihar and Orissa Research Society*, 15, 1929. pp. 541-45.

———. 'A Note on the Recent Instance of a Human Sacrifice to a Village Deity in Southern India'. *J. of the Anthropological Society of Bombay*, 15, 1932-1940, pp. 380-383.

———. 'A Note on the Curious Custom of the Santal Parganas'. *J. Bihar & Orissa Research Society*, 23, 1937, pp. 324-429.

Modi, Jivanji Jamshedji. 'A Custom of Previleged Thefts'. *J. of the Anthropological Society of Bombay*, 13, 1924-1928, pp. 34-41.

Moore, S.F. *Power and Property in Inca Peru*. New York: Columbia University Press, 1958.

Moorthy, Satyanarayana. 'Rites of Social Control of the Koyas : In the Agency Area of Andhra Pradesh'. *Folklore*, 23:6, June 1982, pp. 127-32.

Morgan, L.H. 'The Systems of Consanguinity and Affinity'. *Smithsonian Institution Contributions to Knowledge*. Vol. XVII, Washington, 1971.

Morgenstierne, George. 'A Kafir on Kafir Laws and Customs: Goteborgs Hogokolas Arsakrift 39'. *Donum Natalicium Oseari Von Sydow Oblatum*, 1933, pp. 195-203.

Mukherjee, Anima. 'Aboriginal Crime'. *Man in India*, 29, 1949, pp. 199-208.

———. 'The Pattern of a Polyandrous Society with Particular Reference to Tribal Crime'. *Man in India*, 30, 1950, pp. 56-65.

Mukherjee, Bhabananda. 'Marriage Customs and Kinship Organization of the Urali of Travancore'. *Bulletin of the Department of Anthropology*, Government of India, 1:2, 1952, pp. 37-51.

———. 'Kinship Terminology'. *Journal of the Indian Anthropological Society*, 8:1, 1973, pp. 45-59.

——— 'Family Structure and Laws of Residence, Succession and Inheritance Among the Urali of Travancore'. *Vanyajati*, 3, 1955, pp. 90-104.

Nadel, S.F. *The Nuba*. London, Oxford University Press, 1947.

Nader, Laura and Banbara Yngvesson. 'On Studying the Ethnography of Law and its Consequences'. Honigman, J.J., ed. *Handbook of Social and Cultural Anthropology*, Chicago: Rand Mehally and Co., pp. 883-923.

Nader, Laura. 'Choices in Legal Procedure : Shia Moslem and Mexican Zapotec'. *American Anthropologist*. 1965, 67:2, pp. 394-99.

Nader, Laura. *'Introduction' to Law in Culture and Society*. Chicago: Aldine Publishing Company, 1969.

Naik, T.B. 'Territorial Exogamy'. *Man in India*, 29, 1949, pp. 6-17.

———. *Leena Vinchehed One Porinaya*: in Gujarati. Prasthana, 1950.

———. *The Bhils : A Study*. Delhi: Bhartiya Adimjati Sevak Sangh, 1956.

Nanjundayya, H.V., et al. *The Mysore Tribes and Castes*. Vols. I-IV. Mysore: Mysore University, 1935.

Nasfield, John C. 'Description of the Manners, Industries and Religion of the Tharu and Bhogsa Tribes of Upper India'. Calcutta, Reprinted from *Calcutta Review*, January 1885, 46.

Nathubai, T.N. 'Certain Social Questions Connected With Marriage and Inheritance Among the Hindus'. *J. of the Anthropological Society of Bombay*, 3, 1893-1894, pp. 392-417.

———. 'Ancestral Property Among The Hindus'. *J. of the Anthropological Society of Bombay*, 4, 1895-1899, pp. 90-104.

———. 'On Aurusa-Dutra or The Hindu Law of Inheritance as Based on Religious Belief and Custom'. *J. of the Anthropological Society of Bombay*, 4, 1895-1899, pp. 329-56.

———. 'On Hindu Wills'. *J. of the Anthropological Society of Bombay*, 5, 1899-1901, pp. 29-50.

Navlakha, Surendra K. 'The Authority Structure among the Bhumy and Bhil: A Study of Historical Causations'. *Eastern Anthropologist*, 13, 1959-1960, pp. 27-40.

Needham, R. *An Investigation into the Social Sanctions of the Naga Tribes of the Indo-Burman Border*. Dissertation, University of Oxford, 1952.

Nicholas, Ralph W., and T. Mukhopadhyay. 'Politics and Law in Two West Bengal Villages'. *Bulletin of the Anthropological Survey of India*, 2:1, 1962, pp.15-40.

Northey, W. Brook and Morris, C.J. *The Gurkhas, Their Manners, Customs and Country*. London: John Lane, The Bodley Head, 1928, p. 282.

O'Malley, Lewis Sidney Steward. 'Inheritance and Partition of Property Among Aboriginal Races'. in: *Census of India, 1911*, Vol. 1.5, Part I, *Report, Bengal, Bihar, Orissa & Sikkim*. Calcutta: Bengal Secretariat Book Depot, 1912.

Pais, Alexander A. 'The Navayats, An Account of Their History and Their Customs'. *Quarterly Journal of the Mythic Society*, 10, 1919-1920, pp. 41-58.

Parikh, H. *Light in Darkness*, 1973.

Parry, N.E. *The Lakhers*. London: Macmillan & Co., 1932, pp. 229-348.

Pathak, Manjushree. *Crimes, Customs and Justice in Tribal India — A Teleogical Study of Adis*, New Delhi: Mittal Publications, 1991.

Pathak, Ram Deo. 'Determinants Associated with Agro- technologically Mobilised Traditionally Alienated and Tradi- tionally Affiliated Tribal Farmer'. *Psychological Studies* 22:2, July 1977, pp. 17-23.

Peal, S.E. 'On the 'Morong' as Possibly a Relic of Pre-marriage Communism'. *J. of the Anthropological Institute*, 22, 1893, pp. 244-61.

———. 'Identical Customs of the Dyaks and the Races Around Assam'. *Nature*, 56, 1897, pp. 53-4.

Playfair, A. *The Garos*. London: David Nutt, 1909, pp. 59-79.

Pospisil, Leopold. *The Ethnology of Law*. An Addission Wesley Module in Anthropology. Massachusets: Addission-Wesley Publishing Company, 1972.

Rabha Rajen. *Rabha Janajati*. in Assamese. Jorhat Assam Sahitya Sabha, 1974.

Radcliffe-Brown, A.R. 'The Study of Kinship Systems' in *Structure and Function in Primitive Society*. London: Cohen and West Ltd., 1952.

———. 'Primitive Law', in *Structure and Function in Primitive Society*. London, Cohen and West Ltd., 1952.

———. 'Social Sanction' in *Structure and Function in Primitive Society*. London: Cohen and West Ltd., 1952.

Rajkhowa, S.C. 'Ahom Kinship'. *J. of the Assam Research Society*, 9, 1942, pp. 31-40.

Rao, R. Prakash. 'Village Organization and Authority Among the Lambadas of the Deccan'. *Eastern Anthropologist*, 8, 1954-1955, pp. 3-12.

Ratan, Ram. 'Abjudication of Disputes and Justice Among the Kumarbagh Paharias'. *Anthropos*, 55, 1960, pp. 874-75.

Raturi, Pandit H.S. *Narendra Hindu Law*: in Hindi, 1918.

Raval, Indubhai B. 'A Study of Crime Among the Bhils'. *Man in India*, 44, 1964, pp. 221-32.

Rawlins, J. 'On the Manners, Religion and Laws of the Cucis or Mountaineers of Tipra'. *Asiatik Researches*, 2, 1790, pp. 137-93.

Reddy, A.M. 'The Tribal Hierarchy in the Bagata Region in the Visakhapatnam Agency'. *Journal of Social Research*, XV:1, 1972.

Reddy, N.S. 'Caste in a Tribal Society : The Formative Processes'. *Contributions to Indian Sociology*, N.S., VII, 1973, pp 159-67.

Rice, Stauly. *Hindu Customs and Their Origins*. London, G. Allen & Unwin, 1937, p. 219.

Risley, H.H. *People of India*. Second edition, London: W. Thacker & Co., 1915.

Risley, H.H. *Tribes and Castes of Bengal*, Vols. I-II. Calcutta: Bengal Secretariat Press, 1891; Reprint. Calcutta: Firma Mukhopadhyay, 1981.

Rodman. 'Bigmen and Middlemen : The Politics of Law in Longana'. *American Ethnologist*. 4:3, 1977.

Roe, C.A. and H.A.B. Rattigan. *Tribal Law in the Punjab*, 1895

Rose, R.A. 'Chankhandu: Legitimacy'. *Indian Antiquary*, 31, 1902, p. 359.

Rosser, K. C. 'An Aspect of the Political Organizations of Malana'. *Anthropologist*, 60, 1952-53, pp. 66-82.

Roy Chaudhury, P.C. *Bihar District Gazetteers, Santal Parganas*. Patna: Secretariat Press, 1965.

———. 'Civil Rights and the Tribal Women'. *Shakti*, 2, Aug. 1965, pp. 36-39.

Roy, Jatirmoy. 'Economic and Social Customs of the Rajbasis'. *Modern Review*, 96, 1954, pp. 129-36.

Roy, Sachin. *Aspects of Padam-Minyong Culture*. Shillong: N.E.F.A., 1960, pp. 222-34.

Roy, Shibani and S.H.M. Rizvi. *Tribal Customary Laws of North-East India*, Delhi: B.R. Publishing Corporation, 1990.

Roy, Sripati. *Customs and Customary Law in British India*. Calcutta: Hare Press, 1911; Reprint. New Delhi: Mittal Publications, 1986.

Russell, R.E. *Report of the Santal Parganas Inquiry Committee*. Patna: Govt. Press, 1938.

Russel. R.V. & R.B. Hiralal. *The Tribes and Castes of Central Provinces*, Vol. I-III. London: Macmillian and Co., 1916.

Rustomji, N.K. 'Tribal Administration in the North-East Frontier Agency', *March of India*, 6:2, 1953, pp. 24-8.

Sachchidananda. 'Crime and Punishment in a Munda Village'. *Man in India*, 37, 1957, pp. 124-32.

Sachchidananda. 'Values, Morality and Ethics Among the Munda of Chotanagpur'. Adrian C. Mayer, ed. *Culture and Morality : Essays in Honour of Christoph Von. Furer-Haimendorf*, Delhi: Oxford University Press, 1981, pp. 209-211.

Saha, N. 'Nature of Punishment in Nocte Laws : Anthropological Analysis'. *Journal of N.E.J.S.S.R.*, 1976.

Sahay, B.N. 'Authority Pattern in Maler Villages'. *Man in India*, 37, 1957, pp. 124-32.

———. 'Political Institutions and Tribal Development'. L.P. Vidyarthi, ed. *Tribal Development and its Administration*, New Delhi: Concept Pub. Co., 1981, pp. 287-96.

Saikia, Padmadhar. 'Justice by Oaths and Ordeals Among Daflas'. *Adivasi*, 3:1, 1958-1959. pp. 16-21.

Saksena, R.N. 'Marriage and Divorce in Jaunsar-Bawar'. *Vanyajati*, 1, 1953, pp. 94-98.

Saldanha, J.A. 'Racial Origins of Indian Statutory and Customary Laws'. *J. of the Anthropological Society of Bombay*, 12, 1921-1924, pp. 68-69.

Sapir, E. 'Customary Law' *in Encyclopaedia of Social Sciences*, VI (3-4), p. 658.

Shah, P.G. *Tribal Life in Gujarat*. Bombay: Gujarat Research Society, 1964.

Sarma, Jyotimoyce. 'The Village Organization of the Kanikkars'. *Man in India*, 32, 1958, pp. 64-81.

Sarkar, S.S. *The Malers of the Rajmahal Hills*. Calcutta: The Book Company Ltd., 1938

Sarkar, J.K. . *The Khamti: Ethnography of a Foot Hills Buddhist Tribe*, 1975, (Unpublished).

———. 'A Note on Avoidance of Direct Exchange of Bride Among the Khamti of Arunachal Pradesh'. *Man In India*, 57:3, 1977.

Schapera, I. *A Hand Book of Ishwara Law and Custom*. London: University Press for the Internal African Institute, 1938.

Schneider, D.M. 1957. 'Political Organization, Supernatural Sanctions and the Punishment for Incest on Yap'. *American Anthropologist*, 59:5, 1957, pp. 791-800.

Sengupta, Syamalkanti. *The Social Profiles of the Mahalis*. Calcutta: Firma K.L.Mukhopadhyay, 1960, pp. 187-201.

Shah, P.G. *Tribal Life in Gujarat*, 1964.

Shakespeare, J. *The Lushai Kuki Claus*. London: Macmillan & Co., Ltd., 1912, pp. 41-60.

Sharma, Piare Lal. *The Punjab Customary Law, Containing the Latest Case Law Up to 1966*. Chandigarh: Jain Law Agency, 1967.

Sharma, R.R.P. *The Sherdukpens*. Shilong: Research Deptt., N.E.F.A., 1961, pp. 69-72.

Sharma, T.R. 'Tribal Customary Law in India: A Preliminary Statement'. *Journal of Social Research*, 22:2, Sept. 1979, pp. 1-38.

Shukla, B.K. *The Daflas*. Shillong: N.E.F.A., 1959, pp. 87-94.

Singh K.S. (Ed.). *Tribal Movements in India*, Vol. I, Manohar, 1982.

———. *Tribal Movements in India*, Vol. II, Manohar, 1983.

———. *Economies of the Tribes and their Transformation*, 1982, Concept Publishing Company.

———. Introduction, W.G. Archer, *Tribal Law and Justice, A Report on the Santal*, 1984, Concept Publishing Company.

Singh, Sher. 'Ex-Criminal Tribes of Northern India Need Reclassification on More Authentic and Scientific Grounds. *J. Social Research*, 3:2, 1960, pp. 35-42.

Singh, Bajarang Bhadur. 'Sarguja ke Adivasiyo me Aparadh Evam Nyay Vyavastha' in Hindi. *Vanyajati*, 25:2, April 1977, pp. 8-11.

Singh, Brij Nath. 'Delinquency and Juvenile Pattern in Primitive Society'. *Eastern Anthropologist*, 2, 1948-1949, pp. 104-14.

Sinha, Anand Prasad. 'Crime and Custom in the Tribal Society: Some Reflections'. L.P. Vidyarthi, ed. *Tribal Development and its Administration*, New Delhi: Concept Pub. Co., 1981, pp. 297-311.

Sinha, D. 'Problem of a Marginal Tribe: The Kharias of Purulia'. *Era*, 1:4, 1976, pp. 7-12.

———. *The Hill Kharias of Purulia: A Study on the Impact of Poverty on a Hunting and Gathering Tribe*. Calcutta: Anthropological Survey of India, 1978 (Unpublished report).

Sinha, Raghuvir. *The Akas*. Shillong: Research Deptt., N.E.F.A., 1962, pp. 100-10.

Snyder, Francis G. 'Land Law and Economic Change in Rural Senegal : Diola Pledge Transactions and Disputes'. Ian Hamnett, ed. *Social Anthropology and Law*. A.S.A. Monograph. 14, Academic Press, 1976.

Somasundaram, A.M. 'Lambadis and Crime'. *Eastern Anthropologist*, 1, 1947-1948, pp. 18-25.

Srivastava, L.R.N. *The Gallongs*. Shillong: Research Deptt., N.E.F.A., 1962, pp. 87-99.

Srivastava, R.P. 'Marriage and Divorce Among the Eastern Bhotia'. *Anthropologist*, 4:1 & 2, 1957, pp. 34-43.

Srivastava, S.K. *The Tharus : A Study in Culture Dynamics*. Agra: Univ. Press, 1958, pp. 76-85.

Steele, Arthur. *Law and Custom of Hindu Castes Within Dethin Dekhun Provinces Subject of the Presidency of Bombay, Chiefly Affecting Civil Suits*. London: William H. Allen, 1868, p. 460.

Stewell, V.A. *A Manual of the Land Tenures of the Kumaon Division*. Allahabad: Government Press, 1919.

———. *Kumaon Rulings for Civil Courts with Commentary*. Allahabad: Government Press, (Not Dated).

Stock, Edward. *The Mikire*. London: David Nutt, 1908, pp. 15-23.

Strickland-Anderson, Lily. *Some Notes on the Customs of the Khasi People Studies. Ist 1966 Proceedings*. Kaula Lampur, 1968, 352-375.

Swartz. 'The Political Middlemen.' Maro Swarts, ed. *Local Level Politics*. Chicago: Aldine Publishing Company, 1968, pp. 199-204.

Temple, Richard C. 'Murder in Order to Procure a Son'. *Indian Antiquary*, 27, 1898, p. 336.

——— 'Ritual Murder as a Means of Procuring Children. *Indian Antquiary*, 58, 1923, pp. 113-15.

Thapar, P.N. *General Code of Tribal Custom in the Jhelum District, Punjab*. Lahore: Supdt., Government Printing Press, Punjab, 1946.

Thurston, E. *Castes and Tribes of Southern India*, Vol. III. Madras: Government Press, 1909; Reprint. Delhi: Cosmo Publications 1975.

Thusu, K.N. 'Land-ownership in a Tribal Village of Bastar, M.P.' paper read in the Seminar on Tribal Economy, February, 1977.

Tomasic, Roman, *The Sociology of Law*. New Delhi: Sage Publications, 1985.

Tripathy, B.K. 'Administration of Criminal Justice in Tribal Areas'. *Ind. J. Pub. Adm.*, 23:3, 1977, pp. 723-34.

Tupper, C.L. *Punjab Customary Law*, Vol. I-III. Government Press, 1881.

Turner, A.C. 'Note on Criminal Tribe Settlements'. in *Census of India, 1931*, Vol. 18, The United Provinces of Agra and Oudh. Part 1. - Report. Allahabad: Supdt. Printing & Stationery, U.P. pp. 607-08.

Upadhyaya, D.S. 'The Concept of *Divya* in Bhojpuri Folklore'. *J.B.R.S.*, 53, 1967, pp. 264-69.

Vidyarthi, L.P. *The Maler : A Study in Nature-Man Spirit Complex of a Hill Tribe*. Calcutta: Bookland Private Limited, 1963.

Veena, S. 'Law and Justice in the Tribal Community of Patalkot'. *Vanyajati*, 9, 1961, pp. 145-48.

Vyas, N.N. 'Protective Legislation'. N.N. Vyas and R.S. Mann, ed. *Indian Tribes in Transition*, Jaipur: Rewat Publications, 1980.

Wahi, Laxmi Nath. 'The Bhatus - A Criminal Tribe of the United Provinces'. *Man in India*, 29, 1949, pp. 84-91.

Watts, Neville A. *The Half-Clad Tribals of Eastern India*. Bombay: Orient Longmans, 1970, p. 153.

Wigram, Herbert. *Malabar Law and Customs*. Lewis Moore, ed. Madras: Higginbotham & Co., 1900, p. 318.

INDEX